D0828449

the improbability of GOD

the improbability of GOD

edited by
Michael Martin
&
Ricki Monnier

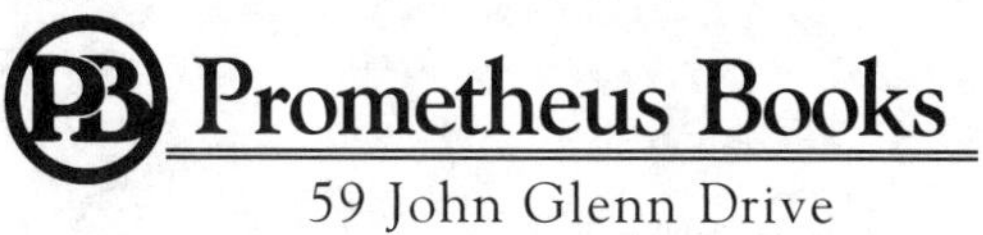

Prometheus Books
59 John Glenn Drive
Amherst, New York 14228–2197

Published 2006 by Prometheus Books

Inquiries should be addressed to
Prometheus Books
59 John Glenn Drive
Amherst, New York 14228–2197
VOICE: 716–691–0133, ext. 207
FAX: 716–564–2711
WWW.PROMETHEUSBOOKS.COM

10 09 08 07 06 5 4 3 2 1

Library of Congress Cataloging-in-Publication Data

The impossibility of God / edited by Michael Martin and Ricki Monnier.
p. cm.
Includes bibliographical references.
ISBN 1–59102–381—5 (hardcover : alk. paper)
1. Atheism. 2. God—Proof. I. Martin, Michael, 1932 Feb. 3– II. Monnier, Ricki.

BL2775.3.I47 2006
212'.1—dc22

2005032632

Printed in the United States of America on acid-free paper

To those who question and wonder.

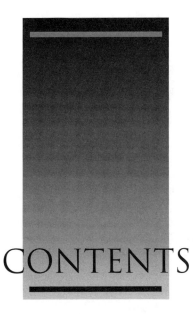

CONTENTS

APPENDIX

PREFACE

This anthology is the indirect result of many years of stimulating talks and lively discussions among the participants of *The Disproof Atheism Society*, an independent network of disproof atheists founded in 1994. We are indebted to the authors whose previously published papers and book selections are collected here as well as the authors who contributed new papers. We thank the various publishers for granting us permission to republish materials and Steven L. Mitchell, editor in chief of Prometheus Books, for assistance in publishing this anthology. We are grateful, above all, to our families for their patience, encouragement, and support.

Michael Martin
Ricki Monnier

2005

GENERAL INTRODUCTION

The philosophy of religion gives extensive treatment to the arguments for the existence of God. Above all, these include the ontological, cosmological, teleological, and moral arguments and the arguments from religious experience and miracles. Among the arguments for the nonexistence of God, however, only the evidential argument from evil receives comparable attention, and a few others, such as the logical argument from evil and the stone argument against omnipotence, are occasionally mentioned and peremptorily dismissed. This preferential treatment of the arguments for the existence of God has persisted despite the strengthening of old arguments and the development of powerful new arguments for the nonexistence of God.

There are basically two kinds of arguments for the nonexistence of God: arguments for the improbability of God and arguments for the impossibility of God. Briefly, an argument for the improbability of God assumes that God *can* exist but argues that the weight of the evidence is against God's *actual* existence; an argument for the impossibility of God argues that the concept of God is *logically contradictory* and therefore God, like a square circle, *cannot* exist. This anthology, *The Improbability of God*, collects in one volume most of the important arguments for the *improbability* of God that have been published since the mid-1900s. Its companion volume, *The Impossibility of God*, published in 2003, collects most of the important published arguments for the *impossibility* of God.

In the interest of clarity and to facilitate discussion the arguments for the improbability of God have been arranged into four main groups: Part 1 contains *cosmological arguments* that the weight of the evidence relative to the origin of the universe is against the existence of a God who is the creator of the universe; Part 2 contains *teleological arguments* that the weight of the evidence relative to the order in the universe is against the existence of a God who is the designer of the universe; Part 3 contains *inductive evil arguments*, or *evidential arguments from evil*, that the weight of the evidence relative to the widespread and horrendous evil in the world is against the existence of a God who possesses certain attributes; and Part 4 contains *nonbelief arguments* that the weight of the evidence relative to the widespread nonbelief or the reasonable nonbelief in the world is against the existence of a God who possesses certain attributes. Of course, the reader who is not satisfied with this arrangement of the arguments or the placement of an individual argument is welcome to make changes.

Each of the four parts begins with an introduction by the editors that briefly summarizes the papers and book selections that follow. Within each paper and book selection itself, the author identifies the concept of God and specific empirical facts or scientific theories that are being considered and then argues that the weight of the evidence from these sources makes the existence of God improbable. The author then usually replies to some possible objections. In many cases there is a follow-up paper that clarifies and develops the argument in response to published objections.

The reader might wonder why there are so many arguments for the improbability of God. Wouldn't just one argument, if supported by the weight of the evidence, be sufficient to establish that God is improbable? There are several answers to this question. First, arguments for the improbability of God are directed at different concepts of God held by the world's major religions and leading theologians. Second, arguments for the improbability of God draw on different empirical facts and scientific theories whose relevance and significance might change over time. Third, arguments for the improbability of God sometimes directly complement and reinforce one another. Finally, every argument for the improbability of God adds to the collective strength of the growing number of arguments for the nonexistence of God (see the references on page 15).

This anthology is an invitation to explore and ponder the probability of God. Is the evidential argument from evil against the existence of God, as Charles Darwin concluded, "a strong one"? Is theism built upon the very idea that is disconfirmed by the evidence? Arguments for the improbability of God are not about certainty but rather about rational justification. They challenge us to think deeply and critically about the plausibility of an idea that has preoccupied much of humanity.

Recommended books presenting arguments for the nonexistence of God:

Drange, Theodore M. *Nonbelief and Evil: Two Arguments for the Nonexistence of God*. Amherst, NY: Prometheus Books, 1998.

Everitt, Nicholas. *The Non-existence of God*. London and New York: Routledge, 2004.

Kenny, Anthony. *The God of the Philosophers*. Oxford: Clarendon Press, 1979.

Mackie, J. L. *The Miracle of Theism: Arguments For and Against the Existence of God*. Oxford: Clarendon Press, 1982.

Martin, Michael. *Atheism: A Philosophical Justification*. Philadelphia: Temple University Press, 1990.

Martin, Michael, and Ricki Monnier, eds. *The Impossibility of God*. Amherst, NY: Prometheus Books, 2003.

Matson, Wallace I. *The Existence of God*. Ithaca and London: Cornell University Press, 1965.

Rowe, William L. *Can God Be Free?* Oxford: Clarendon Press, 2004.

Schellenberg, J. L. *Divine Hiddenness and Human Reason*. Ithaca and London: Cornell University Press, 1993.

Sobel, Jordan Howard. *Logic and Theism: Arguments For and Against Beliefs in God*. Cambridge: Cambridge University Press, 2003.

Stenger, Victor J. *God: The Failed Hypothesis*. Amherst, NY: Prometheus Books, forthcoming.

Weisberger, A. M. *Suffering Belief: Evil and the Anglo-American Defense of Theism*. New York: Peter Lang Publishing, 1999.

PART 1

COSMOLOGICAL ARGUMENTS AGAINST THE EXISTENCE OF GOD

INTRODUCTION

This section contains new and previously published papers and book selections presenting and defending cosmological arguments against the existence of God. A cosmological argument against the existence of God is an inductive argument based on the weight of the evidence relative to the origin of the universe.

A cosmological argument against God's existence takes the following general form:

1. If God exists,
   then God is the creator of the universe.
2. Based on the weight of the evidence relative to the origin of the universe, God is not the creator of the universe.
3. Therefore, God does not exist.

Here are brief summaries of the papers and book selections contained in this section.

Victor J. Stenger in "The Scientific Case against a God Who Created the Universe," a selection from *God: The Failed Hypothesis* (forthcoming), criticizes the kalâm cosmological argument *for* the existence of a creator God popularized by William Lane Craig and argues that the weight of the cosmological evidence and current scientific theories based on that evidence is *against* the existence of such a God. For example, according to modern cosmology, the origin of the universe did *not* involve a miraculous violation of the natural law of conservation of energy and was spontaneous, accidental, and chaotic—which disconfirms the idea of a supernatural creation. Therefore, taking into account this and other cosmological evidence relative to the origin of the universe, God probably does not exist.

Theodore Schick Jr. in a 1998 paper "The Big Bang Argument for the Existence of God" begins by critiquing two cosmological arguments *for* the existence of God. The traditional first-cause argument of Thomas Aquinas is shown to be self-contradictory and incompatible with quantum theory, and Hugh Ross's recent big bang argument is shown to be circular and incompatible with both quantum and relativity theories; further, each argument, even if sound, establishes only a first cause, not God. Schick then presents a cosmological case *against* the existence of God by arguing that Lee Smolin's recent multiverse theory that our universe is just one of an endless series of big bang universes evolving by cosmic natural selection is better than theistic theories because it is simpler, noncircular, self-consistent, testable, and compatible with both quantum and relativity theories.

Quentin Smith in a 1993 paper "Atheism, Theism, and Big Bang Cosmology" presents a relativistic cosmological argument for the nonexistence of God. Working from the classical big bang theory, which, as a scientific theory, is subject to revision or replacement, Smith argues that the inherent unpredictability of the big bang singularity derived from the general theory of relativity makes the classical big bang theory incompatible with the existence of God, understood as an omniscient, omnipotent, and omnibenevolent being who created the universe with the intent of producing animate life. Four possible objections to this relativistic cosmological argument for the nonexistence of God are then considered and rejected.

In another 1993 paper "A Defense of the Cosmological Argument for God's Nonexistence," Smith restates the atheist argument from the big bang singularity and then critically responds to a number of objections raised primarily by William Lane Craig.

Quentin Smith in a 1998 paper "Big Bang Cosmology and Atheism" begins with a criticism of the kalâm cosmological argument *for* the existence of God popularized by William Lane Craig. A quantum cosmological argument *against* the existence of God is then sketched based on Stephen Hawking's theory of the wave function of the universe. According to this theory, which is confirmed by observational evidence, there is a very high, but less than 100 percent, probability that the universe began to exist naturally and uncaused. This is incompatible with the theistic idea that the existence of the universe was supernaturally caused by an omnipotent God who willed it, and therefore weighs against the existence of a God who created the universe.

In a 1994 paper "Stephen Hawking's Cosmology and Theism," Smith presents more of the details of Hawking's theory of the wave function of the universe and how the theory can be employed in a quantum cosmological argument against the existence of God. After revealing the inadequacy of one possible objection by classical theism, Smith goes on to demonstrate how the argument can also be directed against acausal theism, which holds that God creates the probabilistic wave function so that the universe begins to exist uncaused with a very high probability, and various causal versions of nonclassical theism, which abandon such classical beliefs as that God necessarily exists and everything that begins to exist has a cause.

In a 1998 paper "Why Stephen Hawking's Cosmology Precludes a Creator," Smith summarizes the quantum cosmological argument against the existence of God and then considers a number of objections raised by prominent theists. Among these are William Lane Craig, who claims that Hawking's wave function theory involves a conditional probability that allows for divine creation, and William Alston, who claims that God created and designed the probabilistic laws of quantum theory to allow for divine intervention in the universe. Smith meticulously examines and criticizes these objections and concludes that quantum cosmology is incompatible with theism and provides a better explanation of the origin of the universe than theism, and therefore God probably does not exist.

1

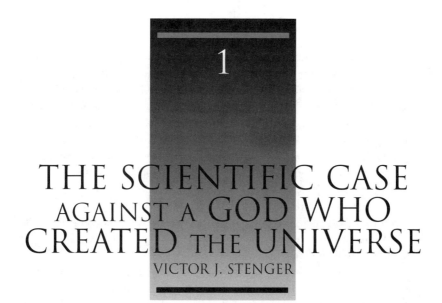

THE SCIENTIFIC CASE AGAINST A GOD WHO CREATED THE UNIVERSE

VICTOR J. STENGER

Presented here is an argument based on modern physics and cosmology against the existence of a God who created the universe. It can be summarized as follows:

1. Hypothesize a God who is the highly intelligent and powerful supernatural creator of the physical universe.
2. We can reasonably expect that empirical evidence should exist for a purposeful and supernatural creation of this cosmos, such as the observed violation of one or more laws of physics.
3. No empirical evidence for a purposeful and supernatural creation of the cosmos can be found. No universal laws of physics were violated at the origin of the universe in which we reside.
4. Modern cosmology indicates that the initial state of our universe was one of maximum chaos so that it contains no memory of a creator.
5. Scientists can provide plausible, purely natural scenarios based in well-established cosmological theories that show how our universe may have arisen out of an initial state of nothingness.
6. We can conclude beyond a reasonable doubt that a God who is the highly intelligent and powerful supernatural creator of the physical universe does not exist.

From a chapter (slightly revised) in *God: The Failed Hypothesis* by Victor J. Stenger (forthcoming).

From a modern scientific perspective, what are the empirical and theoretical implications of a supernatural creation? We need to seek evidence that (1) the universe had an origin and (2) that origin cannot have happened naturally. One sign of a supernatural creation would be a direct empirical confirmation that a miracle was necessary in order to bring the universe into existence. That is, cosmological data should either show evidence for one or more violations of well-established laws of nature or the theories that successfully describe those data should require some causal ingredient that cannot be understood in purely material or natural terms.

Now, as philosopher David Hume pointed out centuries ago, many problems exist with the whole notion of miracles. Three types of possible miracles can be identified: (1) violations of established laws of nature, (2) inexplicable events, and (3) highly unlikely coincidences.

If a violation of an established law of nature is observed, then we might more reasonably surmise that the law was wrong rather than conclude that an occurrence of divine intervention has taken place. If we simply define a miracle as an inexplicable occurrence, then how can we be sure that an explanation will not someday be found? If we view some highly unlikely coincidence as a miracle, how can we know it still was not a random accident? These pose serious questions for anyone arguing from miracles to the existence of God.[1]

However, that is not the task I have undertaken.

Theologian Richard Swinburne, who has undertaken that task, suggests that we define a miracle as a nonrepeatable exception to a law of nature.[2] Of course, we can always redefine the law to include the exception, but that would be somewhat arbitrary. Laws are meant to describe repeatable events. So we will seek evidence for violations of well-established laws that do not repeat themselves in any lawful pattern.

No doubt God, if he exists, is capable of repeating miracles if he so desires. However, repeatable events provide more information that may lead to an eventual natural explanation, while an unexplained, unrepeated event is likely to remain unexplained. Let us give the God hypothesis every benefit of the doubt and keep open the possibility of a miraculous origin for inexplicable events and unlikely coincidences, examining any such occurrences on an individual basis. If even with the loosest definition of a miracle none is observed to occur, then we will have obtained strong support for the case against the existence of a God who directs miraculous events.

Let us proceed to look for evidence of a miraculous creation in our observations of the cosmos.

CREATING MATTER

The universe currently contains a large amount of matter that is characterized by the physical quantity we define as mass. Prior to the twentieth century, it was believed that matter could neither be created nor destroyed, just changed from one type to another. So the very existence of matter seemed to be a miracle, a violation of the assumed law of conservation of mass that occurred just once—at the creation.

However, in his special theory of relativity published in 1905, Albert Einstein showed that matter can be created out of energy and can disappear into energy. His famous formula $E = mc^2$ relates the mass m of a body to an equivalent rest energy, E, where c is a universal constant, the speed of light in a vacuum. That is, for all practical purposes, mass and rest energy are equivalent, with a body at rest still containing energy.

When a body is moving, it carries an additional energy of motion called *kinetic energy*. In chemical and nuclear interactions, kinetic energy can be converted into rest energy, which is equivalent to generating mass.[3] Also, the reverse happens; mass or rest energy can be converted into kinetic energy. In that way, chemical and nuclear interactions can generate kinetic energy, which then can be used to run engines or blow things up.

So the existence of mass in the universe violates no law of nature. It can come from energy. But where does the energy come from? One of the most important principles of physics is the law of *conservation of energy*, also known as the *first law of thermodynamics*, which requires that energy come from somewhere. In principle, the creation hypothesis could be confirmed by the direct observation or theoretical requirement that conservation of energy was violated 13.7 billion years ago at the start of the big bang.

However, neither observations nor theory indicate this to have been the case. The first law allows energy to convert from one type to another as long as the total for a closed system remains fixed. Remarkably, the sum of the measured sums of the rest and kinetic energies of the bodies in the universe seems to be exactly canceled by the negative potential energy that results from their mutual gravitational interactions. Within small measurement errors and quantum uncertainties, the mean energy density of the universe is exactly what it should be for a universe that appeared from an initial state of zero energy, within a small quantum uncertainty.

Furthermore, a close balance between positive and negative energy is predicted by the modern version of the big bang theory called the *inflationary big bang*, according to which the universe underwent a period of rapid, exponential inflation during a tiny fraction of its first second. The inflationary theory has recently undergone a number of stringent observational tests that would have been sufficient to prove it false. So far, it has passed these tests with flying colors.[4]

In short, the existence of matter in the universe did not require the violation of energy conservation at the assumed creation. In fact, the data strongly support the hypothesis that no such miracle occurred. If we regard such a miracle as predicted by the creator hypothesis, then that prediction is not confirmed.

CREATING ORDER

Another prediction of the creator hypothesis also fails to be confirmed by the data. If the universe were created, then it should have possessed some degree of order at the creation—the design that was inserted at that point by the Grand Designer. This expectation of order is usually expressed in terms of the *second law of thermodynamics*, which states that the total *entropy* or *disorder* of a closed system must remain constant or increase with time. It would seem to follow that, if the universe today is a closed system, it could not always have been so. At some point in the past, order must have been imparted from the outside.

Prior to 1929, this was a strong argument for a creation. However, in that year, astronomer Edwin Hubble reported that the galaxies are moving away from one another at speeds approximately proportional to their distance, indicating that the universe is expanding. This formed the earliest evidence for the big bang. For example, an expanding universe can have started in total chaos and still form localized order consistent with the second law.

The simplest way to see this is with a (literally) homey example. Suppose that whenever you clean your house, you empty the collected rubbish by tossing it out the window into your yard. Eventually the yard would be filled with rubbish. However, you can continue doing this with a simple expedient. Just keep buying up the land around your house and you will always have more room to toss the rubbish. You are able to maintain localized order—in your house—at the expense of increased disorder in the rest of the universe.

Similarly, parts of the universe can become more orderly as the rubbish, or entropy, produced during the ordering process (think of it as disorder being removed from the system being ordered) is tossed out into the larger, ever-expanding surrounding space. The total entropy of the universe increases as the universe expands, as required by the second law. However, the maximum possible entropy increases even faster, leaving increasingly more room for order to form. The reason for this is that the maximum entropy of a sphere of a certain radius (we are thinking of the universe as a sphere) is that of a black hole of that radius. The expanding universe is not a black hole and so has less than maximum entropy. Thus, while becoming more disorderly on the whole as time goes by, our expanding universe is not maximally disordered. But once it was.

Suppose we extrapolate the expansion back 13.7 billion years to the earliest definable moment when the universe was confined to the smallest possible region of space that can be operationally defined, a *Planck sphere* that has a radius equal to the *Planck length*, 1.6×10^{-35} meter. As expected from the second law, the universe at that time had lower entropy than it has now. However, that entropy was also as high as it possibly could have been for an object that small because a sphere of Planck dimensions is equivalent to a black hole.

This may require further elaboration. We seem to be saying that the entropy of the universe was maximal when the universe began, yet it has been increasing ever since. Indeed, that's exactly what we are saying. When the universe began, its entropy was the highest it could be for an object of that size because the universe was equivalent to a black hole from which no information can be extracted. Currently, the entropy is higher, but not maximal, that is, not as high as it could be for an object of the universe's current size. The universe is no longer a black hole.

When, at the beginning of the big bang, the entropy was maximal, the disorder was complete and no structure was present. So the universe began with no structure but has structure today because its entropy is no longer maximal.

In short, according to our best current cosmological understanding, our universe began with no structure or organization, designed or otherwise. It was a state of chaos.

We are thus forced to conclude that the order we now observe could *not* have been the result of any initial design built into the universe at the so-called creation. The universe preserves no record of what went on before the big bang. The creator, if he existed, left no imprint.

BEGINNING AND CAUSE

The empirical fact of the big bang has led some theists to argue that this, in itself, demonstrates the existence of a creator. In 1951, Pope Pius XII told the Pontifical Academy, "Creation took place in time, therefore there is a Creator, therefore God exists."[5] The astronomer/priest Georges-Henri Lemaître, who first proposed the idea of a big bang, wisely advised the pope not to make this statement "infallible."

Christian apologist William Lane Craig has made a number of sophisticated arguments that he claims show that the universe must have had a beginning and that beginning implies a personal creator.[6] One argument is based on *general relativity*, the modern theory of gravity that was published by Einstein in 1916 and that has, since then, passed many stringent empirical tests.[7]

In 1970, cosmologist Stephen Hawking and mathematician Roger Penrose, using a theorem derived earlier by Penrose, proposed that a *singularity* exists at the beginning of the big bang.[8] Extrapolating general relativity back to zero time, the universe gets smaller and smaller while the density of the universe and the gravitational field increases. As the size of the universe goes to zero, the density and gravitational field, at least according to the mathematics of general relativity, become infinite. At that point, Craig claims, time must stop, and, therefore, no prior time can exist.

However, Hawking has repudiated his own earlier proof. In his best-seller *A Brief History of Time*, he avers, "There was in fact no singularity at the beginning of the universe."[9] This revised conclusion, concurred to by Penrose, follows from quantum mechanics, the theory of atomic processes that was developed in the years following the introduction of Einstein's theories of relativity. Quantum mechanics, which also is now confirmed to great precision, tells us that general relativity, at least as currently formulated, must break down at times less than the *Planck time*, 6.4×10^{-44} second, and distances smaller than the Planck length, mentioned earlier. It follows that general relativity cannot be used to imply that a singularity occurred prior to the Planck time, and Craig's use of the singularity theorem for a beginning of time is invalid.

Craig and other theists also make another related argument that the universe had to have had a beginning at some point because, if it were infinitely old, it would have taken an infinite time to reach the present. However, as philosopher Keith Parsons has pointed out, "To say the universe is infinitely old is to say that it had no beginning—not a beginning that was infinitely long ago."[10]

Infinity is an abstract mathematical concept that was precisely formulated in the work of mathematician Georg Cantor in the late nineteenth century. However, the symbol '∞' is used in physics simply as a shorthand for "a very big number." Physics is counting. In physics, time is simply the count of ticks on a clock. You can count backward as well as forward. Counting forward you can get a very big but never mathematically infinite positive number, and time "never ends." Counting backward you can get a very big but never mathematically infinite negative number, and time "never begins." Just as we never reach positive infinity, we never reach negative infinity. Even if the universe does not have a mathematically infinite number of events in the future, it still need not have an end. Similarly, even if the universe does not have a mathematically infinite number of events in the past, it still need not have a beginning. We can always have one event follow another, and we can always have one event precede another.

Craig claims that, if it can be shown that the universe had a beginning, this is sufficient to demonstrate the existence of a personal creator. He casts this in terms of the *kalâm cosmological argument*, which is drawn from Islamic theology.[11] The argument is posed as a syllogism:

1. Whatever begins to exist has a cause.
2. The universe began to exist.
3. Therefore, the universe has a cause.

The kalâm argument has been severely challenged by philosophers on logical grounds,[12] which need not be repeated here since we are focusing on the science. In his writings, Craig takes the first premise to be self-evident, with no justification other than common, everyday experience. That's the type of experience that tells us the world is flat.

In fact, physical events at the atomic and subatomic level are observed to have no evident cause. For example, when an atom in an excited energy level drops to a lower level and emits a photon, a particle of light, we find no cause of that event. Similarly, no cause is evident in the decay of a radioactive nucleus.

Craig has retorted that quantum events are still "caused," just caused in a non-predetermined manner—what he calls "probabilistic causality." In effect, Craig is thereby admitting that the "cause" in his first premise could be an accidental one, something spontaneous—something not predetermined. By allowing probabilistic cause, he destroys his own case for a predetermined creation.

We have a highly successful theory of probabilistic causes—quantum mechanics. It does not predict when a given event will occur and, indeed, assumes that individual events are not predetermined. The one exception occurs in the interpretation of quantum mechanics given by David Bohm.[13] This assumes the existence of yet undetected sub-quantum forces. While this interpretation has some supporters, it is not generally accepted because it requires superluminal connections that violate the principles of special relativitiy.[14] More important, no evidence for sub-quantum forces has been found.

Instead of predicting individual events, quantum mechanics is used to predict the statistical distribution of outcomes of ensembles of similar events. This it can do with high precision. For example, a quantum calculation will tell you how many nuclei in a large sample will have decayed after a given time. Or you can predict the intensity of light from a group of excited atoms, which is a measure of the total number of photons emitted. But neither quantum mechanics nor any other existing theory—including Bohm's—can say anything about the behavior of an individual nucleus or atom. The photons emitted in atomic transitions come into existence spontaneously, as do the particles emitted in nuclear radiation. By so appearing, without predetermination, they contradict the first premise.

In the case of radioactivity, the decays are observed to follow an exponential decay "law." However, this statistical law is exactly what you expect if the probability for decay in a given small time interval is the same for all time intervals of the same duration. In other words, the decay curve itself is evidence for each individual event occurring unpredictably and, by inference, without being predetermined.

Quantum mechanics and classical (Newtonian) mechanics are not as separate and distant from one another as is generally thought. Indeed, quantum mechanics changes smoothly into classical mechanics when the parameters of the system, such as masses, distances, and speeds, approach the classical regime.[15] When that happens, quantum probabilities collapse to either zero or 100 percent, which then gives us certainty at that level. However, we have many examples where the probabilities are not zero or 100 percent. The quantum probability calculations agree precisely with the observations made on ensembles of similar events.

Note that, even if the kalâm conclusion were sound and that the universe had a cause, why could that cause itself not be natural? As it is, the kalâm argument fails both empirically and theoretically without ever having to bring up the second premise about the universe having a beginning.

Nevertheless, another nail in the coffin of the kalâm argument is provided by the fact that the second premise also fails. As we saw above, the claim that the universe began with the big bang has no basis in current physical and cosmological knowledge. The observations confirming the big bang do not rule out the possibility of a prior universe. Theoretical models have been published suggesting mechanisms by which our current universe appeared from a pre-existing one, for example, by a process called quantum tunneling or so-called quantum fluctuations.[16] The equations of cosmology that describe the early universe apply equally for the other side of the time axis, so we have no reason to assume that the universe began with the big bang.

We have already seen that no miracle is evident in the big bang. It follows that its appearance could have been natural. Indeed, this is the more rational conclusion based on the absence of any violation of known physical principles. Prominent physicists and cosmologists have published, in reputable scientific journals, a number of proposals for how the universe could have come about "from nothing" naturally.[17] These are speculative, to be sure, but they are speculations based on established knowledge. None violate any known laws of physics. These authors do not claim to "prove" that this is how it all happened. The burden of proof is on those who wish to claim these scenarios are impossible.

In short, empirical data and the theories that successfully describe those data indicate that the universe did not come about by a purposeful creation. Based on our best current scientific knowledge, we conclude beyond a reasonable doubt that a God who is the highly intelligent and powerful supernatural creator of the physical universe does not exist.

NOTES

1. For a discussion of these problems, see Nicholas Everitt, *The Non-existence of God* (London: Routledge, 2004), chap. 6.

2. Richard Swinburne, *The Existence of God* (Oxford, UK: Clarendon, 1979), p. 229.

3. It is commonly thought that only nuclear reactions convert between rest and kinetic energy. This also happens in chemical reactions. However, the changes in the masses of the reactants in that case are too small to be generally noticed.

4. See, for example, Alan Guth, *The Inflationary Universe* (New York: Addison-Wesley, 1997).

5. Pius XII, "The Proofs for the Existence of God in the Light of Modern Natural Science," Address of Pope Pius XII to the Pontifical Academy of Sciences, November 22, 1951, reprinted as "Modern Science and the Existence of God," *Catholic Mind* 49 (1972): 182–92.

6. *Theism, Atheism, and Big Bang Cosmology*, ed. William Lane Craig and Quentin Smith (Oxford, UK: Clarendon, 1993).

7. See, for example, Clifford M. Will, *Was Einstein Right? Putting General Relativity to the Test* (New York: Basic, 1986).

8. Stephen Hawking and Roger Penrose, "The Singularities of Gravitational Collapse and Cosmology," *Proceedings of the Royal Society of London*, series A, 314 (1970): 529–48.

9. Stephen Hawking, *A Brief History of Time: From the Big Bang to Black Holes* (New York: Bantam, 1988), p. 50.

10. Keith Parsons in J. P. Moreland and Kai Nielson, *Does God Exist? The Debate between Theists and Atheists* (Amherst, NY: Prometheus, 1993), p. 187.

11. William Lane Craig, *The Kalâm Cosmological Argument* (London: Macmillan, 1979), and *Reasonable Faith* (Wheaton, IL: Crossways, 1994). See also William Lane Craig, *The Cosmological Argument from Plato to Leibniz* (London: Macmillan, 1980), for a history of cosmological arguments.

12. Quentin Smith in *Theism, Atheism, and Big Bang Cosmology*; Everitt, *Non-existence of God*, pp. 68–72; Graham Oppy, "Arguing *About* the Kalâm Cosmological Argument," *Philo* 5, no. 1 (2002): 34–61.

13. David Bohm and B. J. Hiley, *The Undivided Universe: An Ontological Interpretation of Quantum Mechanics* (London: Routledge, 1993).

14. Discussed in detail in Victor J. Stenger, *The Unconscious Quantum: Metaphysics in Modern Physics and Cosmology* (Amherst, NY: Prometheus, 1995).

15. Quantum mechanics becomes classical mechanics when Planck's constant h is set equal to zero.

16. David Atkatz and Heinz Paegels, "Origin of the Universe as Quantum Tunneling Event," *Physical Review* D25 (1982): 2065–73; Alexander Vilenkin, "Birth of Inflationary Universes," *Physical Review* D27 (1983): 2848–55; David Atkatz, "Quantum Cosmology for Pedestrians," *American Journal of Physics* 62 (1994): 619–27.

17. Edward P. Tryon, "Is the Universe a Vacuum Fluctuation?" *Nature* 246 (1973): 396–97; Vilenkin, "Birth of Inflationary Universes"; Andre Linde, "Quantum Creation of the Inflationary Universe," *Lettere Al Nuovo Cimento* 39 (1984): 401–405.

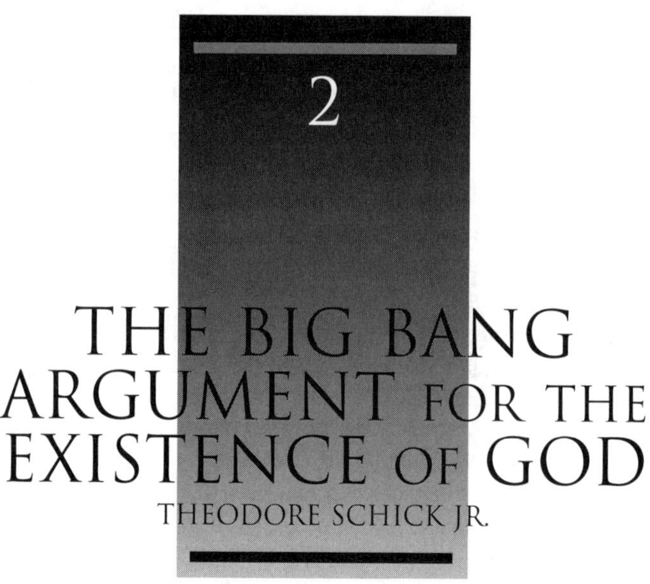

2

THE BIG BANG ARGUMENT FOR THE EXISTENCE OF GOD

THEODORE SCHICK JR.

The evidence is in. There is now little doubt that our universe was brought into existence by a "big bang" that occurred some 15 billion years ago. The existence of such a creation event explains a number of phenomena, including the expansion of the universe, the existence of the cosmic background radiation, and the relative proportions of various sorts of matter. As the theory has been refined, more specific predictions have been derived from it. A number of these predictions have recently been confirmed. Although this is a major scientific achievement, many believe that it has theological implications as well. Specifically, they believe that it provides scientific evidence for the existence of god. Astronomer George Smoot suggested as much when he exclaimed at a press conference reporting the findings of the Cosmic Background Explorer (COBE) satellite, "If you're religious, it's like looking at the face of God."[1] Why? Because something must have caused the big bang, and who else but god could have done such a thing? Astronomer Hugh Ross in his book, *The Creator and the Cosmos*, puts the argument this way: "If the universe arose out of a big bang, it must have had a beginning. If it had a beginning, it must have a beginner."[2] So beguiling is this argument that astronomer Geoffrey Burbridge has lamented that his fellow scientists are rushing off to join the "First Church of Christ of the Big Bang."[3] In what follows, I will attempt to determine whether such a conversion is the most rational response to the evidence.

From *Philo* 1, no. 1 (1998): 95–104.

THE TRADITIONAL FIRST-CAUSE ARGUMENT

The problems with the traditional first-cause or cosmological argument for the existence of god are legion. Before we examine the merits of the big bang argument, it will be helpful to have them before us.

The traditional first-cause argument rests on the assumption that everything has a cause. Since nothing can cause itself, and since the string of causes can't be infinitely long, there must be a first cause, namely, god. This argument received its classic formulation at the hands of the great Roman Catholic philosopher Thomas Aquinas. He writes:

> In the world of sensible things, we find there is an order of efficient causes. There is no case known . . . in which a thing is found to be the efficient cause of itself; for so it would be prior to itself, which is impossible. Now in efficient causes it is not possible to go to infinity, because . . . the first is the cause of the intermediate cause, and the intermediate is the cause of the ultimate cause. . . . Now to take away the cause is to take away the effect. Therefore, if there be no first cause among efficient causes, there will be no ultimate, nor any intermediate, cause . . . therefore it is necessary to admit a first efficient cause, to which everyone gives the name God.[4]

Saint Thomas's argument is this:

1. Everything is caused by something other than itself.
2. Therefore, the universe was caused by something other than itself.
3. The string of causes cannot be infinitely long.
4. If the string of causes cannot be infinitely long, there must be a first cause.
5. Therefore, there must be a first cause, namely, god.

The most telling criticism of this argument is that it is self-refuting. If everything has a cause other than itself, then god must have a cause other than himself. But if god has a cause other than himself, he cannot be the first cause. So if the first premise is true, the conclusion must be false.

To save the argument, the first premise could be amended to read:

1'. Everything except god has a cause other than itself.

But if we're willing to admit the existence of uncaused things, why not just admit that the universe is uncaused and cut out the middleman? David Hume wondered the same thing:

> But if we stop, and go no farther, why go so far? Why not stop at the material world? . . . By supposing it to contain the principle of its order within itself, we

> really assert it to be god; and the sooner we arrive at that Divine Being, so much the better. When you go one step beyond the mundane system, you only excite an inquisitive humor, which it is impossible ever to satisfy.[5]

The simplest way to avoid an infinite regress is to stop it before it starts. If we assume that the universe has always existed, we don't need to identify its cause.

Even if the universe is not eternal (as the big bang suggests), 1' is still unacceptable because modern physics has shown that some things are uncaused. According to quantum mechanics, subatomic particles like electrons, photons, and positrons come into and go out of existence randomly (but in accord with the Heisenberg uncertainty principles). As Edward Tryon reports:

> . . . quantum electrodynamics reveals that an electron, positron, and photon occasionally emerge spontaneously in a perfect vacuum. When this happens, the three particles exist for a brief time, and then annihilate each other, leaving no trace behind. (Energy conservation is violated, but only for a particle lifetime Δt permitted by the uncertainty $\Delta t \, \Delta E \sim h$ where ΔE is the net energy of the particles and h is Planck's constant.) The spontaneous, temporary emergence of particles from a vacuum is called a vacuum fluctuation, and is utterly commonplace in quantum field theory.[6]

A particle produced by a vacuum fluctuation has no cause. Since vacuum fluctuations are commonplace, god cannot be the only thing that is uncaused.

Premise 1, in either its original or its amended version, is unacceptable. But even if it could be salvaged, the argument would still not go through because premise 3 is false. An infinitely long causal chain is not a logical impossibility. Most of us have no trouble conceiving of the universe existing infinitely into the future. Similarly we should have no trouble conceiving of it existing infinitely into the past. Aquinas's view that there must be a first cause rests on the mistaken notion that an infinite series of causes is just a very long finite one.

Consider a single-column stack of children's blocks resting on a table. Each block rests on the block below it except for the block that rests on the table. If the bottom block were taken away, the whole stack would fall down. In a finite stack of blocks, there must be a first block.

In an infinite causal chain, however, there is no first cause. Aquinas took this to mean that an infinite causal chain is missing something. But it is a mistake to think that anything is missing from an infinite causal chain. Even though an infinite causal chain has no first cause, there is no event that doesn't have a cause. Similarly, even though the set of real numbers has no first member, there is no number that doesn't have a predecessor. Logic doesn't demand a first cause any more than it demands a first number.

Finally, even if this argument did succeed in proving the existence of a first cause, it wouldn't succeed in proving the existence of god because there is no reason to believe that the cause of the universe has any of the properties traditionally associated with god. Aquinas took god to be all-powerful, all-knowing, and all-good. But from the existence of the universe, we cannot conclude that its creator had any of these properties.

An all-powerful being should be able to create an infinite number of different universes. But we are acquainted with only one. Maybe our universe is the only one the creator had the power to create. In the absence of any knowledge of other universes, we are not justified in believing that the creator is all-powerful.

Similarly, an all-knowing being should know everything there is to know about every possible universe. But our universe gives us no reason to think that the creator has this kind of knowledge. Maybe our universe is the only universe he knew how to make. Without further information about the cognitive capacity of the creator, we can't conclude that the creator is all-knowing.

Finally, a universe created by an all-powerful, all-knowing, all-good being should be perfect. But the universe as we know it seems flawed. It certainly doesn't seem particularly hospitable to humans. Clarence Darrow explains:

> Even a human being of very limited capacity could think of countless ways in which the earth could be improved as the home of man, and from the earliest time the race has been using all sorts of efforts and resources to make it more suitable for its abode. Admitting that the earth is a fit place for life, and certainly every place in the universe where life exists is fitted for life, then what sort of life was this planet designed to support? There are some millions of different species of animals on this earth, and one-half of these are insects. In numbers, and perhaps in other ways, man is in a great minority. If the land of the earth was made for life, it seems as if it was intended for insect life, which can exist almost anywhere. If no other available place can be found they can live by the million on man, and inside of him. They generally succeed in destroying his life, and, if they have a chance, wind up by eating his body.[7]

Every place on Earth is subject to natural disasters, and there are many places where humans cannot live. Insects, on the other hand, seem to thrive most everywhere. When the great biologist G. B. S. Haldane was asked what his study of living things revealed about god, he is reported to have said, "An inordinate fondness for beetles." If Earth was created for us (as many theists, including Ross, believe), it certainly leaves something to be desired.

Not only might the first cause be something less than perfect, it might be something less than human. David Hume provides the following example:

> The Brahmins assert, that the world arose from an infinite spider, who spun this whole complicated mass from his bowels, and annihilates afterwards the whole or any part of it, by absorbing it again, and resolving it into his own essence.[8]

This is a coherent account of the creation of the world. It is logically possible that everything in the universe came from the belly of an infinite spider. So even if there was a first cause, it need not have been god.

THE BIG BANG ARGUMENT

The big bang argument for the existence of god is supposed to succeed where the traditional first-cause argument fails. Let's see if it does. Ross's version of the argument goes like this:

6. Everything that had a beginning in time has a cause.
7. The universe had a beginning in time.
8. Therefore, the universe had a cause.
9. The only thing that could have caused the universe is god.
10. Therefore, god exists.

Unlike the traditional first-cause argument, this argument is not self-refuting because it does not imply that god has a cause. If god had no beginning in time, he need not have a cause. Moreover, this argument doesn't deny the possibility of an infinite causal chain. It simply denies that the actual chain of causes is infinite. While this represents an improvement over the traditional first-cause argument, the big bang argument runs into difficulties of its own.

Premise 6 conflicts with quantum mechanics because, as we have seen, quantum electrodynamics claims that subatomic particles can come into existence through a vacuum fluctuation. These particles have a beginning in time, but they have no cause because vacuum fluctuations are purely random events. Such particles, then, serve as a counterexample to premise 6.

Premise 7 conflicts with relativity theory because the general theory of relativity claims that there was no time before there was a universe. Time and the universe are coterminous—they came into existence together. This finding of Einstein's was anticipated by Augustine, who proclaimed, "The world and time had both one beginning. The world was made, not in time, but simultaneously with time."[9] If there was no time before there was a universe, the universe can't have a beginning in time.

Ross tries to avoid this conclusion by claiming that although the universe did not have a beginning in time as we know it, it had a beginning in another time dimension. He writes:

> By definition, time is that dimension in which cause-and-effect phenomena take place. No time, no cause and effect. If time's beginning is concurrent with the beginning of the universe, as the space-time theorem says, then the cause of the

> universe must be some entity operating in a time dimension completely independent of and preexistent to the time dimension of the cosmos. This conclusion is powerfully important to our understanding of who God is and who or what God isn't. It tells us that the Creator is transcendent, operating beyond the dimensional limits of the universe.[10]

Ross needs the premise that the universe has a beginning in time to arrive at the conclusion that the universe has a cause. But the general theory of relativity prohibits the universe from having a beginning in its own time dimension. So he postulates a higher time dimension that is independent of and preexistent to the time dimension of the universe.

As confirming evidence for the existence of this higher time dimension, Ross cites the Bible:

> Again, by definition, time is that realm or dimension in which cause-and-effect phenomena take place. According to the space-time theorem of general relativity, such effects as matter, energy, length, width, height, and time were caused independent of the time dimension of the universe. According to the New Testament (2 Timothy 1:9, Titus 1:2), such effects as grace and hope were caused independent of the time dimension of the universe. So both the Bible and general relativity speak of at least one additional time dimension for God.[11]

Whether the Bible speaks of an additional time dimension for god, the general theory of relativity does not. It makes no mention of an agent that exists outside of the space-time continuum. God is not written into the general theory of relativity.

Ross's argument here is a transcendental one, in both the logical and the theological senses of the word. It goes like this:

11. There can be no cause and effect unless there is time.
12. The universe has a cause.
13. Therefore the universe has a beginning in time.
14. The universe cannot have a beginning in its own time dimension.
15. Therefore the universe has a beginning in a time dimension independent of and preexistent to its own time dimension.

This argument arrives at the conclusion that the universe has a beginning in time by assuming that the universe has a cause. But the big bang argument uses the premise that the universe has a beginning in time to arrive at the conclusion that the universe has a cause. So Ross is arguing in a circle. He is assuming that the universe has a cause to prove that the universe has a cause. Because Ross begs the question about whether the universe has a cause, he does not succeed in proving the existence of a higher dimensional time, let alone the existence of a transcendental god.

Even if Ross's argument were not circular, it would still be equivocal because it uses the words 'time' and 'cause' in two different senses. Ordinary time is one-dimensional because it flows in only one direction. Ross's hypothetical time is two-dimensional because it flows in an infinite number of directions, just as the lines on a plane point in an infinite number of directions.[12] Cause, as ordinarily understood, requires a one-dimensional time because a cause must always precede its effects. (An effect cannot precede its cause.) In a two-dimensional time, however, the notion of precession or succession (before or after) makes no sense. So from the fact that the universe has a beginning in a higher time dimension, it doesn't follow that it has a cause (in the ordinary sense), and that is what must be shown in order for the argument to succeed.

Furthermore, Ross's appeal to the Bible is unwarranted. Before we can accept the Bible as a source of data, we need some reason for believing it to be true. Traditionally, the truth of the Bible has been justified on the grounds that god wrote it. But this approach is not available to Ross because the existence of god is what he is trying to prove. He cannot assume the existence of god to prove the existence of god. So he can't appeal to the Bible for evidential support.

The claim that the universe has a cause is essential to the big bang argument. Premises 6 and 7 do not justify this claim, for neither of them is true. But the failure of these premises to justify that claim does not necessarily mean that it is false.

There are good reasons for believing that the universe does not have a cause, however. Edward Tryon and others have suggested that the universe is the result of a vacuum fluctuation. Ross considers this theory but rejects it on the grounds that a vacuum fluctuation the size of the universe could only exist for 10^{-103} seconds, "a moment a bit briefer than the age of the universe."[13] But this follows only if we consider mass-energy to be the only type of energy in the world. Tryon suggests, however, that there is "another form of energy which is important for cosmology, namely gravitational potential energy."[14] If the total amount of gravitational potential energy in the universe is equivalent to the total amount of mass-energy, then the universe may have a zero net value for all conserved quantities. But if it does, then a vacuum fluctuation the size of the universe could exist for a very long time. Tryon summarizes his reasoning as follows:

> If it is true that our Universe has a zero net value for all conserved quantities, then it may simply be a fluctuation of a vacuum, the vacuum of some larger space in which our universe is imbedded. In answer to the question of why it happened, I offer the modest proposal that our Universe is simply one of those things which happen from time to time.[15]

So not only can subatomic particles be uncaused, so can the universe.

Premise 9 is also suspect because even if the universe has a cause, it need not be god. Like the traditional first-cause argument, the big bang argument tells us nothing about the nature of the creator. Specifically, it doesn't tell us whether he (she, it?) is all-powerful, all-knowing, or all-good. And the universe itself gives us no reason to believe that the creator has any of those qualities.

Ross's argument, if successful, would give us reason to believe that the creator is transcendent, at least in the sense that he exists outside of the normal time dimension. On the basis of scripture, Ross makes the further claim that god is a person.[16] But if god is transcendent in Ross's sense, it's hard to see how he can also be a person. Paul Davies explains:

> The problem about postulating a god who transcends time is that, though it may bring him into the "here and now," many of the qualities which most people attribute to God only make sense within the context of time. Surely God can plan, answer prayers, express pleasure or anxiety about the course of human progress, and sit in judgment afterwards? Is he not continually active in the world, doing work "oiling the cogs of the cosmic machine" and so on? All of these activities are meaningless except in a temporal context. How can God *plan* and *act* except *in time*? Why, if God transcends time and so knows the future, is he concerned about human progress or the fight against evil? The outcome is already perceived by God.[17]

Ross's god exists in a two-dimensional time—like a plane—in which he can travel an infinite number of directions.[18] Thus Ross's god knows the future as well as the past. How such a being can plan, act, hope, or even think is a mystery. In the absence of an explanation of how such a being can be a person, Ross's claim is incoherent.

Not only does the cause of the universe not have to be god, it does not have to be supernatural. It has long been known that if the amount of matter in the universe is great enough, then the universe will someday stop expanding and start contracting. Eventually, all the matter in the universe will be drawn back to a single point in what has come to be known as "the big crunch." Since matter supposedly cannot be crushed out of existence, the contraction cannot go on indefinitely. At some point the compressed matter may rebound in another big bang. If so, the big bang would have been caused by a prior state of the universe rather than some external agency.

This bounce theory of the universe has fallen on hard times, however. In a paper entitled "The Impossibility of a Bouncing Universe," Marc Sher and Alan Guth argued that the universe is not mechanically efficient enough to bounce.[19] In terms of mechanical efficiency, the universe appears to be more like a snowball than a superball. Moreover, recent estimates indicate that there is not enough mass in the universe to stop its expansion. So it is doubtful that the big bang was the result of a prior big crunch.

Although the universe as a whole may never contract, we know that certain parts of it do. When a star has used up its fuel, the force of gravity causes it to contract. If the star is massive enough, this contraction results in a black hole. The matter in a black hole is compressed toward a point of infinite density known as a "singularity." Before it reaches the singularity, however, some physicists, most notably Lee Smolin, believe that it may start expanding again and give rise to another universe. In a sense, then, according to Smolin, our universe may reproduce itself by budding off. He writes:

> A collapsing star forms a black hole, within which it is compressed to a very dense state. The universe began in a similarly very dense state from which it expands. Is it possible that these are one and the same dense state? That is, is it possible that what is beyond the horizon of a black hole is the beginning of another universe?
>
> This could happen if the collapsing star exploded once it reached a very dense state, but after the black hole horizon had formed around it. . . .
>
> What we are doing is applying this bounce hypothesis, not to the universe as a whole, but to every black hole in it. If this is true, then we live not in a single universe, which is eternally passing through the same recurring cycle of collapse and rebirth. We live instead in a continually growing community of "universes," each of which is born from an explosion following the collapse of a star to a black hole.[20]

Smolin's vision is an appealing one. It suggests that the universe is more like a living thing than an artifact and thus that its coming into being doesn't require an external agent.

Smolin's theory has the advantage of simplicity over Ross's. Because it does not postulate the existence of any supernatural entities, it has less ontological baggage than Ross's. It also has the advantage of conservatism over Ross's theory. Because it doesn't contradict any laws of science, such as the conservation laws (which must be rejected by anyone who believes in creation ex nihilo), it fits better with existing theory. Other things being equal, the simpler and more conservative a theory, the better. The fewer independent assumptions made by a theory and the less damage it does to existing theory, the more it systematizes and unifies our knowledge. And the more it systematizes and unifies our knowledge, the more understanding it produces. Since Smolin's theory is simpler and more conservative than Ross's, it is the better theory.

Smolin's theory is also potentially more fruitful than Ross's because it is possible to draw testable predictions from it. But what if these predictions are not born out? Does that mean that we must embrace the god hypothesis? No, because our inability to explain a phenomenon may simply be due to our ignorance of the operative laws. Augustine concurs. "A miracle," he tells us, "is not contrary to nature but contrary to our knowledge of nature."[21]

We would be justified in believing that an inexplicable event is the work of god only if we were justified in believing that a natural explanation of it would never be found. But we can never be justified in believing that, because we can't predict what the future will bring. We can't rule out the possibility that a natural explanation will be found, no matter how incredible the event. When faced with an inexplicable event, it is always more rational to look for a natural cause than to attribute it to something supernatural. Appealing to the supernatural does not increase our understanding. It simply masks the fact that we do not yet understand.

What's more, any supposed miracle could be the result of a super-advanced technology rather than a supernatural being. Arthur C. Clarke once said that any sufficiently advanced technology is indistinguishable from magic. So the seemingly inexplicable events that many attribute to god could simply be the work of advanced aliens. Erik von Däniken argues as much in his book *Chariots of the Gods*, where he claims that the wheel that Ezekiel saw in the sky was really a UFO. Explanations that appeal to advanced aliens are actually superior to explanations that appeal to supernatural beings because they are simpler and more conservative—they do not postulate any nonphysical substances and they do not presuppose the falsity of any natural laws. If astronomers feel the need to join a church, they would do better to join the First Church of Space Aliens than the First Church of Christ of the Big Bang.

NOTES

1. Thomas H. Maugh, "Relics of 'Big Bang' Seen for First Time," *Los Angeles Times*, April 24, 1992, p. A30.

2. Hugh Ross, *The Creator and the Cosmos* (Colorado Springs: Navpress, 1995), p. 14.

3. Stephen Strauss, "An Innocent's Guide to the Big Bang Theory: Fingerprint in Space Left by the Universe as a Baby Still Has Doubters Hurling Stones," *Globe and Mail* (Toronto), April 25, 1992, p. 1.

4. Thomas Aquinas, *Summa Theologica* (New York: Benziger Bros., 1947).

5. David Hume, *Dialogues Concerning Natural Religion*, edited by Norman Kemp Smith (Indianapolis: Bobbs-Merrill, 1947), pp. 161–62.

6. Edward P. Tryon, "Is the Universe a Vacuum Fluctuation?" *Nature* 246 (1973): 396–97.

7. Clarence Darrow, *The Story of My Life* (New York: Charles Scribner's Sons, 1932), pp. 419–20.

8. Hume, *Dialogues Concerning Natural Religion*, p. 180.

9. Augustine, *The City of God* (trans. Dods), 11.6.

10. Ross, *The Creator and the Cosmos*, p. 76.

11. Ibid., p. 80.

12. Ibid., p. 81.

13. Ibid., p. 96.

14. Tryon, "Is the Universe a Vacuum Fluctuation?"

15. Ibid.

16. Ross, *The Creator and the Cosmos*, pp. 77f.

17. Paul Davies, *God and the New Physics* (New York: Simon and Schuster, 1983), pp. 38–39.

18. Ross, *The Creator of the Cosmos*, p. 81.

19. Alan H. Guth and Marc Sher, "The Impossibility of a Bouncing Universe," *Nature* 302 (1983): 505–507.

20. Lee Smolin, *The Life of the Cosmos* (New York: Oxford University Press, 1997), pp. 87–88.

21. Augustine, *The City of God*, 21.8.

3

ATHEISM, THEISM, AND BIG BANG COSMOLOGY

QUENTIN SMITH

1. INTRODUCTION

The idea that the Big Bang theory allows us to infer that the universe began to exist about 15 billion years ago has attracted the attention of many theists. This theory seemed to confirm or at least lend support to the theological doctrine of creation ex nihilo. Indeed, the suggestion of a divine creation seemed so compelling that the notion that "God created the Big Bang" has taken a hold on popular consciousness and become a staple in the theistic component of "educated common sense." By contrast, the response of atheists and agnostics to this development has been comparatively lame. Whereas the theistic interpretation of the Big Bang has received both popular endorsement and serious philosophical defense (most notably by William Lane Craig and John Leslie[1]), the non-theistic interpretation remains largely undeveloped and unpromulgated. The task of this article is to fill this lacuna and develop a non-theistic interpretation of the Big Bang. I shall argue that the non-theistic interpretation is not merely an alternative candidate to the theistic interpretation, but is better justified than the theistic interpretation. In fact, I will argue for the strong claim that Big Bang cosmology is actually *inconsistent* with theism.

The cosmological theory that has been endowed with the theistic interpreta-

---

From *Theism, Atheism, and Big Bang Cosmology*, edited by William Lane Craig and Quentin Smith (Oxford, UK: Clarendon Press, 1993), pp. 195–217.

tion is the *classic Big Bang theory* (also known as the standard hot Big Bang theory), which is based on the Friedman models with their prediction of an original Big Bang singularity. In this paper I shall also work with this theory, as supplemented (as is now standard practice) with the singularity theorems and Hawking's principle of ignorance. But we must be careful about how we view the significance of this classical theory. We cannot say that it is "the final truth" about the universe, since it is thought by many cosmologists that this classical theory will one day be replaced by a quantum cosmology that is based on a fully developed quantum theory of gravity. Accordingly, my argument in this essay cannot be "If the classical Big Bang theory is true, God does not exist; the classical theory is true, therefore God does not exist." Rather, my argument is simply that the existence of God is inconsistent with the classical Big Bang theory. I aim to produce a valid argument for God's nonexistence, not a sound one.

There is also a second reason why the classical Big Bang theory cannot be viewed as the definitive theory of the universe. There are many other competing theories of the universe currently being considered, and some of these have at least as good a claim as the classical theory to be regarded as "the best currently available theory" and "the theory we should provisionally accept until the complete quantum cosmology is developed." These competitors[2] include (1) Guth's original inflationary theory, (2) Linde's and Albrecht and Steinhardt's new inflationary theory, (3) Linde's theory of chaotic inflation, (4) Tryon's, Gott's and others' theories that there are many universes (one of which is ours) that emerged as "vacuum fluctuations" from a background empty space, (5) Hartle and Hawking's theory that the universe's wave function is a function of three-dimensional spatial geometries but not of a fourth temporal dimension, (6) Everett's theory of branching universes, and many other theories of current interest. In order to keep this essay within manageable limits, I shall not consider these competing theories but shall confine myself to the classical Big Bang theory. This confinement is consistent with my limited aim of counteracting the theistic interpretation of this classical theory.

In Section 2 I set forth, in a relatively non-technical manner, the pertinent cosmological concepts. In Section 3 I offer an argument that these concepts are inconsistent with theism. In Sections 4–7 I state and respond to some objections to this argument.

2. THE BIG BANG COSMOLOGICAL THEORY

The Big Bang theory is largely based on Friedman's solutions to the so-called Einstein equation that lies at the heart of the General Theory of Relativity.[3] The ideas I wish to emphasize are the Hawking-Penrose singularity theorems and especially Hawking's principle of ignorance. The solutions for the Hawking-Penrose theorems in the general case show that there is a singularity that intersects every past-directed spacetime path and constitutes the beginning of time. These solutions demonstrate, in Hawking's words, that even for imperfectly homogeneous universes "general relativity predicts a beginning of time."[4]

The singularity theorems are the part of Big Bang cosmology that support the claim that *there is* a Big Bang singularity. But the part of Big Bang cosmology that shall be crucial to my atheistic argument is the conception of the *nature* of this singularity. This conception is embodied in Hawking's principle of ignorance, which states that singularities are inherently chaotic and unpredictable. In Hawking's words,

> A singularity is a place where the classical concepts of space and time break down as do all the known laws of physics because they are all formulated on a classical space-time background. In this paper it is claimed that this breakdown is not merely a result of our ignorance of the correct theory but that it represents a fundamental limitation to our ability to predict the future, a limitation that is analogous but additional to the limitation imposed by the normal quantum-mechanical uncertainty principle.[5]

One of the quantum-mechanical uncertainty relations is $\Delta p \cdot \Delta q \geq h/4\pi$, which implies that if the position q of a particle is definitely predictable, then the momentum p of the particle is not, and vice versa. The principle of ignorance implies that one can definitely predict neither the position nor the momentum of any particle emitted from a singularity.[6] All possible values of the particle's position and momentum that are compatible with the limited information (if any) available about the interaction region are equally probable. But the principle of ignorance has further consequences. It implies that none of the physical values of the emitted particles are definitely predictable. The Big Bang singularity "would thus emit all configurations of particles with equal probability."[7]

If the singularity's emissions are completely unpredictable, then we should expect a totally chaotic outpouring from it. This expectation is consistent with Big Bang cosmologists' understanding of the early universe, for the early universe is thought to be in a state of maximal chaos (complete entropy). Particles were emitted in random microstates, which resulted in an overall macrostate of thermal equilibrium.[8]

It is important to understand the full significance of the principle of ignorance. If the Big Bang singularity behaves in a completely unpredictable manner, then no physical laws govern its behavior. There is no law to place restrictions on what it can emit. As Paul Davies aptly comments, "anything can come out of a naked singularity—in the case of the Big Bang the universe came out. Its creation represents the instantaneous suspension of physical laws, the sudden, abrupt flash of lawlessness that allowed something to come out of nothing."[9] Here 'nothing' should be understood metaphorically as referring to something not a part of the four-dimensional spacetime continuum; the singularity is not a part of this continuum since it occupies less than three spatial dimensions. But Davies is literally correct in implying that the singularity entails an instantaneous state of lawlessness. The singularity exists for an instant and during this instant no physical law obtains that could connect the singularity to later instants. Given the initial conditions of the singularity, nothing can be predicted about the future state of the universe. Each possible configuration of particles has the same probability of being emitted by the singularity. (If there are uncountably infinite possible configurations, then we must speak instead of the probability density of each possible configuration and assign probabilities to each of the countable number of intervals of possible configurations, given an appropriate partition.) At any instant arbitrarily close to the instant at which the singularity exists, physical laws do obtain and they govern the particles actually emitted from the singularity. This means that for any physical configuration *C* that occupies an instant arbitrarily close to the instant occupied by the singularity from which *C* was emitted, there obtain laws connecting *C* to the configurations occupying later instants but there obtains no law connecting *C* to the earlier singularity. *C* adopts a lawful evolution but has its ultimate origin in primordial lawlessness.

3. THE ATHEISTIC ARGUMENT

I shall use the aspects of Big Bang cosmology explicated in the last section as the scientific premises of my atheistic argument. In this section I will add two theological premises and deduce the statement that God does not exist. Following the construction of this argument, I will state and respond to several objections to it (Sections 4–7). The real force of the argument will not become apparent until the responses to these objections are given.

The two theological premises I need are

(1) If God exists and there is an earliest state *E* of the universe, then God created *E*.
(2) If God created *E*, then *E* is ensured either to contain animate creatures or to lead to a subsequent state of the universe that contains animate creatures.

Premise (2) is entailed by two more basic theological premises, namely,

(3) God is omniscient, omnipotent, and perfectly benevolent.
(4) An animate universe is better than an inanimate universe.

Given (4), if God created a universe that was not ensured to be animate, then he would have created a universe not ensured to be of the better sort and thereby would be limited in his benevolence, power, or wisdom. But this contradicts (3). Therefore, (2) is true.

Some of the scientific ideas articulated in the last section, mainly the Hawking-Penrose singularity theorems, provide us with the summary premise

(5) There is an earliest state of the universe and it is the Big Bang singularity.

(5) requires a terminological clarification regarding "the universe." By this phrase I mean the four-dimensional spacetime continuum and any *n*-dimensional physical state that is earlier or later than the four-dimensional continuum. Since the universe has a zero radius at the singularity, it is not then four-dimensional, but since the singularity is a physical state earlier than the four-dimensional continuum it can be considered to be the first state of the universe (this is discussed further in Section 6).

The scientific ideas also give us the premise

(6) The earliest state of the universe is inanimate since the singularity involves the life-hostile conditions of infinite temperature, infinite curvature, and infinite density.

Another scientific idea enunciated in the last section, the principle of ignorance, gives us the summary premise

(7) The Big Bang singularity is inherently unpredictable and lawless and consequently there is no guarantee that it will emit a maximal configuration of particles that will evolve into an animate state of the universe. (A maximal configuration of particles is a complete state of the universe, the universe as a whole at one time.)

(5) and (7) entail

(8) The earliest state of the universe is not ensured to lead to an animate state of the universe.

We now come to the crux of our argument. Given (2), (6), and (8), we can infer that God could not have created the earliest state of the universe. It then follows, by (1), that God does not exist.

I will now state and respond to four objections to this atheistic argument.

4. FIRST OBJECTION: ANIMATE UNIVERSES ARE NOT REQUIRED BY GOD

This objection is based on the principle that there is no universe that is the best of all possible universes. For each universe U_1 there is a better universe U_2. Consequently, the fact that there is some universe better than whatever universe is the actual one is not only compatible with divine creation but is entailed by it. Therefore, the objection goes, the fact that an animate universe is better than an inanimate one is compatible with God creating as the earliest state something that by chance leads to an inanimate universe. Premises (3) and (4) do not entail (2) and the atheistic argument therefore fails.

In response, I note first that many theists claim that there is a best of all possible universes and that God ensures that the one he creates is the best one. My argument implies at least that these theologies are mistaken. But it also tells against theologies that entail there is no best possible universe. These theologies, if they are at all consistent with what is ordinarily meant by 'God' and what most philosophers and theologians mean by 'God', must impose some minimal constraint on the value of the universe God creates. I believe the overwhelming majority of theists explicitly or implicitly accept the minimal constraint that the universe contain living creatures. The idea that God has no more reason to create an animate universe than an inanimate one is inconsistent with the kind of person we normally conceive God to be. The God of the Judaeo–Christian–Islamic tradition is obviously a God who ensures that there be life in the universe he creates. This requirement conforms to the theism of Swinburne, Craig, Leslie, Plantinga, Adams, Morris, and all or virtually all other contemporary theists. Swinburne, for example, defines 'orderly universes' as the ones required by animate creatures and affirms that "God has overriding reason to make an orderly universe if he makes a universe at all."[10] According to this standard conception of God, premises (3) and (4) come with the suppressed premise

(4*a*) If God chooses to create a universe, he will choose to create an animate rather than an inanimate universe.

Given (4*a*), (3) and (4) do entail (2) and the atheistic argument is valid.

5. SECOND OBJECTION: GOD CAN INTERVENE TO ENSURE AN ANIMATE UNIVERSE

The second objection is that the lawlessness of the Big Bang singularity is not logically incompatible with its being ensured by God to emit a life-producing maximal configuration of particles. For God could intervene at the instant of the singularity and supernaturally constrain the singularity to emit a life-producing configuration.

I believe this objection is incompatible with the rationality of God. If God intends to create a universe that contains living beings at some stage in its history, then there is no reason for him to begin the universe with an inherently unpredictable singularity. Indeed, it is positively irrational. It is a sign of incompetent planning to create as the first natural state something that requires immediate supernatural intervention to ensure that it leads to the desired result. The rational thing to do is to create some state that *by its own lawful nature leads* to a life-producing universe.

This response to the second objection can be developed in the context of a discussion of John Leslie's interpretation of Big Bang cosmology. Leslie points to data or figures (the "anthropic coincidences") that suggest it is *highly improbable* that an animate universe would result from a Big Bang singularity.[11] There are many possible maximal configurations of particles that might be emitted from the singularity and only an extremely small number of these, Leslie suggests, lead toward animate states. But Leslie argues that this improbability tells *for* rather than against the hypothesis of divine creation. (I should note that Leslie works with a "Neoplatonic" conception of God[12] but that makes no substantive difference to the validity of the arguments I shall examine.) He implies that if we suppose that God constrained the singularity's explosion to be directed away from the more probable alternatives of lifelessness and toward the very narrow range of alternatives that lead to life, then we can "explain away" the apparent improbability of an animate universe evolving from the singularity. The alleged simplicity of this explanation, the distinctive value of life, and other relevant premises are regarded as making this explanation a credible one. But this fails to take into account the above-mentioned problem regarding God's rationality and competence, which appears here in an aggravated form. It seems to me that Leslie's premise that it is highly improbable that the Big Bang singularity would (if left to evolve naturally) lead to an animate universe is *inconsistent* with the conclusion that God created the singularity. If God created the universe with the aim of making it animate, it is illogical that he would have created as its first state *something whose natural evolution would lead with high probability only to inanimate states*. It does not agree with the idea of an efficient creation of an animate universe that life is brought about through the first state being created with a natural tendency toward *lifelessness* and through this tendency being *counteracted* and *overridden* by the very agency that endowed it with this tendency. The following two propositions appear to be logically incompatible:

(1) God is a rational and competent creator and he intends to create an animate universe.

(2) God creates as the first state of the universe a singularity whose natural tendency is toward lifelessness.

The problem involved here is essentially a problem of divine interference in or "correction of" the divine creations. Leslie is "opposed"[13] to the idea of "divine interference" with natural processes and is unsympathetic to the idea that "God occasionally intervenes [in the natural universe] with a helpful shove"[14] so as to ensure that life evolves. Leslie states that the hypothesis of such intervention involves an unsimple theory and for this reason is to be dispreferred. But such intervention is precisely what is required by his own account of the evolution of the early universe. His account supposes that God not only interferes with the singularity's explosion but also interferes with the subsequent evolution of the maximal configuration of particles that was emitted from the singularity. For example, Leslie mentions the theory that the early universe underwent a number of "spontaneous symmetry breaking phases" during the first 10^{-4} seconds after the Big Bang singularity and that during these phases the four forces (gravitational, strong, weak, and electromagnetic) became separated. In the GUT era (from 10^{-43} seconds after the singularity to 10^{-35} seconds) the gravitational force is separated from the strong-electroweak force. During the electroweak era (from 10^{-35} seconds to 10^{-10} seconds) the strong force is separated from the electroweak force. During the free quark era (from 10^{-10} seconds to 10^{-4} seconds) the electromagnetic force is separated from the weak force. Each of these separations is a breaking of a symmetry (the unification of two or more forces) and each symmetry is broken in a random way. This means, in effect, that the strengths of the four forces are determined in random ways at the time they become separated. This is significant, Leslie indicates, since only a small range of the values these forces may possess are consistent with a life-supporting universe. For example, if the actual value of the weak fine structure constant ($a_{\omega} \sim 10^{-11}$) were slightly larger, supernovae would have been unable to eject the heavy materials that are necessary for organisms. If this value were slightly smaller, no hydrogen would have formed and consequently no stars and planets would have evolved. Similar considerations hold for the gravitational, electromagnetic, and strong forces. Given this, Leslie continues, it is "exceedingly improbable"[15] that these symmetry-breaking phases would have resulted in the very narrow range of values required by a life-supporting universe. This improbability could be eliminated if we supposed that these values were not selected by natural random processes but were "selected by God." But this requires divine interference on a grand scale in the evolution of the universe. God would have to intervene in his creation at the Big Bang singularity to ensure that it emitted a maximal configuration of particles capable of undergoing the symmetry-breaking phases, *then again* during the GUT era to ensure that the separating gravitational force acquires the right value, *and then once again* during the electroweak era to ensure that the separating strong force acquires the right value, *and then once more* during the free quark era to ensure that the separating electromagnetic and weak forces acquire the right value. And these are only some of the interventions required (I have not even mentioned, for example, the interventions required to ensure that the elementary particles acquire the right masses). But why does Leslie think his theory avoids the implausibly complex theory of repeated divine interventions in natural processes? Because he *stipulates* that God's fixing of the values of the constants are not instances of such interventions. Interventions he defines as applying to less basic aspects of nature (such as creations of individual animal organisms).[16] But this stipulation seems arbitrary and implausible. If God's interference with the singularity's emission of particles and with the several symmetry-breaking phases are not examples of God interfering with natural states and processes, then I don't know what is.

Leslie suggests that the notion of divine interference with the processes of nature is implausible because it is less simple than the idea that God lets nature evolve on its own. But it seems to me there is a more fundamental problem with this notion, at least as it applies to Leslie's scenario. This notion, in the context of Leslie's scenario, implies that the universe God created was so bungled that it needed his repeated intervention to steer it away from disaster and toward the desired life-producing states. God created a universe that time and again was probably headed toward *the very opposite result than the one he wanted* and only through interfering with its natural evolution could he ensure that it would lead to the result he desired. But this contradicts the principle that God is not a bungler ("a competent Creator does not create things he immediately or subsequently needs to set aright").

I should make explicit that the key idea in my argument is not that God is incompetent if he creates a universe whose laws he must *violate* if his intentions are to be realized, but that he is incompetent if he creates a universe requiring his *intervention* if his intentions are to be realized. A divine intervention in natural events is entailed by, but does not entail, a divine violation of natural laws, since God may intervene in an event (e.g., the explosion of the singularity) not governed by laws. Thus, the possible objection to my argument that "if physical laws under-constrain the evolution of the universe, then God can constrain the universe to evolve into animate states without violating his physical laws" misses the point, that *intervention*, not violation, is the problem. However, if we assume Leslie's scenario, then we can say there are not only interventions but also violations, since in his scenario there are probabilistic laws governing the early evolution of the universe (which includes the symmetry-breaking phases) and God suspends (violates) these laws to ensure that the improbable life-producing outcomes result.

My conclusion is this. There are countless logically possible initial states of the universe that lead by a natural and lawlike evolution to animate states and if God had created the universe he would have selected one of these states. Given that the initial state posited by Big Bang cosmology is not one of these states, it follows that Big Bang cosmology is inconsistent with the hypothesis of divine creation.[17]

6. THIRD OBJECTION: THE SINGULARITY IS A THEORETICAL FICTION

The theist may attempt to avoid the difficulties of an unpredictable initial state and a divine intervention by supposing that the initial state of the universe is not an unpredictable singularity. The theist may continue to accept Big Bang cosmology except that she adopts rules for the interpretation of this theory that forbid reality to the singularity. These rules are based on a criterion of physical existence that the singularity fails to meet but which is met by the Big Bang explosion. These rules allow the theist to regard the Big Bang explosion, not the singularity, as the earliest state of the universe. (But now 'state' must be understood as a temporally extended state of a certain length rather than as an instantaneous one since the explosion is extended.) The Big Bang explosion is governed by physical laws and this explosion leads by a natural and lawful evolution to a state of the universe that contains animate creatures. The problem of God creating as the first state some totally unpredictable state is thereby avoided and the theist is able to ascribe a rational behavior to God in creating as the first state something that naturally evolves into an animate universe.

In dealing with this third objection I shall ignore the problem of the unpredictable symmetry-breaking phases that Leslie introduces into his scenario and that would seem to vitiate the hypothesis that the Big Bang explosion predictably evolves into animate states. Although it is widely—but not universally—accepted today that such phases occur, these phases are not entailed by classical Big Bang cosmology and accordingly it is not appropriate to introduce them when criticizing theistic interpretations of this cosmology that do not themselves introduce the phases. Thus, in responding to the third objection I will not argue that there remain unpredictabilities even if the singularity is omitted but will argue instead that there is no justification for rejecting the singularity with its unpredictability.

Let me begin by noting that the description or definition of the Big Bang singularity as a mere idealization does *not* belong to Big Bang cosmology itself and thus that if this view of the singularity is to be justified some strong and independent philosophical arguments will be needed. Big Bang cosmology represents the singularity as a unique sort of reality, a *physical singularity*, but it is represented as real nonetheless. This is evinced by the fact that past-directed spacetime paths in the early universe are not modeled on half-open intervals that approach arbitrarily close to but never reach the ideal limit, but on closed intervals one of the end-points of which is the singularity. In the words of Penrose, "the essential feature of a past spacelike singularity [the Big Bang singularity] is that it supplies a past singular end-point to the otherwise past-endless timelike curve."[18] (A timelike curve is a spacetime path of a particle.) In the words of Geroch and Horowitz, converging past-directed spacetime paths are not commonly thought to merely approach with arbitrary closeness the same singular point but are thought to actually "*reach* the same singular point,"[19] which requires the actual physical existence of the singular point. Furthermore, this point is thought by physicists to be earlier in time than the Big Bang explosion. Penrose articulates the common view that in the case of a finite universe "we think of the initial singularity as a single point . . . [which] *gives rise to an infinity of causally disconnected regions at the next instant*,"[20] a conception that clearly entails the physical and temporal reality of the initial singularity.

Given this realist representation of the singularity, the theists must have strong reasons indeed to support the interpretation of the singularity as a mere idealization. They must establish some convincing criterion of physical existence and show that the singularity fails to meet this criterion. This has been attempted by William Lane Craig. Craig argues that no infinitely complex object can be real and the singularity cannot be real since it has infinite values, such as infinite density; "there can be no object in the real world that possesses infinite density, for if it had any size at all, it would not be *infinitely* dense."[21] Craig's arguments against infinite realities in his book are aimed at showing that no reality can be mapped onto a Cantorian transfinite set. I have elsewhere[22] countered Craig's arguments but I would like to show here that even if his arguments were sound they would not count against the reality of the Big Bang singularity. When it is said that the Big Bang singularity has an infinite density, infinite temperature, and infinite curvature, it is not being said that the singularity has parts or properties that map onto a set with an aleph-zero or aleph-one cardinality. Rather, three things are implied and each of them is compatible with Craig's rejection of Cantorian realities.

The theory that there is an infinite singularity implies, first of all, that at any instant arbitrarily close to the Big Bang singularity the density, temperature, and curvature of the universe have arbitrarily high finite values. The values become higher and higher as we regress closer and closer to the singularity, such that for any arbitrarily high finite value there is an instant at which the density, temperature, and curvature of the universe possess that value.

The theory of the infinite singularity implies, second, that when the singularity is reached the values become infinite. But this does *not* mean that the density, temperature, and curvature of the universe have values involving the numbers $\aleph_0$ or $\aleph_1$. Consider the phenomenon of density, which is the ratio of mass to unit volume (density = mass/volume). If the universe is finite and the Big Bang singularity a single point, then at the first instant the entire mass of the universe is compressed into a space with zero volume. The density of the point is $n/0$, where n is the extremely high but finite number of kilograms of mass in the universe. Since it is impermissible to divide by zero, the ratio of mass to unit volume has no meaningful and measurable value and *in this sense is infinite.* Although philosophers frequently misunderstand this use of the word 'infinite' by physicists, this usage has been clearly grasped by Milton Munitz in his recent discussion of the Big Bang theory. He notes that

> the density of a homogeneous material is mass per unit volume—for example, grams per cubic centimeter. Given both a zero value and the conservation of the mass-energy of the universe [at the Big Bang singularity], no finite value can be given to the ratio of the latter to the former (it is forbidden to divide by zero). This is normally expressed by saying that the density becomes *infinite.* It would be more accurate to say the standard meaning of 'density' cannot be employed in this situation. The density cannot be assigned a finite measurable value, as is the case in all standard applications of the concept.[23]

The theory of the infinite singularity implies, third, that the space of the singularity topologically transforms into the three-dimensional space of the universe at the Big Bang explosion. It is a familiar notion in the mathematical discipline of topology that a space with a topology of a point can assume the topology of a finite three-dimensional space. The topological transformation of the zero-dimensional space to the three-dimensional space is precisely the Big Bang explosion. But I am not saying here that the zero-dimensional space is homeomorphic to the three-dimensional space, where x is homeomorphic to y if there exists a continuous bijective map f of x onto y such that the inverse map f^{-1} is also continuous. Rather, I am saying that a space with the topology of a point assumes, at a subsequent time, the topology of a finite three-dimensional space. Such topological transformations are possible but it is not possible, for instance, for a space with the topology of a point to assume, at a subsequent time, the topology of an infinite three-dimensional space (where 'infinite' is used in the Cantorian sense). If our universe is infinite, then the Big Bang singularity must have consisted of an infinite number of points and must have been at least one dimension, with each of the points "topologically exploding" into a different finite three-dimensional region. Paul Davies comments that if the universe is finite

> one can really suppose that the entire universe began compressed into one point. On the other hand, if space is infinite, we have the mathematically delicate issue of conflicting infinities, because infinitely extended space becomes infinitely compressed at the beginning of the Big Bang. This means that any given *finite* volume of the present universe, however large one chooses it to be, was compressed to a single point at the beginning. Nevertheless, it would not be correct to say *all* the universe was at one place then, for there is no way that a space with the topology of a point can suddenly assume the topology of a space with infinite extent.[24]

It might be conceded that the notion that the singularity is real escapes Craig's criticism, since it is not 'infinite' in a Cantorian sense, but argued that the concept of the singularity is defective for other reasons. For example, how can the entire mass of a finite universe be compressed into a point? The mass is three-dimensional and the point is zero-dimensional, which involves a contradiction. But this is a misunderstanding. The mass as compressed into the point is not ordinary mass, three-dimensional mass, but *infinitely compressed mass*, which means that it has lost its three-dimensionality and assumed the dimensionality of the point it occupies. The assertion that at the instant of the singularity *n* kilograms of mass is infinitely compressed in a zero volume implies in part that (1) at this instant there exists no three-dimensional mass, (2) at this instant there exists only one zero-dimensional point, that (3) this point subsequently assumes the topology of a three-dimensional space, and that (4) this subsequent three-dimensional space is occupied by *n* kilograms of mass. Of course this singular point can assume the topology of a three-dimensional space that contains *any* finite number of kilograms of mass—the actual number, *n*, is randomly "selected" from the range of possibilities—and this is one of the reasons the singularity is wholly unpredictable.

I believe, therefore, that there is no good reason for rejecting the reality of the Big Bang singularity and the attendant unpredictability. If Craig is to justify his claim that the assumption that it is real is an illegitimate "ontologizing" of a mathematical construct, he must provide some reason to support this claim other than his arguments against Cantorian infinities. His recent and related claim that "a physical state in which all spatial and temporal dimensions are zero is a mathematical idealization whose ontological counterpart is nothing"[25] is made with no effort to support it and should be rejected as an unjustified skepticism about a widely held scientific thesis.

7. FOURTH OBJECTION: UNPREDICTABILITY DOES NOT ENTAIL THERE IS NO DIVINE KNOWLEDGE

I have said the Big Bang singularity is unpredictable. It might be objected that the fact that *we* cannot predict what comes out of the singularity is consistent with God being able to predict what will emerge from it. God is omniscient, which implies he can know things that are unknowable by humans.

But this objection is based on several questionable assumptions, one of which concerns the meaning of the word 'unpredictable' as it is used in the formulation of Hawking's principle of ignorance. What is meant is *unpredictability in principle*, which entails but is different from *unpredictability by us*. The qualifier "in principle" is added to indicate that the unpredictability is due to the fact that *no natural laws govern the state(s)*. If something is merely unpredictable by us, that is consistent with saying that it is governed by a natural law that is not knowable by humans. But if there is an "in principle" unpredictability, then there is no natural law to be known, by God or any other knower. Since there is no natural law governing the singularity, God has no basis on which to compute what will emerge from the singularity. As Davies says, the instantaneous existence of the singularity and the subsequent explosion is an "abrupt flash of lawlessness."

Some might claim that 'unpredictability in principle' as used in quantum mechanics (and thus in Hawking's theory, which is partly based on quantum mechanics) should be interpreted as meaning the same as 'unpredictability by us' since the most plausible interpretations of quantum mechanics (e.g., the Copenhagen interpretation) are anti-realist. But this claim, while perhaps justified on the old assumption that the Everett interpretation is the only realist one consistent with quantum mechanics, is not justified today, given that some plausible realist interpretations have been recently developed, such as, for example, Storrs McCall's "branched model" interpretation.[26]

But this reference to a realist interpretation of the singularity's unpredictability does not do full justice to the objection that "unpredictability does not entail there is no divine knowledge." For the objector might claim that God can "know in advance" the result of the singularity's explosion *even if there is no law on the basis of which he can form a prediction*. It might be said that just as God knows, logically prior to creation, the free decisions humans would make if they were in certain circumstances, so he knows, logically prior to creation, the way the singularity would explode if it were to be the first state of the universe. The theist may allege that in addition to the familiar sorts of counterfactuals, we may introduce a new sort, "counterfactuals of singularities," one of which is the counterfactual

(1) If a Big Bang singularity were to be the earliest state of the universe, this singularity would emit a life-producing configuration of particles.

The theist may allege that (1) is true logically prior to creation and that God's pre-creation knowledge of (1) serves as his reason for his creation of a universe with a Big Bang singularity.

But this argument is unsound, since the supposition that (1) is true logically prior to creation is inconsistent with the semantic properties of counterfactuals. As Jonathan Bennett and Wayne Davies have argued,[27] counterfactuals are true iff the antecedent and consequent are both true in the possible world most similar to the actual world *before* the time specified in the antecedent. This entails that there are no possible conditions in which (1) is true, since the time specified in its antecedent is the earliest time.

But the theist need not accept the Bennett-Davies theory of counterfactuals. He may accept one of the theories of Robert Stalnaker and Richmond Thomason and Frank Jackson,[28] according to which a counterfactual is true iff its antecedent and consequent are both true in a possible world whose *total history* is most similar to that of the actual world. Or the theist may accept David Lewis's theory,[29] that counterfactuals are true iff some world in which the antecedent and consequent are both true is more similar in its overall history to the actual world than any world in which the antecedent is true and the consequent false.

But these theories of counterfactuals are of no avail since they one and all entail that a counterfactual is true only if *there is an actual world* that serves as a relatum of the similarity relation. According to the Bennett-Davies theories, the relatum is all the states of the actual world up to a certain time and according to the theories of Stalnaker, Lewis, and others, the relatum is all the states of the actual world. Since (1) is supposed to be true logically prior to creation, its truth-conditions cannot include all the states (or all the states up to a time) of the actual world, which contradicts the truth-condition requirements of counterfactuals.

But a theist familiar with the corpus of William Lane Craig might be able to come up with a response to this argument. Craig does not discuss "counterfactuals of singularities" but he does discuss counterfactuals of freedom and some of his arguments may be borrowed by a defender of the truth of (1). In response to the objection that there is no actual world logically prior to creation in relation to which counterfactuals of freedom could be evaluated as true, Craig maintains that a part of our world is actual prior to creation, namely, the part consisting of logically necessary states of affairs and counterfactual states of affairs concerning the free decisions of creatures.

> Since the relevant states of affairs are actual, one can hold to both the doctrine of divine middle knowledge [i.e., that God knows counterfactuals of freedom prior to creation] and the current explanation of what it means for a counterfactual to be true: in those possible worlds which are most similar to the actual world (insofar as it exists at [this logical] moment [prior to creation]) and in which the antecedent is true, the consequent is also true.[30]

But this response is untenable, since the current explanation of counterfactuals is that their truth conditions include either *all the states of the actual world* or *all the states of the actual world earlier than a certain time*, and the counterfactuals that are allegedly objects of God's middle knowledge meet neither of these two requirements. They are supposed to be true logically prior to the creation of the earliest state and therefore cannot include in their truth conditions all the states of the actual world or all the states earlier than a certain time.

Of course, the theist may reject the current explanation of counterfactuals. He may hold that counterfactuals of freedom (or of singularities) are true iff their antecedents and consequents are both true in the possible world most similar to the actual world *insofar as the actual world exists at the moment logically prior to creation*. This seems to be Craig's position, although he mistakenly claims it is consistent with "the current explanation of what it means for a counterfactual to be true." Now Craig holds, as we have seen, that at this logically prior moment there obtain all logically necessary states of affairs and all counterfactual states of affairs concerning free decisions of creatures. In response to the objection that counterfactuals of freedom cannot be true at this logically prior moment, since the actual world is not then actual, he claims that it is partly actual, since it includes in part the counterfactual states of affairs, i.e., the "states of affairs corresponding to true counterfactuals concerning creaturely freedom."[31] But this argument is viciously circular. In order to demonstrate that counterfactuals of freedom are true logically prior to creation, it is assumed that counterfactuals of freedom are true logically prior to creation, i.e., that prior to creation there are "states of affairs corresponding to true counterfactuals concerning creaturely freedom." To avoid this vicious circle, we must allow only the premise that there obtain logically necessary states of affairs prior to creation. But this premise is insufficient to establish the desired conclusion, since these states of affairs cannot ground the relations of transworld similarity required by logically contingent counterfactuals, the counterfactuals of freedom. It follows, then, that no sound argument can be constructed, in analogy to Craig's argument about counterfactuals of freedom, for the thesis that the "counterfactual of singularity" (1) is true logically prior to creation. It is logically incoherent to suppose that (1) is true logically prior to creation and therefore the fact that God is omniscient does not entail that he knows, logically prior to creation, that the Big Bang singularity would evolve into an animate universe.

8. CONCLUSION

If the arguments in this paper are sound, then God does not exist if Big Bang cosmology, or some relevantly similar theory, is true. If this cosmology is true, our universe exists without cause and without explanation.[32] There are numerous possible universes, and there is possibly no universe at all, and there is no reason why this one is actual rather than some other one or none at all. Now the theistically inclined person might think this grounds for despair, in that the alleged human need for a reason for existence, and other alleged needs, are unsatisfied. But I suggest that humans do or can possess a deeper level of experience than such anthropocentric despairs. We can forget about ourselves for a moment and open ourselves up to the startling impingement of reality itself. We can let ourselves become profoundly astonished by the fact that this universe exists at all. It is arguably a truth of the "metaphysics of feeling" that this fact is indeed "stupefying" and is most fully appreciated in such experiences as the one evoked in the following passage:

> [This world] exists nonnecessarily, improbably, and causelessly. It exists *for absolutely no reason at all*. It is *inexplicably* and *stunningly actual*. . . . The impact of this captivated realization upon me is overwhelming. I am completely stunned. I take a few dazed steps in the dark meadow, and fall among the flowers. I lie stupefied, whirling without comprehension in this world through numberless worlds other than this one.[33]

NOTES

1. See William Lane Craig, *The Kalam Cosmological Argument* (New York: Harper and Row, 1979); "God, Creation and Mr. Davies," *British Journal for the Philosophy of Science* 37 (1986): 163–75; "Barrow and Tipler on the Anthropic Principle vs. Divine Design," *British Journal for the Philosophy of Science* 39 (1988): 389–95; "The Caused Beginning of the Universe," in *Theism, Atheism, and Big Bang Cosmology*, edited by William Lane Craig and Quentin Smith (Oxford: Clarendon Press, 1993), pp. 141–60; "'What Place, then, for a Creator?': Hawking on God and Creation," in *Theism, Atheism, and Big Bang Cosmology*, pp. 279–300. Also see John Leslie, "Anthropic Principle, World Ensemble, Design," *American Philosophical Quarterly* 19 (1982): 141–51; "Modern Cosmology and the Creation of Life," in *Evolution and Creation*, edited by E. McMullin (South Bend, IN: University of Notre Dame Press, 1985); and numerous other articles.

2. See (1) A. Guth, "Inflationary Universe: A Possible Solution to the Horizon and Flatness Problems," *Physical Review* D23 (1981): 347–56; (2) A. D. Linde, "A New Inflationary Universe Scenario," *Physical Letters* 108B (1982): 389–93, and A. Albrecht and P. I. Steinhardt, *Physical Review Letters* 48 (1982): 1220ff.; (3) A. D. Linde, "The Inflationary Universe," *Reports on Progress in Physics* 47 (1984): 925–86; (4) E. P. Tryon, "Is the Universe a Vacuum Fluctuation?" *Nature* 246 (1973): 396–97, and J. R. Gott, "Creation of Open Universes from de Sitter Space," *Nature* 295 (1982): 304–307; (5) J. B. Hartle and S. W. Hawking, "Wave Function of the Universe," *Physical Review* D28

(1983): 2960–75; (6) H. Everett, "'Relative State' Formulation of Quantum Mechanics," *Reviews of Modern Physics* 29 (1957): 454–62. Some of these theories are discussed in Quentin Smith, "World Ensemble Explanations," *Pacific Philosophical Quarterly* 67 (1986): 73–86, and "The Uncaused Beginning of the Universe," in *Theism, Atheism, and Big Bang Cosmology*, pp. 108–40.

3. The details may be found in Smith, "The Uncaused Beginning of the Universe," and "A Criticism of A Posteriori and A Priori Arguments for a Cause of the Big Bang Singularity," in *Theism, Atheism, and Big Bang Cosmology*, pp. 161–91, and need only be mentioned in passing here.

4. S. W. Hawking, "Theoretical Advances in General Relativity," in *Some Strangeness in the Proportion*, edited by H. Woolf (Reading, MA: Addison-Wesley, 1980), p. 149.

5. S. W. Hawking, "Breakdown of Predictability in Gravitational Collapse," *Physical Review* D14 (1976): 2460.

6. See S. W. Hawking, "Is the End in Sight for Theoretical Physics?" in *Stephen Hawking's Universe*, edited by John Boslough (New York: William Morrow, 1985), p. 145.

7. Hawking, "Breakdown of Predictability," p. 2460.

8. Ibid., p. 2463.

9. P. Davies, *The Edge of Infinity* (New York: Simon and Schuster, 1981), p. 161.

10. R. Swinburne, *The Existence of God* (Oxford: Clarendon Press, 1979), p. 147. Swinburne's full definition is that orderly universes are those required by both natural beauty and life. Cf. p. 146.

11. See Leslie's articles mentioned in note 1.

12. For Leslie, 'God' means one of two things. God "may be identified as the world's creative ethical requiredness [i.e., the ethical requiredness that created the universe]. . . . Alternatively [God may be identified] as an existing person, a person creatively responsible for every other existence, who owed his existence to his ethical requiredness." See his "Efforts to Explain All Existence," *Mind* 87 (1978): 93. On the second conception of God, God as a person, it is appropriate to refer to him with a personal pronoun ('he'). But on the first conception, the impersonal pronoun 'it' is more appropriate. For simplicity's sake, I use 'he' in the main body of the paper.

13. Leslie, "Modern Cosmology and the Creation of Life," p. 112.

14. Ibid., p. 92.

15. Ibid., p. 95.

16. Ibid., pp. 91 and 112.

17. I would add that my argument does not require that God create an animate universe in the most efficient way possible, since there may be no "most efficient way possible," but merely that he create it in an efficient way (which minimally requires that no interventions be needed). Somewhat analogously, Keith Chrzan has soundly argued that "there is no best possible world" does not entail "there is no world without evil" and therefore that the "no best possible world" theodicy fails to demonstrate that evil is a necessary implication of creation and thus fails to explain how God's existence is compatible with the actual world. See Keith Chrzan, "The Irrelevance of the No Best Possible World Defense," *Philosophia* 17 (1987): 161–67. The analogy can be seen if we substitute "most efficient" for "best possible" and "without divine intervention" for "without evil" in the

above sentences. I also reject the supposition that the Hawking-Penrose theorems and the principle of ignorance are *metaphysically necessary* laws of nature and therefore that God had no alternative to creating a singularity that required his intervention. In his interesting article on "Explaining Existence," *Canadian Journal of Philosophy* 16 (1986): 713–22, Chris Mortensen entertains the supposition that the laws governing the beginning of the universe are necessary, but concludes, soundly I believe, that this supposition is not particularly credible. I would add that the Kripke-Putnam argument that some laws are necessary (e.g., that water is H_2O), even if sound, does not apply to the singularity theorems, for the Kripke-Putnam argument applies only to laws involving ostensively defined terms (e.g., 'water') and 'singularity' is not ostensively defined. See Jarrett Leplin, "Is Essentialism Unscientific?" *Philosophy of Science* 55 (1988): 493–510, and "Reference and Scientific Realism," *Studies in History and Philosophy of Science* 10 (1979): 265–85.

18. R. Penrose, "Singularities in Cosmology," in *Confrontation of Cosmological Theories with Observational Data*, edited by M. S. Longair (Dordrecht: Reidel, 1974), p. 264. Penrose shows how the zero dimensional singularity can be conformally rescaled as a three-dimensional singularity, which testifies further to the fact that the singularity is thought of as something real.

19. R. Geroch and G. Horowitz, "Global Structure of Spacetime," in *General Relativity*, edited by S. W. Hawking and W. Israel (New York: Cambridge University Press, 1979), p. 267. Geroch and Horowitz go on to argue for the nonstandard position that a study of the global properties of singular spacetimes is a more fruitful line of research than attempts to provide constructions of local singular points.

20. Penrose, "Singularities in Cosmology," p. 264; the italics are mine. Penrose is best interpreted as speaking loosely in this passage, for strictly speaking there is no "next instant" after the instant of the singularity (if time is dense or continuous) and the singular point does not topologically transform to an "infinite" number of causally disconnected regions but to an arbitrarily large finite number.

21. William Lane Craig, "The Finitude of the Past and the Existence of God," in *Theism, Atheism, and Big Bang Cosmology*, p. 43.

22. See "Infinity and the Past," in *Theism, Atheism, and Big Bang Cosmology*, pp. 77–91, and "A New Typology of Temporal and Atemporal Permanence," *Noûs* 23 (1989): 307–30, sect. 6. For a correction to one of my arguments in "Infinity and the Past," see E. Eells, "Quentin Smith on Infinity and the Past," *Philosophy of Science* 55 (1988): 453–55.

23. Milton Munitz, *Cosmic Understanding* (Princeton: Princeton University Press, 1986), p. 111.

24. Davies, *The Edge of Infinity*, p. 159.

25. Craig, "The Caused Beginning of the Universe," sect. 2.

26. Storrs McCall, "Interpreting Quantum Mechanics Via Quantum Probabilities," mimeograph, 1989.

27. Jonathan Bennett. "Counterfactuals and Possible Worlds," *Canadian Journal of Philosophy* 4 (1974): 381–402; Wayne Davies, "Indicative and Subjunctive Conditionals," *Philosophical Review* 88 (1979): 544–64.

28. Robert Stalnaker, "A Theory of Conditionals," in *Studies in Logical Theory*, edited by N. Rescher (Oxford: Blackwell, 1968), pp. 92–112; Richmond Thomason and Robert Stalnaker, "A Semantic Analysis of Conditional Logic," *Theoria* 36 (1970):

23–42; Frank Jackson, "On Assertion and Indicative Conditionals," *Philosophical Review* 88 (1979): 565ff.

29. David Lewis, *Counterfactuals* (Cambridge, MA: Harvard University Press, 1973).

30. William Lane Craig, *The Only Wise God: The Compatibility of Divine Foreknowledge and Human Freedom* (Grand Rapids: Baker Book House, 1987), p. 144.

31. Ibid., p. 143.

32. Big Bang cosmology may be modified in certain fundamental respects so that our universe has an explanation in terms of other universes, but the set of all universes will nonetheless remain unexplained. See Quentin Smith, "A Natural Explanation of the Existence and Laws of Our Universe," *Australasian Journal of Philosophy* 68 (1990): 22–43.

33. Quentin Smith, *The Felt Meanings of the World: A Metaphysics of Feeling* (West Lafayette: Purdue University Press, 1986), pp. 300–301. In an important study, Milton Munitz has plausibly argued that it is *possible* that there is a reason for the existence of the universe, such that this reason is not a 'reason' in the sense of a purpose, cause, scientific explanation or evidence (justification) for a belief or statement, but in some unique sense not fully comprehensible by us. This argument is consistent, of course, with the position that there actually is no reason for the existence of the Big Bang universe and that it is not possible that this universe has a cause or purpose. See his *The Mystery of Existence: An Essay in Philosophical Cosmology* (New York: Appleton-Century-Crofts, 1965), especially Part 4 and the conclusion.

I am grateful to Richard Fallon and two anonymous referees for the *Australasian Journal of Philosophy* for helpful comments on an earlier version of this essay.

4

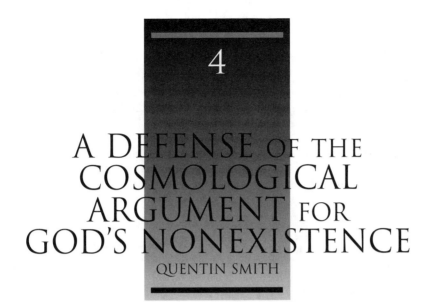

A DEFENSE OF THE COSMOLOGICAL ARGUMENT FOR GOD'S NONEXISTENCE

QUENTIN SMITH

1. INTRODUCTION

The advent of Big Bang cosmology in this century was a watershed for theists. Since the times of Copernicus and Darwin, many theists regarded science as hostile to their world-view and as requiring defense and retrenchment on the part of theism. But Big Bang cosmology in effect reversed this situation. The central idea of this cosmology, that the universe exploded into existence in a "Big Bang" about 15 billion years ago or so, seemed tailor-made to a theistic viewpoint. Big Bang cosmology seemed to offer empirical evidence for the religious doctrine of creation ex nihilo. The theistic implications seemed so clear and exciting that even Pope Pius XII was led to comment that "True science to an ever increasing degree discovers God as though God were waiting behind each door opened by science."[1] But the theistic interpretation of the Big Bang has received not only widespread dissemination in popular culture and official sanction but also a sophisticated philosophical articulation. Richard Swinburne, John Leslie, and especially William Lane Craig[2] have developed powerful arguments for theism based on a well-grounded knowledge of the cosmological data and ideas.

The response of atheists and agnostics to this development has been comparatively weak, indeed, almost invisible. An uncomfortable silence seems to be the

From *Theism, Atheism, and Big Bang Cosmology*, edited by William Lane Craig and Quentin Smith (Oxford: Clarendon, 1993), pp. 232–55.

rule when the issue arises among nonbelievers or else the subject is briefly and epigrammatically dismissed with a comment to the effect that "science has no relevance to religion." The reason for the apparent embarrassment of nontheists is not hard to find. Anthony Kenny suggests it in this summary statement:

> According to the big bang theory, the whole matter of the universe began to exist at a particular time in the remote past. A proponent of such a theory, at least if he is an atheist, must believe that the matter of the universe came from nothing and by nothing.[3]

This idea disturbs many for the reason it disturbs C. D. Broad:

> I must confess that I have a very great difficulty in supposing that there was a first phase in the world's history, i.e. a phase immediately before which there existed neither matter, nor minds, nor anything else. . . . I suspect that my difficulty about a first event or phase in the world's history is due to the fact that, whatever I may *say* when I am trying to give Hume a run for his money, I cannot really *believe* in anything beginning to exist without being *caused* (in the old-fashioned sense of *produced* or *generated*) by something else which existed before and up to the moment when the entity in question began to exist. . . . I . . . find it impossible to give up the principle; and with that confession of the intellectual impotence of old age I must leave this topic.[4]

Motivated by concerns such as Broad's, some of the few nontheists who have been vocal on this subject have gone so far as to deny, without due justification, central tenets of Big Bang cosmology. Among physicists, the most notorious example is Fred Hoyle, who vehemently rejected the suggestion of a Big Bang that seemed to imply a Creator and unsuccessfully attempted to construe the evidence for a Big Bang as evidence for an evolving "bubble" within a larger unchanging and infinitely old universe (I am referring to his 1970s post-steady state theory[5]). An example of this contrary approach among philosophers is evinced by W. H. Newton-Smith. Newton-Smith felt himself compelled to maintain, in flat contradiction to the singularity theorems of Big Bang cosmology (which entail that there can be no earlier state of the universe than the Big Bang singularity), that the evidence that macroscopic events have causal origins gives us "reason to suppose that some prior state of the universe led to the production of this particular singularity."[6]

It seems to me, however, that nontheists are not put in such dire straits by Big Bang cosmology. Nontheists are not faced only with the alternatives of embarrassed silence, confessions of impotence, epigrammatic dismissals, or "denial" when confronted with the apparently radical implications of Big Bang cosmology. It will be my purpose in this paper to show this by further developing a coherent and plausible atheistic interpretation of the Big Bang,[7] an interpretation that is not only able to stand up to the theistic interpretation but is in fact *better justified* than the theistic interpretation. But my argument is intended to establish even more than this, namely, that Big Bang cosmology is actually *inconsistent* with theism. I will argue that if Big Bang cosmology is true, then God does not exist.

2. THE ARGUMENT

This argument was initially presented in "Atheism, Theism, and Big Bang Cosmology"[8] and I shall briefly restate it and then offer a more comprehensive defense of the argument than was offered in that essay.

The argument involves the idea that the Big Bang singularity is inherently unpredictable, as is implied by Hawking's principle of ignorance. The significance of this principle can be easily missed. It implies that the Big Bang singularity behaves in a completely unpredictable manner *in the sense that no physical laws govern its behavior.* The unpredictability of the singularity is not simply an epistemic affair, meaning that "we humans cannot predict what will emerge from it, even though there is a law governing the singularity which, if known, would enable precise predictions to be made." William Lane Craig assumes unpredictability to be merely epistemic; he writes that "unpredictability [is] an epistemic affair which may or may not result from an ontological indeterminism. For clearly, it would be entirely consistent to maintain determinism on the quantum level even if *we* could not, even in principle, predict precisely such events."[9] Now I grant that there are legitimate uses of 'unpredictability' that are merely epistemic in import, but this is not how the word is used in Hawking's principle of ignorance. The unpredictability that pertains to Hawking's principle of ignorance is an unpredictability that is a consequence of lawlessness, not of human inability to know the laws. There is no law, not even a probabilistic law, governing the singularity that places restrictions on what it can emit. Hawking writes that

> A singularity can be regarded as a place where there is a breakdown of the classical concept of space-time as a manifold with a pseudo-Riemannian metric. Because all known laws of physics are formulated on a classical space-time background, they will all break down at a singularity. This is a great crisis for physics because it means that one cannot predict the future. One does not know what will come out of a singularity.[10]

Deterministic or even probabilistic laws cannot obtain on the quantum level in the singularity, since *there is no quantum level* in the singularity; the space-time manifold that quantum processes presuppose has broken down. The singularity is a violent, terrifying cauldron of lawlessness. As Paul Davies notes, "anything can come out of a naked singularity—in the case of the Big Bang the universe came out. Its creation represents the instantaneous suspension of physical laws, the sudden, abrupt flash of lawlessness that allowed something to come out of nothing."[11] The question I shall examine is whether this primordial lawlessness is consistent with the hypothesis of divine creation. I shall argue it is not.

The cosmological argument for God's nonexistence has two premises that are based on classical Big Bang cosmology, namely,

(1) The Big Bang singularity is the earliest state of the universe.
(2) The earliest state of the universe is inanimate.

(2) follows from (1) since the singularity involves the life-hostile conditions of infinite temperature, infinite curvature, and infinite density.

The principle of ignorance gives us the summary premise

(3) No law governs the Big Bang singularity and consequently there is no guarantee that it will emit a configuration of particles that will evolve into an animate universe.

(1)–(3) entail

(4) The earliest state of the universe is not guaranteed to evolve into an animate state of the universe.

My argument is that (4) is inconsistent with the hypothesis that God created the earliest state of the universe, since it is true of God that *if he created the earliest state of the universe, then he would have ensured that this state is animate or evolves into animate states of the universe*. But this conditional may be doubted and the argument rejected.

3. THE QUESTION OF GOD'S INTENTION TO CREATE AN ANIMATE UNIVERSE

I believe it is essential to the idea of God as the perfect being that if he creates a universe, he creates an animate universe, and therefore that if he creates a first state of the universe, he creates a state that is, or is guaranteed to evolve into, an animate state. If somebody says, "It does not matter to God whether the universe he creates is animate or inanimate," the person is operating with a concept of

God different from that embodied in the definition of God as the perfect being, as omniscient, omnibenevolent, omnipotent, etc. Even if there is no best possible world, it does not follow that it is consistent with the divine nature to create just any world. There are different types of worlds and God is constrained by his nature to create a world of a certain type (even though there may be no best world within the class of possible worlds constituting the type in question). William Craig admits that the divine perfections impose some constraint upon which type of world God creates. "The most that his omnibenevolence would seem to require is that he create a world in which the evil is not on balance greater than the good."[12] However, I believe these perfections impose further constraints, for example, that the type of world God creates be one in which there is no gratuitous evil. If the evil is not on balance greater than the good, but the world contains some gratuitous evil, then this world cannot be created by an omnibenevolent being. I believe a further constraint imposed by God's omnibenevolence is that the type of world he creates be animate. Omnibenevolence requires living creatures in relation to which God can exercise his benevolence. How can God be benevolent to a cloud of hydrogen gas? Divine benevolence involves advancing the good of creatures and in order to have *a good* a creature must have some desires or goals that God can enable it to attain by creating it and placing it in the appropriate circumstances. A cloud of hydrogen gas, however, has no good that God can advance.

It might be responded that God's benevolence need not require him to advance the good of his creatures. Divine benevolence requires only that God do something that is good. Since a lifeless universe is better than no universe at all, God is doing something good by creating a lifeless universe.

I reject the idea that God's benevolence does not require that he advance the good of his creatures and thus I reject the idea that God would create only creatures that have no good. But even waiving this objection, the above response is unsound. I would grant that a lifeless universe is better than no universe at all, but deny that God is being good or benevolent if he creates such a universe rather than an animate universe. In assessing whether or not the creation of a universe containing only hydrogen gas is an act of benevolence we must take into account not only that an inanimate universe is better than no universe but also that an animate universe is better than an inanimate universe. Is it consistent (in the broadly logical sense) with omnibenevolence to bring into existence nothing but a cloud of hydrogen gas, when one could have instead brought into existence a world with animals and intelligent and moral organisms? I think it is not consistent, but is instead a sign of moral callousness or indifference or a failure to recognize the distinctive value of intelligent and moral organisms; these signified characteristics are not consistent with a god that is all-knowing and supremely good. It would be a gratuitous evil of omission if God created merely an inanimate world.

Craig writes that:

> All that Smith's reasoning proves is
>
> > (4") If God chose to create the universe, he had a reason to create an animate rather than an inanimate one.
>
> But it does not follow from (4") that necessarily, if God chose to create the universe, then its first state is either animate or leads by physical necessity to an animate state. For there is no inconsistency in His choosing to create an inanimate universe.[13]

I agree that this "does not follow," but for reasons not mentioned by Craig. It does not follow because God may choose to create a universe with no first state, but infinite in its past-direction. It also does not follow since God may create a first state that leads with high probability (rather than physical necessity) to an animate state. Craig's reason seems to be that if God actually had a reason to create an animate rather than an inanimate universe, this is consistent with his choosing to create an inanimate rather than animate universe in some merely possible world. I do not think so, since God does not contingently, but necessarily, have a reason to create an animate rather than an inanimate universe. It contradicts his omnibenevolence to suppose there is a possible world where God has a reason to create an inanimate rather than an animate universe, or has no reason to create an animate rather than inanimate universe. And if God has a reason (an overriding reason is the sort we have in mind) to create an animate rather than an inanimate universe, then it would be irrational to create an inanimate universe. (A person is irrational if he has an overriding reason to do *A* and chooses to do not-*A* instead.) Thus, I believe that necessarily, if God chose to create a universe that has a beginning in time, then its first state is either animate or leads by physical necessity or high probability to an animate state. In "Atheism, Theism, and Big Bang Cosmology" I said that God would *ensure* the first state is or leads to an animate state, but this constraint can be interpreted broadly so as to allow for "high probability" as well as "physical necessity."

I shall now respond to further objections to the atheistic cosmological argument. Some of these objections have been made by Craig,[14] some are suggested by the writings of Swinburne, and still others are formulated independently.

4. THE QUESTION OF DIVINE INTERVENTION

One objection to the argument of Section 2 is that it does not take into account the possibility of divine intervention. If the Big Bang singularity is lawless, then it is feasible for God to intervene at the instant of the singularity and supernaturally constrain it to explode in a certain way, namely, to explode by emitting a life-producing maximal configuration of particles. In this way, God can guarantee that the earliest state of the universe will evolve into an animate state.

But it is not at all obvious that this objection is consistent with the classical theist conception of the divine nature. God is omniscient, omnipotent, and perfectly rational and it is not a sign of a being with these attributes to create as the first state of the universe some inherently unpredictable entity that requires immediate "corrective" intervention in order that the universe may be set on the right course. It is a mark of inefficiency, incompetent planning, and poor design to create as the first natural state something that needs supernatural intervention "right off the bat" to ensure that it leads to the desired outcome.

William Craig objects to this argument that it counts against deism, but not against classical theism. The god of the deists creates the first state (if there is a first state) and allows the universe to evolve henceforth on its own, without requiring any further divine activity. The god of the classical theists, on the other hand, is ceaselessly active in the universe, for this god is *continuously creating (conserving)* the universe. Accordingly, Craig concludes, the classical theist "will therefore tend to welcome Smith's case for the necessity of divine interventions as a confirmation of God's intimate involvement with creation at a very fundamental level."[15]

But this response is based on a failure to distinguish in a relevant way *divine intervention* from *divine conservation (continuous creation)*. The two concepts are incompatible in a certain respect, i.e., that an intervention is possible only if conservation is not being realized in a rational way. God intervenes in a natural process if and only if God violates a natural law governing that process or alters a natural process or state that is not governed by any law. Divine conservation requires that God sustains the universe in existence throughout the time that the universe exists, such that each subsequent state of the universe is produced by God as following upon the prior state. If the universe is conserved by a perfectly rational being, then the sequence of states (the way in which they follow upon one another) will be lawlike and rationally explicable rather than haphazard. If a branch is falling to the ground at time *t*, then at *t* + 1 the universe is conserved in such a way that the branch hits the ground rather than vanishes into nothingness and is replaced by an instantaneously appearing three-headed bat. The materials for a definition of a rational conservation are provided by Swinburne's remarks in this passage:

> An argument from the universe to God may start from the existence of the universe today, or from its existence for as long as it has existed—whether a finite or an infinite time. Leibniz considers the argument in the latter form, and I shall

> follow him. So let us consider the series of states of the universe starting from the present and going backwards in time, S_1, S_2, S_3, and so on. (We can suppose each to last a small finite time.) Now clearly there are laws of nature *L* which bring about the evolution of S_3 from S_4, S_2 from S_3, and so on. (I shall assume for the purpose of simplicity of exposition that this process is a deterministic process, viz., that *L* and S_5 together provide a full explanation of S_4, *L* and S_4 a full explanation of S_3, and so on; we can ignore any minor element of indeterminism—nothing will turn on it.) So we get the following picture:
>
> $$.>\ldots S_5 \overset{L}{\rightarrow} S_4 \overset{L}{\rightarrow} S_3 \overset{L}{\rightarrow} S_2 \overset{L}{\rightarrow} S_1.$$
>
> The series of states may be finite or infinite—which, we do not know. Now God might come into the picture in one of two ways, as responsible for *L*, and so as providing a complete explanation of the occurrence of each state *S*; or at the beginning of the series (if it has one) as starting the process off.[16]

If the universe has a beginning and classical theism is true, then God will come into the picture in both ways.

These remarks suggest the following definition of conservation by a perfectly rational (powerful, good, etc.) being. God conserves the universe if and only if for any two states *S* and *S′* of the universe, where *S′* is the immediate successor of *S*, God creates *S′* and *S′* has the property of *being the nomological consequent of S*. (If time is dense or continuous, then *S′* must be understood as a temporally extended state, for there is no instantaneous state *S′* that immediately succeeds an instantaneous or extended state *S* if time is dense or continuous.) *S′* is the nomological consequent of *S* if and only if there is a set of laws *L* such that the premises that *L* obtains and *S* exists wholly or partially entail that *S* is succeeded by *S′*. The premises that *L* obtains and *S* exists wholly entail that *S′* is the successor if *L* is a set of deterministic laws and these premises partially entail (i.e., render probable to some degree) that *S′* is the successor if *L* is a set of probabilistic laws.

If God interferes with the universe by violating or suspending his laws, or by altering the natural tendency of a lawless state, then he is not engaged in a rational continuous creation of the universe (i.e., a producing of a subsequent state as a nomological consequent of a prior state). Now the "god" of popular imagination or various religious scriptures is thought to interfere in such ways with the universe (e.g., by causing a bush to combust spontaneously or by enabling a person to survive a plane crash in which two hundred other people are killed), but the god with the attributes assigned by classical theism (omniscience, etc.) should not be understood in this way. This god is perfectly rational and conserves the universe in a lawlike and rationally explicable way. It is not consistent with the concept of this god that he[17] should create a lawless first state (the Big Bang singularity) that naturally tends toward the opposite state he desires and thereby requires a divine correction.

I would note that this argument need not be made to hinge upon the reality of the Big Bang singularity. If the singularity is ontologically nothing, as Craig argues, then divine interference still shows up in the symmetry-breaking phases, as I argued in "Atheism, Theism, and Big Bang Cosmology." It would make no clear sense for God to ordain that S_1 follow upon S_2 by a probabilistic law L and at the same time for God to violate L and provide a force or particle mass with a value it probably would not have possessed if L were left unviolated. However, I believe the singularity exists (as I shall further argue in a later section) and shall continue to assume this.

I would emphasize that my argument does not presuppose that there is a "most rational, competent, or efficient way of creating an animate universe" and therefore does not succumb to an analogue of the "no best possible world" theodicy, such as the one developed by George Schlesinger.[18] My argument presupposes only that there are efficient ways and inefficient ways, where an efficient way is one whereby animate states evolve in accordance with natural laws and an inefficient way one whereby animate states do not evolve in accordance with natural laws but require divine intervention.

Craig rejoins to this that efficiency is not one of the divine perfections. He refers to Thomas Morris's theory that an efficient person is one who husbands his energy and time, achieving his ends with as little energy and time as possible. It is good to be efficient if one has limited time and energy, but if one's power and time is unlimited, then there is no reason to think efficiency is better than inefficiency.

I believe there is such a reason, namely, that efficiency is of positive aesthetic value and inefficiency of negative aesthetic value (apart from any considerations of whether one's power and time is limited or unlimited). Efficiency, like gracefulness, is one of the positive aesthetic values that supervene upon personal activities and all else being equal it is irrational for a good person to realize a negative value when he could have realized a positive one instead.

But the premise that "God is inefficient" is not necessary to conclude that "God is irrational" if he creates an initial state that is not naturally tended toward an animate universe. One needs only the principles of rational action. Consider this argument:

(1) God intends to create an animate universe.

(2) It is possible for God to create an initial state S that deterministically or probably evolves toward an animate universe and it is possible for God to create an initial state S' that does not deterministically or probably evolve toward an animate universe.

(3) If it is within any person's power to do *A* or (exclusive disjunction) *B*, and *A* certainly or probably advances the person's goals and *B* does not, then (all other things being equal) the person is rational with respect to *A* and *B* if and only if the person does *A* rather than *B*.

(4) God creates *S'*.

Therefore,

(5) God is irrational.

Since (5) contradicts the definition of God, it follows that *S'* is uncreated by God and thus that God does not exist. (I respond to the objection that it is not possible for God to create *S* in a later section.)

Craig suggests that God may have reasons for creating *S'* "of which we have no idea,"[19] reasons which would show that it is one of God's goals to have a first state that does not deterministically or probably evolve toward an animate universe. Craig's suggestion at best may block a deductive "Big Bang cosmological argument" against God's existence, but not a probabilistic argument. I may grant that it is logically possible that God has reasons for creating *S'* of which we have no idea, but I would affirm there is not the slightest evidence of any such reason and therefore that it is rational to believe that this is improbable. (The difference between a deductive and probabilistic "Big Bang cosmological argument against God's existence" is not material to the main thrust of my argument, since "Big Bang cosmology is inconsistent with theism" may be read as "Big Bang cosmology is certainly or probably inconsistent with theism.")

However, Craig does introduce a possible reason for God's creation of *S'*, namely, that God "wanted to leave a general revelation of himself in nature by creating a world which would never in all probability have resulted from the natural tendencies of things alone."[20] But this gets things backwards; the fact that the evolution of an animate universe appears to be due to random chance and improbable occurrences suggests that the universe is *not* designed for humans or other living creatures and therefore that God does not exist. If the universe is to manifest a "general revelation" of God, then it must appear designed by God and it does not appear designed if the evolution of living creatures appears to be rendered improbable by the very nature of things.

The further possible reason Craig offers for God's creation of *S'*, that "Perhaps God delights in the creative activity of fashioning a world"[21] runs foul of the above-mentioned points, namely, that the "creative activity" alluded to involves interfering with the natural tendency with which God endowed things and that this entails inefficiency, the performance of an aesthetically disvaluable action, and the performance of an action that conflicts with the principles of rational activity. God would not "delight" in doing something inefficient, irrational, or aesthetically disvaluable.

Accordingly, while my argument against the hypothesis of divine intervention in the singularity and the symmetry-breaking phases may be a "glaring weakness"[22] in an argument against the god of popular imagination or religious scriptures, it is not a weakness in an argument against a god conceived as possessing the divine perfections of perfect rationality, omniscience, omnipotence, and omnibenevolence.

5. THE QUESTION OF THE REALITY OF THE SINGULARITY

Craig argues that a crucial premise of the atheistic argument, premise (1) that "The Big Bang singularity is the earliest state of the universe," is false since it is based on a reification of the singularity. Although I argued that physicists represent the singularity as real, Craig thinks certain statements by physicists lend themselves to the interpretation that the singularity is unreal. But the statements he quotes imply no such thing. He quotes Geroch to the effect that a space traveler *C* is "snuffed out of existence" when *C* hits a black hole singularity.[23] This is indeed true, but not because the singularity does not exist. Rather, it is because the space traveler *C* becomes crushed to a dimensionless point and no person can exist if she is crushed to a point. But the singular point still exists. Craig also quotes Kanitscheider to the effect that the singularity is not an element of the spacetime manifold and is not an event, but this is something I have insisted myself and it certainly does not entail that the singularity does not exist. The singularity is not an event or an element in the manifold since all such events belong to a four-dimensional continuum, whereas the singularity does not. In the case of a finite universe, it is a pointlike object that exists by itself for an instant before exploding and emitting a four-dimensional continuum.

Craig proceeds to assert that something with no duration and no spatial dimensions does not exist. "Simply put, an object which has no spatial dimensions and no temporal duration hardly seems to qualify as a physical object at all, but is rather a mathematical conceptualization. . . . [S]uch a point could hardly be called a physical object and seems ontologically equivalent to nothing."[24] But this assertion flies in the face of Special and General Relativity, which represents spacetime as a continuum of instantaneous spatial points. Each "event" in the spacetime is a spatial point (something with zero spatial dimensions) and is instantaneous (something with zero temporal duration). The difference between the Big Bang singularity and elements of spacetime is that the elements have four coordinates and the singularity has no coordinates; this difference is reflected in the fact that the singularity is a boundary or edge of spacetime and an event or element is a part of spacetime. Each event is a spatial point that is connected to other spatial points along the dimensions of height, width, and depth, but the initial singularity of a finite universe is a spatial point that exists in isolation. But each element of the manifold and the singularity are similar in that each is spatially and temporally pointlike. Thus, if Craig's assertion is true, not only would the singularity be ontologically equivalent to nothing but everything that exists (every event) would be equivalent to nothing. This shows his statement is false. I conclude that there is reason to believe that the singularity is real (namely, that it follows from the Hawking-Penrose singularity theorems and is treated as real by physicists) and no reason to believe it is unreal. (Recall that I am working with classical Big Bang cosmology in this essay and am not taking into account quantum models, such as the Hartle-Hawking model, which result in the singularity being "smeared out.")

Richard Swinburne also believes that the singular point is a mathematical idealization. He provides an argument for this, namely, that it is logically necessary that space be three-dimensional. Swinburne presents an argument against the logical possibility of two-dimensional objects and suggests that analogous arguments can be constructed against one-dimensional and zero-dimensional objects. He asks us to consider a two-dimensional surface that contains two-dimensional objects:

> it is clearly logically possible that the two-dimensional "material objects" should be elevated above the surface or depressed below it . . . the logical possibility exists even if the physical possibility does not. Since it is logically possible that the "material objects" be moved out of the surface, there must be places, and so points, outside the surface, since a place is wherever, it is logically possible, a material object could be.[25]

Therefore, Swinburne concludes, if there exists a two-dimensional object or surface there must also exist a third spatial dimension. Swinburne's argument instantiates the following invalid argument form:

(1) *Fx* is logically possible (i.e., it is logically possible for *x* to possess the property *F*).
(2) *C* is a necessary condition of *Fx*.
(3) *x* exists.
(4) Therefore, *C* exists.

The fact that Swinburne's argument has this form becomes clear if we state his argument as follows:

(1') It is logically possible for any object on a two-dimensional surface to possess the property of *moving above or below the surface.*
(2') A third spatial dimension is a necessary condition of any object on a two-dimensional surface moving above or below the surface.

(3') There exists an object on a two-dimensional surface.
(4') Therefore, there exists a third spatial dimension.

If (1')–(4') proves that objects on two-dimensional surfaces require a third spatial dimension, then the following argument proves that there is a heaven:

(1") It is logically possible for any human body to be resurrected after death and occupy a heavenly space.
(2") Heaven is a necessary condition of any human body being resurrected.
(3") There are human bodies.
(4") Therefore, there is a heaven.

The fallacy, if the reader has not already grasped it, is the assumption that a necessary condition of an object possessing a certain property must be actual if the object is actual. This of course is not so; the necessary condition need be actual only if the object's possession of the property is actual. I conclude that Swinburne has given us no reason to believe that it is impossible for there to be a Big Bang singularity that occupies fewer than three spatial dimensions. Given that Swinburne's argument fails, and that no other arguments against the coherency of the Big Bang singularity have been presented (at least of which I am aware), the above considerations warrant the conclusion that there is no reason to deny reality to the Big Bang singularity. Thus, the problem of unpredictability remains.

6. COUNTERFACTUALS OF SINGULARITIES

The problem of unpredictability would be solved if counterfactuals of singularities were true logically prior to creation. I argued in "Atheism, Theism, and Big Bang Cosmology" that the supposition that these propositions are true logically prior to creation is inconsistent with possible world semantics (e.g., those of Stalnaker, Lewis, Davies, and others). There is an inconsistency since there are no relevant grounds of similarity among possible worlds that could render the counterfactuals of singularities true logically prior to creation.

I would agree with Craig's remark that "Smith has to treat possible world semantics as the final word on the truth conditions of counterfactual conditionals in order for his anti-theistic argument to go through."[26] Craig rejects my argument by rejecting these semantics, but I am willing to rest my case on the validity of these semantics.

However, Craig attempts to show that the thesis that God knows (logically prior to creation) counterfactuals of singularities is "consistent"[27] with possible

world semantics. The structure of Craig's argument for the consistency is unclear to me, but I will indicate that the various remarks he makes cannot add up to a sound argument for the alleged consistency.

Craig responds to the claim that there are no truth-makers for counterfactuals of singularities (logically prior to creation) by stating that counterfactual states of affairs concerning singularities serve as the truth-makers of the counterfactual propositions. "The counterfactuals are true because the relevant states of affairs obtain." The counterfactual proposition *If a Big Bang singularity were to be the earliest state of the universe, this singularity would emit a life-producing configuration of particles* is made true by virtue of corresponding to the state of affairs *If a Big Bang singularity were to be the earliest start of the universe, this singularity would emit a life-producing configuration of particles.* According to Craig, similarity relations among worlds do not constitute "a reason *why* certain counterfactuals are true or false."[28] The reason why a counterfactual is true is that the corresponding counterfactual state of affairs obtains. However, I would object that this position is *not* consistent with the standard possible worlds semantics. According to these semantics, "counterfactual states of affairs" are not the truth-makers of counterfactual propositions. There are no such states of affairs. Rather, relations of similarity among possible worlds are the truth-makers. The similarity relations have for their relata the histories of the worlds and the natural laws. These relations are the reason why the relevant counterfactual propositions are true.

But Craig (following Plantinga) seems to see an opening here since natural laws entail counterfactuals. Given this entailment, it seems possible to argue that the counterfactual states of affairs grounded in the natural laws help determine the similarity among worlds and function as truth-makers of the counterfactual propositions entailed by natural laws. The move is then made to the claim that counterfactuals of singularities also have counterfactual states of affairs for their truth-makers, states of affairs that obtain logically prior to creation.

Although I have difficulty with each of the moves in this argument, I will confine myself to pointing out that its initial move is untenable; the fact that natural laws are among the relata of the similarity relations and entail counterfactual propositions does not imply that there are counterfactual states of affairs that serve as the truth-makers of the entailed propositions. The truth-makers are rather the similarity relations among worlds that are grounded upon the world histories and the laws themselves. The truth-maker of *If a light ray were emitted from this flashlight, it would travel at 186,000 m.p.s.* is not a counterfactual state of affairs (it is not the putative state of affairs *If a light ray were emitted from this flashlight, it would travel at 186,000 m.p.s.*); rather, it is a certain similarity relation between the actual world and a world in which there obtains the natural law that light travels at 186,000 m.p.s. and in which a light ray is emitted from this

flashlight. Craig says that "one measure of similarity between worlds is the degree to which they share their counterfactuals."[29] This is true in the sense that one measure of similarity between worlds is the degree to which they share their natural laws, which entail counterfactual propositions. But Craig does not show us how to get from this claim to the thesis that there are counterfactual states of affairs. Nor does he show us how to get from the claim that there are counterfactual states of affairs corresponding to the propositions entailed by natural laws to the further claim that there obtain (logically prior to creation) counterfactual states of affairs concerning singularities. He simply asserts that there are such states of affairs and that they obtain logically prior to creation. Thus, I do not think Craig has established his claims or demonstrated that his assertions are consistent with the possible worlds semantics of counterfactuals.

7. THE QUESTION OF THE RELATIVE SIMPLICITY OF THE THEISTIC AND ATHEISTIC HYPOTHESES

I shall turn now to an issue not previously discussed, namely, whether considerations of simplicity support the theistic or atheistic interpretation of Big Bang cosmology. Swinburne has advanced the argument that the hypothesis of divine creation is simpler than the atheistic hypothesis and more likely to be true. He claims that God is simpler than the physical universe and therefore is more likely than it to exist unexplained. "If something has to occur unexplained, a complex physical universe is less to be expected than other things (e.g., God)."[30] If the physical universe is created by God, then it has its explanation in God and consequently does not exist unexplained; in this case, only God exists unexplained. Since the hypothesis that only God exists unexplained is simpler than the atheistic hypothesis, it is more likely to be true.

The principle Swinburne is appealing to is

(1) The simpler an existent is, the more likely it is to exist unexplained.

I believe, however, that even if we grant Swinburne this and other of his premises it can be shown that considerations of simplicity support atheism rather than theism. Swinburne's criterion of simplicity is that there is a simplicity "about zero and infinity which particular finite numbers lack."[31] For example, "the hypothesis that some particle has zero mass, or infinite velocity is simpler than the hypothesis that it has a mass of 0.34127 of some unit, or a velocity of 301,000 km/sec."[32] Likewise, a person with infinite power, knowledge, and goodness is simpler than a person with a certain finite degree of power, knowledge, and goodness. Furthermore, a person with infinite power, knowledge, etc., is simpler than a physical object that has particular finite values for its size, duration, velocity, density, etc. Assuming these premises, let us examine the hypothesis that a finite universe begins with an uncaused singularity. The singularity in question has *zero* spatial volume and *zero* temporal duration and *does not have particular finite values* for its density, temperature, or curvature. It seems reasonable to suppose that by virtue of these zero and non-finite values this instantaneous point is the simplest possible physical object. If we grant to Swinburne that God is the simplest possible person and hold that God and the uncaused singularity cannot both exist (for reasons stated in the atheistic argument in Section 2), then our alternatives are to suppose that either the simplest person exists and creates the four-dimensional spatiotemporal universe or the simplest physical object exists and emits the four-dimensional spatiotemporal universe. If we use criteria of simplicity, are there any reasons to prefer one of these hypotheses over the other? It seems reasonable to suppose that the simplest possible physical object is equally as simple as the simplest possible person, such that there is no basis to prefer one over the other on grounds of intrinsic simplicity. Swinburne holds that God exists unexplained and so God and the simplest physical object are also on a par in this respect. But the hypothesis that the four-dimensional spatiotemporal universe began from the simplest physical object is in one crucial respect simpler than the theistic hypothesis. It is simpler to suppose that the four-dimensional physical universe began from the simplest instance of the same basic kind as itself, namely, something physical, than it is to suppose that this universe began from the simplest instance of a different basic kind, namely, something nonphysical and personal. The atheistic account of the origin of the four-dimensional universe posits phenomena of only one basic kind (physical phenomena), whereas the theistic account of its origin posits phenomena of two basic kinds (physical phenomena and disembodied personal phenomena). Thus on grounds of simplicity the postulation of a singularity that explodes in a Big Bang wins out over the postulation of a deity that creates the Big Bang explosion ex nihilo.

8. THE QUESTION OF THE METAPHYSICAL NECESSITY OF A BIG BANG UNIVERSE

According to essentialism, natural laws, such as the law that water is H_2O, are metaphysically necessary; they hold in all possible worlds, such that God could not have created a universe in which they are violated. Consequently, if it is a natural law that a universe obeying the Friedman solutions to Einstein's equation and the Hawking-Penrose singularity theorems begins in a singularity, then God could not have created a Friedman–Hawking–Penrose (FHP) universe otherwise than by first creating an unpredictable singularity. Given this, and given his desire that the universe be animate, he would then have to intervene to ensure that the universe be animate. This would not be a sign of inefficiency or bungling since this would be the only possible way in which an animate universe could be guaranteed.

My response to this objection is that even if its essentialist assumption is sound, it does not follow that God must create a Big Bang singularity if he intends to create an animate universe. For the fact that certain natural laws are metaphysically necessary does not entail that they are necessarily instantiated. If we borrow the symbolism, if not the position, of D. M. Armstrong,[33] we may say that a metaphysically necessary natural law is of a form such as

(*L*) $\Box(N\,(F,G))$,

where *F* and *G* are universals and *N* a relation between them. *N* is the relation of nomic necessitation. Armstrong takes *N* to be primitive, but I think we can define *N* in terms of coexemplification. (*L*) means that in every possible world in which *F* is exemplified, *G* is coexemplified. If *F* is water and *G* H_2O, then (*L*) says that in each world in which *being water* is exemplified, *being H_2O* is exemplified by whatever exemplifies *being water*. But (*L*) does not entail that *F* or *G* is *exemplified*. The fact that water is H_2O in every world in which there is water does not entail that there is water in every world. Analogously, the fact that a universe that satisfies the FHP laws begins in a Big Bang singularity in every world in which such a universe exists does not entail that there is an FHP universe in every world. For other sorts of universe are also possible, ones that satisfy other sets of laws, including sets of laws that enable an earliest state to be, or evolve predictably into, an animate state. If God exists and intended there to be an animate universe, he would have created one of these universes (or a beginningless animate universe).

This response to the essentialist objection might be rejected on the grounds that essentialism and the FHP theory jointly entail that the only metaphysically possible universes are FHP universes. Let *F* be the property *being a universe* and *G* the property *being an FHP universe*. According to (*L*), *being a universe* cannot be exemplified unless *being an FHP universe* is coexemplified.

I believe, however, that we can concede even this objection consistently with the soundness of the atheological argument. To see this, we must reflect on the evidence adduced for the metaphysical necessity of natural laws. Kripke, Putnam, and other originators of essentialism have recognized that some *reason* must be given for holding a natural law to be necessary that defeats the standard reason for regarding them to be contingent, namely, that they can be coherently conceived not to obtain. The reason for holding some principles to be necessary, such as tautologies (all unmarried men are men), analytic principles (all unmarried men are bachelors), and synthetic a priori principles (all completely green objects are not simultaneously completely red), is that they cannot coherently be conceived to be false. But this is not the case for natural laws. As Putnam remarks, "we can perfectly well imagine having experiences that would convince us (and that would make it rational to believe that) water *isn't* H_2O. In that sense, it is conceivable that water isn't H_2O."[34] But in this case, conceivability of being otherwise is a defeated guide to contingency, for considerations of how the reference of 'water' is established, in conjunction with scientific observations, show that water is necessarily H_2O. But I will not strictly follow Putnam in presenting "the argument from the rigidity of 'water'" since subsequent formulations have provided improved versions. Keith Donnellan[35] offered a version improving on Putnam's, and Nathan Salmon[36] has improved upon Donnellan's version. But Paul Copeck[37] has recently improved upon Salmon's version and I shall partly borrow from Copeck's version in the following summary statement of this argument. The first premise is a formalization of the rigid meaning of 'water' in terms of the word's ostensive definition and the second premise is borrowed from current scientific theory:

(1) It is necessarily the case that: something is a sample of water iff it exemplifies dthat (the properties $P_1, \ldots, P_n$, such that $P_1, \ldots, P_n$ are causally responsible for the observable properties [e.g., being tasteless, odorless, and clear] of the substance of which *that* is a sample).

(2) This (liquid sample) has the chemical structure H_2O, such that *being H_2O* is the property causally responsible for the observable properties of being tasteless, odorless, clear, etc.

Therefore,

(3) It is necessarily the case that: every sample of water has the chemical structure H_2O.

The word 'dthat' in premise (1) is Kaplan's rigidifying functor, which operates on 'that' to produce a demonstrative reference that is rigid. Now if we construct an analogous argument for the necessity of a universe being FHP, it would appear as

(4) It is necessarily the case that: something is an instance of a universe iff it exemplifies dthat (the properties $P_1, \ldots, P_n$, such that $P_1, \ldots, P_n$ are causally responsible for the observable properties [e.g., receding galactic clusters, the background microwave radiation of 2.7 K] of the kind of which that is an instance).

(5) This instance of a universe has an FHP structure, such that *being an FHP universe* is the property causally responsible for the observable properties of receding clusters, background radiation, etc.

Therefore,

(6) It is necessarily the case that: every instance of a universe has the property of *being an FHP universe*.

I shall not challenge the soundness of (4)–(6) but merely show its soundness is consistent with the soundness of the Big Bang cosmological argument for God's nonexistence. It will be helpful if a parallel with the example of water is drawn. As Putnam has pointed out, there is another possible world *W* in which a substance has a certain chemical structure *XYZ*, such that *XYZ* is causally responsible for the substance's observable properties of being a clear, odorless, tasteless liquid. This substance is not water but something whose observational properties are indistinguishable from those of water. This substance may be called $water_1$, such that it is metaphysically necessary that $water_1$ is *XYZ*. Analogously, there is another possible world *W* in which the cosmic structure responsible for the observable properties of receding clusters, background radiation, etc., is not an FHP structure but some other structure, say, *ABC*. That which has this structure is not a universe, since 'universe' rigidly refers to something with an FHP structure. But we can call it a $universe_1$, just as we can call *XYZ* $water_1$. There are still other worlds in which the relevant observational properties do not include receding clusters and background radiation but such properties as the systems of Ptolemy, Copernicus, or Newton were thought to exemplify. What is causally responsible for these properties may be called a $universe_2$, a $universe_3$, etc. Accordingly, the proponent of the atheological argument may grant that God could not have created an animate universe without creating a Big Bang singularity, but he will point out that it would be irrational and incompetent on the part of God to create an animate universe; the rational thing to do is to create an animate $universe_1$ or an animate $universe_2$, etc., such that these systems do not require divine interventions for animate states to be ensured.

For the reasons adduced in this section and earlier sections, I believe it rational to hold that the Big Bang cosmological argument for God's nonexistence is defensible.

NOTES

1. Pope Pius XII, *Bulletin of the Atomic Scientists* 8 (1952): 143–46.

2. See Richard Swinburne, *The Existence of God* (Oxford: Clarendon Press, 1979), and *Space and Time* (New York: St. Martin's Press, 1982). Swinburne doubts that the prediction of a first event by Big Bang cosmology is probably true but nonetheless shows how this prediction can be theologically construed. Also see John Leslie, "Anthropic Principle, World Ensemble, Design," *American Philosophical Quarterly* 19 (1982): 141–51, and "Modern Cosmology and the Creation of Life," in *Evolution and Creation*, edited by

E. McMullin (South Bend: University of Notre Dame Press, 1985), and numerous other articles. Leslie, of course, operates with a Neoplatonic conception of God, but his arguments are obviously relevant to classical theism. The most developed theistic interpretation of Big Bang cosmology is William Lane Craig's. See his *The Kalam Cosmological Argument* (New York: Harper and Row, 1979); "God, Creation and Mr. Davies," *British Journal for the Philosophy of Science* 37 (1986): 163–75; "Barrow and Tipler on the Anthropic Principle vs. Divine Design," *British Journal for the Philosophy of Science* 39 (1988): 389–95; "The Caused Beginning of the Universe," in *Theism, Atheism, and Big Bang Cosmology*, edited by William Lane Craig and Quentin Smith (Oxford: Clarendon Press, 1993), pp. 141–60; "'What Place, then, for a Creator?': Hawking on God and Creation," in *Theism, Atheism, and Big Bang Cosmology*, pp. 279–300.

3. Anthony Kenny, *The Five Ways* (New York: Schocken Books, 1969), p. 66.

4. C. D. Broad, "Kant's Mathematical Antinomies," *Proceedings of the Aristotelian Society* 40 (1955): 1–22.

5. See Fred Hoyle, *Astrophysical Journal* 196 (1975): 661.

6. W. H. Newton-Smith, *The Structure of Time* (London: Routledge and Kegan Paul, 1980), p. 111.

7. Quentin Smith, "The Anthropic Principle and Many Worlds Cosmologies," *Australasian Journal of Philosophy* 63 (1985): 336–48; "World Ensemble Explanations," *Pacific Philosophical Quarterly* 67 (1986): 73–86; "A Natural Explanation of the Existence and Laws of Our Universe," *Australasian Journal of Philosophy* 68 (March 1990): 22–43; "The Uncaused Beginning of the Universe," in *Theism, Atheism, and Big Bang Cosmology*, pp. 108–40.

8. Quentin Smith, "Atheism, Theism, and Big Bang Cosmology," in *Theism, Atheism, and Big Bang Cosmology*, pp. 195–217. Reprinted as the previous paper in the current anthology.

9. Craig, "The Caused Beginning of the Universe," p. 142, note 4.

10. S. W. Hawking, "Breakdown of Predictability in Gravitational Collapse," *Physical Review* D14 (1976): 2460.

11. P. Davies, *The Edge of Infinity* (New York: Simon and Schuster, 1981), p. 161.

12. William Lane Craig, "Theism and Big Bang Cosmology," in *Theism, Atheism, and Big Bang Cosmology*, pp. 218–31, sect. 1.

13. Ibid.

14. Craig, "Theism and Big Bang Cosmology."

15. Ibid.

16. Swinburne, *The Existence of God*, p. 120.

17. At some juncture I should mention that by always referring to God as 'he' rather than 'she' I am calling attention to the fact that the god of classical theism has its roots in the patriarchal religions of the Judaeo–Christian–Islamic traditions. Distinct from these religions are the goddess religions of early Crete, Malta, Sumer, Canaan, etc. I would reserve 'she' for the deity of goddess religions.

18. George Schlesinger, *Religion and the Scientific Method* (Dordrecht: Reidel, 1977).

19. Craig, "Theism and Big Bang Cosmology," sect. 1.

20. Ibid.

21. Ibid.
22. Ibid.
23. Ibid., pp. 497–98.
24. Ibid., p. 499.
25. Swinburne, *Space and Time*, p. 125.
26. Craig, "Theism and Big Bang Cosmology," sect. 1.
27. Ibid.
28. Ibid., p. 496.
29. Ibid., p. 495.
30. Swinburne, *The Existence of God*, p. 130.
31. Ibid., p. 94.
32. Ibid.
33. D. M. Armstrong, *What Is a Law of Nature?* (Cambridge: Cambridge University Press, 1983), p. 163. Armstrong rejects the idea that laws of nature are metaphysically necessary. Alfred J. Freddoso, on the other hand, argues that natural laws are correctly represented by (*L*). See his "The Necessity of Nature," in *Midwest Studies in Philosophy XI*, edited by P. French, T. Uehling, and H. Wettstein (Minneapolis: University of Minnesota Press, 1986), pp. 215–42.
34. Hilary Putnam, *Philosophical Papers*, vol. 2 (Cambridge: Cambridge University Press, 1975), p. 233.
35. Keith Donnellan, "Substance and Individuals," APA address, 1973.
36. Nathan Salmon, *Reference and Essence* (Princeton: Princeton University Press, 1981).
37. Paul Copeck, "Review of Nathan Salmon's *Reference and Essence*," *Journal of Philosophy* 81 (1984): 261–70.

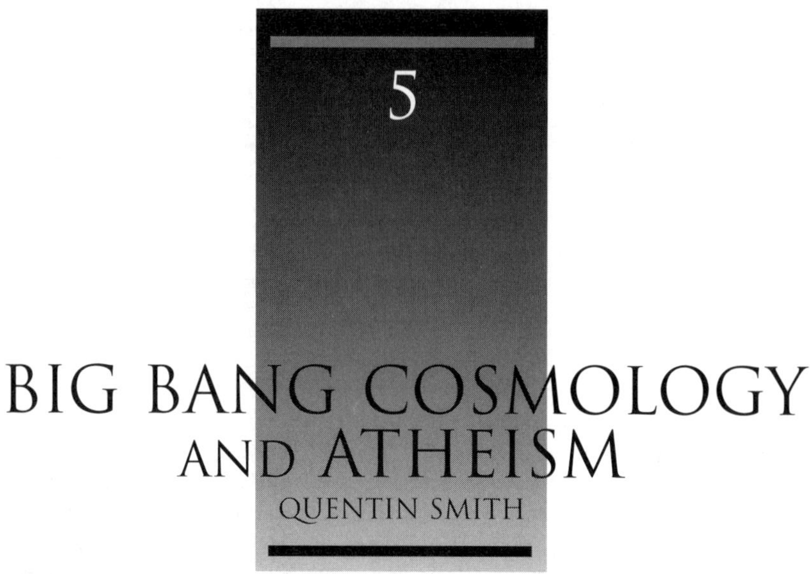

5

BIG BANG COSMOLOGY AND ATHEISM

QUENTIN SMITH

Since the mid-1960s, scientifically informed theists have been ecstatic because of Big Bang cosmology. Theists believe that the best scientific evidence that God exists is the evidence that the universe began to exist in an explosion about 15 billion years ago, an explosion called the Big Bang. Theists think it obvious that the universe could not have begun to exist uncaused. They argue that the most reasonable hypothesis is that the cause of the universe is God. This theory hinges on the assumption that it is obviously true that whatever begins to exist has a cause.

The most recent statement of this theist theory is in William Lane Craig's 1994 book *Reasonable Faith*.[1] In it Craig states his argument like this:

1. Whatever begins to exist has a cause.
2. The universe began to exist.
3. Therefore, the universe has a cause.[2]

In a very interesting quote from this book he discusses the first premise and mentions me as one of the perverse atheists who deny the obviousness of this assumption:

The first step is so intuitively obvious that I think scarcely anyone could sincerely believe it to be false. I therefore think it somewhat unwise to argue in favor of it, for any proof of the principle is likely to be less obvious than the principle itself. And as Aristotle remarked, one ought not to try to prove the obvious via the less obvious. The old axiom that "out of nothing, nothing comes" remains as obvious today as ever. When I first wrote *The Kalam Cosmological Argument*, I remarked that I found it an attractive feature of this argument that it allows the atheist a way of escape: he can always deny the first premise and assert the universe sprang into existence uncaused out of nothing. I figured that few would take this option, since I believed they would thereby expose themselves as persons interested only in academic refutation of the argument and not in really discovering the truth about the universe. To my surprise, however, atheists seem to be increasingly taking this route. For example, Quentin Smith, commenting that philosophers are too often adversely affected by Heidegger's dread of "the nothing," concludes that "the most reasonable belief is that we came from nothing, by nothing, and for nothing"—a nice ending to a sort of Gettysburg address of atheism, perhaps.[3]

A BASELESS ASSUMPTION

I'm going to criticize this argument from scientific cosmology, which is the most popular argument that scientifically informed theists and philosophers are now using to argue that God exists.

Let's consider the first premise of the argument, that whatever has a beginning to its existence must have a cause. What reason is there to believe this causal principle is true? It's not self-evident; something is self-evident if and only if everyone who understands it automatically believes it. But many people, including leading theists such as Richard Swinburne, understand this principle very well but think it is false. Many philosophers, scientists, and indeed the majority of graduate and undergraduate students I've had in my classes think this principle is false. This principle is not self-evident, nor can this principle be deduced from any self-evident proposition. Therefore, there's no reason to think it's true. It is either false or it has the status of a statement that we do not know is true or false. At the very least, it is clear that we do not know that it is true.

Now suppose the theist retreats to a weaker version of this principle and says, "Whatever has a beginning to its existence has a cause." Now, this does not say that whatever has a beginning to its existence *must* have a cause; it allows that it is possible that some things begin to exist without a cause. So we don't need to consider it as a self-evident, necessary truth. Rather, according to the theists, we can consider it to be an empirical generalization based on observation.

But there is a decisive problem with this line of thinking. There is absolutely no evidence that it is true. All of the observations we have are of changes in things—of something changing from one state to another. Things move, come to a rest, get larger, get smaller, combine with other things, divide in half, and so on. But we have no observation of things coming into existence. For example, we have no observations of people coming into existence. Here again, you merely have a change of things. An egg cell and a sperm cell change their state by combining. The combination divides, enlarges, and eventually evolves into an adult human being. Therefore, I conclude that we have no evidence at all that the empirical version of Craig's statement, "Whatever begins to exist has a 'cause,'" is true. All of the causes we are aware of are changes in pre-existing materials. In Craig's and other theists' causal principle, 'cause' means something entirely different: it means creating material from nothingness. It is pure speculation that such a strange sort of causation is even possible, let alone even supported in our observations in our daily lives.

AN UNCAUSED UNIVERSE

But the more important point is this: not only is there no evidence for the theist's causal assumption, there's evidence against it. The claim that the beginning of our universe has a cause conflicts with current scientific theory. The scientific theory is called the Wave Function of the Universe. It has been developed in the past 15 years or so by Stephen Hawking, Alexander Vilenkin, Andre Linde, and many others. Their theory is that there is a scientific law of nature called the Wave Function of the Universe that implies that it is *highly probable* that a universe with our characteristics will come into existence without a cause. Hawking's theory is based on assigning numbers to all possible universes. All of the numbers cancel out except for a universe with features that our universe possesses, such as containing intelligent organisms. This remaining universe has a very high probability—near 100 percent—of coming into existence uncaused.

Hawking's theory is confirmed by observational evidence. The theory predicts that our universe has evenly distributed matter on a large scale—that is, on the level of super-clusters of galaxies. It predicts that the expansion rate of our universe—our universe has been expanding ever since the Big Bang—would be almost exactly between the rate of the universe expanding forever and the rate where it expands and then collapses. It also predicts the very early area of rapid expansion near the beginning of the universe called "inflation." Hawking's theory exactly predicted what the COBE satellite discovered about the irregularities of the background radiation in the universe.[4]

So scientific theory that is confirmed by observational evidence tells us that the universe began without being caused. If you want to be a rational person and accept the results of rational inquiry into nature, then you must accept the fact that God did not cause the universe to exist. The universe exists uncaused, in accordance with the wave function law.

Now Stephen Hawking's theory dissolves any worries about how the universe could begin to exist uncaused. He supposes that there is a timeless space, a four-dimensional hypersphere, near the beginning of the universe. It is smaller than the nucleus of an atom. It is smaller than 10^{-33} centimeters in radius. Since it was timeless, it no more needs a cause than the timeless god of theism. This timeless hypersphere is connected to our expanding universe. Our universe begins smaller than an atom and explodes in a Big Bang, and here we are today in a universe that is still expanding.

Is it nonetheless possible that God could have caused this universe? No. For the Wave Function of the Universe implies that there is a 95 percent probability that the universe came into existence uncaused. If God created the universe, he would contradict this scientific law in two ways. First, the scientific law says that the universe would come into existence because of its natural, mathematical properties, not because of any supernatural forces. Second, the scientific law says that the probability is only 95 percent that the universe would come into existence. But if God created the universe, the probability would be 100 percent that it would come into existence because God is all-powerful. If God wills the universe to come into existence, his will is guaranteed to be 100 percent effective.

So contemporary scientific cosmology is not only *not* supported by any theistic theory, it is actually logically inconsistent with theism.

NOTES

1. William Lane Craig, *Reasonable Faith* (Wheaton, IL: Crossway, 1994).
2. Ibid., p. 92.
3. Ibid.
4. Confirmation of Hawking's theory is consistent with this theory being a reasonable proposal for the form that an (as yet) undeveloped theory of quantum gravity will take, as Hawking himself emphasizes. See chap. 12, William Lane Craig and Quentin Smith, *Theism, Atheism, and Big Bang Cosmology* (Oxford: Clarendon Press, 1993).

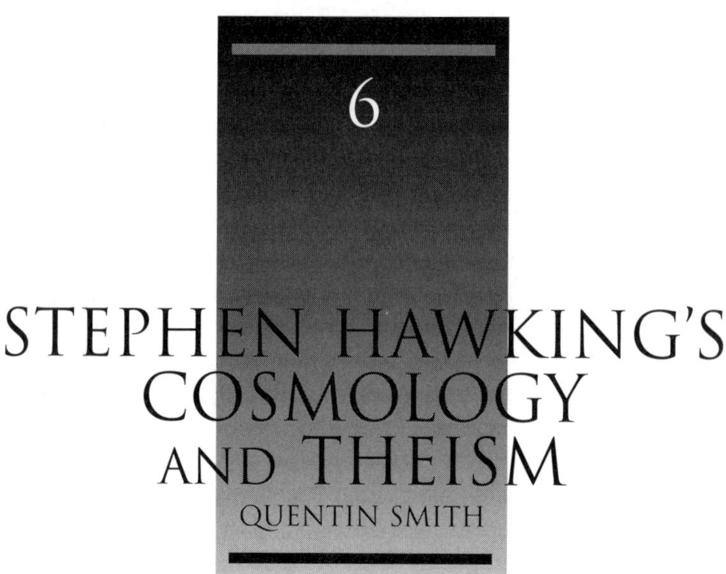

6

STEPHEN HAWKING'S COSMOLOGY AND THEISM

QUENTIN SMITH

1. Stephen Hawking has recently argued that there is "no place for a creator," that God does not exist. In his quantum cosmology

> there would be no singularities at which the laws of science broke down and no edge of space-time at which one would have to appeal to God or some new law to set the boundary conditions for space-time. . . . The universe would be completely self-contained and not affected by anything outside itself. It would neither be created nor destroyed. It would just BE. . . . What place, then, for a creator?[1]

This does not seem much like an argument, let alone a rigorous argument, for atheism, and theists have jumped all over it, claiming it blatantly fails as an argument for God's nonexistence.[2] Specifically, they have argued that even if Hawking's physical laws are true, that fact does not entail that the God of classical theism does not exist or even disconfirm the classical theistic hypothesis.

It seems to me that a case can be made that Hawking's physical laws are inconsistent with classical theism. I shall develop an argument to this effect in the present paper. Although this argument is not explicit in Hawking's writings, it is arguably implicit in or based upon his theory. I shall argue that

---

(P) Hawking's wave function law obtains.

entails

(C) God does not exist.

Some defenders of classical theism have not attacked (P) but have attacked the claim that (P) entails (C). It is not part of my argument to defend (P), although I believe (P) is confirmed by observational evidence, e.g., by the COBE satellite observations of the density fluctuations in the background radiation, by the observed large-scale homogeneity and isotropy of the universe, by the evidence for an early inflationary era, and by the evidence that the critical density is near to one.

2. Hawking's atheistic dreadnaught is a "wave function of the universe." The wave function is $\psi[h_{ij},\varphi]$. Without bothering overly much about technical niceties,[3] we may take φ as representing the matter field of the initial state of the universe, roughly, how much matter this state contains and how it is distributed. h_{ij} may be regarded as representing the metrical structure of the initial state of the universe, that is, the sort of curvature possessed by the three-dimensional space of this state. ψ is the amplitude, which is important since the square of the modulus of the amplitude gives a probability, namely, the probability that the universe will begin to exist with the metric h_{ij} and the matter field φ.

The square of the modulus of the amplitude is $|\psi[h_{ij},\varphi]|^2$. As Hartle and Hawking say, this gives us the probability "for the Universe to appear from nothing,"[4] specifically, it gives us the unconditional probability that a universe begins to exist with the metric h_{ij} and matter field φ. The reason this equation is inconsistent with classical theism is related to the respect in which quantum cosmology has superior explanatory value to classical general relativistic cosmology (the "standard hot Big Bang model"). According to the standard hot Big Bang model, the universe began to exist about 15 billion years ago from a physical singularity, the Big Bang singularity. At this singularity, all physical laws break down and thus it is in principle impossible to predict what will emerge from the singularity. Furthermore, the existence of the singularity itself is an unexplained given.[5] Hawking's quantum cosmology omits the initial singularity and implies that it is probable (to a degree less than one) that the universe begins to exist with a nonsingular state, namely, h_{ij},φ, in accordance with the wave function law $\psi[h_{ij},\varphi]$.

3. It is precisely this implication that precludes the existence of God. Let us suppose (for the sake of illustration) that the probability value the wave function gives us is 95 percent. The wave function law would then entail:

(1) The probability that a universe begin to exist with the metric h_{ij} and matter field φ is 95 percent.

Now consider the hypothesis that God ordains that Hawking's wave function law obtains. Assuming this hypothesis, God could create the sort of universe that is most probable or the one that is second most probable, etc., as specified by the law he chose to make obtain. Suppose he decides to create the most probable one. It follows that the universe has a sufficient condition of its existence, not a probabilistic one. Note that

(2) God wills that a universe begin to exist with a metric h_{ij} and matter field φ.

entails

(3) The probability that a universe begin to exist with the metric h_{ij} and matter field φ is 100 percent.

God is omnipotent and thus his willing cannot fail to be effective and thus the probability value is 100 percent. Now (3) is inconsistent with (1). Since (1) is true if Hawking's wave function law obtains and (2) entails (3), it follows that (2) is false if Hawking's wave function law obtains. Put another way, it is implicitly self-contradictory that

(4) God wills that Hawking's wave function law obtains and that a universe begin to exist with the metric h_{ij} and matter field φ.

since if the law obtains, the probability is 95 percent, and if God wills that this universe exist, the probability is 100 percent.

Suppose the defender of classical theism responds that (1) really means

(5) The probability that a universe begin to exist without supernatural causation and with the metric h_{ij} and matter field φ is 95 percent.

and that the probability estimate stated in (3) is more explicitly stated by

(6) The probability that a universe begin to exist with the metric h_{ij} and matter field φ, given that God wills such a universe to begin to exist, is 100 percent.

Since (5) is consistent with (6), it follows that (1) is consistent with (2) and thereby that Hawking's quantum cosmology has a place for a creator.

However, this response conflicts with the various propositions entailed by classical theism. Classical theism is the theory that there necessarily exists a disembodied person who is necessarily omniscient, omnipotent, and omnibenevolent and necessarily the cause of whatever universe there is. Accordingly, classical theism entails

(7) Necessarily, there is no universe that begins to exist without supernatural causation.

Given (7), it is true that, in the absence of supernatural causation, the probability that a universe begins to exist with the metric h_{ij} and matter field φ is 0 percent. If the wave function is "the amplitude for the Universe to appear [supernaturally uncaused] from nothing" and the modulus of the amplitude squared gives the probability, then the probability contra Hartle and Hawking is zero if it is true that the universe cannot begin to exist supernaturally uncaused.

Thus, if Hawking's wave function law obtains, there is "no place for a creator" and classical theism is false. Indeed, if it is even possible that the wave function law obtains, classical theism is false, since classical theism entails that there is no possible world in which a universe begins to exist supernaturally uncaused. Accordingly, we should conclude that theists are mistaken if they think that Hawking's quantum cosmology is consistent with classical theism.

4. The fact that classical theism is inconsistent with Hawking's cosmology does not entail that every version of theism is inconsistent with this cosmology. I shall discuss acausal and causal versions of nonclassical theism and determine the respects in which they are consistent with the obtaining of the wave function law.

An acausal version of nonclassical theism may include the proposition that God is responsible for instituting the laws that govern whatever universe exists, but that God does not create the universe. In the actual world, God wills that the wave function law obtains but does not will that the universe exist. Rather, God leaves it to chance, a 95 percent chance, that the universe with the specified metric and matter field will begin to exist uncaused.

It is important to emphasize that this version of theism, although consistent with Hawking's cosmology, is fundamentally at odds with central tenets of classical theism and is even more dissimilar to classical theism than is deism. It is central to classical theism and deism that God is the cause of the universe. This tenet is inconsistent with acausal theism, since according to acausal theism the universe is not created by God but instead came into existence uncaused in accordance with a probabilistic law. On the acausal version of theism, God does not will that some concrete objects exist but merely that some abstract object possesses a certain property; God wills merely that the wave function law has the property of obtaining. If God wills that this law obtain, there is a 100 percent probability that it obtain and if it obtains, there is a 95 percent chance that a universe with the metric h_{ij} and matter field φ will come into existence uncaused.

Acausal theism also rejects the classical doctrine of continuous creation (divine conservation). As Phillip Quinn represents this theory, it holds that "God not only creates the cosmos of contingent things but also conserves it in existence at every instant when it exists."[6] The rejection of this doctrine is motivated by considerations similar to the rejection of the doctrine that God causes the universe to begin to exist. Hawking's wave function law enables the probabilistic history of the universe to be calculated once the initial state of the universe is known. Given the initial state, we have certain probability values (each less than 100 percent) for possible subsequent states and histories of the universe. This is inconsistent with continuous creation, since God's willing of any state or history is guaranteed to be effective and thus the probability value of any state or history he willed would be 100 percent. If God willed that some subsequent state, say S, follow upon the initial state, then the existence of S would have the probability of 100 percent, inconsistently with the wave function law, which gives the existence of S a probability less than 100 percent. According to acausal theism, God does not continuously create the universe but instead leaves it to chance (specifically, the chances specified by the wave function he ordained to obtain) as to whether the universe will continue existing and as to which state will follow upon a prior state. Once the wave function law is decreed to obtain by God, a probability distribution for possible histories of the universe is determined and God sits back and watches as chance takes its course.

5. The classical theist may resist the suggestion that she must retreat to an acausal version of theism in order to retain a theistic belief that is consistent with Hawking's cosmology. It may be argued that a central tenet of classical theism, that God is actually the original and continuous creator of the universe, may be retained consistently with the obtaining of Hawking's wave function law if we reject the idea that God necessarily exists and the idea that it is a necessary truth that everything that begins to exist has a cause. According to this causal version of nonclassical theism, God actually causes the universe to begin to exist but there is some possible world in which God does not exist and in which there is a universe that begins uncaused. Alternatively, the theist could retain the idea that God actually causes the universe and necessarily exists but reject the idea that he necessarily causes the universe; according to this version, there is some possible world in which God exists but in which the universe begins to exist uncaused. Each of these two causal versions of nonclassical theism is arguably consistent with Hawking's cosmology since we cannot infer from either of these two versions that

(7) Necessarily, there is no universe that begins to exist without supernatural causation,

and thus cannot infer that the probability of a supernaturally uncaused universe is 0 percent. Since the possibility of an uncaused universe is granted, these versions of theism are consistent with

(5) The probability that a universe begin to exist without supernatural causation and with the metric h_{ij} and matter field φ is 95 percent.

The key to these causal versions of nonclassical theism is the argument that (5) is true even if the universe actually begins to exist by supernatural causation. The truth of (5) may be explained in terms of a quantification over merely possible worlds, namely, in terms of the assertion that a universe with the metric h_{ij} and matter field φ begins to exist uncaused in 95 percent of all the possible worlds in which the wave function law obtains and in which it is not the case that God causes a universe to exist. This is consistent with the claim that in 100 percent of the possible worlds in which God wills that such a universe begin to exist, it does begin to exist, and with the claim that the actual world is one of these worlds. Hartle and Hawking may have believed that in the actual world, the universe begins uncaused, but this proposition is not entailed by their wave function law. Their law states the probability of the universe beginning to exist under the condition that the universe not be supernaturally caused, but this condition is not met in the actual world, at least according to the causal versions of nonclassical theism.

However, this attempt to preserve God's classical role as the cause of the universe is inconsistent with two of the divine attributes, viz., the rationality and goodness of God.

If God is rational, then each law instituted by God is instituted for a reason. The conjunction of either of the two causal versions of nonclassical theism with Hawking's cosmology is inconsistent with the rationality of God since this conjunction implies that God ordains that the wave function law $\psi[h_{ij},\varphi]$ obtain but that God has no reason for ordaining that it obtain. There is no reason for instituting a law that makes it 95 percent probable that a universe with the metric h_{ij} and matter field φ will come into existence uncaused, under the condition that God not will that this universe come into existence, if God intends to bring this universe into existence by his will and thereby vitiate the condition laid down in the law.

A second respect in which the hypothesis that God actually causes the universe is problematic is that it is inconsistent with God's goodness. There is abundant observational evidence that confirms the hypothesis that the universe began to exist uncaused in accordance with Hawking's wave function law. The early inflationary era, the density fluctuations in the background radiation discovered by the COBE satellite, the large-scale homogeneity and isotropy of the universe, the fact that the universe is nearly flat, etc., all confirm the hypothesis that the universe began uncaused in accordance with $\psi[h_{ij},\varphi]$. If God nonetheless caused the universe to begin to exist, he would have created a universe that appeared to come into existence by virtue of a scientific law but in reality did not come into existence in this way. This would constitute a deception of human beings and would defeat the quintessentially human project of rational scientific inquiry. We would have a situation analogous to Descartes's scenario about the evil demon, who deceives human beings by making it delusively appear as if there is an external world. However, God is good, as Descartes noted, and thus would not deceive human beings.

6. For these two reasons, the endeavor to preserve God's classical theistic role as original and continuous creator of the universe cannot succeed. If there is a theism consistent with the obtaining of the law $\psi[h_{ij},\varphi]$, it must be an acausal theism.

But the fact of this consistency does not show there is a positive reason to believe that acausal theism and Hawking's wave function are both true. In order to establish this, one would have to show that the wave function law $\psi[h_{ij},\varphi]$ obtains because some mind wills it to obtain. But it is hard to see how this could be shown. Clearly, that $\psi[h_{ij},\varphi]$ obtains does not entail that some mind wills $\psi[h_{ij},\varphi]$ to obtain. Furthermore, there seems to be no empirical evidence that would confirm the conjunction of acausal theism and the wave function law to an equal or greater degree than it would confirm the wave function law alone. The anthropic coincidences[7] and the existence of intelligent organisms do not count as separate evidence for theism, since these are predicted by the wave function law. As Hawking writes, "Each history in the sum over histories will describe not only the space-time but everything in it as well, including any complicated organisms like human beings who can observe the history of the universe. . . . [Calculations show] that, using the sum over histories, our universe is not just one of the possible histories but one of the most probable ones."[8] Accordingly, there seem to be no logical or empirical reasons to support a belief that there is a deity who instituted the wave function law. It seems we are left with the belief that $\psi[h_{ij},\varphi]$ alone is responsible for the existence of the universe.[9]

NOTES

1. Stephen W. Hawking, *A Brief History of Time* (New York: Bantam Books, 1988), pp. 136, 141.

2. See Christopher Isham, "Creation of the Universe as a Quantum Tunneling Process," in *Physics, Philosophy, and Theology*, edited by R. J. Russell et al. (Notre Dame: Notre Dame University Press, 1988); William Lane Craig, "'What Place, then, for a Creator?': Hawking on God and Creation," in *Theism, Atheism, and Big Bang Cosmology*, edited by William Lane Craig and Quentin Smith (Oxford: Clarendon Press, 1993), pp. 279–300; W. B. Drees, *Beyond the Big Bang* (La Salle: Open Court, 1990); Robin Le Poidevin, "Creation in a Closed Universe; or, Have Physicists Disproved the Existence of God?" *Religious Studies* 27 (1991): 39–48; Robert J. Deltete, "Hawking on God and Creation," *Zygon* 28 (1993): 485–506. See also William Lane Craig on theism and cosmology, "God and the Initial Cosmological Singularity: A Reply to Quentin Smith," *Faith and Philosophy* 9 (1992): 238–48; "The Origin and Creation of the Universe: A Reply to Adolf Grünbaum," *British Journal for the Philosophy of Science* 43 (1992): 233–40; "The Caused Beginning of the Universe," in *Theism, Atheism, and Big Bang Cosmology*, pp. 141–60; "Theism and Big Bang Cosmology," in *Theism, Atheism, and Big Bang Cosmology*, pp. 218–31.

3. For a technical discussion of Hawking's quantum cosmology, see Quentin Smith, "The Wave Function of a Godless Universe," in *Theism, Atheism and Big Bang Cosmology*, pp. 301–37; also see Quentin Smith and Adolf Grünbaum, *The Uncreated Universe* (New York: Oxford University Press, forthcoming).

4. J. Hartle and S. W. Hawking, "Wave Function of the Universe," *Physical Review* D28 (1983): 2961.

5. This assumes a realist interpretation of the Big Bang singularity. For further discussion, see Quentin Smith, "A Natural Explanation of the Existence and Laws of Our Universe," *Australasian Journal of Philosophy* 68 (1990): 22–43; "The Uncaused Beginning of the Universe," in *Theism, Atheism, and Big Bang Cosmology*, pp. 108–40; "Atheism, Theism and Big Bang Cosmology," in *Theism, Atheism, and Big Bang Cosmology*, pp. 195–217; "A Defense of the Cosmological Argument for God's Nonexistence," in *Theism, Atheism, and Big Bang Cosmology*, pp. 232–55; "Did the Big Bang Have a Cause?" *British Journal for the Philosophy of Science* 45 (1994): 649–68; "Can Everything Come to Be without a Cause?" *Dialogue: Canadian Philosophical Review* 33 (1994): 313–23.

6. Phillip Quinn, "Divine Conservation, Continuous Creation, and Human Action," in *The Existence and Nature of God*, edited by A. Freddosa (Notre Dame: University of Notre Dame Press, 1983), p. 55.

7. See Quentin Smith, "The Anthropic Coincidences, Evil and the Disconfirmation of Theism," *Religious Studies* 28 (1992): 347–50.

8. Hawking, *A Brief History of Time*, p. 137.

9. I should like to thank an anonymous referee for *Analysis*, William F. Vallicella, Christopher Isham, and the Department of Philosophy at Western Michigan University for helpful comments on earlier versions of this paper.

7

WHY STEPHEN HAWKING'S COSMOLOGY PRECLUDES A CREATOR

QUENTIN SMITH

1. EXPLAINING THE UNIVERSE

Atheists have traditionally conceded in advance the theoretical arena in cosmology to the theists. Atheists have offered no explanation of why the universe exists, and theists have offered an explanation. It can be argued that since theism has greater explanatory power, it is preferable according to this theoretical criterion. Atheists have traditionally taken a merely negative route, arguing that the theistic explanation is false, disconfirmed, or meaningless. But this seems to be a tacit admission that theism is prima facie theoretically superior to atheism, since theism at least purports to explain something that atheism does not even attempt to explain.

But I think this prima facie superiority of theism to atheism can be countered by showing that atheism offers an explanation of the universe, and a better explanation, than theism. I believe that contemporary physical cosmology *can* explain (in principle and in simplified models) the universe's existence. Quantum gravity cosmology, I believe, does show how the universe can be explained in atheistic terms.

In Fang and Wu's introduction to the book *Quantum Cosmology*, which collects the major technical papers by Stephen Hawking, James Hartle, John Wheeler, and others, they say quantum cosmology implies that "in principle, one

---

can predict everything in the universe solely from physical laws. Thus, the long-standing 'first cause' problem intrinsic in cosmology has been finally dispelled."[1] This cosmology has eliminated the need to postulate (or even the possibility of postulating) a first cause (originating cause) of the universe's beginning. Stephen Hawking has famously said that "there is no place for a Creator." However, there are few or no actual arguments to be found either in their technical or popular writings to support such "atheistic" claims. Apparently they want to leave to philosophers the task of figuring out how their mathematical equations both imply that there is no First Cause and that there is an atheistic explanation of the universe's existence. Some attempts to carry out this task in partial form will be made in this paper. I will also show that the very explanation of the universe offered by quantum cosmology implies that quantum cosmology is logically incompatible with theism, that is, implies that God does not exist.

2. THE UNCONDITIONAL PROBABILITY OF THE EXISTENCE OF A UNIVERSE

I shall concentrate on the cosmology developed by Hawking[2] and Hartle and Hawking[3] and later elaborated upon by Hawking and other coauthors. The wave function of the universe in Hartle and Hawking's paper gives a probabilistic and noncausal explanation of why our universe exists. More precisely, it provides an unconditional probability for the existence of a universe of our sort (i.e., an expanding [and later contracting] universe with an early inflationary era and with matter that is evenly distributed on large scales). Given only their functional law of nature, there is a high probability that a universe of this sort begins to exist uncaused.

This can be explained more exactly. In their formalism, $\psi[h_{ij},\phi]$ gives the probability amplitude for a certain three-dimensional space S that has the metric h_{ij} and matter field ϕ.

A *probability amplitude* ψ gives a number that, when squared, is the probability that something exists. This is often put by saying that the square of the modulus of the amplitude gives the probability. The square of the modulus of the amplitude is $|\psi[h_{ij},\phi]|^2$.

In the case at hand, the probability is for the existence of the three-dimensional spatial slice S (the "three-geometry S" in Hartle and Hawking's parlance), from which the probability of the other states of the universe can be calculated. The three-dimensional space S is the first state of the temporally evolving universe, i.e., the earliest state of the temporal length 10^{-43} second (the Planck length). S is the state of the universe that may be called the "Big Bang"; it precedes the inflationary epoch and gives rise to inflation.

The *metric* is the degree of curvature of spacetime; the metric h_{ij} Hartle and Hawking derive is that of an approximately smooth sphere (like the earth) that is much smaller than the head of a pin.

The *matter field* ϕ is equivalent to an approximately homogeneous distribution of elementary particles throughout the small sphere S.

Hartle and Hawking derive the probability amplitude by adding up or summing over all the possible metrics and matter fields of all the possible, finite, four-dimensional spacetimes which have a three-dimensional space S with metric h_{ij} and matter field ϕ as a boundary. The square of the modulus of the amplitude, $|\psi[h_{ij},\phi]|^2$, gives the probability that a universe begins to exist with a three-dimensional space S that possesses this metric and matter field. The probabilities for the history of the rest of the universe can be calculated once we know the metric and matter field of the initial state S.

Since the wave function includes the three-dimensional space S as the boundary of all *merely possible* four-dimensional, finite spacetimes, we can calculate the "unconditional probability" of the 3-space S, in the sense that we do not need to presuppose some *actually existent* earlier 3-space S* as the initial condition from which the probability of the final condition S is calculated. The probability of the existence of the 3-space S is not conditional upon the existence of any concrete object (body or mind) or concrete event (state of a body or mind) or even upon the existence of any quantum vacuum, empty space or time; the probability follows only from the mathematical properties of possible universes. The probability of S is conditional only upon certain abstract objects, numbers, operations, functions, matrices, and other mathematical entities that comprise the wave-function equation. This gives us a probabilistic explanation of the universe's existence that is based solely on laws of nature, specifically the functional law of nature called "the wave function of the universe." . . .

3. THE INCONSISTENCY OF THE HARTLE-HAWKING MODEL WITH CLASSICAL THEISM

The Hartle-Hawking derivation of the unconditional probability of the existence of a universe of our sort is inconsistent with classical theism. The unconditional probability is very high, near to 1. For purposes of simplification, we are saying the probability is 99 percent; there is a 99 percent probability that a universe of our sort—I will call it a Hartle-Hawking universe—exists uncaused.

The universe exists uncaused since the probability amplitude is determined by a summation or path integral over all possible histories of a finite universe. That is, the probability that a Hartle-Hawking universe exists follows directly from the natural-mathematical properties of possible finite universes; there is no need for a cause, probabilistic or otherwise, for there to be a 99 percent probability that a Hartle-Hawking universe will exist.

This is not consistent with classical theism. According to classical theism, if a universe is to have any probability of existing, this probability is dependent on God's dispositions, beliefs, or choices. But the Hartle-Hawking probability is not dependent on any supernatural states or acts; Hartle and Hawking do not sum over anything supernatural in their path integral derivation of the probability amplitude.

Furthermore, according to classical theism, the probability that a universe exist without divine causation is 0, and the probability that if a universe exists, it is divinely caused, is 1. Thus, the probabilities that are implied by classical theism are inconsistent with the probabilities implied by the Hartle-Hawking wave function of the universe.

It may be said that God could will that the Hartle-Hawking wave function law obtain and leave it to chance, a 99 percent chance, that a Hartle-Hawking universe begin to exist uncaused. But then God is not the creator of the universe, and we no longer have the god of classical theism. According to traditional theism, it is a contradiction to suppose that the universe exists without being created by God.

Some may suggest a scenario where there is a 99 percent probability that God shall *create* a Hartle-Hawking universe. Ned Markosian has developed such a scenario.[4] Imagine there are 100 possible universes tied for best in intrinsic value-ranking, and 99 of them are Hartle-Hawking type universes. According to Markosian, since God is omnipotent, God could see to it that, for each of these universes, there is a 1 percent chance that she will create (on a whimsy) that universe. It follows that there is a 99 percent probability that a Hartle-Hawking type universe will be created by God. As it happens, God *does* will that a Hartle-Hawking universe exist. Markosian thinks this scenario makes classical theism consistent with Hartle and Hawking's cosmology.

But it does not, for the wave function states that the natural-mathematical properties of the possible universes make it 99 percent probable that a Hartle-Hawking universe exist uncaused. This probability statement is not consistent with the classical theist position that there is 0 percent probability that a Hartle-Hawking universe exist uncaused or with Markosian's scenario where the 99 percent probability obtains only because it is derived from supernatural considerations. Further, since God is omniscient, she knows by middle knowledge or foreknowledge which universe she will create and thus the probability of the Hartle-Hawking universe existing is not 99 percent but 100 percent.

Graham Oppy says that if the Hartle-Hawking theory is true, the probability that a Hartle-Hawking universe exists is 100 percent since such a universe does exist.[5] But this *conditional* probability is not the one I am talking about. Given the condition that a Hartle-Hawking universe exists, the probability of its existing is 100 percent. But the unconditional probability of such a universe, i.e., its probability not conditional upon anything but the wave function of the universe, is 99 percent. It is this latter probability that allows for an atheistic and acausal explanation of why the universe exists.

4. WILLIAM LANE CRAIG'S CLAIM THAT THE HARTLE-HAWKING PROBABILITY IS MERELY CONDITIONAL

William Lane Craig[6] and many others (e.g., Robert Deltete and Reed Guy[7]) argue that the probability implied by the wave function of the universe is not unconditional and is conditional in a way that allows for a divine creation of the universe ex nihilo. Their claim is that I have misunderstood the Hartle-Hawking model. According to Craig, the only probabilities that follow from their model are conditional in the sense that they are transition probabilities for one state of the universe to follow another state. He writes:

> Smith interprets Hawking's model as establishing a certain probability for the first three-dimensional slice of spacetime to appear uncaused out of nothing. But this is a mistake, for the probability of finding any three-dimensional cross-section of spacetime in such quantum models is only relative to some other cross-section given as one's point of departure.[8]

Craig does not refer to Hawking's articles in support of this claim, but to the quantum cosmologist Christopher Isham's article on the Hartle-Hawking theory. What shall we say about Craig's argument? Craig is wrong both about the Hartle-Hawking theory and about Isham's interpretation of it.

First, Hawking and Hartle do say the probability is unconditional; in their 1983 article, they write about an unconditional probability amplitude, a probability "amplitude for the Universe to appear from nothing."[9] More fully, they say:

> One can interpret the functional integral over all compact four-geometries bounded by a given three-geometry as giving the amplitude for that three-geometry to arise from a zero three-dimensional geometry, i.e., a single point. In other words, the ground state is the amplitude for the Universe to appear from nothing.[10]

Hartle has written to Grünbaum about the odd statement he and Hawking made that nothing is a "single point" and has rejected this identification; Hartle writes: "the 'nothing' is not realized as a physical state in the formalism"[11] and thus that the misleading statement about nothing being a physical state, a "single point," should be omitted.

Hawking also recently emphasizes that the universe "would quite literally be created out of nothing: not just out of the vacuum, but out of absolutely nothing at all, because there is nothing outside the universe."[12] By 'be created' Hawking, like other physicists, means began to exist. The statement that the universe is 'created out of nothing' means (in the familiar terms of analytic philosophy) that the universe (a maximal spacetime containing mass-energy) began to exist and that it is not the case that the universe is caused to exist or consists of anything that exists temporally prior to the universe or that there is time prior to the universe.

The only "single point" or zero three-geometry in the Hartle-Hawking model is one predicted with a certain degree of (unconditional) probability by the wave function, and thus is not an unexplained given or brute fact. Hartle and Hawking write in their original paper: "In the case of the Universe we would interpret the fact that the wave function [the probability amplitude] can be finite and nonzero at the zero three-geometry as allowing the possibility of topological fluctuations of the three-geometry."[13] This predicted fluctuation to a zero three-geometry is not the referent of "nothing" in the "appear from nothing" phrase, since "nothing" has no referent (or, in Hartle's words, "the 'nothing' is not realized as a physical state in the formalism"[14]).

As I said, Craig does not refer to the Hartle-Hawking article to support his contention about the probabilities being conditional, but to Christopher Isham's article. Did Isham get it wrong, or did Craig misread Isham?

Craig refers to pages 395–400 in Isham's "Creation as a Quantum Process."[15] On pages 395–97, Isham is talking about how the probability of one state of the universe can be predicted from another state. But on page 398 he starts talking about the Hartle-Hawking theory of the uncaused beginning of the universe and says the wave function that gives the probability amplitude for the beginning of the universe does *not* make reference to, or depend upon, any earlier configuration or time from which the first physical state has evolved. Isham writes about the Hartle-Hawking concept K(c,f), where K is the probability, c the curvature, and f the matter field of a certain three-dimensional space. Isham writes:

> Note that the "transition" probability [Isham puts "transition" in scare quotes, since there is no transition from anything else] associated with this state-function is $K(c,f) = |\psi(c,f)|^2$. . . . Hence, K(c,f) is a function of just a *single* configuration point (c,f) [i.e., a single point in superspace, where each point represents a 3-space]: there is no (c_1,f_1) corresponding to an *earlier configuration and time* from which the system has "evolved." This is the precise sense in which the theory is said to predict the probability that the universe is created in various configurations "from nothing."[16]

So Craig misinterprets both Isham and Hawking; Hawking's theory does give us an unconditional probability that a Hawking-type universe begins to exist uncaused and Isham correctly recognizes and states this fact in his interpretation of Hawking's theory. This also shows that Deltete and Guy[17] are wrong when they say the Hartle-Hawking theory is analogous to ordinary quantum mechanics in that it is about merely "a transition between two real states" and thus that the "probability amplitude is conditional."[18]

5. ALVIN PLANTINGA'S CRITICISM OF THE ATHEIST ARGUMENT FROM QUANTUM COSMOLOGY

Craig asserts that "Plantinga pointed out to Smith that since according to classical theism God exists in all possible worlds, the probability of the universe on the wave function cannot differ from its probability on the wave function plus theism."[19] Exactly what did Plantinga point out and how should we evaluate his argument? Plantinga states that the relevant unconditional probability is (to quote Plantinga's own words):

> the proportion of possible worlds in which the universe has the characteristics [specified by the H-H wave function]. (Of course the figure of proportions of possible worlds here is just that—a figure; we have no reason to think possible worlds occupy something like a space, and no reason to think that there are at most continuum many possible worlds.) So the absolute probability of there being such a universe is, say, .95. But according to theism, God's existence is a necessary truth; so the probability that there be such a universe on the existence of God is the same as its probability on any necessary truth, which is just its absolute probability. So where's the inconsistency [that Smith alleges]? Of course the probability that there is such a world, given that God wills that there be such a world, is 1. But that's not an absolute probability, but a probability conditional on the (contingent) truth that God wills there be such a world.[20]

I am sympathetic with the "possible-worlds" approach to probability sketched (but not endorsed) by Plantinga in this passage and I think Plantinga's ideas are more nearly in line with the probability theory required by quantum gravity cosmology than are Deltete and Guy's or Oppy's. However, I believe there are several ways to respond to Plantinga's argument that there is no inconsistency between classical theism and quantum cosmology.

To begin with, the argument that theism and quantum cosmology are consistent is invalid in relevance logic. Let p be the complex proposition that states the Hartle-Hawking theory. For any conjunction of p with any necessary truth q, p by itself will *entail* (in the sense of relevance logic) the statement r of the probability value. The proposition r is:

(*r*) The probability that a universe begins to exist with the matter field ϕ and metric h_{ij} is .99.

However, if theism is true, *p* does not entail *r*. There must be a theistic proposition q_1 that entails *r*, since the probability of a universe existing based solely on natural-mathematical truths and without divine causation is zero. Thus, quantum gravity cosmology and theism will differ as regards to which conjunct in the conjunctive proposition, *p and* q_1, entails *r*, which prevents the two theories from being consistent in relevance logic.

Another problem is that there is no candidate for the theistic necessary truth q_1. Since the theist cannot allow that *p*, in the conjunction *p and* q_1, entails *r*, the theist must find some necessary truth of theism that entails *r*. Plantinga's proposition, *God exists*, does not entail *r*; nor does the theistic necessary proposition *whatever universe that exists is created by God.* Contingent propositions about God's decision to create a universe are not candidates, precisely because they are not necessary truths.

In fact, there is even an inconsistency *in standard propositional logic* between theism and quantum cosmology. I have been using 'conditional probability' to mean a probability that is dependent on the existence of some concrete things or events (bodies, minds, or events involving bodies or minds). I will now use 'conditional probability' to refer instead to any probability of the form *c(h/e & b)*, where *c* is the probability value, *h* a contingent hypothesis, *e* a contingent evidence statement, and *b* the "background knowledge" of necessary truths. An 'unconditional probability' now refers to probabilities of the form *c(h/b)*, which can be abbreviated as *c(h)* to highlight their unconditional nature (they are not conditional on any contingent proposition). I will assign the following values to these letters:

h = *there exists a Hartle-Hawking universe.*
e = *there obtains the wave function of the universe* $\psi[h_{ij}, \phi]$.
b = *small houses are houses, and . . . , etc. (the conjunction of all necessary truths).*

The proposition *c(h/e & b)* = .99 is true if Hawking's quantum cosmology is true and it is no part of Plantinga's argument to argue this cosmology is false. But if classical theism is true, *b* will include some truths that are incompatible with *c(h/e & b)* = .99, since it is a necessary truth of classical theism that for any possible universe U, the conditional probability that U exists is zero unless the conditions include some positive, contingent truths about divine dispositions, states, or acts. A positive, contingent truth about divine acts is any truth of the form, *God exists and contingently performs the act* A. If theism is true, *c(h/e & b)* = 0, since *e* includes no positive, contingent truths about divine dispositions, states, or acts. Thus if quantum cosmology and theism are both true, it follows both that $c(h/e \ \& \ b) = .99$ and that it is not the case that $c(h/e \ \& \ b) = .99$. This shows that we need not rely on relevance logic to show that quantum cosmology and theism are logically inconsistent.

6. WILLIAM ALSTON AND THE PROBLEM OF CONSERVING A QUANTUM UNIVERSE

God cannot conserve (in the sense of continuous creation) the successive states of the universe if the wave function law is true.

It is part of quantum mechanics that any quantum mechanical system Q is governed by a wave function, and that the wave function evolves in accordance with the Schrodinger equation *unless interfered with by an outside influence.* Now the evolution of the quantum mechanical system Q in quantum cosmology is governed by the gravitational Schrodinger equation (the Wheeler-DeWitt equation). Since the system Q that is the subject of quantum cosmology involves a physically closed system, the entire universe, there can be no outside influences. The evolution of the probabilities of the metric and matter field of the universe *cannot* be due to divine influence.

This argument can be presented more formally.

1a. The universe is a physically closed system that is described by the Hartle-Hawking "no-boundary" wave function of the universe.
2a. The probability distribution of the metrical and matter properties of any given three-dimensional spatial slice of the universe that has a preceding three-dimensional spatial slice, follow deterministically from the metrical and matter properties of the preceding 3-space in accordance with the "no-boundary" solution of the Wheeler-DeWitt equation.

Therefore,

3a. There are always sufficient conditions for the probabilistic evolution of the universe that are physical.

Therefore,

4a. There is no causal role for the god of classical theism to play in determining the probabilistic evolution of the universe.

Note that if we introduce at this point a theological ceteris paribus clause about divine conservation, we are introducing an argument that science is false, and are not showing how science is consistent with theism. Note, first, that there cannot be a theological ceteris paribus clause about divine conservation that is logically consistent with quantum cosmology, for such a clause would entail that the probabilities of the successive 3-spaces of the universe *never* evolve in accordance with initial conditions and the "no-boundary" solution of the Wheeler-DeWitt equation. But if they never evolve in this way, Hawking's "no-boundary" quantum cosmology is false.

If an alleged natural law L is never instantiated, despite the fact that its antecedent is instantiated (the antecedent referring to the initial conditions), then the alleged law is false. Consider this alleged law: "If there is a 3-space S_1 with the property F, then there is a subsequent 3-space S_2 that is probabilistically caused by S_1 in accordance with the probability distribution specified by the 'no-boundary' solution of the Wheeler-DeWitt equation." Now if the 3-space S_1 mentioned in the antecedent exists, but the subsequent 3-space S_2 is caused by God and is not probabilistically caused by S_1 in accordance with the Hartle-Hawking "no-boundary" solution of the Wheeler-DeWitt equation, then the quantum cosmological law is false.

William Alston states that quantum mechanics allows for divine intervention. Divine intervention would be ruled out, Alston says, if "the universe as a whole [is] a closed system vis-à-vis our body of physical laws. That, in effect, is what is envisaged by the Laplacean formulation of determinism."[21] If the universe is a closed system vis-à-vis our body of physical laws, then "the total state of the universe at one moment is a determinate function of its state at any other moment."[22] Alston regards quantum mechanics as refuting this view and allowing that "God designed the universe to operate in accordance with probabilistic laws so as to give room for God to enter the process as an agent."[23]

Thus, we would have it that the wave function of the 3-space S determines the probabilities for the next 3-space. Suppose the 3-space that actually occurs after S is S_1. We may suppose that the probability of S_1, conditional upon S and the wave function, is 85 percent. But God wants to bring about a different 3-space S_2. Thus the probability of S_1 conditional upon S, the wave function, and God's volition that S_2 occur, is 0 percent. Let us suppose that this is true for each 3-space, so that the probability of a 3-space, p(h/e & b & G), is 100 percent, where h is the hypothesis that the 3-space occurs, e is the evidence that the earlier 3-space occurred, b is the relevant background knowledge (in this case, the wave function), and G is God's willing that h be true.

But in this case quantum cosmology would be false. It never succeeds in giving us the correct probability for any hypothesis h. Quantum cosmology is false since it includes among its conditions e + b, and omits G. It is not the mere omission of G that renders quantum cosmology a false theory; it is the inclusion of probabilistically irrelevant conditions e and b as the conditions for h. Since p(h/e & b & G) = p(h/G), it follows that e and b are probabilistically irrelevant. Quantum cosmology is thus false for two reasons; it omits a relevant condition of p(h), and it includes only irrelevant conditions of p(h).

The theist may respond to this that "science is true since it is only about the natural universe, and does not take into account supernatural activity." But this response is offered as a panacea to disguise the implication of theism, namely, that science is false. Theism implies that science gives us a false theory of the natural universe, since science asserts that probabilistically *irrelevant* conditions of natural occurrences are the only probabilistically *relevant* conditions. The reason the theist cannot admit this, I submit, is sociological. Anybody who says "science is false and religion is true" immediately puts themselves beyond the pale of academic respectability and is dismissed as a "religious kook." I submit the theist ought to brave this negative peer pressure and "come out of the closet" about the implications of her theism.

Thus, Alston is mistaken that quantum mechanics can allow divine activity in a way that classical determinism cannot. But Alston puts forth another line of argument, that no scientific law specifies "unqualifiedly" conditions for a natural occurrence, be these conditions sufficient or probabilistic. Alston writes: "The most we are ever justified in accepting is a law that specifies what will be the outcome of certain conditions in the absence of any relevant factor other than those specified in the law." "None of our laws take account of all possible influences." Thus, "it can hardly be claimed that such a law will be violated if a divine outside force intervenes."[24] But this does not solve the problem, since, if theism is true, the conditions mentioned in the law are probabilistically irrelevant to the outcome, and the law is false. If the law is true, then the conditions are probabilistically relevant; but in that case, God cannot intervene since his intervention, being omnipotent, makes any other conditions probabilistically irrelevant.

Now, does quantum cosmology bring any new twist to this argument? This argument holds for ordinary quantum mechanics as well as quantum cosmology, but what quantum cosmology adds to this is that the wave function of the universe is a unique sort of law in that it *does* take account of *all possible influences* and does offer *unqualified* conditions for occurrences of states of the universe and of the universe as a whole. The qualified laws are those that purport to describe some part of the universe, since they allow that some other part may be influential and thus change the outcome specified by the law. But the wave function of the universe is about the whole universe. It is the one law that incorporates the clause that there are no other possible outside influences. If it did not incorporate this clause, it would not be a wave function of the universe but a wave function of a subsystem of the universe.

The response that the law means no other "natural influences" is unsuccessful, since the law, as a universal generalization, does not have for its domain only some of the things that exist—God's creatures. The variable ranges over everything. The natural/supernatural distinction is not made by the wave function, but is invented by the theist, limiting the actually unlimited domain of quantification of the variables in the wave function law. But this law in fact has no limits to its domain of quantification. For the theist to stipulate that it does not range over everything, but only some things—the things belonging to God's creation—is to change the law—or more exactly, is to say the law is false since it ranges over everything and thus over God and thus fails to account for God's activities in what it mentions.

This fact is illustrated by one point. As Hawking says in *A Brief History of Time*,[25] the wave function gives in principle the probabilities of the histories of intelligent organisms: "Each history in the sum over histories will describe not only the space-time but everything in it as well, including any complicated organisms like human beings who can observe the history of the universe." Some of these histories include, to borrow Alston's phrase, "the many occasions on which human beings take themselves to be in communication with God, receiving messages from God and speaking to God in turn, being aware of God's activity towards them . . . these events involve God's doing something at a particular time and place to bring something about."[26] The histories of intelligent organisms not only include their interactions with other intelligent organisms, but also their interactions with God (or what they believe is a god). If they receive a message from God, the description of this event involves the description of the organism receiving the message from God and (as a part of this complex event) God giving the message. A complete wave function of the universe would thus include these human-divine interactions; otherwise, it would not be complete. Thus, the universal variables in the complete wave function do range over *all* events (which include, if theism is true, creaturely events and the Creator's events). Accordingly, a theist has to say that if a complete wave function does not incorporate reference to divine activity, it is not true. It is not a wave function that describes the complete histories of intelligent organisms; it has gaps in it, gaps at every moment when someone stoops to prayer or hears a message from God. But the complete wave function purports to have no gaps, and thus the theist must say that this complete wave function is false.

The moral of this story is that quantum cosmology and classical theism cannot both be true. One has two choices: become an atheist or else argue that science, in the form of quantum cosmology, is false. However, since Copernicus and Galileo, any time that religion has opposed science, religion has lost.

NOTES

1. L. Z. Fang and Z. C. Wu, "An Overview of Quantum Cosmology," in *Quantum Cosmology*, edited by L. Z. Fang and Remo Ruffini (Singapore: World Scientific, 1986), p. 3.

2. Stephen W. Hawking, "The Boundary Conditions of the Universe," in *Astrophysical Cosmology* (Vatican City: Pontifica Academiae Scientarium, 1982), pp. 563–72.

3. J. Hartle and Stephen W. Hawking, "Wave Function of the Universe," *Physical Review* D28 (1983): 2960–75.

4. Ned Markosian, "On the Argument from Quantum Cosmology against Atheism," *Analysis* 55 (1995): 247–51.

5. Graham Oppy, "Some Questions about 'The Hartle-Hawking Cosmology,'" *Sophia* 36 (1997): 84–95.

6. William Lane Craig, "The Caused Beginning of the Universe: A Response to Quentin Smith," *British Journal for the Philosophy of Science* 44 (1993): 623–39; "Hartle-Hawking Cosmology and Atheism," *Analysis* 57 (1997): 291–95.

7. Robert Deltete and Reed Guy, "Emerging from Imaginary Time," *Synthese* 108 (1996): 185–203; "Hartle-Hawking Cosmology and Unconditional Probabilities," *Analysis* 57 (1997): 304–15.

8. Craig, "The Caused Beginning of the Universe," p. 637.

9. Hartle and Hawking, "Wave Function of the Universe," p. 2961.

10. Ibid.

11. Hartle, letter to Adolf Grünbaum, 1990.

12. Stephen Hawking and Roger Penrose, *The Nature of Space and Time* (Princeton, NJ: Princeton University Press, 1996).

13. Hartle and Hawking, "Wave Function of the Universe," p. 2962.

14. Hartle, letter to Adolf Grünbaum.

15. Christopher Isham, "Creation of the Universe as a Quantum Tunneling Process," in *Physics, Philosophy and Theology*, edited by R. J. Russell et al. (Vatican City: Vatican Observatory, 1988).

16. Ibid., pp. 399–400.

17. Deltete and Guy, "Hartle-Hawking Cosmology," p. 306.

18. Ibid.

19. Craig, "Hartle-Hawking Cosmology and Atheism," p. 292, note 2.

20. Alvin Plantinga, quoted with permission from a private communication to Quentin Smith about quantum cosmology and theism, 1996.

21. William Alston, "Divine Action, Human Freedom, and the Laws of Nature," in *Quantum Cosmology and the Laws of Nature*, edited by R. Russell, N. Murphy, and C. Isham (Vatican City: Vatican Observatory, 1993), p. 190.

22. Ibid., p. 188.

23. Ibid., p. 189.

24. Ibid., p. 190.

25. Stephen W. Hawking, *A Brief History of Time* (New York: Bantam Books, 1988), p. 137.

26. Alston, "Divine Action," pp. 186–87.

PART 2

TELEOLOGICAL ARGUMENTS AGAINST THE EXISTENCE OF GOD

INTRODUCTION

This section contains new and previously published papers and book selections presenting and defending teleological arguments against the existence of God. A teleological argument against God's existence is an inductive argument based on the weight of the evidence relative to the order in the universe.

A teleological argument against God's existence takes the following general form:

1. If God exists,
   then God is the designer of the universe.
2. Based on the weight of the evidence relative to the order in the universe, God is not the designer of the universe.
3. Therefore, God does not exist.

Here are brief summaries of the papers and book selections contained in this section.

Nicholas Everitt in a selection "The Argument from Scale" from *The Non-existence of God* (2004) considers a God who created the universe with the intention of making humanity its centerpiece. Drawing on the findings of modern cosmology, Everitt argues that the incredible length of time that the universe, and even nonhuman life on earth, has existed compared to the relatively very short time that humans have existed and the enormous volume of the universe compared to the relatively minuscule volume that is needed by and accessible to humans are both very inapt design features. The conclusion is that the immense temporal and spatial dimensions of the universe revealed by science weigh against the existence of God.

Victor J. Stenger in a 1999 paper "The Anthropic Coincidences: A Natural Explanation" discusses the so-called anthropic coincidences (the delicate connections between certain physical constants and life), the anthropic principles (hypotheses about the meaning of these coincidences), and the fine-tuning argument for God's existence (divine design is the best explanation of these coincidences). The fine-tuning argument is criticized for making several unwarranted assumptions, such as that life must be carbon-based and certain physical constants must take on values within only a very narrow range for life to arise naturally. Stenger then argues that modern physics, besides providing a simpler and naturalistic explanation for the physical constants, has shown that the conservation laws of energy, momentum, and so on, describe global symmetries in our universe (e.g., space, time, and rotational symmetries) and these symmetries occur precisely because the universe is *not* being acted upon or disturbed by external forces, such as a designing agent, and therefore God probably does not exist.

Michael Ikeda and Bill Jefferys in a 2002 paper "The Anthropic Principle Does Not Support Supernaturalism," published on the Web, begin with a critique of the fine-tuning argument for God's existence: it unjustifiably assumes that no other universes exist and that certain physical constants must take on values within only a very narrow range for life to arise naturally; it fails to take into account possible universes that do not allow life to arise naturally but that still contain life due to divine intervention; and it invalidly infers the improbability of a naturalistic universe with life-friendly conditions from the improbability of life-friendly conditions in a naturalistic universe. They then use Bayes's theorem to argue that, even assuming only one universe exists, since our universe both contains life and allows life to arise naturally and since the number of possible universes that allow life to arise naturally is greatly exceeded by the number of possible universes that do not allow life to arise naturally but that still contain life due to divine intervention, the probability of our universe existing if God *does not* exist, although small, is much larger than the probability of our universe existing if God *does* exist. Since our universe exists, it follows that God probably does not exist.

Wesley C. Salmon in a 1978 paper "Religion and Science: A New Look at Hume's *Dialogues*" reformulates Philo's analogical argument from experience in Hume's *Dialogues Concerning Natural Religion* in terms of Bayes's theorem to show that the existence of a God who designed the universe is improbable. Salmon argues that since nearly all objects exhibiting order that we observe (atoms, molecules, cells, plants, animals, galaxies, etc.) appear to be produced naturally and only a tiny percentage of all objects exhibiting order that we observe (watches, skyscrapers, etc.) are the product of intelligent design, it is very unlikely that the universe was intelligently designed. Moreover, even granting that the universe is intelligently designed, since all designers we observe have bodies and all large, complexly designed objects have multiple designers, the universe was probably not designed by a single disembodied designer. Therefore, God probably does not exist.

In a short 1979 paper "Experimental Atheism" that addresses several objections raised by Nancy Cartwright, Salmon argues that no questions are begged, an experiment suggested by Cartwright is irrelevant, and the best cosmological evidence available supports the view that the universe was not designed by God, and thus God probably does not exist.

Michael Martin in "Atheistic Teleological Arguments," a selection from *Atheism: A Philosophical Justification* (1990), formalizes and expands the analogical argument from experience against the existence of God. According to the common definition, God created and designed the universe from nothing, did so alone, and possesses such attributes as disembodiedness, omnipotence, and infallibility. However, if God created and designed the universe, then, in analogy with extensive human experience of beings that create and design, one would expect God to have utilized preexisting material, collaborated with peers, have a body, be limited in power, and make mistakes—all of which conflicts with the common definition of God. Therefore, God probably does not exist.

Bruce and Frances Martin in a 2003 paper "Neither Intelligent nor Designed" consider whether the biological diversity and complexity of organisms on the earth reveals "Intelligent Design" (i.e., purposeful planning) by God. They argue that the fossil evidence of many unsuccessful species that have become extinct and the physiological evidence of vestigial (useless) organs and anatomical inefficiencies in existing organisms is incompatible with "Intelligent Design" by an omnibenevolent, omniscient, and omnipotent being, and therefore God, so conceived, probably does not exist.

Richard Dawkins in a 1998 paper "The Improbability of God" begins by pointing out that the evidence is overwhelming that the biological diversity and complexity of organisms on the earth is the result of evolution by natural selection. Such evidence includes the layered fossil record, the geographical distribution of plants and animals, and the common genetic code of all creatures that indicates descent from a single ancestor. On the strength of this evidence Dawkins then argues that God is either *unnecessary* in the production of biological order or necessary somehow in its production but *deceptive* in planting evidence that makes it appear as though God is unnecessary, so that in either case God is unworthy of worship, and therefore God probably does not exist.

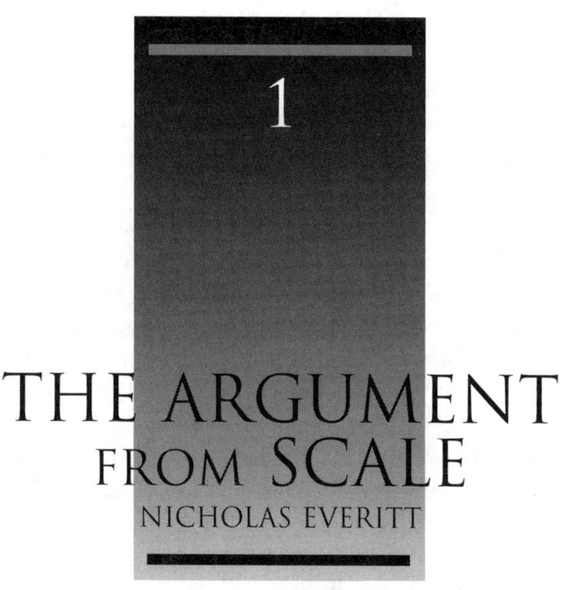

1

THE ARGUMENT FROM SCALE

NICHOLAS EVERITT

INTRODUCTION

The first argument against theism which we consider is a modest science-based argument, and it aims to show that the picture of the universe with which modern science presents us constitutes evidence against the truth of theism. The evidence by itself is not very strong, certainly not overwhelming, but it is nonetheless significant. Traditional theism presents us with a certain picture of God and of his intentions in creating the universe at large, and in creating human beings in particular. In general, if someone hypothesizes that there is an agent with a certain nature and a certain set of intentions, then we can form some idea of what the agent is likely to do—in what respect things will be different just in virtue of the hypothesized agent's having that nature, those beliefs, and that intention. If we then discover that the world is not as we have predicted, then we have evidence that the initial hypothesis that there was such an agent is mistaken. The argument thus has the form:

(1) If there is an agent with nature N, beliefs B, and intention I, then he will produce change C in the world.
(2) The world does not display C. So:
(3) There is evidence against the hypothesis that there is an agent with N and I and B.

As an example of the argument at work in an uncontroversial context, consider an updated Robinson Crusoe. Suppose he considers the hypothesis that elsewhere on the island with him is another survivor of the shipwreck similar to Crusoe himself in his physical and mental capacities, including his beliefs, and with the intention of making contact with any other survivors, such as Crusoe. Even given as vague and impoverished a hypothesis as this, Crusoe can make *some* predictions about what the hypothetical survivor will do. He can formulate in his mind a range of what he might call apt behavior, and a range of inapt behavior, which the survivor might display—apt and inapt relative to the intention with which Crusoe has tentatively credited him. It would be apt if, for example, the survivor left visible signs of his presence on the island (marks on trees, scratchings on rocks, carefully arranged pieces of wood or stone). It would be apt if he emitted characteristically human noises (whistling, singing, shouting, etc.). It would be apt if he lit a fire and tried to send smoke signals. These would be apt pieces of behavior because they are just the sorts of things which a Crusoe-like survivor would do if he were trying to let other possible survivors know of his existence on the island. By contrast, it would not be apt if the hypothetical survivor, for example, found some deep undergrowth and lay in it, quiet and still, for the greater part of each day. It would not be apt if after being in any location on the island, he carefully removed all signs of his presence (footprints, ashes from fires, etc.). And so on. These are not apt ways of realizing the intention of making your presence known to another human who might be in the vicinity. They are not the kind of actions which it would be reasonable for Crusoe to expect another survivor to pursue, given the intentions and beliefs with which Crusoe is crediting him.

So, even before starting his empirical investigation of the island, Crusoe can formulate to himself a description of what evidence would help to confirm his initial hypothesis, and what evidence would help to disconfirm it. If he looks hard and carefully for evidence of what we have called apt behavior, and finds none, that constitutes some evidence against his initial hypothesis that there is another survivor. It is evidence for saying that either there is no actual survivor, or if there is one, the initial hypothesis was wrong about either his capacities or his intentions. In saying that some kinds of behavior by the hypothetical survivor would be 'inapt', we do not mean that it *absolutely disproves* the initial hypothesis about the survivor's capacities and intentions, but rather that it constitutes *evidence against* the hypothesis. The evidence is defeasible in that it is possible that there is some factor of which Crusoe is unaware which would explain away its initial anti-hypothesis import. (Perhaps the survivor is injured or even unconscious.) But if he does not discover any such factor, he would be justified in concluding that the initial hypothesis is to some degree disconfirmed.

Let us see now how considerations of this kind can be applied on a cosmic scale, and how the nature of the universe as revealed by modern science gives us reason to reject traditional theism.

THE ARGUMENT FROM SCALE

Consider, first, the account of God's nature and purposes with which theism presents us. Theism tells us that God is a being who is omnipotent and omniscient, wholly self-sufficient, with no needs, or lacks, or deficiencies of any kind. For reasons that are not entirely clear, God decides to create a universe in which human beings will be the jewel. Although he will have a care for the whole of his creation, God will have an especial care for human beings. He will give these creatures the power of free choice. Exactly what this power is, no one can agree. Some think that it is a capacity the possession of which is incompatible with the truth of determinism; others think that it is a kind of freedom which is compatible with determinism, and which perhaps even requires determinism. Because humans are the jewel of creation, the rest of the universe will be at least not unremittingly hostile or even indifferent to human flourishing. Even if the universe will not make such flourishing immediately and easily and painlessly accessible, it will make it at least accessible in principle for humanity at large. The question then to ask is: given this much information about God and his nature and his purposes, what sort of a universe would you expect to find? Which of all the possible worlds that God could create would you expect him to create, given this much knowledge of his nature and of his overall plan?

As with our example of Robinson Crusoe, it is difficult to answer this question in any great detail. The description of God is so sketchy, and in particular the theistic hypothesis gives us so little information about his aims, that a large number of possible worlds are left equally likely. But among the more likely scenarios is a universe somewhat like the one presented to us in the story of Genesis. In particular, traditional theism would lead you to expect human beings to appear fairly soon after the start of the universe. For, given the central role of humanity, what would be the point of a universe which came into existence and then existed for unimaginable eons without the presence of the very species that supplied its rationale? You would expect humans to appear after a great many animals, since the animals are subordinate species available for human utilization, and there would be no point in having humans arrive on the scene needing animals (e.g., as a source of food, or clothing, or companionship) only for them to discover that animals had not yet been created. But equally, you would not expect humans to arrive *very* long after the animals, for what would be the point of a universe existing for eons full of animals created for humanity's delectation, in the absence of any humans? Further, you would expect the earth to be fairly near the center of the universe if it had one, or at some similarly significant location if it did not have an actual center. You would expect the total universe to be not many orders of magnitude greater than the size of the earth. The universe would be on a *human* scale. You would expect that even if there are regions of the created world which are hostile to human life, and which perhaps are incompatible with it, the greater part of the universe would be accessible to human exploration. If this were not so, what would the point be of God creating it?

These expectations are largely what we find in the Genesis story (or strictly, stories) of creation. There is, then, a logic to the picture of the universe with which the Genesis story presents us: given the initial assumptions about God, his nature, and his intentions, the Genesis universe is pretty much how it would be reasonable for God to proceed. Given the hypothesis of theism and no scientific knowledge, and then asked to construct a picture of the universe and its creation, it is not surprising that the author(s) of Genesis came up with the account which they did. It is not that God would have *had* to proceed in the Genesis way (just as there is not just one kind of behavior which a possible island survivor would need to produce to confirm Crusoe's initial hypothesis), and it is not that *every* non-Genesis way would be extremely puzzling. There is in fact a wide range of possible universes which God could have created and about which there would not be a puzzle of the form "But how could a universe like *that* be an expression of a set of intentions like *those*?" Nevertheless, we can still draw a distinction between universes which would be apt, given the initial hypothesis, and universes which would be inapt. The Genesis universe is clearly an apt one, given the theistic hypothesis; but a universe in which (say) most humans could survive only by leading lives of great and endless pain would be a surprising one for God to choose, given the other assumptions we make about him.

The question now to raise is, "Is the universe as it is revealed to us by modern science roughly the sort of universe which we would antecedently expect a God of traditional theism to create? Is it an apt universe, given the admittedly sketchy conception we have of his nature and his intentions?"

The short answer to this is "No." In almost every respect, the universe as it is revealed to us by modern science is *hugely* unlike the sort of universe which the traditional thesis would lead us to expect. Although the bare quantitative facts will be familiar to many readers, it is worth repeating them. First, in terms of age: our best estimates are that the universe itself is very roughly 15 billion years, and the earth is roughly 5 billion years old. How long humans have existed will depend partly on what we take a human to be. But if we take humans to be *Homo sapiens*, and if we take them to be creatures with some sort of language and some sort of social culture, then realistic estimates would allow that they have existed for no more than 100,000 years. So if we imagine the history of the universe represented by a line which is roughly 24 miles long, human life would occupy only the last inch. Or if we imagine this history of the universe represented by a single year, humanity would emerge only in the last few seconds of the last minute of the last hour of the last day of the year. So for something more than 99.999 percent of the history of the universe, the very creatures which are meant to be the jewel of creation have been absent from it. The question that at once arises is "What, given the hypothesis of theism, was the point of this huge discrepancy between the age of the universe and the age of humanity?" How very inapt a creation of that kind must strike us.

The same story recurs if we turn to the size of the universe. Suppose we take the size of our solar system to be within the expectable parameters of the theistic hypothesis. (This might seem over-generous to theism: why would God need a solar system as big as ours to achieve any of his purposes? Why does he need a sun that is 93 *million* miles from earth? Why wouldn't 93 thousand miles have been enough? Of course the laws of physics would then have had to be different if the sun were to make earth habitable—but as an omnipotent being, God could easily have adjusted the laws of physics. However, let us overlook this and allow that a distance of 93 million miles counts as intelligible—it is intelligible, that is, that a God with the nature and intentions ascribed by traditional theism should create a universe that big.) But of course, we know now that the universe is staggeringly larger than any such intelligible size. The sun is about 8 light minutes from us, the next nearest star is about 4.3 light years, the next nearest galaxy to the Milky Way is scores of light years away. Current findings indicate that the furthest star visible from earth is about 3 billion light years away. In other words, the most distant star is very roughly some 200,000,000,000,000,000 times (two hundred thousand trillion times) as far from us as the sun. This sort of scale to the universe makes no conceivable sense on the theistic hypothesis. Nor should we assume that the most distant visible star is the most distant detectable entity. The furthest galaxy, detectable only by radio telescopes, is reckoned to be about three times further away—9 billion light years. The possible limits of the universe lie further away still. If the Big Bang occurred about 15 billion years ago, and if the expansion had occurred at the speed of light, the limits of the universe would be about 30 billion light years. Assuming that the expansion was at less than the speed of light, that still leaves the possibility of a universe whose overall size is between 10 billion and 30 billion light years across (i.e., up to two million trillion miles). Why would a God make it that big?

Further, astronomers tell us that there are about 100 trillion galaxies, each with a billion stars (giving us something of the order of 100,000,000,000,000,000,000,000 stars).[1] It could count as apt if a creator created a universe with one star or perhaps a few dozen or even a few hundred, so that the night sky were as beautiful as we now find it. But what could be the point of the huge superabundance of celestial matter, especially given the fact that the very great majority of humanity will never be aware of most of it? Again, given the theistic hypothesis, it is strikingly inapt.

If we confine our attention to the earth, the same extraordinary inaptness confronts us. The Genesis story presents God's actions as apt in relation to the non-human creatures who share the planet with humans: they all emerge at about the same time; and all the creatures which surround humanity in that story share a human scale—none are so tiny that it is impossible to detect them by the senses, and none are so huge (e.g., thousands or millions of times larger than humans) as to be unrecognizable as organisms at all. But again, modern science reveals this to be deeply wrong—not just in points of detail, but in almost every major respect. Life has existed on the planet for something like 3 billion to 3.5 billion years. For roughly half of that time, it has been solely bacterial in form. Given that humans have emerged only in the last 100,000 years, that means that for 99.99 percent of the history of life on earth, there have been no humans. How very bizarre, given the theistic hypothesis! Further, from a biological point of view, "On any possible or reasonable or fair criterion, bacteria are—and always have been—the dominant forms of life on earth."[2] In terms of their numbers, their longevity, their ability to exploit the widest variety of habitats, their degree of genetic variation, and even (amazingly, give how tiny they are individually) their total biomass, they outstrip every other kind of life. If God had intended any species to flourish, the obvious candidate for divine favor would be bacteria, not humans.

In short, then, everything that modern science tells us about the size and scale and nature of the universe around us reveals it to be strikingly inapt as an expression of a set of divine intentions of the kind that theism postulates. Let us emphasize that the claim here is not that there is a logical incompatibility between these modern scientific findings and traditional theism. It is not that the findings *disprove* theism. The claim is weaker than that. The claim is only that the findings of modern science *significantly reduce the probability* that theism is true, because the universe is turning out to be very unlike the sort of universe which we would have expected, had theism been true. However, before accepting this conclusion, let us see what responses the theist might make.

REPLY 1: MODERN SCIENCE IS FALLIBLE

A first reply would complain that the argument places too much reliance on modern science. This is a mistake, the theist may say, for two reasons. First, all of the figures used in the above arguments are subject to huge margins of uncertainty. For example, although it is customary for the age of the universe to be given as 15 billion years, estimates by wholly reputable experts range between

12 billion and 18 billion years. Similarly with the other figures for the size of the universe, the amount of matter it contains, the age of life on earth, and so on. All of the figures have a "back of an envelope" quality to them. They are, the theist may complain, little more than ballpark figures, on which no reliance can be placed. Second, even if the figures could be made more precise, they are derived only from current scientific theories; and scientific theories, the theist can rightly point out, change constantly. They do not constitute secure knowledge, they are fleeting "best bet" guesses all of which will probably be rejected in time as science advances. So, in the light of these two objections, the theist might conclude that the argument from scale is built on sand.

The atheist, however, should be unmoved by these objections. She can concede the essence of what they say, but reject the conclusions which the theist draws from them. Take first the uncertainty about the numbers employed. Even if the numbers are inaccurate, even if they are hugely inaccurate, the atheist's argument is largely unaffected. Suppose, for example, that the universe is not 15 billion years old but only one tenth as old or one hundredth or one thousandth as old. That would still leave it at 15 million years old. That may not sound much to modern ears, accustomed to the huge dimensions which cosmology introduces. But it still gives us a universe that is still *massively* inapt on the theistic hypothesis. One way of seeing how this is so, is to reflect on the estimates of the age of the universe provided by those who did not have access to modern science. From Scaliger and Spanheim in the fifteenth and sixteenth centuries, through the famous Ussher discussion of the seventeenth, and on to a number of competent and respectable Victorian scientists, the consensus figure was that the universe began in about 4000 BC. Reflective thinkers clearly believed that a universe with roughly this sort of timescale is what the theistic hypothesis would lead one to expect. That would be an apt universe in terms of age, given theism. So even if current estimates of the age of the universe were out by a factor of a thousand, that would still give us a universe that was roughly 3,000 times older than pre-scientific theists thought made sense from a theistic point of view. So the power of the argument from scale does not depend on the figures it uses being correct, or even approximately correct. They could be a thousand times too big, and the argument would still be a good one.

The theist's second objection to reliance on science was that science presents us with a set of constantly changing, constantly refuted hypotheses; it does not give us knowledge. This again the atheist can concede, while denying that it carries the implications which the theist supposes. For in the first place, although theories are constantly being superseded, the *general picture* of which they are a transitory part does not fundamentally change. Although it is possible that future estimates of the age or size of the universe may be greater or smaller than those which we now accept, there is no possibility that we will return to the scales which would deprive the argument from scale of its force. There is no possibility that future scientific theories will tell us that the universe started in about 4000 BC. There is no possibility that future theories will tell us that it is only about one million, or ten million, or a hundred million, or a thousand million miles across. In short, there is no possibility that future theories will tell us that the scale of the universe is what it would need to be, to be apt for the theistic hypothesis. So even if the details of current scientific theorizing cannot be taken as secure knowledge, the general picture which science presents can be so taken; and it is that general picture which presents us with a universe inapt for theism.

REPLY 2: THEISM IS NOT COMMITTED TO WHAT SCIENCE HAS DISPROVED

A second natural response would be for the theist to deny that she is committed to what the argument is attacking. The theist might, for example, point out that theism per se has no commitment to any specifically Christian doctrines, even less to the truth of any specifically Biblical claims. To believe in God is not to be committed to any claims about prophets or messiahs, or any empirical or quasi-empirical claims about the age of the universe, the origin of humanity, or even God's special and unique concern for humanity. As a matter of historical fact, the theist may be willing to concede, the vast majority of theists *have* accorded special status to the Bible—but that was in virtue of their acceptance of further claims which were not entailed by theism itself. It is possible to be a theist without being a Jew, or a Christian, or a Moslem. So, whatever may be the relations between Biblical claims on the one hand, and the doctrines of these specific religions on the other, is completely independent of theism. Modern science is incompatible with, for example, a literal reading of Genesis—but that is a problem for Fundamentalist Christians and Jews (the theist may say) and not for theism per se.

There is a sense in which this theistic response is correct and a sense in which it is wrong. It is correct in the sense that it is of course right to say that theism is not committed to the literal truth of the Genesis creation story. But it is wrong to think that the argument from scale makes this assumption. Rather, what the argument from scale assumes is that the theist is committed to the universe being an apt expression of the nature and intention of God, where it was allowed that a wide variety of possible universes would count as apt. The point was only that some universes must count as inapt (such as the universe in which every human being could survive only by leading a life of great and ceaseless pain); and that the universe that modern science reveals falls into the inapt category.

For surely the theist must concede that her assumptions about the nature and

purposes of a creator and sustainer of all things carry *some* empirical implications, however vague and however defeasible. She surely does not want to say that the character of the universe would have been just as it is if there had been no God, or if there had been a creator with a very different nature, and with very different intentions. Once the theist concedes that her theistic hypothesis does carry *some* empirical implications, then we can test those empirical implications, and when we find that they are false, carry the disconfirmation back to theism itself.

Even so, the theist may reply, the argument as presented assumes that theism is committed to more than in fact it is. Certainly theism is committed to the view that God is benign, and hence will have a concern with human welfare. But it is not committed to the view that God is concerned only or even specially with humanity. It is not committed, as the Genesis story is, to the claim that life appears only on earth. So it is not committed to there being anything surprising in the fact that the universe is very much bigger than it apparently needs to be for specifically human flourishing; or in the fact that specifically human life has appeared very late in the history of the universe, and indeed very late in the history of life.

This response has some force—but not much. First, it seems that theism *is* committed to certain evaluations on God's part. One of his defining attributes is omniscience; and this suggests that God thinks knowledge is a valuable attribute. . . . So, all other things being equal, he will think that species which are capable of knowledge are better than species which are not capable of knowledge. So, given that humans are the supremely knowledge-possessing species as far as we know, theism must think that God will regard them as especially valuable. And in that case, the puzzle for theism returns: why in the three-billion-year history of life have intelligent, knowledgeable humans existed only for the last 100,000 years? To use the same analogy we used above: if the history of life on earth is represented by a year, humans have appeared only in the final few seconds of the year. Why the delay, given that theism must think that humans are the most valuable species created so far? Who or what has gained, and how, from that colossal delay?

Similar puzzles return if we look out to the stars. The theist could plausibly say that God places no special value on humans, if it were the case that when we scanned the heavens we found it teeming with intelligent life comparable to and perhaps greater than ourselves. But that is exactly what we do not find. What we find are unimaginably huge volumes of space with no sign of intelligent life at all—in fact, no sign of any kind of life. Of course, there *may* be life elsewhere, and conceivably there may also be intelligent life elsewhere. But we have as yet nothing but the barest circumstantial evidence for thinking that there is. So, of everything which we know to exist in the universe, it seems that theism is committed to saying that humans are the most valuable things in creation. They are the nearest to God—they are made in his image.

REPLY 3: THERE *IS* A DIVINE PURPOSE IN THE SCALE OF THINGS

A third theistic response would allow what the second response denied, namely, that theism does carry some implications about what the universe will turn out to be like. But it would deny that the universe as we find it is different from the universe as theism would predict it to be. It would seek to show that the universe as we find it is very much as theism would predict it to be—or at least, even if theism could not have predicted that God would choose to create the universe which he has created, it would try to show ex post facto that it is not surprising that God has chosen to create a universe of this kind. How might such an argument go in detail? The theist might point to the fact that God's omniscience is a sign that knowledge is a valuable commodity. So, God would want his creatures to acquire it, so it is explicable that he would create a world of relatively high complexity. The world would be complex enough for the pursuit of knowledge to be a taxing and worthwhile human pursuit, but not so taxing that it was wholly or largely beyond human power. And that is just the degree of complexity which we find the world to have. Cosmology, physics, chemistry, biology, and other sciences studying the natural world *are* intellectually challenging: they do require discipline, imagination, and rational thought; but they are to some degree within the compass of a significant and expandable proportion of humanity.

There are, however, several problems which the atheist will find with an ex post facto justification such as this. She might point out in the first place that it is a purported justification of *complexity*, rather than of *scale*, and that a universe on a human scale could certainly display plenty of complexity (in such domains as say, mathematics and history, biography and literary criticism—and even philosophy). But second and more importantly, the weakness of all such ex post justifications is revealed in the very fact that they are ex post. Those early theists (in fact, right up to the nineteenth century) who never thought that God might make such a colossally huge universe knew perfectly well that omniscience was one of God's defining properties, that he was therefore likely to regard knowledge as a good thing, and that he would therefore create a universe in which human knowledge would be attainable, albeit with some effort. Why did it never cross their minds that given these initial assumptions, God might create a universe billions of times bigger and older than their contemporary cosmologists were contemplating? Surely, the atheist will claim, it is because it is simply arbitrary to try and connect any supposed value placed by God on knowledge on the one hand, with the huge dimensions of the universe on the other.

REPLY 4: SCIENCE USES THE WRONG CRITERION OF SIGNIFICANCE

A different line of reply for the theist is to challenge the significance of the findings of modern science, at least as they have been used here by the atheist. What the atheist has implicitly been doing (the critic will allege) is asking us to be impressed by sheer size—either temporal or spatial. Thus, the atheist draws our attention to the fact that the universe is very big by human standards; or to the fact that the duration of humanity compared with other life forms is very small; or to the fact that in numbers and variety, lowly species of life like bacteria show much greater richness than humanity. The implication which the atheist wants us to draw is that human beings are insignificant in the cosmic scheme of things. But, the theist will object, this conclusion cannot be drawn. What gives value to something is not how big it is, or how long it has lasted, or whether it exists everywhere, or exists in huge numbers. What gives value to it is a set of qualities such as intelligence, creativity, and morality. These are qualities which are found uniquely, or to a unique degree, in human beings. For that reason, no findings about the huge size of the universe or the vast age of the earth, or the biological success of lowly life forms could in any way undermine the importance and significance of human life. Human life would not become more significant if science were to discover that the universe was very much smaller or younger than we now take it to be; nor would it become less significant and less valuable if we were to discover the universe to be larger and older than we now take it to be. In short (the theist will say), the atheist has been over-impressed by big numbers, and ignored the fact that these have no necessary connection with significance or value.

However, the atheist can object that this misrepresents his position. The point about the argument from scale is not that it shows human beings to be unimportant or insignificant, even less that they are unimportant or insignificant *because* they are small in space and time. Rather, the aim of the argument is to show that there is a mismatch between the kind of universe which one would expect, given the theistic conception of God and his purposes, and the kind of universe which modern science reveals to us. The atheist can happily concede all the theist's claims about the value of humanity, and how that is unaffected by the scale of the universe within which it finds itself. The inaptness which the atheist wants to insist on concerns the size of the universe (in space and time) and the position of humanity within the domain of life, given the hypothesized existence and purposes of God. Given that God wants to create beings akin to human beings, with certain features which give them value and significance, why does he set these beings in a universe whose spatio-temporal dimensions are so hugely in excess of what is needed? Why does he precede these human beings with vast multitudes of life forms, most of which simply become extinct, and none of which display any intrinsically admirable features?

REPLY 5: GOD IS INSCRUTABLE

The final line of reply which the theist might make is to concede that there *is* a prima facie inaptness about the scale of the universe, given the nature and purposes which theism attributes to God, but to claim that this is wholly inconclusive. We should not presume, the theist may say, to understand *everything* about God's reasons and purposes. We may be unable to see why God should make a universe as big or as old as the one in which we find ourselves, a universe in which so much of what has existed and does now exist has nothing at all to do with humanity—or indeed with life. But that just shows, the theist may say, that God surpasses all human understanding. It is wholly unsurprising, given what theism tells us about God, that we should find him largely inscrutable. Clearly, he will have had his reasons for creating a universe as big and as old as the one we have, and the fact that we have no idea what those reasons are simply reflects our own limited intelligence: it does not discredit the doctrine of theism at all.

But again, the atheist should be unmoved. In the first place, she can legitimately press the theist for some details of what these further divine purposes might be. The point here is that it is not enough for the theist to say, "There *could* be some intention which would render the scale of the universe intelligible to us." Whether or not we have any grounds for thinking that God has any of these intentions is a further question: the prior question is whether the theist is right to say that there could be some such intentions. If she cannot actually specify what intentions she has in mind, then her claim that there are such intentions is simply frivolous.

Let us assume that the theist can specify what these possible intentions are. The atheist will now ask what grounds there are for thinking that God actually has any of them. She will object that there is no independent evidence for thinking that God *does* have these extra inscrutable purposes, purposes which would explain the otherwise puzzling features of the universe. This extra hypothesis which the theist is forced to adopt is thus entirely ad hoc and unreasonable. And if the only way to prevent considerations of scale from reducing the probability of theism is by adopting a further hypothesis for which there is no evidence, then the theist is unreasonable in adopting that further hypothesis. So, the atheist will conclude, she is either unreasonable if she denies that considerations of scale reduce the probability of theism, or she is unreasonable because in trying to block that charge of unreasonableness, she accepts a hypothesis which there is no reason to accept.

We can think again here of the Crusoe analogy with which we started. Suppose that in spite of careful searching, Crusoe finds no evidence of a survivor (no rock scratchings, no smoke signals, no shouts, whistles, etc.), and infers that this reduces the probability of his initial hypothesis that there was another survivor who was trying to contact him. It then occurs to him that if he attributed some further strange intentions to the hypothetical survivor, then the lack of obvious signs on the island of another person would be exactly what he would expect. Suppose, for example, that the survivor does not simply want to make contact with Crusoe, but to make contact *by using a method which would initially lead Crusoe to think that there was no survivor*. This would be a strange intention for the survivor to have, and there is no reason for Crusoe to think that the survivor, if there is one, has such an intention. But if there were a survivor, and if he had this strange intention, then the absence of signs on the island of the survivor would precisely be an apt expression of the survivor's strange intention. But we can see that in such a situation, Crusoe would be unreasonable in adding to his initial hypothesis this further unsupported hypothesis, just to make the original hypothesis square with the lack of evidence which he found for the existence of the supposed survivor. And in a similar way, the atheist can insist, the theist who attributes arbitrary further intentions to God, in order to square the hypothesis of God's existence with the scale of the universe, is being unreasonable.

The atheist might also note in passing how an appeal to divine inscrutability appears as a deus ex machina argument. Historically, theists have claimed to have a very detailed knowledge of God's intentions and preferences. They have claimed to know, for example, that he does not want humans to consume certain sorts of foods and drink, that he objects to some specific kinds of contraception but not to others, that he has firm views on the cutting or non-cutting of (some) hair of (some) people, that it matters to him on which days of the week people perform certain tasks, and so on. How very strange that God's mind should be so transparent on such small-scale and local issues, and yet opaque on much larger issues.

CONCLUSION

The upshot of this line of thought, then, is that there is indeed a mismatch between the universe as revealed to us by modern science and the universe which we would expect, given the hypothesis of theism. Utilizing the argument schema with which we started, we can say:

(1) If the God of classical theism existed, with the purposes traditionally ascribed to him, then he would create a universe on a human scale, i.e.,

one that is not unimaginably large, unimaginably old, and in which human beings form an unimaginably tiny part of it, temporally and spatially.

(2) The world does not display a human scale. So:

(3) There is evidence against the hypothesis that the God of classical theism exists with the purposes traditionally ascribed to him.

We need to notice the limited nature of this conclusion. We have already emphasized that it is not a *proof* of the falsity of theism. We can also add that as presented, it does not even claim that theism is *probably* false. For it could quite well be the case that there was evidence against theism, but not of such a weight as to make the falsity of theism more probable than not. On the other hand, the argument is not negligible. It shows that those who think that science and theism can be kept wholly insulated from each other are mistaken. Science *does* reveal to us unobvious facts about the nature of the universe; the nature of the universe *is* relevant to the question of whether theism is a possible, or a good, or the best explanation of the existence and nature of the universe; and the argument of this paper shows why the findings of modern science tell against the truth of theism.

NOTES

1. Sarah Woodward, "Things to Come," *Cambridge Alumni Magazine* 30 (2000): 25.
2. Stephen Jay Gould, *Life's Grandeur* (London: Jonathan Cape, 1996), p. 176.

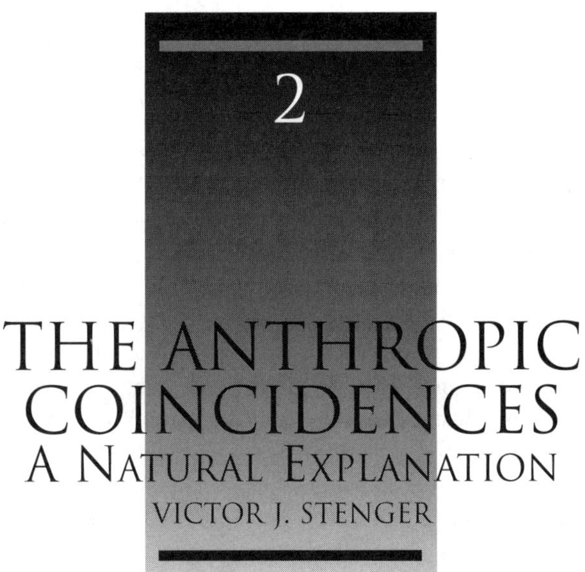

2

THE ANTHROPIC COINCIDENCES

A Natural Explanation

VICTOR J. STENGER

Recently the media have reported that scientists have discovered supernatural purpose to the universe. The so-called anthropic coincidences, in which the constants of nature seem to be extraordinarily fine-tuned for the production of life, are cited, in these reports, as evidence. However, no such interpretation can be found in scientific literature. Based on all we currently know about fundamental physics and cosmology, the most logically consistent and parsimonious picture of the universe as we know it is a natural one, with no sign of design or purposeful creation provided by scientific observations.

POKING OUT OF THE NOISE

At least two-and-a-half millennia have passed since a few thinkers, such as Thales and Heraclitus in ancient Greece, had the idea that the world around us might be understood wholly in terms of familiar substances and forces such as water and fire. They were the first to grasp the possibility that mysterious, undetectable agents need not be invoked in the explanation of phenomena. It was a revolutionary notion—and the world was far from ready to embrace it. At this stage, humanity still clutched the superstitions carried out of cave and forest. And so, with a few exceptions, *naturalism* lay largely dormant for two millennia while human cultures continued to be dominated by supernatural thinking.

In Christian Europe during the Middle Ages, the study of empirical phenomena did not necessarily exclude the supernatural. Indeed, most if not all of the scientists, or "natural philosophers," of the period were clerics or otherwise connected with the Church. Nevertheless, serious conflict between the fledgling science and religion broke out in the sixteenth century when the Church condemned Galileo for maintaining that Copernicus's proposition that the earth circled the sun represented a *physical* and not just *mathematical* description of the solar system. However, religion and science soon reconciled. Newton interpreted his great mechanical discoveries, which were based on the earlier work of Descartes, Galileo, and others, as uncovering God's design for the physical universe. The success of Newtonian science was rapid and dramatic. People began to speak of the need to read two books authored by God—Scripture and the Book of Nature.

Science offers natural explanations for phenomena previously attributed to supernatural agency. Static electricity, not Thor's spear, produces a lightning flash. Natural selection, not divine intervention, impels the development of life. The neural network of the brain, not some disembodied spirit, enables mental processes. Scientific explanations are frequently unpopular; witness Darwinism. It seems that they occupy a privileged place for the simple reason that they work so well, not because people find them appealing. Technological progress, fed by scientific discovery, testifies to the power of natural explanations for events. This has given science enormous stature and credibility. People listen to what science has to say, even if they do not always like what they hear, in particular, that they are not the center of the universe.

With the exception of the minority who insist on literal interpretation of scripture, religious scholars have largely deferred to science on those matters where the scientific consensus has spoken. Theologians are quite adept at reinterpreting the teachings of their faiths in the light of new knowledge. There is nothing wrong with this. Most scientists and theologians agree that both groups are in the business of learning, not preaching. Theologians argue, with some merit, that religion still has a role to play in moral matters and in the search to find the place of humanity in the scheme of things. Most scientists regard questions about the purpose of the universe to be beyond the scope of science. Nevertheless, when they read the press reports about science and religion converging, some religious believers take heart that, when everything is said and done, the purpose they desire will stick its head up out of the scientific background noise.

THE SUPPOSED SIGNAL OF PURPOSE

For about a decade now, an ever-increasing number of scientists and theologians have been asserting, in popular articles and books, that they can detect a signal of cosmic purpose poking its head out of the noisy data of physics and cosmology. This claim has been widely reported in the media,[1] perhaps misleading lay people into thinking that some kind of new scientific consensus is developing in support of supernatural beliefs. In fact, none of this reported evidence can be found in the pages of scientific journals, which continue to successfully operate within an assumed framework in which all physical phenomena are natural.

The purported signal of cosmic purpose cannot be demonstrated from the data alone. Such observations require considerable interpretation to arrive at that conclusion. Those not very familiar with recent deliberations in the philosophy of science might be inclined to scoff and say that the observations speak for themselves, with no interpretation necessary. Facts are facts, they might argue, and neither God nor purpose are scientific facts.

However, scientists and philosophers of science have been unable to define a clear demarcation between observation and theory. Most now agree that all scientific observations are "theory-laden." That is, empirical results cannot be cleanly separated from the theoretical framework used to classify and interpret them. This new development in the philosophy of science has opened the door for theologians and believing scientists to reinterpret scientific data in terms of their preferred model of intelligent design and divine purpose to the universe. Some claim the data fit this model better than alternatives. Most say it is at least as good.

The data whose interpretation is being debated in the religion-science dialogue are not scraps of fading documents, nor the uncertain translations of ancient fables that over time have evolved into sacred texts. Rather, they consist of measurements made by sophisticated research teams using advanced scientific instruments. The new theistic argument is based on the fact that earthly life is so sensitive to the values of the fundamental physical constants and properties of its environment that even the tiniest changes to any of these would mean that life as we see it around us would not exist. This is said to reveal a universe in which the fundamental physical constants of nature are exquisitely fine-tuned and delicately balanced for the production of life. As the argument goes, the chance that any initially random set of constants would correspond to the set of values they happen to have in our universe is very small; thus this precise balancing act is exceedingly unlikely to be the result of mindless chance. Rather, an intelligent, purposeful, and indeed personal Creator probably made things the way they are. The argument is well captured by a cartoon in mathematician Roger Penrose's book *The Emperor's New Mind* which shows the Creator pointing a finger toward an absurdly tiny volume in the "phase space of possible universes" to produce the universe in which we live.[2]

Most who make the fine-tuning argument are content to say that intelligent, purposeful, supernatural design has become an equally viable alternative to a random, purposeless, natural evolution of the universe and humankind suggested by conventional science. However, a few theists have gone much further to insist that God is now *required* by the data. Moreover, this God must be the God of the Christian Bible. No way, this group says, can the universe be the product of purely natural, impersonal processes. Typical of this view is *The Creator and the Cosmos: How the Greatest Scientific Discoveries of the Century Reveal God*, a book by physicist and astronomer Hugh Ross. Ross cannot imagine fine-tuning happening any other way than by a "personal Entity . . . at least a hundred trillion times more 'capable' than are we human beings with all our resources." He concludes that "the Entity who brought the universe into existence must be a Personal Being, for only a person can design with anywhere near this degree of precision."[3]

The delicate connections among certain physical constants, and between those constants and life, are collectively called the *anthropic coincidences*. Before examining the merits of the interpretation of these coincidences as evidence for intelligent design, I will review how the notion first came about. For a detailed history and a wide-ranging discussion of all the issues, see *The Anthropic Cosmological Principle*, by John D. Barrow and Frank J. Tipler.[4] I also refer the reader there for the original references. But be forewarned that this exhaustive tome has many errors, especially in equations, some of which remain uncorrected in later editions.

THE ANTHROPIC COINCIDENCES

In 1919, Hermann Weyl expressed his puzzlement that the ratio of the electromagnetic force to the gravitational force between two electrons is such a huge number, $N_1 = 10^{39}$.[5] This means that the strength of the electromagnetic force is greater than the strength of the gravitational force by 39 orders of magnitude. Weyl wondered why this should be the case, expressing his intuition that "pure" numbers, like pi, that do not depend on any system of units, occurring in the description of physical properties should most naturally occur within a few orders of magnitude of unity. Unity, or zero, you can expect "naturally." But why 10^{39}? Why not 10^{57} or 10^{-123}? Some principle must select out 10^{39}.

In 1923, Arthur Eddington commented: "It is difficult to account for the occurrence of a pure number (of order greatly different from unity) in the scheme of things; but this difficulty would be removed if we could connect it to the number of particles in the world—a number presumably decided by accident."[6] He estimated that number, now called the "Eddington number," to be $N = 10^{79}$. Well, N is not too far from the square of N_1. This was the first of the anthropic coincidences, that N approximately equals the square of N_1.

These musings may bring to mind the measurements made on the Great

Pyramid of Egypt in 1864 by Scotland's Astronomer-Royal, Piazzi Smyth. He found accurate estimates of pi and the distance from the earth to the sun, and other strange "coincidences" buried in his measurements.[7] However, we now know that these were simply the result of Smyth's selective toying with the numbers.[8] Still, even today some people believe that the pyramids hold secrets about the universe. Ideas like this never seem to die, no matter how deep in the sand they may be buried.

Look around at enough numbers and you are bound to find some that appear connected. Most physicists, therefore, did not regard the large-numbers puzzle seriously until one of their most brilliant members, Paul Dirac, took an interest. Few physicists ignored anything Dirac had to say.

Dirac discovered that N_1 is the same order of magnitude as another pure number N_2 that gives the ratio of a typical stellar lifetime to the time for light to traverse the radius of a proton. That is, he found two seemingly unconnected large numbers to be of the same order of magnitude.[9] If one number being large is unlikely, how much more unlikely is another to come along with about the same value?

In 1961, Robert Dicke pointed out that N_2 is necessarily large in order that the lifetime of typical stars be sufficient to generate heavy chemical elements such as carbon. Furthermore, he showed that N_1 must be of the same order of N_2 in any universe with heavy elements.[10]

The heavy elements did not get fabricated straightforwardly. According to the big bang theory (despite what you may hear, the consensus of cosmologists now regard the big bang as very well established), only hydrogen, deuterium (the isotope of hydrogen consisting of one proton and one neutron), helium, and lithium were formed in the early universe. Carbon, nitrogen, oxygen, iron, and the other elements of the chemical periodic table were not produced until billions of years later. These billions of years were needed for stars to assemble these heavier elements out of neutrons and protons. When the more massive stars expended their hydrogen fuel, they exploded as supernovae, spraying the manufactured elements into space. Once in space, these elements cooled and accumulated into planets.

Billions of additional years were needed for our home star, the sun, to provide a stable output of energy so that at least one of its planets could develop life. But if the gravitational attraction between protons in stars had not been many orders of magnitude weaker than the electric repulsion, as represented by the very large value of N_1, stars would have collapsed and burned out long before nuclear processes could build up the periodic table from the original hydrogen and deuterium. The formation of chemical complexity is only possible in a universe of great age—or at least in a universe with other parameters close to the values they have in this one.

Great age is not all. The element-synthesizing processes in stars depend sensitively on the properties and abundances of deuterium and helium produced in the early universe. Deuterium would not exist if the difference between the masses of a neutron and a proton were just slightly displaced from its actual value. The relative abundances of hydrogen and helium also depend strongly on this parameter. The relative abundances of hydrogen and helium also require a delicate balance of the relative strengths of gravity and the weak interaction, the interaction responsible for nuclear beta decay. A slightly stronger weak force and the universe would be 100 percent hydrogen. In that case, all the neutrons in the early universe will have decayed, leaving none around to be saved in deuterium nuclei for later use in the element-building processes in stars. A slightly weaker weak force and few neutrons would have decayed, leaving about the same numbers of protons and neutrons. In that case, all the protons and neutrons would have been bound up in helium nuclei, with two protons and two neutrons in each. This would have led to a universe that was 100 percent helium, with no hydrogen to fuel the fusion processes in stars. Neither of these extremes would have allowed for the existence of stars and life as we know it based on carbon chemistry.

The electron also enters into the tightrope act needed to produce the heavier elements. Because the mass of the electron is less than the neutron-proton mass difference, a free neutron can decay into a proton, electron, and anti-neutrino. If this were not the case, the neutron would be stable and most of the protons and electrons in the early universe would have combined to form neutrons, leaving little hydrogen to act as the main component and fuel of stars. It is also essential that the neutron be heavier than the proton, but not so much heavier that neutrons cannot be bound in nuclei, where conservation of energy prevents the neutrons from decaying.

In 1952, astronomer Fred Hoyle used anthropic arguments to predict that an excited carbon nucleus has an excited energy level at around 7.7 MeV. I have already noted that a delicate balance of physical constants was necessary for carbon and other chemical elements beyond lithium in the periodic table to be cooked in stars. Hoyle looked closely at the nuclear mechanisms involved and found that they appeared to be inadequate.

The basic mechanism for the manufacture of carbon is the fusion of three helium nuclei into a single carbon nucleus:

$$3He^4 \rightarrow C^{12}$$

(The superscripts give the number of *nucleons*, i.e., protons and neutrons in each nucleus, which is indicated by its chemical symbol; the total number of nucleons is conserved, i.e., remains constant, in a nuclear reaction). However, the probability of three bodies coming together simultaneously is very low and some catalytic process in which only two bodies interact at a time must be assisting. An intermediate process had earlier been suggested in which two helium nuclei first fuse into a beryllium nucleus, which then interacts with the third helium nucleus to give the desired carbon nucleus:

$$2He^4 \rightarrow Be^8$$
$$He^4 + Be^8 \rightarrow C^{12}$$

Hoyle showed that this still was not sufficient unless the carbon nucleus had an excited state at 7.7 MeV to provide for a high reaction probability. A laboratory experiment was undertaken, and sure enough a previously unknown excited state of carbon was found at 7.66 MeV.[11]

Nothing can gain you more respect in science than the successful prediction of a new phenomenon. Here, Hoyle used standard nuclear theory. But his reasoning contained another element whose significance is still hotly debated. Without the 7.7 MeV nuclear state of carbon, our form of life based on carbon would not have existed. Yet nothing in fundamental nuclear theory, as it is still known today, directly determines the existence of this state. It cannot be deduced from the axioms of the theory.

Like the other coincidences, this particular nuclear state seems hardly likely to be the result of chance. In 1974, Brandon Carter[12] introduced the notion of the *anthropic principle* which hypothesized that the anthropic coincidences are not the result of chance but somehow built into the structure of the universe. Barrow and Tipler[13] have identified three different forms of the anthropic principle and refer to Carter's version as the "strong" anthropic principle, defined as follows:

> *Strong Anthropic Principle* (SAP): *The Universe must have those properties which allow life to develop within it at some stage in its history.*

This suggests that the coincidences are not accidental but the result of a law of nature. But it is a strange law indeed, unlike any other in physics. It suggests that life exists as some Aristotelian "final cause."

Barrow and Tipler[14] claim that this can have three interpretations:

> (A) *There exists one possible Universe "designed" with the goal of generating and sustaining "observers."*

This is the interpretation adopted by most theistic believers.

> (B) *Observers are necessary to bring the Universe into being.*

This is traditional solipsism, but also is a part of today's New Age mysticism.

> (C) *An ensemble of other different universes is necessary for the existence of our Universe.*

This speculation is part of contemporary cosmological thinking, as I will discuss below. It represents the idea that the coincidences are accidental. We just happen to live in the particular universe that was suited for us.

The current dialogue focuses on the choice between (A) and (C), with (B) not taken seriously in the scientific community. However, before discussing the relative merits of the three choices, let me complete the story on the various forms of the anthropic principle discussed by Barrow and Tipler. They identify two other versions:

> *Weak Anthropic Principle* (WAP): *The observed values of all physical and cosmological quantities are not equally probable but take on values restricted by the requirement that there exist sites where carbon-based life can evolve and by the requirement that the Universe be old enough for it to have already done so.*

The WAP has not impressed too many people. All it seems to say is that if the universe was not the way it is, we would not be here talking about it. If the fine structure constant were not 1/137, people would look different. If I did not live at 508 Pepeekeo Place, I would live someplace else.

> *Final Anthropic Principle* (FAP): *Intelligent information-processing must come into existence in the Universe, and, once it comes into existence, it will never die out.*

This is sometimes also referred to as the *Completely Ridiculous Anthropic Principle.*

PREDICTIONS OF THE FAP

In *The Anthropic Cosmological Principle*, Barrow and Tipler speculated only briefly about the implications of the FAP. Tipler later propounded its consequences in a controversial book with the provocative title: *The Physics of Immortality: Modern Cosmology, God and the Resurrection of the Dead.* Here Tipler carries the implications of the FAP about as far as one can imagine they could go.[15]

Tipler argues that the robots that will evolve from our current computer technology will ultimately spread themselves throughout the universe, each new generation of robot producing ever superior versions of itself. After the passage of a billion billion years or so, the universe will become uniformly populated with an extremely advanced life form. Humanity, of course, will be long gone.

At that point, Tipler assumes the universe will begin to contract toward what is called the "big crunch," the reverse of the big bang. The collapse of the universe does not happen in any old way, however. It is very carefully controlled in order to maintain causal contact across the universe and provide sufficient energy for what life must then accomplish in order to avoid extinction.

The advanced life form that has evolved from our twenty-first-century robots should be able to manage this, according to Tipler. Who can deny the possibility of anything a billion billion years in the future? The universe then converges on what the French Jesuit Pierre Teilhard de Chardin called the *Omega Point*. Tipler associates the Omega Point, as did Teilhard, with God.

Being the ultimate form of power and knowledge, the Omega Point would also be the ultimate in Love. Loving us, it would proceed to resurrect all humans who ever lived (along with their favorite pets and popular endangered species). This is accomplished by means of a perfect computer simulation, what Tipler calls an *emulation*.

Since each of us is defined by our DNA, the Omega Point simply emulates all possible humans that could ever live, which of course includes you and me in every variation. Our memories have long since dissolved into entropy, but Omega has us relive our lives in an instant, along with all the other possible lives we could have lived. Those that Omega-God deems deserving will get to live even better lives, including lots of sex with the most desirable partners we can imagine.

All this, Tipler claims, is a predictable consequence of the FAP. Fortunately, we do not have to wait a billion billion years to test the theory. One prediction is that the universe is "closed." That is, someday in the distant future it will stop expanding and begin contracting. This depends on the average density of matter and energy in the universe, a quantity which can be estimated from a wide range of observations that are improving every year.

When Tipler wrote his book, a closed universe was not supported by the data, but the uncertainties were still large enough that the possibility could not be strongly ruled out. Since then, observations have made it even more unlikely that the universe is closed. An open, "flat" universe that is poised just on the border between expansion and contraction is predicted by the inflationary big bang theory. Right now, the FAP prediction of a closed universe does not look as if it will be fulfilled.

You might ask if an ever-expanding universe can be made consistent with the FAP. No doubt it can, but then it makes no testable predictions and so it becomes little more than speculation. Tipler's theory at least had the virtue of being falsifiable. It now seems to be heading for falsification.

INTERPRETING THE COINCIDENCES: (A) THEY ARE DESIGNED

Let us now review the first of the three possible explanations for the anthropic coincidences listed by Barrow and Tipler: (A) *There exists one possible Universe "designed" with the goal of generating and sustaining "observers."*

Many theists see the anthropic coincidences as evidence for purposeful design to the universe. They ask: how can the universe possibly have obtained the unique set of physical constants it has, so exquisitely fine-tuned for life as they are, except by purposeful design—design with life and perhaps humanity in mind?[16]

Let us examine the implicit assumptions here. First and foremost, and fatal to the design argument all by itself, we have the wholly unwarranted assumption that only *one type of life is possible*—the particular form of carbon-based life we have here on earth.

Carbon would seem to be the chemical element best suited to act as the building block for the type of complex molecular systems that develop lifelike qualities. Even today, new materials assembled from carbon atoms exhibit remarkable, unexpected properties, from superconductivity to ferromagnetism. However, to assume that only carbon life is possible is simply "carbocentrism" that results from the fact that you and I are structured on carbon.

Given the known laws of physics and chemistry, we can easily imagine life based on silicon (computers, the Internet?) or other elements chemically similar to carbon. However, these still require cooking in stars and thus a universe old enough for star evolution. The $N_1 = N_2$ coincidence would still hold in this case, although the anthropic principle would have to be renamed the "cyberthropic" principle, or some such, with computers rather than humans and cockroaches the purpose of existence. Indeed, Tipler would probably agree with this.

Only hydrogen, helium, and lithium were synthesized in the early big bang. They are probably chemically too simple to be assembled into diverse structures. So, it seems that any life based on chemistry would require an old universe, with long-lived stars producing the needed materials.

Still, it seems like "chemicentrism" to rule out other forms of matter than molecules in the universe as building blocks of complex systems. While atomic nuclei, for example, do not exhibit the diversity and complexity seen in the way atoms assemble into molecular structures, perhaps they might be able to do so in a universe with different properties.

Sufficient complexity and long life may be the only ingredients needed for a universe to have *some* form of life. Those who argue that life is highly improbable need to open their minds to the fact that life might be likely with many different configurations of laws and constants of physics. Furthermore, nothing in anthropic reasoning indicates any special preference for human life, or indeed intelligent or sentient life of any sort. As Earmon has expressed this: "Imagine, if you will, the wonderment of a species of mud worms who discover that if the constant of thermometric conductivity of mud were different by a small percentage they would not be able to survive."[17]

The development of intelligent life does not seem to have proceeded smoothly and elegantly from the fundamental constants in the way that the phrase "fine-tuning" may be thought to imply. Several billion years elapsed before the conditions of intelligent life came together, and the process of fashioning these conditions seems to have been accompanied by a staggering degree of waste (all that space, dust, and seemingly dead cosmic bodies). By human standards, it seems remarkably inefficient. Also, in the case of human life, it appears that (amongst other things) earth would have suffered frequent catastrophic collisions with comets had it not been for the gravitational effect of Jupiter. This hardly seems consistent with divine creation. Setting in motion a myriad threatening comets and then positioning a huge planet as a protection against the danger you have thus created seems like the work of a cosmic jerry-builder.[18]

Even before we examine the other possibilities in detail, we can see another fatal fallacy in the fine-tuning argument. It is a probability argument that rests on a misconception of the concept of probability. Suppose we were to begin with an ensemble of universes in which the physical constants for each vary over a wide range of possible values. Then the probability that one universe selected randomly from that set would be our universe is admittedly very small. The fine-tuning argument then concludes that our specific universe was deliberately selected from the set by some external agent, namely, God.

However, a simple example shows that this conclusion does not logically follow. Suppose that a lottery is conducted in which each entrant is assigned a number from one to one million. Each has kicked in a dollar and the winner gets the whole pot of $1 million. The number is selected and you are the lucky winner! Now it is possible that the whole thing was fixed and your mother chose the winning number. But absent any evidence for this, no one has the right to make that accusation. Yet that's what the fine-tuning argument amounts to. Without any evidence, God is accused of fixing the lottery.

Somebody had to win the lottery, and you lucked out. Similarly, if a universe was going to happen, some set of physical constants was going to be selected. The physical constants, randomly selected, could have been the ones we have. And they led to the form of life we have.

In another example, estimate the probability that the particular sperm and egg that formed you would unite—that your parents, grandparents and all your ancestors down to the primeval stew that formed the first living things would come together in the right combination. Would that infinitesimally small number be the probability that you exist? Of course not. You exist with 100 percent probability.[19]

Michael Ikeda and Bill Jefferys[20] have done a formal probability theory analysis that demonstrates these logical flaws and others in the fine-tuning argument. They have also noted an amusing inconsistency that shows how promoters of design often use mutually contradictory logic.

On the one hand you have the creationists and god-of-the-gaps evolutionists who argue that nature is too *uncongenial* for life to have developed totally naturally, and so therefore supernatural input must have occurred. Then you have the fine-tuners (often the same people) arguing that the constants and laws of nature are exquisitely *congenial* to life, and so therefore they must have been supernaturally created. They can't have it both ways.

The fine-tuning argument rests on the assumption that *any* form of life is possible only for a very narrow, improbable range of physical parameters. We can safely conclude that this assumption is completely unjustified. None of this rules out option (A) as the source of the anthropic coincidences. But it does show that the arguments that are used to support that option are very weak and certainly insufficient to rule out of hand all alternatives. If all those alternatives are to fall, making (A) the choice by default, then they will have to fall of their own weight.

INTERPRETING THE COINCIDENCES: (B) THEY ARE ALL IN THE HEAD

Let us look next at the second of the explanations for the anthropic coincidences listed by Barrow and Tipler: (B) *Observers are necessary to bring the Universe into being.*

As the philosophers Berkeley and Hume realized, the possibility that reality is all in the mind cannot be disproved. However, any philosophy based on this notion is wrought with problems, not the least of which is why then is the universe not the way each of us wants it to be? Furthermore, whose mind is the one that is doing the imagining? Berkeley decided it had to be the mind of God, which makes this interpretation of the anthropic coincidences indistinguishable from the previous one. However, another possibility that is more in tune with Eastern religion than Western is that we are all part of a single cosmic mind.

This idea has become very popular in the New Age movement. Triggered by the publication of *The Tao of Physics* by physicist Fritjof Capra,[21] a whole industry has developed in which the so-called mysteries and paradoxes of quantum mechanics are used to justify the notion that our thoughts control reality. The most successful practitioner of this philosophy is Dr. Deepak Chopra, who has done very well promoting what he calls "quantum healing."[22]

Option (B) is certainly not taken seriously in the current science-religion dialogues. However, let me include a brief discussion for the sake of completeness.[23]

Basically, the new ideas on cosmic mind and the quantum begin with the confusing interpretive language used by some of the founders of quantum mechanics, most particularly Niels Bohr. In what is termed the *Copenhagen interpretation*, a physical body does not obtain a property, such as position in space, until it is observed. Although quantum mechanics has continued to agree with all measurements to very high precision, the Copenhagen interpretation has been further interpreted to mean that reality is all in our heads.

Moreover, according to the idea of "quantum consciousness," our minds are all tuned in holistically to all the minds of the universe, with each individual forming part of the cosmic mind of God. As applied to the anthropic coincidences, the constants of physics are what they are because the cosmic mind wills them so.

Today few quantum physicists take the notion of a cosmic quantum mind seriously. The success of quantum mechanics does not depend in any way on the Copenhagen interpretation or its more mystical spinoffs. Other interpretations exist, like Bohm's hidden variables, the many worlds interpretation, and the consistent histories interpretation.[24] Unfortunately, no consensus interpretation of quantum mechanics exists among physicists and philosophers. Suffice it to say that the admittedly "strange" behavior of the quantum world is mysterious only because it is unfamiliar, and can be interpreted without the introduction of any mystical ideas, including cosmic mind.

INTERPRETING THE COINCIDENCES: (C) THEY ARE NATURAL

Finally let me move to the possibility that we can understand the anthropic coincidences naturally. I have very carefully discussed the other options first in order to make it clear that, by themselves, they are highly flawed and provide us little reason to accept their premises. I might stop here and claim the natural explanation wins by default. This can be somewhat justified on the principle of parsimony. Since all scientific explanations until now have been natural, then it would seem that the best bet is a natural explanation for the anthropic coincidences. Such an explanation would probably require the fewest in the way of extraordinary hypotheses—such as the existence of a spirit world either inside or outside the physical universe.

The Laws of Nature

The standard model of elementary particles and fields has, for the first time in history, given us a theory that is consistent with all experiments. More than that, in developing the standard model physicists have gained significant new insights into the nature of the so-called laws of nature.

Prior to these recent developments, the physicist's conception of the laws of nature was pretty much that of most lay people: They were assumed to be rules for the behavior of matter and energy that are part of the very structure of the universe, laid out at the creation. However, in the past several decades we have gradually come to understand that what we call "laws of physics" are basically our own descriptions of certain symmetries observed in nature and how these symmetries, in some cases, happen to be broken. And, as we will see, the particular laws we have found do not require an agent to bring them into being. In fact, they are exactly what would be expected in the absence of an agent.

The most powerful of all the laws of nature are the great conservation principles of energy, momentum, angular momentum, charge, and other quantities that are measured in fundamental interactions. These apply whenever a system of bodies is sufficiently isolated from its environment. Thus the total energy, momentum, angular momentum, charge, etc. of the molecules in a completely insulated chamber of fixed volume will remain constant as the molecules move about. Individual molecules can exchange these quantities when they interact with others. Thus a molecule can lose energy and momentum by colliding with another, while the struck molecule will gain the same amounts. A chemical reaction can occur in which the charges of the molecules also change, but the total charge remains constant.

The position of a body in space is usually represented in terms of coordinates, such as the latitude, longitude, and altitude of an aircraft in the sky. For over a century now, physicists have known that whenever their description of a body does not depend on a particular coordinate, say x, then the momentum that corresponds to that coordinate, p_x, is conserved. That is, this particular momentum component, called the "momentum conjugate to x," does not change as the body moves.

For example, consider a space probe far from earth moving in a straight line at constant velocity v_x with respect to its home ship in which we are riding. Let the position of the probe with respect to some arbitrary marker, say asteroid Randi, be x. The motion of the probe will look the same whether viewed from our ship at $x = 0$ or another vessel at $x = 137{,}000$ kilometers. The probe's velocity v_x and momentum $p_x = mv_x$, where m is the mass of the probe, will be the same independent of x.

Similarly, our description of the probe's motion need not include the time at which it is being observed. As long as it keeps moving with constant velocity, in magnitude and direction, its motion will look the same whether viewed at UT0645 or UT1720. This independence of the time "coordinate" is expressed as conservation of energy, where energy is "the momentum conjugate to t." (In relativistic kinematics, energy is the "timelike coordinate" of a four-dimensional momentum in which each component is conjugate to four-dimensional spacetime.)

The motion of the probe in this example is said to possess both *space-translation* and *time-translation* symmetries. This means that our description of its motion does not depend on any special position in space or moment in time. Under the same conditions, the probe would behave the same way on a planet in the Andromeda galaxy a million years in the future.

The probe also possesses *rotational symmetry*, behaving the same way when observed from other angles where its motion points in a different direction. Rotational symmetry implies angular momentum conservation.

Now consider the universe as a whole. Unless it is being acted on by some outside agent, it will behave the same regardless of where we place it in some imagined super spacetime or how we happen to orient it. That is, the universe is expected to possess all three symmetries described above. It follows that energy, momentum, angular momentum, and any other quantities of the type that are conjugate to these coordinates will be conserved *globally*, that is, as a whole and at each point in space and time.

In other words, the global conservation "laws" are exactly what one expects for an isolated universe with no outside agent acting. Only a *violation* of these laws would imply an outside agent. The data so far are consistent with no agent.

Global conservation laws follow from what we call global symmetries, like space translation and time translation. As I said, this was pretty much known a hundred years ago but not much was made of it. In this century, with the development of quantum mechanics, the same connection between symmetries and conservation laws was shown to still exist and to be even more profound.

In more recent years, the importance of *broken symmetries* has come to be recognized. This has been put together with our understanding of unbroken global symmetries to produce a coherent scheme in which everything we know seems to broadly fit.

Broken symmetry is actually very common at the everyday scale. Not all cars travel in straight lines at constant speed. They roll to a stop when the engine cuts off, as energy is lost to friction. Neither are the material structures we see around us fully symmetric. The earth is not a sphere but a flattened spheroid. A tree looks different from different angles. Our faces look different in a mirror. Mirror symmetry is broken when a system is not precisely left-right or mirror symmetric, like our faces. That is no surprise, and indeed we can view much of what we call material structure as a combination of broken and unbroken symmetries. Again, think of a snowflake. Structure and beauty seem to be combinations of both unbroken and broken symmetries, of both order and randomness.

The big revelation to physicists in the 1950s was that a few rare nuclear and fundamental particle interactions are not mirror symmetric. This discovery triggered an awakening to the possibilities of symmetry breaking at the fundamental scale in other situations. In many cases, this was merely a re-expression of old facts in a new language. For example, a symmetry such as momentum conservation can be broken *locally* without destroying the overall space-translation symmetry of the universe. When momentum conservation is locally broken, as with a falling body, we say we have a force acting. Indeed Newton's second law of motion specifies that force is equal to the time rate of change of momentum. In this case global momentum conservation is maintained, as interacting bodies in an isolated system have an equal and opposite reaction, as expressed by Newton's third law.

Thus gravity, and the other forces of nature, came to be recognized—and described theoretically—as broken local symmetries. The standard model was built on a framework of local broken symmetry.

Symmetry breaking can be likened to a pencil balanced vertically on its eraser end. This situation possesses rotational symmetry about the vertical axis, that is, it looks the same from any angle you view it as you walk around the table holding the pencil. However, the balance is precarious. With no help from the outside other than random breezes, the pencil will eventually fall over. The direction it points along is random—unpredictable, undesigned—but the symmetry is broken and a new, special direction is then singled out.

In the Beginning

For almost two decades, the *inflationary big bang* has been the standard model of cosmology.[25] We keep hearing, again from the unreliable popular media, that the big bang is in trouble and the inflationary model is dead. In fact, no viable substitute has been proposed that has near the equivalent explanatory power.

The inflationary big bang offers a plausible, natural scenario for the uncaused origin and evolution of the universe, including the formation of order and structure—without the violation of any laws of physics. Indeed, as we saw above, these laws themselves are now understood far more deeply than before and we are beginning to grasp how they too could have come about naturally. This particular version of a natural scenario for the origin of the universe has not yet risen to the exalted status of a scientific theory. However, the fact that it is consistent with all current knowledge and cannot be ruled out at this time demonstrates that no rational basis exists for introducing the added hypothesis of supernatural creation. Such a hypothesis is simply not required by the data.

According to this scenario, by means of a random quantum fluctuation the universe "tunneled" from pure vacuum ("nothing") to what is called a *false vacuum*, a region of space that contains no matter or radiation but is not quite "nothing." The space inside this bubble of false vacuum was curved, or warped. A small amount of energy was contained in that curvature, somewhat like the energy stored in a strung bow. This ostensible violation of energy conservation is allowed by the Heisenberg uncertainty principle for sufficiently small time intervals.

The bubble then inflated exponentially and the universe grew by many orders of magnitude in a tiny fraction of a second.[26] As the bubble expanded, its curvature energy was converted into matter and radiation, inflation stopped, and the more linear big bang expansion we now experience commenced. The universe cooled and its structure spontaneously froze out, as formless water vapor freezes into snowflakes whose unique patterns arise from a combination of symmetry and randomness. The first galaxies began to assemble after about a billion years, eventually evolving into stable systems where stars could live out their lives and populate the interstellar medium with the heavier chemical elements such as carbon which are needed for the formation of life.

So how did our universe happen to be so "fine-tuned" as to produce these wonderful, self-important carbon structures? As I explained above, we have no reason to assume that ours is the only possible form of life and perhaps life of some sort would have happened whatever form the universe took—however the crystals on the arm of the snowflake happened to be arranged by chance.

At some point, according to this scenario, the symmetries of the initial nothingness began to be "spontaneously" broken. Those of the current standard model of elementary particles and forces were among the last broken, when the universe was about 10^{-12} second old and much "colder" than earlier. The distances and energies involved at this point have been probed in existing colliding beam accelerators, which represents about the deepest into big bang physics we have so far been able to explore in detail. Higher energy colliders will be necessary to push farther, and we are far from directly probing the earliest time scales where the ultimate symmetry breakdown can be explored. Still, it may surprise the reader that the physical principles which have been in place since a trillionth of a second after the universe began are very well understood.

By about 10^{-6} second, the early universe had gone through all the symmetry breaking required to produce the fundamental laws and constants we still observe today, 13–15 billion years later. Nuclei and atoms still needed more time to get organized, but after 300,000 years the lighter atoms had assembled and ceased to interact with the photons that went off on their own to become the cosmic microwave background.

Regardless of the fact that we cannot explore the origin of the universe by any direct means, the undoubted success of the theory of broken symmetry as manifested in the standard model of particle physics provides us with a mechanism that we can apply, at least in broad terms, to provide a natural explanation for the development of natural laws within the universe, without a lawgiver being invoked to institute those laws from the outside.

We have seen that the conservation laws correspond to global symmetries that would automatically be present in the absence of any outside agent. The total chaos that was the state of the universe at the earliest definable time possessed space translation, time translation, rotational, and all the other symmetries that result when a system depends on none of the corresponding coordinates. Nothing is more symmetric than nothing. Nothing has more conservation laws than nothing. Expressing this in an information science context, total chaos and complete symmetry correspond to zero information. Any kind of action by an external agent would result in non-zero information and some broken symmetry. We have no evidence for this, again no need to introduce the uneconomical hypothesis of a creator.

The force laws as exist in the standard model are represented as spontaneously broken symmetries, that is, symmetries that are broken randomly and without cause or design. When the pencil fell over, the direction it pointed to broke the original symmetry and selected out a particular axis. In a more apt example, consider what happens when a ferromagnet cools below a certain critical temperature called the *Curie point*. The iron undergoes a change of phase and a magnetic field suddenly appears that points in a specific, though random, direction, breaking the original symmetry in which no direction was singled out ahead of time, none predictable by any known theory.

The forces of nature are akin to the magnetic field of a ferromagnet. The "direction" they point to after symmetry breaking was not determined ahead of time. The nature of the forces themselves was not pre-specified. They just happened to freeze out the way they did. Just as no agent is implied by the global symmetries, in fact quite the opposite, none is implied by the broken symmetries, which in fact look very much like the opposite.

Now theists may argue that I am simply assuming the absence of divine causation and not proving it. I am not claiming to prove that such causation does not exist. Rather I am simply demonstrating that, based on current scientific knowledge, none is necessary.

In the natural scenario I have provided, the values of the constants of nature in question are not the only ones that can occur. A huge range of values are in fact possible, as are all the possible laws that can result from symmetry breaking. The constants and forces that we have were selected by accident—as the pencil fell—when the expanding universe cooled and the structure we see at the fundamental level froze out. Just as the force laws did not exist before symmetry breaking, so too the constants did not exist. They, after all, come along with the forces. In the current theoretical scheme, particles also appear, with the forces, as the carriers of the quantities like mass and charge and indeed the forces themselves. They provided the means by which the broken symmetries materialize and manifest their structure.

What about Life?

Someday we may have the opportunity to study different forms of life that evolved on other planets. Given the vastness of the universe, and the common observation of supernovas in other galaxies, we have no reason to assume life only exists on earth. Although it seems hardly likely that the evolution of DNA and other details were exactly replicated elsewhere, carbon and the other elements of our life form are well distributed, as evidenced by the composition of cosmic rays and the spectral analysis of interstellar gas.

We also cannot assume that life would have been impossible in our universe had the symmetries broken differently. Certainly we cannot speak of such things in the normal scientific mode in which direct observations are described by theory. But, at the same time, it is not illegitimate, not unscientific, to examine the logical consequences of existing theories that are well-confirmed by data from our own universe.

The extrapolation of theories beyond their normal domains can turn out to be wildly wrong. But it can also turn out to be spectacularly correct. The fundamental physics learned in earthbound laboratories has proved to be valid at great distances from earth and at times long before the earth and solar system had been formed. Those who argue that science cannot talk about the early universe, or life on the early earth because no humans were there to witness these events, greatly underestimate the power of scientific theory.

I have made a modest attempt to obtain some feeling for what a universe with different constants would be like. It happens that the physical properties of matter, from the dimensions of atoms to the length of the day and year, can be estimated from the values of just four fundamental constants. Two of these constants are the strengths of the electromagnetic and strong nuclear interactions. The other two are the masses of the electron and proton.[27]

Of course, many more constants are needed to fill in the details of our universe. And our universe, as we have seen, might have had different physical laws. We have little idea what those laws might be; all we know is the laws we have. Still, varying the constants that go into our familiar equations will give many universes that do not look a bit like ours. The gross properties of our universe are determined by these four constants, and we can vary them to see what a universe might grossly look like with different values of these constants. . . .

As an example, I have analyzed 100 universes in which the values of the four parameters were generated randomly from a range five orders of magnitude above to five orders of magnitude below their values in our universe, that is, over a total range of ten orders of magnitude. Over this range of parameter variation, N_1 is at least 10^{33} and N_2 at least 10^{20} in all cases. That is, both are still very large numbers. Although many pairs do not have $N_1 = N_2$, an approximate coincidence between these two quantities is not very rare.[28]

The distribution of stellar lifetimes for these same 100 universes has also been examined. While a few are low, most are probably high enough to allow time for stellar evolution and heavy element nucleosynthesis. Over half the universes have stars that live at least a billion years. Long life is not the only requirement for life, but it certainly is not an unusual property of universes.

Recall Barrow and Tipler's option (C), which held that an ensemble of other, different universes is necessary in any natural explanation for the existence of our universe. Another myth that has appeared frequently in the literature[29] holds that only a multiple-universe scenario can explain the coincidences without a supernatural creator. No doubt this can do it, as we will see below. But even if there were only one universe, the likelihood of *some* form of life in that single universe is not necessarily small. If many universes beside our own exist, then the anthropic coincidences are a no-brainer.

An Infinity of Universes

Within the framework of established knowledge of physics and cosmology, our universe could be one of many in an infinite super universe or "multiverse."[30] Each universe within the multiverse can have a different set of constants and physical laws. Some might have life of a different form than us, others might have no life at all or something even more complex or so different that we cannot even imagine it. Obviously we are in one of those universes with life.

Several commentators have argued that a multiverse cosmology violates Occam's Razor.[31] This is wrong. The entities that Occam's law of parsimony forbids us from "multiplying beyond necessity" are theoretical hypotheses, not universes. For example, although the atomic theory of matter multiplied the number of bodies we must consider in solving a thermodynamic problem by 10^{24} or so per gram, it did not violate Occam's Razor. Instead, it provided for a simpler, more powerful, more economic exposition of the rules that were obeyed by thermodynamic systems.

As Max Tegmark[32] has argued, a theory in which all possible universes exist is actually more parsimonious than one in which only one exists. Just as was the case for the breaking of the global conservation laws, a single universe requires more explanation—additional hypotheses.

Let me give a simple example that illustrates his point. Consider the two statements: (a) $y = x^2$ and (b) $4 = 2^2$. Which is simpler? The answer is (a), because it carries far more information with the same number of characters than the special case (b). Applied to multiple universes, a multiverse in which all possible universes exist is analogous to (a), while a single universe is analogous to (b).

The existence of many universes is in fact consistent with all we know about physics and cosmology. No new hypotheses are needed to introduce them. It takes an added hypothesis to rule them out—a super law of nature that says only one universe can exist. That would be an uneconomical hypothesis! Another way to express this is with lines from T. H. White's *The Once and Future King*: "Everything not forbidden is compulsory."

An infinity of random universes is suggested by the modern *inflationary model* of the early universe.[33] As we have seen, a quantum fluctuation can produce a tiny, empty region of curved space that will exponentially expand, increasing its energy sufficiently in the process to produce energy equivalent to all the mass of a universe in a tiny fraction of a second. André Linde proposed that a background spacetime "foam" empty of matter and radiation will experience local quantum fluctuations in curvature, forming many bubbles of false vacuum that individually inflate into mini-universes with random characteristics.[34] In this view, our universe is one of those expanding bubbles, the product of a single monkey banging away at the keys of a single word processor.

The Descent of the Universe

Quentin Smith and Lee Smolin[35] have independently suggested a mechanism for the evolution of universes by natural selection. They propose a multi-universe scenario in which each universe is the residue of an exploding black hole that was previously formed in another universe.

An individual universe is born with a certain set of physical parameters—its "genes." As it expands, new black holes are formed within. When these black holes eventually collapse, the genes of the parent universe get slightly scrambled by fluctuations that are expected in the state of high entropy inside a black hole. So when the descendant black hole explodes, it produces a new universe with a different set of physical parameters—similar but not exactly the same as its parent universe. (To my knowledge, no one has yet developed a sexual model for universe reproduction.)

The black hole mechanism provides for both mutations and progeny. The rest is left to survival of the survivor. Universes with parameters near their "natural" values can easily be shown to produce a small number of black holes and so have few progeny to which to pass their genes. Many will not even inflate into material universes, but quickly collapse back on themselves. Others will continue to inflate, producing nothing. However, by chance some small fraction of universes will have parameters optimized for greater black hole production. These will quickly predominate as their genes get passed from generation to generation.

The evolution of universes by natural selection provides a mechanism for explaining the anthropic coincidences that may appear far out, but Smolin suggests several tests. In one, he predicts that the fluctuations in the cosmic microwave background should be near the value expected if the energy fluctuation responsible for inflation in the early universe is just below the critical value for inflation to occur.

It is no coincidence that the idea of the evolution of universes is akin to Darwin's theory of biological evolution. In both cases we are faced with explaining how unlikely, complex, non-equilibrium structures can form without invoking even less likely supernatural forces. Natural selection may offer a natural explanation.

Tegmark's Ensembles

Tegmark has recently proposed what he calls "the ultimate ensemble theory" in which all universes that mathematically exist also physically exist.[36] By "mathematical existence," Tegmark means "freedom from contradiction." So, universes cannot contain square circles, but anything that does not break a rule of logic exists in some universe.

Tegmark claims his theory is scientifically legitimate since it is falsifiable, makes testable predictions, and is economical in the sense that I have already mentioned above—a theory of many universes contains fewer hypotheses than a theory of one. He finds that many mathematically possible universes will not be suitable for the development of what he calls "self-aware structures," his euphemism for intelligent life. For example, he argues that only a universe with three spatial and one time dimension can contain self-aware structures because other combinations are too simple, too unstable, or too unpredictable. Specifically, in order that the universe be predictable to its self-aware structures, only a single time dimension is deemed possible. In this case, one or two space dimensions is regarded as too simple, and four or more space dimensions is reckoned as too unstable. However, Tegmark admits that we may simply lack the imagination to consider universes radically different from our own.

Tegmark examines the types of universes that would occur for different values of key parameters and concludes, as have others, that many combinations will lead to unlivable universes. However, the region of the parameter space where ordered structures can form is not the infinitesimal point only reachable by a skilled artisan, as asserted by proponents of the designer universe.

CONCLUSION

The new convergence of science and religion that has been reported in the media is more between believing scientists and theologians than believers and nonbelievers. Theistic scientists who deeply wish to find evidence for design and purpose to the universe now think they have. Many say that they see strong hints of purpose in the way the physical constants of nature seem to be exquisitely fine-tuned for the evolution and maintenance of life. Although not so specific that they select out human life, these properties are called the "anthropic coincidences" and various forms of the "anthropic principle" have been suggested as the underlying rationale.

Theists argue that the universe seems to have been specifically designed so that intelligent life would form. Some have gone so far as to claim that this is already "proved" by the existence of the anthropic coincidences. The theist claim translates into a modern version of the ancient argument from design for the existence of God. However, the new version is as deeply flawed as its predecessors, making many unjustified assumptions and being inconsistent with existing knowledge. One gross and fatal assumption is that only one kind of life, ours, is possible in every configuration of possible universes.

Another form of the anthropic principle holds that observers, by their very act of observation, bring the universe into being. This has become a popular notion in New Age philosophy and is supposedly justified by certain interpretations of quantum mechanics. However, other interpretations of quantum mechanics are viable and the best evidence that we do not make our own universe is the fact that the universe is not what most of us want it to be.

We have examined possible natural explanations for the anthropic coincidences. A wide variation of constants of physics has been shown to lead to universes that are long-lived enough for life to evolve and exhibit "anthropic" coincidences, though human life would certainly not exist in such universes.

The most powerful "laws of physics," the conservation laws, were shown to be evidence against design rather than for it. They are directly related to the "symmetries of nothing" that would exist in the absence of design. Furthermore, the observed forces, particles, and other structure in our universe are consistent with the accidental, or spontaneous, breaking of symmetries at local points in spacetime. This also mitigates against design or creation.

Although not needed to negate the fine-tuning argument, which falls of its own weight, from all that we know of fundamental physics and cosmology other universes besides our own are not ruled out. The theory of a multiverse composed of many universes with different laws and physical properties is actually more parsimonious, more consistent with Occam's Razor, than a single universe. We would need to hypothesize a new principle to rule out all but a single universe. If, indeed, there exist multiple universes, then we are simply in that particular universe of all the logically consistent possibilities that had the properties needed to produce us.[37]

NOTES

1. See, for example, Sharon Begley, "Science Finds God," *Newsweek* (July 20, 1998): 46.

2. Roger Penrose, *The Emperor's New Mind: Concerning Computers, Minds, and the Laws of Physics* (Oxford: Oxford University Press, 1989), p. 343.

3. Hugh Ross, *The Creator and the Cosmos: How the Greatest Scientific Discoveries of the Century Reveal God* (Colorado Springs: Navpress, 1995), p. 118.

4. John D. Barrow and Frank J. Tipler, *The Anthropic Cosmological Principle* (Oxford: Oxford University Press, 1986).

5. H. Weyl, *Ann. Physik* 59 (1919): 101.

6. A. S. Eddington, *The Mathematical Theory of Relativity* (London: Cambridge, 1923), p. 167.

7. Piazzi Smyth, *The Great Pyramid: Its Secrets and Mysteries Revealed* (New York: Bell Publishing Company, 1978).

8. William H. Steibling, *Ancient Astronomers, Cosmic Collisions and Other Popular Theories about Man's Past* (Amherst, NY: Prometheus Books, 1994), pp. 108–10; Cornelius De Jager, "Adventures in Science and Cyclosophy," *Skeptical Inquirer* 16, no. 2 (1992): 167–72.

9. P. A. M. Dirac, "The Cosmological Constants," *Nature* 139 (1937): 323.

10. R. H. Dicke, "Dirac's Cosmology and Mach's Principle," *Nature* 192 (1961): 440.

11. Barrow and Tipler, p. 252.

12. Brandon Carter, "Large Number Coincidences and the Anthropic Principle in Cosmology," in *Confrontation of Cosmological Theory with Astronomical Data*, edited by M. S. Longair (Dordrecht: Reidel, 1974), pp. 291–98, reprinted in *Physical Cosmology and Philosophy*, edited by John Leslie (New York: Macmillan, 1990).

13. Barrow and Tipler, *The Anthropic Cosmological Principle*, p. 21.

14. Ibid., p. 22.

15. Frank J. Tipler, *The Physics of Immortality: Modern Cosmology, God and the Resurrection of the Dead* (New York: Doubleday, 1994).

16. See, for example: Richard Swinburne, "Argument from the Fine-Tuning of the Universe," in *Physical Cosmology and Philosophy*, pp. 154–73; George Ellis, *Before the Beginning: Cosmology Explained* (London, New York: Boyars/Bowerdean, 1993); Ross, *The Creator and the Cosmos*.

17. John Earmon, *Philosophical Quarterly* 24.4 (1987): 314.

18. For more about the contingency of life on earth, see Stuart Ross Taylor, *Destiny or Chance: Our Solar System and Its Place in the Cosmos* (Cambridge: Cambridge University Press, 1998).

19. For further discussion of probability and the fine-tuning argument, see Robin Le

Poidevin, *Arguing for Atheism: An Introduction to the Philosophy* (London: Routledge, 1996), and Keith M. Parsons, "Lively Answers to Theists," *Philo* 1, no. 1 (1998): 115–21.

20. Michael Ikeda and Bill Jefferys, "The Anthropic Principle Does Not Support Supernaturalism" [online], http://quasar.as.utexas.edu/anthropic.html [2002].

21. Fritjof Capra, *The Tao of Physics* (Boulder: Shambhala, 1975).

22. Deepak Chopra, *Quantum Healing: Exploring the Frontiers of Mind/Body Medicine* (New York: Bantam, 1989), and *Ageless Body, Timeless Mind: The Quantum Alternative to Growing Old* (New York: Random House, 1993).

23. For more details, see Victor J. Stenger, *The Unconscious Quantum: Metaphysics in Modern Physics and Cosmology* (Amherst, NY: Prometheus Books, 1995).

24. D. Bohm and B. J. Hiley, *The Undivided Universe: An Ontological Interpretation of Quantum Mechanics* (London: Routledge, 1993); David Deutsch, *The Fabric of Reality* (New York: Allen Lane, 1997); R. J. Omnès, *The Interpretation of Quantum Mechanics* (Princeton: Princeton University Press, 1994).

25. Alan Guth, "Inflationary Universe: A Possible Solution to the Horizon and Flatness Problems," *Physical Review* D 23 (1981): 347–56, and *The Inflationary Universe* (New York: Addison-Wesley, 1997); André Linde, "Particle Physics and Inflationary Cosmology," *Physics Today* 40 (1987): 61–68, *Particle Physics and Inflationary Cosmology* (New York: Academic Press, 1990), and "The Self-Reproducing Inflationary Universe," *Scientific American* 271 (Nov. 1994): 48–55.

26. For a not-too-technical discussion, see Victor J. Stenger, "The Universe: The Ultimate Free Lunch," *European Journal of Physics* 11 (1990): 236.

27. W. H. Press and A. P. Lightman, *Phil. Trans. R. Soc. Lond.* A 310 (1983): 323.

28. For more details, see Stenger, *The Unconscious Quantum*.

29. See, for example, Swinburne, "Argument from the Fine-Tuning of the Universe."

30. Linde, "The Self-Reproducing Inflationary Universe."

31. See, typically, Ellis, *Before the Beginning*, p. 97.

32. Max Tegmark, "Is 'The Theory of Everything' Merely the Ultimate Ensemble Theory?" *Annals of Physics* 270 (1998): 1–51.

33. Linde, "Particle Physics and Inflationary Cosmology," *Particle Physics and Inflationary Cosmology*, and "The Self-Reproducing Inflationary Universe"; Guth, "Inflationary Universe: A Possible Solution," and *The Inflationary Universe*; Lee Smolin, "Did the Universe Evolve?" *Classical and Quantum Gravity* 9 (1992): 173–91, and *The Life of the Cosmos* (New York: Oxford, 1997).

34. Linde, "Particle Physics and Inflationary Cosmology" and "The Self-Reproducing Inflationary Universe"; Guth, *The Inflationary Universe*.

35. Quentin Smith, "A Natural Explanation of the Existence and Laws of Our Universe," *Australasian Journal of Philosophy* 68 (1990): 22–43; Smolin, "Did the Universe Evolve?"

36. Tegmark, "Is 'The Theory of Everything' Merely the Ultimate Ensemble Theory?"

37. I have greatly benefited from discussions with Ricardo Aler Mur, Samantha Atkins, John Chalmers, Scott Dalton, Keith Douglas, Ron Ebert, Simon Ewins, Jim Humphreys, Bill Jefferys, Kenneth Porter, Wayne Spencer, and Ed Weinmann.

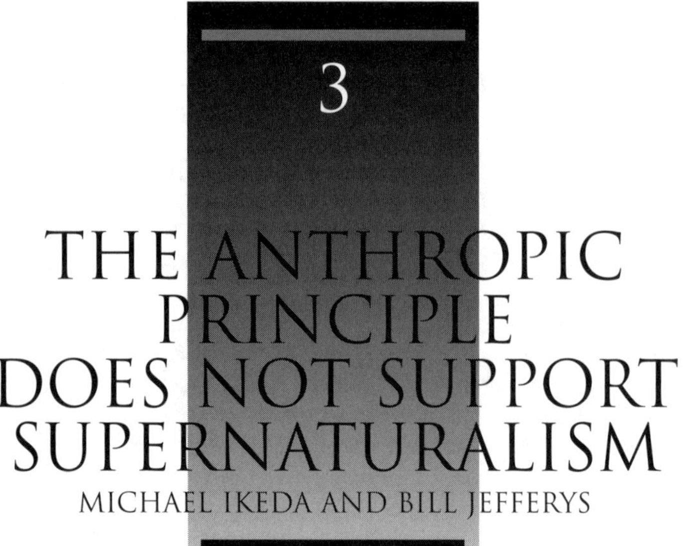

3
THE ANTHROPIC PRINCIPLE DOES NOT SUPPORT SUPERNATURALISM

MICHAEL IKEDA AND BILL JEFFERYS

INTRODUCTION

It has recently been claimed, most prominently by Dr. Hugh Ross,[1] that the so-called "fine-tuning" of the constants of physics supports a supernatural origin of the universe. Specifically, it is claimed that many of the constants of physics must be within a very small range of their actual values, or else life could not exist in our universe. Since it is alleged that this range is very small, and since our very existence shows that our universe has values of these constants that would allow life to exist, it is argued that the probability that our universe arose by chance is so small that we must seek a supernatural origin of the universe.

In this article we will show that this argument is wrong. Not only is it wrong, but in fact we will show that the observation that the universe is "fine-tuned" in this sense can only count against a supernatural origin of the universe. And we shall furthermore show that with certain theologies suggested by deities that are both inscrutable and very powerful, the more "finely-tuned" the universe is, the more a supernatural origin of the universe is undermined.[2]

Our basic argument starts with a few very simple assumptions. We believe that anyone who accepts that the universe is "fine-tuned" for life would find it difficult not to accept these assumptions. They are:

a) Our universe exists and contains life.

---

b) Our universe is "life-friendly," that is, the conditions in our universe (such as physical laws, etc.) permit or are compatible with life existing naturalistically.
c) Life cannot exist in a universe that is governed solely by naturalistic law unless that universe is "life-friendly."

We will discuss only the Weak Anthropic Principle (WAP), since it is uncontroversial and generally accepted. We will not discuss the Strong Anthropic Principle (SAP), much less the Completely Ridiculous Anthropic Principle.

According to the WAP, which is embodied in assumption (c), the fact that life (and we as intelligent life along with it) exists in our universe, coupled with the assumption that the universe is governed by naturalistic law, implies that those laws must be "life-friendly." If they were not "life-friendly," then it is obvious that life could not exist in a universe governed solely by naturalistic law. However, it should be noted that a sufficiently powerful supernatural principle or entity (deity) could sustain life in a universe with laws that are not "life-friendly," simply by virtue of that entity's will and power.

We will show that if assumptions (a–c) are true, then the observation that our universe is "life-friendly" can *never* be evidence *against* the hypothesis that the universe is governed solely by naturalistic law. Moreover, "fine-tuning," in the sense that "life-friendly" laws are claimed to represent only a very small fraction of possible universes, can even undermine the hypothesis of a supernatural origin of the universe; and the more "finely-tuned" the universe is, the more this hypothesis can be undermined.

TRADITIONAL RESPONSES TO THE "FINE-TUNING" ARGUMENT

There are a number of traditional arguments that have been made against the "fine-tuning" argument. We will state them here, and we think that they are valid, although our main interest will be directed toward some new insights arising from a deeper understanding of probability theory.

1) In proving our main result, we do not assume or contemplate that universes other than our own exist (e.g., as in cosmologies such as those proposed by Alexander Vilenkin,[3] André Linde,[4] and most recently Lee Smolin,[5] or as in some kinds of "many worlds" quantum models). One argument against Ross has been to claim that there may be many universes with many different combinations of physical constants. If there are enough of them, a few would be able to support life solely by chance. It is hypothesized that we live in one of those few. Thus, this argument seeks to overcome the low probability of having a universe with life in it with a multiplicity of universes.[6]

2) Others have argued against the assumption that the universe must have very narrowly constrained values of certain physical constants for life to exist in it. They have argued that life could exist in universes that are very different from ours, but it is only our insular ignorance of the physics of such universes that misleads us into thinking that a universe must be much like our own to sustain life. Indeed, virtually nothing is known about the possibility of life in universes that are very different from ours. It could well be that most universes could support life, even if it is of a type that is completely unfamiliar to us. To assert that only universes very like our own could support life goes well beyond anything that we know today.

Indeed, it might well be that a fundamental "theory of everything" in physics would predict that only a very narrow range of physical constants, or even no range at all, would be possible. If this turns out to be the case, then the entire "fine-tuning" argument would be moot.

While recognizing the force and validity of these arguments, the main points we will make go in quite different directions, and show that *even if Ross is correct about "fine-tuning"* and *even if ours is the only universe that exists*, the "fine-tuning" argument fails.

NOTATION AND SOME BASIC PROBABILITY THEORY

In this section, we will introduce some necessary notation and discuss some basic probability theory needed in order to understand our points.

First, some notation. We introduce several predicates (statements which can have values true or false).

Let L = "The universe exists and contains Life." L is clearly true for our universe (assumption a).

Let F = "The conditions in the universe are 'life-Friendly,' in the sense described above." Ross, in his arguments, certainly assumes that F is true. So will we (assumption b). The negation, ~F, would be that the conditions are such that life cannot exist naturalistically, so that if life is present it must be because of some supernatural principle or entity.

Let N = "The universe is governed solely by Naturalistic law." The negation, ~N, is that it is not governed solely by naturalistic law, that is, some non-naturalistic (supernaturalistic) principle or entity is involved. N and ~N are not assumptions; they are hypotheses to be tested. However, we do not rule out either possibility at the outset; rather, we assume that each of them has some non-zero a priori probability of being true.

Probability theory now allows us to write down some important relationships between these predicates. For example, assumption (c) can be written mathematically as N&L ==> F ('==>' means logical implication). In the language of probability theory, this can be expressed as

P(F|N&L) = 1

where P(A|B) is the probability that A is true, given that B is true,[7] and '&' is logical conjunction.

WHY THE "FINE-TUNING" ARGUMENT IS INVALID

Expressed in the language of probability theory, we understand the "fine-tuning" argument to claim that if naturalistic law applies, then the probability that a randomly selected universe would be "life-friendly" is very small, or in mathematical terms, P(F|N) << 1. Notice that this condition is not a predicate like L, N and F. Rather, it is a statement about the *probability distribution* P(F|N), considered as it applies to all possible universes. For this reason, it is not possible to express the "fine-tuning" condition in terms of one of the arguments A or B of a probability function P(A|B). It is, rather, a statement about how large those probabilities are.

The "fine-tuning" argument then reasons that if P(F|N) << 1, then it follows that P(N|F) << 1. In ordinary English, this says that if the probability that a randomly selected universe would be "life-friendly" (given naturalism) is very small, then the probability that naturalism is true, given the observed fact that the universe is "life-friendly," is also very small. This, however, is an elementary if common blunder in probability theory. One cannot simply exchange the two arguments in a probability like P(F|N) and get a valid result. A simple example will suffice to show this.

Example:

Let A = "I am holding a Royal Flush."

Let B = "I will win the poker hand."

It is evident that P(A|B) is nearly 0. Almost all poker hands are won with hands other than a Royal Flush. On the other hand, it is equally clear that P(B|A) is nearly 1. If you have a Royal Flush, you are virtually certain to win the poker hand.

There is a second reason why this "fine-tuning" argument is wrong. It is that for an inference to be valid, it is necessary to take into account *all* known information that may be relevant to the conclusion. In the present case, we happen to *know* that life exists in our universe (i.e., that L is true). Therefore, it is invalid to make inferences about N if we fail to take into account the fact that L, as well as F, are already known to be true. It follows that any inferences about N *must* be conditioned upon *both* F *and* L. An example of this is seen in the next section.

The most important consequence of the previous paragraph is very simple: In inferring the probability that N is true, it is entirely irrelevant whether P(F|N) is large or small. It is entirely irrelevant whether the universe is "fine-tuned" or not. Only probabilities conditioned upon L are relevant to our inquiry.

Richard Harter has suggested a somewhat different interpretation of the "fine-tuning" argument. He writes:

> This takes care of the WAP; if one argues solely from the WAP the argument is correct. However the "fine-tuning" argument is not (despite what its proponents say) a WAP argument; it is an inverse Bayesian argument. The argument runs thusly:
>
> $$P(F|\sim N) >> P(F|N)$$
>
> ergo
>
> $$P(\sim N|F) >> P(N|F).$$
>
> Considered as a formal inference this is a fallacy. Nonetheless it is a normal rule of induction which is (usually) sound. The reason is that for the "conclusion" not to hold we need
>
> $$P(N) >> P(\sim N)$$
>
> (This is not the full condition but it is close enough for government work.)[8]

There are two fallacies in this form of the argument. The first is the failure to condition on L, mentioned above. This in itself would render the argument invalid. The second is that the first line of the argument, $P(F|\sim N) >> P(F|N)$, is merely an unsupported assertion. No one knows what the probability of a supernatural entity creating a universe that is F is! For example, a dilettante deity might never get around to creating any universes at all, much less ones capable of supporting life.[9]

OUR MAIN THEOREM

Having understood the previous discussion, and with our notation in hand, it is now easy to prove that the WAP does not support supernaturalism (which we take to be the negation ~N of N). Recall that the WAP can be written as P(F|N&L) = 1. Then, by Bayes's Theorem[10] we have

$$\begin{aligned} P(N|F\&L) &= P(F|N\&L)P(N|L) / P(F|L) \\ &= P(N|L) / P(F|L) \\ &\geq P(N|L) \end{aligned}$$

where '≥' means "greater than or equal to." The second line follows because P(F|N&L) = 1, and the inequality of the third line follows because P(F|L) is a positive quantity less than or equal to 1.[11]

The inequality P(N|F&L) ≥ P(N|L) shows that the WAP supports (or at least does not undermine) the hypothesis that the universe is governed by naturalistic law. This result is, as we have emphasized, independent of how large or small P(F|N) is. The observation F cannot decrease the probability that N is true (given the known background information that life exists in our universe), and may well increase it.

Corollary: Since P(~N|F&L) = 1 – P(N|F&L) and similarly for P(~N|L), it follows that P(~N|F&L) ≤ P(~N|L). In other words, the observation F does not support supernaturalism (~N), and may well undermine it.

ANOTHER WAY TO LOOK AT IT

The thrust of practically all "intelligent design" and creationist arguments (excepting the anthropic argument and perhaps a few others) is to show ~F, since it is evident, we think, that if ~F then we cannot have both life and a naturalistic universe. We evidently do have life, so the success of one of these arguments would clearly establish ~N. In other words, given our prior opinion P(N&L), where 0 < P(N&L) < 1 but otherwise unrestricted (thus we neither rule in nor rule out N initially), arguments like Michael J. Behe's attempt[12] to support ~F so as to undermine N:

$$P(N|{\sim}F\&L) < P(N|L).$$

But the "anthropic" argument is that observing F also undermines N:

$$P(N|F\&L) < P(N|L).$$

We assert that the intelligent design folks want these inequalities to be strict (otherwise there would be no point in their making the argument!).

From these two inequalities we readily derive a contradiction, as follows. From the definition of conditional probability,[13] the two inequalities above yield

$$P(N\&{\sim}F\&L) < P(N|L)P({\sim}F\&L),\ P(N\&F\&L) < P(N|L)P(F\&L).$$

Adding,

$$\begin{aligned} P(N\&L) &= P(N\&{\sim}F\&L) + P(N\&F\&L) \\ &< P(N|L)(P({\sim}F\&L) + P(F\&L)) \\ &= P(N|L)P(L) = P(N\&L), \end{aligned}$$

a contradiction since the inequality is strict.

If we remove the restriction that the inequalities be strict, then the only case where both inequalities can be true is if

$$P(N|{\sim}F\&L) = P(N|L) \text{ and } P(N|F\&L) = P(N|L).$$

In other words, the only case where both can be true is if the information that the universe is "life-friendly" has *no* effect on the probability that it is naturalistic (given the existence of life); and this can only be the case if neither inequality is strict.

In essence, we see that the intelligent design folks who make the anthropic argument are really trying to have it both ways: They want observation of F to undermine N, and they also want observation of ~F to undermine N. That is, they want any observation whatsoever to undermine N! But the error is that the anthropic argument does *not* undermine N, it supports N. They can have one of the prongs of their argument, but they can't have both.[14]

IMPLICATIONS OF "FINE-TUNING" VERSUS MERE "LIFE-FRIENDLINESS"

Ross's argument discusses the case where the conditions in our universe are not only "life-friendly," but they are also "fine-tuned," in the sense that only a very small fraction of possible universes can be "life-friendly." We have shown that regardless how "finely-tuned" the laws of physics are, the observation that the universe is capable of sustaining life cannot undermine N.

As we have pointed out above, others have responded to the claim of "fine-tuning" in several ways. One way has been to point out that this claim is not corroborated by any theoretical understanding about what forms of life might arise in universes with different physical conditions than our own, or even any theoretical understanding about what kinds of universes are possible at all; it is basically a claim founded upon our own ignorance of physics. To those that make this point, the argument is about whether P(F|N) is really small (as Ross claims), or is in fact large. The point (against Ross) is essentially that Ross's crucial assumption is completely without support.

A second response is to point out that several theoretical lines of evidence indicate that many other, and perhaps even an infinite number of other universes, with varying sets of physical constants and conditions, might well exist, so that even if the probability that a given universe would have constants close to those of our own universe is small, the sheer number of such universes would virtually guarantee that some of them would possess constants that would allow life to arise.

Nevertheless, it is necessary to consider the implications of Ross's assertion that the universe is "fine-tuned." Suppose it is true that amongst all naturalistic universes, only a very small proportion could support life. What would this imply?

We have shown that the WAP tends to support N, and cannot undermine it. This observation is *independent* of whether P(F|N) is small or large, since (as we have seen) the only probabilities that are significant for inference about N are those that are conditioned upon all relevant data at our disposal, including the fact that L is true. Therefore, regardless of the size of P(F|N), valid reasoning shows that observing that F is true cannot decrease the probability that N is true, and may increase it.

We believe that the real import of observing that P(F|N) is small (if indeed that is true) would be to strengthen Vilenkin/Linde/Smolin–type hypotheses that multiple universes with varying physical constants may exist. If indeed the universe is governed by naturalistic laws, and if indeed the probability that a universe governed by naturalistic laws can support life is small, then this supports a Vilenkin/Linde/Smolin model of multiple universes over a model that includes only a single universe with a single set of physical constants.

To see this, let S = "there is only a Single universe," and M = "there are Multiple universes." Let E = "there Exists a universe with life." Clearly, P(E|N) < P(F|N), since it is possible that a universe that is "life-friendly" could still be barren. But, since L is true, E is also true, so observing L implies that we have also observed E.

Then, assuming that P(F|N) < 1 is the probability that a single universe is "life-friendly," that this probability is the same for each "random" multiple universe as it would be for a single universe, and that the probability that a given universe exists is independent of the existence of other universes, it follows that

$P(E|S\&N) = p = P(E|N) < P(F|N) < 1$ (and for Ross, $P(F|N) << 1$);

$P(E|M\&N) = 1 - (1 - p)^m$, where m is the number of universes if M is true. This is less than 1 but approaches 1 (for fixed p) as m gets larger and larger. Since all the multiple universe proposals we have seen suggest that m is in fact infinite, it follows that P(E|M&N) = 1. (If one postulates that m is finite, then the calculation depends explicitly on p and m; this is left as an exercise for the reader.)

Since

P(S|E&N) = P(E|S&N)P(S|N) / P(E|N) and

P(M|E&N) = P(E|M&N)P(M|N) / P(E|N),

with these assumptions it follows by division that

$$\frac{P(M|E\&N)}{P(S|E\&N)} = \frac{1}{p} \times \frac{P(M|N)}{P(S|N)},$$

which shows that observing E (or L) increases the evidence for M against S in a naturalistic universe by a factor of at least 1/p. The smaller P(F|N) = p (that is, the more "finely-tuned" the universe is), the more likely it is that some form of multiple-universe hypothesis is true.

THEOLOGICAL CONSIDERATIONS

The next section is rather more speculative, depending as it does upon theological notions that are hard to pin down, and therefore should be taken with large grains of salt. But it is worth considering what effect various theological hypotheses would have on this argument. It is interesting to ask the question, "given that observing that F is true cannot undermine N and may support it, by how much can N be strengthened (and ~N be undermined) when we observe that F is true?"

It is evident from the discussion of the main theorem that the key is the denominator P(F|L). The smaller that denominator, the greater the support for N. Explicitly we have

P(F|L) = P(F|N&L)P(N|L) + P(F|~N&L)P(~N|L).

But since P(F|N&L) = 1 we can simplify this to

P(F|L) = P(N|L) + P(F|~N&L)P(~N|L).

Plugging this into the expression P(N|F&L) = P(N|L) / P(F|L) we obtain

P(N|F&L) = P(N|L) / [P(N|L) + P(F|~N&L)P(~N|L)]

$$= 1 / [1 + P(F|{\sim}N\&L)P({\sim}N|L) / P(N|L)]$$
$$= 1 / [1 + C\ P(F|{\sim}N\&L)],$$

where C = P(~N|L) / P(N|L) is the prior odds in favor of ~N against N. In other words, C is the odds that we would offer in favor of ~N over N before noting that the universe is "fine-tuned" for life.

A major controversy in statistics has been over the choice of prior probabilities (or in this case prior odds). However, for our purposes this is not a significant consideration, as long as we don't choose C in such a way as to completely rule out either possibility (N or ~N), i.e., as long as we haven't made up our minds in advance. This means that any positive, finite value of C is acceptable.

One readily sees from this formula that for acceptable C

(1) as $P(F|{\sim}N\&L) \to 0$, $P(N|F\&L) \to 1$;
(2) as $P(F|{\sim}N\&L) \to 1$, $P(N|F\&L) \to 1 / [1 + P({\sim}N|L) / P(N|L)] = P(N|L)$,

where '→' means "approaches as a limit" and the last result follows from the fact that P(N|L) + P(~N|L) = 1.

So, P(N|F&L) is a monotonically decreasing function of P(F|~N&L) bounded from below by P(N|L). This confirms the observation made earlier, that noting that F is true can never decrease the evidential support for N. Furthermore, the only case where the evidential support is unchanged is when P(F|~N&L) is identically 1. This is interesting, because it tells us that the only case where observing the truth of F does *not* increase the support for N is precisely the case when the likelihood function P(F|x&L), evaluated at F, and with x ranging over N and ~N, cannot distinguish between N and ~N. That is, the only way to prevent the observation F from increasing the support for N is to assert that ~N&L also *requires* F to be true. Under these circumstances we cannot distinguish between N and ~N on the basis of the data F. In a deep sense, the two hypotheses represent, and in fact, *are* the same hypothesis. Put another way, to assume that P(F|~N&L) = 1 is to concede that life in the world actually arose by the operation of an agent that is observationally indistinguishable from naturalistic law, insofar as the observation F is concerned. In essence, any such agent is just an extreme version of the "God-of-the-gaps," whose existence has been made superfluous as far as the existence of life is concerned. Such an assumption would completely undermine the proposition that it is *necessary* to go outside of naturalistic law in order to explain the world as it is, although it doesn't undermine any argument for supernaturalism that doesn't rely on the universe being "life-friendly."

So, if supernaturalism is to be distinguished from naturalism on the basis of the fact that the universe is F, it must be the case that P(F|~N&L) < 1. Otherwise, we are condemned to an unsatisfying kind of "God-of-the-gaps" theology. But what sort of theologies can we consider, and how would they affect this crucial probability?

To make these ideas more definite, we consider first a specific interpretation that is intended to imitate, albeit crudely, how the assumption of a relatively powerful and inscrutable deity (such as a generic Judeo–Christian–Islamic deity might be) could affect the calculation of the likelihood function P(F|~N&L).

We suggest that any reasonable version of supernaturalism with such a deity would result in a value of P(F|~N&L) that is, in fact, very small (assuming that only a small set of possible universes are F). The reason is that a sufficiently powerful deity could arrange things so that a universe with laws that are not "life-friendly" can sustain life. Since we do not know the purposes of such a deity, we must assign a significant amount of the likelihood function to that possibility. Furthermore, if such a deity creates universes and if the "fine-tuning" claims are correct, then *most* life-containing universes will be of this type (i.e., containing life despite not being "life-friendly"). Thus, all other things being equal, and if this is the sort of deity we are dealing with, we would *expect* to live in a universe that is ~F.

To assert that such a deity *could* only create universes containing life if the laws are "life-friendly" is to restrict the power of such a deity. And to assert that such a deity *would* only create universes with life if the laws are "life-friendly" is to assert knowledge of that deity's purposes that many religions seem reluctant to claim. Indeed, any such assertion would tend to undermine the claim, made by many religions, that their deity can and does perform miracles that are contrary to naturalistic law, and recognizably so.

Our conclusion, therefore, is that not only does the observation F support N, but it supports it overwhelmingly against its negation ~N, if ~N means creation by a sufficiently powerful and inscrutable deity. This latter conclusion is, by the way, a consequence of the Bayesian Ockham's Razor.[15] The point is that N predicts outcomes much more sharply and narrowly than does ~N; it is, in Popperian language, more easily falsifiable than is ~N. (We do not wish to get into a discussion of the Demarcation Problem here since that is out of the scope of this article, though we do not regard it as a difficulty for our argument. For our purposes, we are simply making a statement about the consequences of the likelihood function having significant support on only a relatively small subset of possible outcomes.) Under these circumstances, the Bayesian Ockham's Razor shows that observing an outcome allowed by both N and ~N is likely to favor N over ~N. We refer the reader to the cited paper for a more detailed discussion of this point.

Aside from sharply limiting the likely actions of the deity (either by making it less powerful or asserting more human knowledge of the deity's intentions), we can think of only one way to avoid this conclusion. One might assert that any universe with life would appear to be "life-friendly" from the vantage point of the creatures living within it, regardless of the physical constants that such a universe were equipped with. In such a case, observing F cannot change our opinion about the nature of the universe. This is certainly a possible way out for the supernaturalist, but this solution is not available to Ross because it contradicts his assertions that the values of certain physical constants *do* allow us to distinguish between universes that are "life-friendly" and those that are not. And, such an assumption does not come without cost; whether others would find it satisfactory is problematic. For example, what about miracles? If every universe with life looks "life-friendly" from the inside, might this not lead one to wonder if everything that happens therein would also look to its inhabitants like the result of the simple operation of naturalistic law? And then there is Ockham's Razor: What would be the point of postulating a supernatural entity if the predictions we get are indistinguishable from those of naturalistic law?

BUT WHICH DEITY?

In the previous section, we have discussed just one of many sorts of deities that might exist. This one happens to be very powerful and rather inscrutable (and is intended to be a model of a generic Judeo–Christian–Islamic sort of deity, though believers are welcome to disagree and propose—and justify—their own interpretations of their favorite deity). However, there are many other sorts of deities that might be postulated as being responsible for the existence of the universe. There are somewhat more limited deities, such as Zeus/Jupiter, there are deities that share their existence with antagonistic deities, such as the Zoroastrian Ahura-Mazda/Ahriman pair of deities, there are various Native American deities, such as the trickster deity Coyote, there are Australian, Chinese, African, Japanese, and East Indian deities, and even many other possible deities that no one on earth has ever thought of. There could be deities of life forms indigenous to planets around the star Arcturus that we should consider, for example.

Now when considering a multiplicity of deities, say $D_1, D_2, \ldots, D_i, \ldots$, we would have to specify a value of the likelihood function for each individual deity, specifying what the implications would be if *that* deity were the actual deity that created the universe. In particular, with the "fine-tuning" argument in mind, we would have to specify $P(F|D_i\&L)$ for every i (probably an infinite set of deities). Assuming that we have a mutually exclusive and exhaustive list of deities, we see the hypothesis ~N revealed to be *composite*, that is, it is a combination or union of the individual hypotheses D_i (i = 1, 2, . . .). We then have

$$\sim N = D_1 \vee D_2 \vee \ldots \vee D_i \vee \ldots.$$

Now, the total prior probability of ~N, P(~N|L), has to be divvied up amongst all of the individual sub-hypotheses D_i:

$$P(\sim N|L) = P(D_1|L) + P(D_2|L) + \ldots + P(D_i|L) + \ldots,$$

where $0 < P(D_i) < P(\sim N|L) < 1$ (assuming that we only consider deities that might exist, and that there are at least two of them). In general, each of the individual prior probabilities $P(D_i|L)$ would be very small, since there are so many possible deities. Only if some deities are a priori much more likely than others would any individual deity have an appreciable amount of prior probability.

This means that in general, $P(D_i|L) \ll 1$ for all i.

Now when we originally considered just N and ~N, we calculated the posterior probability of N given L&F from the prior probabilities of N and ~N given L, and the likelihood functions. Here it would be simpler to look at prior and posterior odds. These are derived straightforwardly from probabilities by the relation

$$\text{Odds} = \text{Probability} / (1 - \text{Probability}).$$

This yields a relationship between the prior and posterior odds of N against ~N [using P(N|F&L) + P(~N|F&L) = 1]:

$$\text{Posterior Odds} = \frac{P(N|F\&L)}{P(\sim N|F\&L)} = \frac{P(F|N\&L)}{P(F|\sim N\&L)} \times \frac{P(N|L)}{P(\sim N|L)}$$

$$= (\text{Bayes Factor}) \times (\text{Prior Odds}).$$

The Bayes Factor and Prior Odds are given straightforwardly by the two ratios in this formula.

Since P(F|N&L) = 1 and $P(F|\sim N\&L) \leq 1$, it follows that the posterior odds are greater than or equal to the prior odds (this is a restatement of our first theorem, in terms of odds). This means that observing that F is true cannot decrease our confidence that N is true.

But by using odds instead of probabilities, we can now consider the individual sub-hypotheses that make up ~N. For example, we can calculate prior and posterior odds of N against any individual D_i. We find that

$$\text{Posterior Odds} = \frac{P(N|F\&L)}{P(D_i|F\&L)} = \frac{P(F|N\&L)}{P(F|D_i\&L)} \times \frac{P(N|L)}{P(D_i|L)}.$$

This follows because[16]

$$P(N|F\&L) = P(F|N\&L)P(N|L) / P(F|L),$$

$$P(D_i|F\&L) = P(F|D_i\&L)P(D_i|L) / P(F|L),$$

and the P(F|L)'s cancel out when you take the ratio.

Now, even if $P(F|D_i\&L) = 1$, which is the maximum possible, the posterior odds against D_i may still be quite large. The reason for this is that the prior probability of ~N has to be shared out amongst a large number of hypotheses D_j, each one greedily demanding its own share of the limited amount of prior probability available. On the other hand, the hypothesis N has no others to share with. In contrast to ~N, which is a compound hypothesis, N is a simple hypothesis. As a consequence, and again assuming that no particular deity is a priori much more likely than any other (it would be incumbent upon the proposer of such a deity to explain *why* his favorite deity is so much more likely than the others), it follows that the hypothesis of naturalism will end up being much more probable than the hypothesis of *any particular* deity D_i.

This phenomenon is a second manifestation of the Bayesian Ockham's Razor.[17]

In theory it is now straightforward to calculate the posterior odds of N against ~N if we don't particularly care *which* deity is the right one. Since the D_i form a mutually exclusive and exhaustive set of hypotheses whose union is ~N, ordinary probability theory gives us

$$P(\sim N|F\&L) = P(D_1|F\&L) + P(D_2|F\&L) + \ldots$$
$$= [P(F|D_1\&L)P(D_1|L) + P(F|D_2\&L)\, P(D_2|L) + \ldots] / P(F|L).$$

Assuming we know these numbers, we can now calculate the posterior odds of N against ~N by dividing the above expression into the one we found previously for P(N|F&L). Of course, in practice this may be difficult! However, as can be seen from this formula, the deities D_i that contribute most to the denominator (that is, to the supernaturalistic hypothesis) will be the ones that have the largest values of the likelihood function $P(F|D_i\&L)$ or the largest prior probability $P(D_i|L)$ or both. In the first case, it will be because the particular deity is closer to predicting what naturalism predicts (as regards F), and is therefore closer to being a "God-of-the-gaps" deity; in the second, it will be because we already favored that particular deity over others a priori.

FINAL COMMENTS

Some make the mistake of thinking that "fine-tuning" and the anthropic principle support supernaturalism. This mistake has two sources.

The first and most important of these arises from confusing entirely different conditional probabilities. If one observes that P(F|N) is small (since most hypothetical naturalistic universes are not "fine-tuned" for life), one might be tempted to turn the probability around and decide, *incorrectly*, that P(N|F) is also small. But as we have seen, this is an elementary blunder in probability theory. We find ourselves in a universe that is "fine-tuned" for life, which would be unlikely to come about by chance (because P(F|N) is small), *therefore* (we conclude incorrectly), P(N|F) must also be small. This common mistake is due to confusing two entirely different *conditional* probabilities. *Most* actual outcomes are, in fact, highly improbable, but it does not follow that the hypotheses that they are conditioned upon are themselves highly improbable. It is therefore fallacious to reason that if we have observed an improbable outcome, it is necessarily the case that a hypothesis that generates that outcome is itself improbable. One *must* compare the probabilities of obtaining the observed outcome under *all* hypotheses. In general, most, if not all, of these probabilities will be very small, but some hypotheses will turn out to be much more favored by the actual outcome we have observed than others.

The second source of confusion is that one *must* do the calculations taking into account *all* the information at hand. In the present case, that *includes* the fact that life is known to exist in our universe. The possible existence of hypothetical naturalistic universes where life does not exist is entirely irrelevant to the question at hand, which *must* be based on the data we *actually have*.

In our view, similar fallacious reasoning may well underlie many other arguments that have been raised against naturalism, not excluding design and "God-of-the-gaps" arguments, such as Michael Behe's "Irreducible Complexity" argument and William Dembski's "Complex Specified Information."[18] We conclude that whatever their rhetorical appeal, such arguments need to be examined much more carefully than has happened so far to see if they have any validity. But that discussion is outside the scope of this article.

Bottom line: The anthropic argument should be dropped. It is wrong. "Intelligent design" folks should stick to trying to undermine N by showing ~F. That's their only hope (though we believe it to be a forlorn one).[19]

NOTES

1. Hugh Ross, "Design and the Anthropic Principle" [online], www.reasons.org/resources/apologetics/design.shtml [2003].

2. [We have learned that] the philosopher of science, Elliott Sober, has made some similar points in a recent article written for the *Blackwell Guide to Philosophy of Religion*. A draft copy can be obtained from his Web site: http://philosophy.wisc.edu/sober/blackda.pdf. We have some small differences with Professor Sober (in particular, we think that

his condition (A3) is too strong, and that a weaker version of (A3) actually gives a stronger result), but he has an excellent discussion of the role that selection bias plays where the bias is due to self-selection by sentient observers.

3. Alexander Vilenkin, "Quantum Creation of the Universe," *Physical Review* D30 (1984): 509–11.

4. André Linde, "The self-reproducing inflationary universe," *Scientific American* (November 1994): 48–55.

5. Lee Smolin, *The Life of the Cosmos* (New York: Oxford University Press, 1997).

6. A recent technical discussion of this idea can be found in Jaume Garriga and Alexander Vilenkin, "Many Worlds in One," *Physical Review* D64 (2001): 043511.

7. By definition, P(A|B) = P(A&B) / P(B); it follows that also P(A|B&C) = P(A&B|C) / P(B|C).

8. Richard Harter in an e-mail (reproduced here with permission).

9. We have proved that if You, knowing as a sentient observer that L is true, adopt an a priori position that is neutral between N and ~N, i.e., that P(~N|L) is of the same order of magnitude as P(N|L), then when You learn that F is true *and* that P(F|N) << 1, You will conclude that P(F&L&~N) << 1. For the proof, see "Appendix 1: Reply to Kwon" (April 30, 2001) [online], http://quasar.as.utexas.edu/anthropic.html [2002]. This observation is problematic for Harter's argument. For under these assumptions we have

$$P(F\&L\&{\sim}N) = P(L|F\&{\sim}N)P(F|{\sim}N)P({\sim}N) \ll 1.$$

Thus under these assumptions it follows that at least one of P(L|F&~N), P(F|~N) or P(~N) is quite small. A small P(L|F&~N) says that it is almost certain that the supernatural deity, having created a "life-friendly" universe, would make it sterile (lifeless). A small P(F|~N) says that it is highly *unlikely* that this deity would even create a universe that is "life-friendly." Both of these undermine the usual concepts attributed to the deity by "intelligent design" theorists, although either would be consistent with a deity that was incompetent, a dilettante, or a "trickster." A small P(F|~N) is also consistent with a deity who makes many universes, most of them being ~F, with many of these ~F universes perhaps containing life (that is, ~F&L universes, as we discuss below). A small P(~N) says that it is nearly certain that naturalism is true a priori and unconditioned on L, so that Harter's "escape" condition P(N) >> P(~N) in fact holds.

Please remember that if You are a sentient observer, You must already know that L is true, even before You learn anything about F or P(F|N). Thus it is legitimate, appropriate, and indeed *required*, for You to elicit Your prior on N versus ~N conditioned on L and use that as Your starting point. If You then retrodict that P(~N) << 1 as a consequence, all You are doing is eliciting the prior that You would have had in the absence of Your knowledge that You existed as a sentient observer. This is the only legitimate way to infer Your value of P(~N) unconditioned on L.

10. We use Bayes's Theorem in the form

$$P(A|B\&K) = P(B|A\&K)P(A|K) / P(B|K)$$

which follows straightforwardly from the identity

$$P(A|B\&K)P(B|K) = P(A\&B|K) = P(B|A\&K)P(A|K)$$

(a consequence of note 7) assuming that $P(B|K) > 0$.

11. This demonstration is inspired by a recent article on talk.origins by Michael Ikeda <mmikeda@erols.com>; we have simplified the proof in his article. The message ID for the cited article is <5j6dq8$bvj@winter.erols.com> for those who wish to search for it on dejanews.)

12. Michael J. Behe, *Darwin's Black Box: The Biochemical Challenge to Evolution* (New York: Simon and Schuster, 1996).

13. See note 7.

14. Some people have objected to us that Behe is not making the argument ~F, but is only making a statement that it is *highly unlikely* that certain of his "IC" structures could arise naturalistically. Our reading of Behe is that he is making an argument that it is *impossible* for this to happen (a form of ~F as we understand it), but even if we are wrong and he is not making this argument, the point of our comments in this section is that making the argument that the universe is F or is "fine-tuned" ($P(F|N) << 1$) does not support supernaturalism; the argument that should be made is that the universe is ~F, since this manifestly supports supernaturalism by refuting naturalism. See "Appendix 1: Reply to Kwon."

15. W. H. Jefferys and J. O. Berger, "Ockham's Razor and Bayesian Analysis," *American Scientist* 80 (1992): 64–72.

16. See note 7.

17. As discussed in Jefferys and Berger, "Ockham's Razor and Bayesian Analysis."

18. Behe, *Darwin's Black Box*; William Dembski, dissertation (University of Illinois at Chicago).

19. David Kwon has posted a Web page in which he claims to have refuted the arguments in our article. However, he has made a simple error, which we discuss in detail along with comments on some of his other assertions in "Appendix 1: Reply to Kwon."

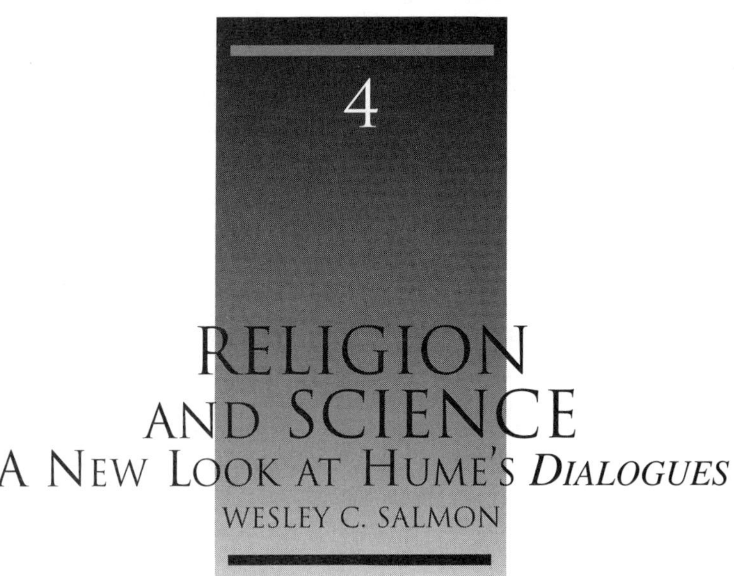

4

Religion and Science: A New Look at Hume's *Dialogues*

Wesley C. Salmon

I. THE DESIGN ARGUMENT

Many different kinds of reasons have been given, in various times and places, for belief in the existence of God. Mystics have sometimes claimed direct experiential awareness of the Deity. Other believers have maintained that faith, not reason, is the proper foundation for religious conviction. Pascal, a devout adherent of this latter group, also claimed that belief could be fostered by a pragmatic "wager." During Hume's lifetime—as well as before and after—"natural religion" enjoyed considerable popularity. According to this approach, the existence of a Supreme Being could be established by rational arguments, either a priori or a posteriori. In Hume's *Dialogues* the a priori arguments—such as Anselm's ontological argument and Aquinas's first cause argument—are treated briefly, but they are given rather short shrift. They are defended by Demea, who is clearly the intellectual inferior of Philo and Cleanthes; they are dispatched quickly and without much ceremony. Indeed, Demea is not even able to stick out the discussion to the end.

The main topic of the *Dialogues* is what Philo calls 'experimental theism'—the thesis that the existence of God can be approached as a scientific hypothesis, and that His existence can be established with a high degree of confirmation by observational evidence. The classic statement of this approach is given by William Paley in 1802 in a book entitled *Natural Theology; or, Evidences of the*

Existence and Attributes of the Deity, Collected from the Appearances of Nature, where he writes,

> In crossing a heath, suppose I pitched my foot against a *stone,* and were asked how the stone came to be there, I might possibly answer, that, for any thing I knew to the contrary, it had lain there forever: nor would it perhaps be very easy to show the absurdity of this answer. But suppose I had found a *watch* upon the ground, and it should be inquired how the watch happened to be in that place, I should hardly think of the answer which I had before given, that, for anything I knew, the watch might have always been there. Yet why should not this answer serve for the watch, as well as for the stone? Why is it not as admissible in the second case, as in the first? For this reason, and no other, viz. that, when we come to inspect the watch, we perceive (what we could not discover in the stone) that its several parts are framed and put together for a purpose, e.g., that they are so formed and adjusted as to produce motion, and that motion is so regulated as to point out the hour of the day; that, if the several parts had been differently shaped from what they are, of a different size from what they are, or placed after any other manner, or in any other order, than that in which they are placed, either no motion at all would have been carried on in the machine, or none which would have answered the use, that is now served by it.[1]

Precisely the same sort of reasoning has, incidentally, been recently applied to Stonehenge. After an elaborate discussion of the workings of the watch, Paley goes on to draw the moral, "... every indication of contrivance, every manifestation of design, which existed in the watch, exists in the works of nature; with the difference, on the side of nature, of being greater and more, and that in a degree which exceeds all computation."[2]

In the second dialogue, Hume puts the same argument in the mouth of Cleanthes:

> I shall briefly explain how I conceive this matter. Look round the world: contemplate the whole and every part of it: you will find it to be nothing but one great machine, subdivided into an infinite number of lesser machines, which again admit of subdivisions, to a degree beyond what human senses and faculties can trace and explain. All these various machines, and even their most minute parts, are adjusted to each other with an accuracy, which ravishes into admiration all men, who have ever contemplated them. The curious adapting of means to ends, throughout all nature, resembles exactly, though it much exceeds, the productions of human contrivance; of human design, thought, wisdom, and intelligence. Since therefore the effects resemble each other, we are led to infer, by all the rules of analogy, that the causes also resemble; and that the Author of Nature is somewhat similar to the mind of men; though possessed of much larger faculties proportioned to the grandeur of the work, which he has executed. By this argument a posteriori, and by this argument alone, do

we prove at once the existence of a Deity, and his similarity to human mind and intelligence.[3]

Throughout the major portions of the *Dialogues*, Cleanthes attempts to defend this type of argument, while Philo launches repeated attacks against it. After some polite preliminaries in the first dialogue, Cleanthes advances the argument near the beginning of the second dialogue. Philo persists in damaging attacks which Cleanthes seems unable to answer until at the opening of the twelfth and final dialogue (after Demea's departure), Philo makes a startling declaration of belief in the argument from design. This sudden apparent reversal of position has led to many disputes about Hume's intention, and many controversies as to whether Philo or Cleanthes is Hume's protagonist. I shall postpone discussion of this historical question until the concluding postscript.[4] My purpose for now is simply to attempt a logical analysis of the arguments presented in the *Dialogues*.

As Cleanthes presents the design argument, it is an instance of argument by analogy. Such arguments have traditionally been classified as an important type of inductive argument, and they seem to occur in certain areas of scientific research. It is often said, for example, that the use of medical experiments on animals in order to ascertain the effects of various substances upon humans constitutes an important application of analogical reasoning. Some of the research on carcinogens seems to proceed in this manner.

To characterize these arguments—the medical arguments as well as the design argument—as mere analogies is, however, to run the risk of seriously misrepresenting them and overlooking much of their force. The strength of a simple argument by analogy depends crucially upon the degree of similarity between the entities with respect to which the analogy is drawn. But mice are strikingly dissimilar to men, and watches are even more dissimilar to universes. Philo is quick to point this out with devastating force.[5] By the end of the second dialogue, it seems to me, both Philo and Cleanthes are fully aware that the argument is more complex. The discussion does not, however, end there. Early in the third dialogue, Cleanthes advances a different form of the design argument—one which Philo, remarkably, does not answer. Cleanthes seems to distinguish it from simple analogies by commenting upon its "irregular nature."[6] I shall return to this version of the argument below.

There is one obvious sense in which the arguments are not simple analogies, namely, it is not the degree of similarity that matters most, but rather the *relevance* of the similarities and the *irrelevance* of the dissimilarities. The fact that men wear neckties and smoke cigarettes, while mice do not, is irrelevant. The fact that the physiological processes in the body of the mouse are similar to those in the human body is highly relevant to the question of whether a substance, such as cigarette tar, which produces cancer in experimental animals, is likely to cause cancer in humans. Such questions of relevance are, obviously, highly theoretical in character—they do not hinge on directly observable similarities or differences. We must conclude that these arguments, initially characterized as analogies, are more subtle and complex. They are arguments whose function is to evaluate *causal hypotheses*; if we wish to understand them, we must try to subject them to the sort of analysis which is appropriate to arguments offered in support of causal hypotheses in science. Hume was aware of this fact, I believe. If we look at the various facets of the discussion between Philo and Cleanthes, we shall find the main constituents of just such arguments.

2. CAUSAL HYPOTHESES AND BAYES'S THEOREM

The question of what argument form is correct for the establishment of causal hypotheses is, of course, still a matter of great controversy. Inasmuch as I have discussed the various approaches in some detail elsewhere,[7] I shall not rehearse the arguments and counterarguments here. Let me simply state my preference, and then proceed to apply it to the discussion of the design argument in Hume's *Dialogues*. The reader may decide at the conclusion whether this approach provides an illuminating analysis. I believe it furnishes a useful framework for fitting together the various arguments that occur throughout the *Dialogues*.

My analysis employs a simple formula in the probability calculus known as Bayes's theorem, after the English clergyman Thomas Bayes (1702–1761), who was roughly a contemporary of Hume. I do not know when Bayes discovered his theorem. It was not published until 1763, so it was in all probability unknown to Hume when he was composing the *Dialogues*. Let me begin by stating the theorem, and illustrating its application by means of a simple fictitious example.

Example: Suppose that a small percentage of pearls have a particular sort of color flaw which renders them worthless. This flaw appears in 1 percent of all cultured pearls, and in 3 percent of all natural pearls. Assume, moreover, that 90 percent of all pearls examined are cultured pearls. Now, a pearl is found which exhibits this undesirable color flaw. What is the probability that it is a cultured pearl?

This problem can be solved by using Bayes's theorem, which reads:

$$\mathrm{P(A \cdot C, B)} = \frac{P(A, B) \times P(A \cdot B, C)}{P(A, B) \times P(A \cdot B, C) + P(A, \bar{B}) \times P(A \cdot \bar{B}, C)}$$

Let A be the class of pearls, B the class of cultured pearls, $\bar{B}$ the class of noncultured (i.e., natural) pearls, and C the class of color-flawed pearls. The formula involves the following probability expressions:

$P(A, B)$ = the probability that a pearl is cultured = 0.9.
$P(A, \bar{B})$ = the probability that a pearl is natural = 0.1.

These two probabilities are called *prior probabilities*.

$P(A \cdot B, C)$ = the probability that a cultured pearl is color-flawed = 0.01.
$P(A \cdot \bar{B}, C)$ = the probability that a natural pearl is color-flawed = 0.03.

These two probabilities are called *likelihoods*. The probability we seek appears on the left-hand side:

$P(A \cdot C, B)$ = the probability that a color-flawed pearl is cultured.

This probability is called the *posterior probability*. The prior probabilities and likelihoods are sometimes called *forward probabilities*, while the posterior probability is sometimes called an *inverse probability*. Substituting the values stipulated, we find that the posterior probability

$$P(A \cdot C, B) = \frac{0.9 \times 0.01}{0.9 \times 0.01 + 0.1 \times 0.03} = 3/4.$$

Notice that, although the probability that a natural pearl is color-flawed is greater than the probability that a cultured pearl is color-flawed, the probability that a color-flawed pearl is cultured is greater than the probability that a color-flawed pearl is natural. In other words, the inverse probabilities invert the order of the likelihoods.

Bayes's theorem is an elementary and non-controversial consequence of the axioms of the mathematical calculus of probability, and its application to examples of the foregoing sort is also non-controversial. Its application to the assessment of serious scientific hypotheses is a matter of dispute, but many twentieth-century inductive logicians have endorsed its use for that purpose in one way or another. Rudolf Carnap, L. J. Savage, and Hans Reichenbach have all accepted this approach even though they disagree about the interpretation of the probability concept that is involved.[8]

It is important to note from the outset that the evaluation of the causal hypothesis—the evaluation of the posterior probability, $P(A \cdot C, B)$—requires three distinct probabilities. (1) We need the value of the prior probability, $P(A, B)$. If this is known the other prior probability, $P(A, \bar{B})$, is also known, for these two probabilities must add up to one. (2) We need the probability, $P(A \cdot B, C)$, that the effect in question would occur if the particular cause is operative. (3) We need the probability, $P(A \cdot \bar{B}, C)$, that the same effect would occur if some other cause were operative. These latter two probabilities, the likelihoods, are independent of one another. In the pearl example, each of these three probabilities was furnished; as a result we could use Bayes's theorem to compute the probability that the flaw occurred in a cultured pearl. If any of these three probabilities had been unknown, we would have been unable to compute the probability.[9]

3. PHILO'S ESTIMATES

My main thesis regarding Hume's *Dialogues Concerning Natural Religion* is that, although Hume must have been unaware of Bayes's theorem, his characters in the *Dialogues* (especially Philo) devote considerable attention to each of these three types of probabilities in their discussion of the hypothesis that a supremely intelligent, powerful, and benevolent Deity created the universe. Although the argument in the *Dialogues* is not cast in formal terms, Hume showed a full appreciation of the three types of considerations which must be brought to bear in order to evaluate the theistic causal hypothesis. Whether, in the end, Hume accepts or rejects the design argument, he certainly recognizes it as something deeper and more subtle than a simple appeal to analogy.

The aim of the design argument, as presented by Cleanthes, is to show that the universe, as an object exhibiting a high degree of orderliness, was very probably the result of intelligent design. Since we cannot observe other worlds coming into being—universes are not as plentiful as blackberries, as Peirce remarked—we cannot perform an induction by simple enumeration on observed births of universes in order to draw a direct conclusion about the creation of our own. "Have worlds ever been formed under your eye," Philo asks at the end of the second dialogue, "and have you had leisure to observe the whole progress of the phenomenon, from the first appearance of order to its final consummation?"[10] The answer, of course, is negative. We must, instead, make an indirect inference from the origins of other types of entities whose beginnings we can observe. Let us, therefore, proceed on that basis.

The first step in our attempt to apply Bayes's theorem is to find meanings for the terms that occur in it. Let '*A*' denote the class of instances of entities coming into being. We shall want to consider quite a broad class, so as not to bias our evidence. The class *A* will include, for example:

(i) The formation of a fetus when a sperm and egg unite.
(ii) The building of a house which was designed by an architect.
(iii) The growth of a tree from a seed.
(iv) The formation of a piece of ice as a lake freezes.
(v) Reduction of buildings to piles of rubble as a tornado tears through a town.
(vi) The carving of a gully by water rushing down a hillside.
(vii) The formation of compost as organic matter decays.

Let 'B' designate the class of instances in which intelligence operates. I shall not include cases of the operation of computing machines, since there is no need to raise the question whether machines have intelligence.

(i) Designing a house.
(ii) Writing a poem.
(iii) Designing and making a telescope.
(iv) Doing a sum.
(v) Proving a mathematical theorem.

In some of these examples a product results, but in others, such as the last, it might be doubtful that anything comes into existence. In the present discussion, however, we will not be concerned with cases in which intelligence does not create an entity—indeed, a material entity.

The letter 'C' will now be taken to represent the class of entities which exhibit order. For example,

(i) A watch.
(ii) A ship.
(iii) A living organism, plant or animal.
(iv) The human eye.
(v) A rainbow.
(vi) The solar system.
(vii) A diamond.

All of the foregoing examples are entities which rather obviously exhibit some sort of order. We shall need to return to the concept of order below, to analyze it with greater precision.

With the foregoing meanings assigned to the letters in Bayes's theorem which designate classes, we can now interpret all of the probability expressions that appear in it:

$P(A, B)$ = the probability that a case of coming-into-being is an instance of the operation of intelligence.

$P(A, \bar{B})$ = the probability that a case of coming-into-being is an instance of the operation of something other than intelligence.

$P(A \cdot B, C)$ = the probability that something produced by intelligence exhibits order.

$P(A \cdot \bar{B}, C)$ = the probability that something produced by some agency other than intelligence exhibits order.

$P(A \cdot C, B)$ = the probability that something which comes into being and exhibits order was produced by intelligence.

This last probability, which appears on the left-hand side of Bayes's theorem, is the one we seek. Proponents of the design argument maintain that it is very high.

With the help of Philo, let us now attempt to assess these various probabilities. We may begin with the prior probabilities, $P(A, B)$ and $P(A, \bar{B})$. Philo furnishes a brief inventory of "springs and principles" from which a variety of entities arise:[11]

(1) *Two types of biological generation, animal and vegetable.* Whenever any organism comes into being, one or the other is operative.
(2) *Instinct.* When bees makes honeycombs, spiders spin webs, birds build nests, or wolves mark out their territories by urinating on trees this principle is operative.
(3) *Mechanical causation.* The formation of snowflakes, diamonds, and other crystals, as well as the formation of galaxies, solar systems, molecules, and atoms, all illustrate this principle.
(4) *Intelligent design.* All types of human artifacts arise from this principle.

When we consider the number of organisms, animal or vegetable, living on the earth—including the millions of microbes which inhabit each human body—we see immediately that biological generation operates in large numbers of instances. Similar considerations apply to instinct. Mechanical causation obviously operates with great frequency upon the earth; for all we know, it may be the only principle which operates anywhere else in this vast universe. Hume knew that the physical universe is enormous, but he could not have guessed its actual size. We now have evidence to indicate that it contains perhaps 10 billion galaxies, and that each of these contains, on the average, from 10 billion to 100 billion stars. And who can say how many atoms have been formed in the interiors of these stars? Our earth alone contains something like 10^{50} atoms.

Although there are many unanswered questions in cosmology and astrophysics concerning the formation of galaxies, stars, and atoms, we have achieved some scientific understanding of these processes. They appear to be mechanical. There is, consequently, a great deal of evidence pointing to the conclusion that the number of instances in which mechanical causation operates is almost incomprehensibly greater than all of the rest combined. All of the evidence indicates that $P(A, B)$ is low—incredibly small—and that $P(A, \bar{B})$ is high. Although he did not have some of the numbers we have today, Hume was clearly aware of the fact. "What peculiar privilege has this little agitation of the brain that we call *thought*," Philo asks in the second dialogue, "that we must thus make it the model of the whole universe?"[12] We now have a rough assessment of the prior probabilities.

The probability, $P(A \cdot \bar{B}, C)$, that the operation of some principle other than intelligence will yield order, cannot be taken as negligible. The examples already cited under biological generation, instinct, and mechanical causation make this point evident. Philo cites such evidence in his discussion of these various "springs and principles."

The probability, $P(A \cdot B, C)$, that a result of intelligent planning and design will exhibit order, may be quite high. That fact, in and of itself, does *not* guarantee that the probability we are attempting to evaluate—the posterior probability, $P(A \cdot C, B)$—will be high. If $P(A, \bar{B})$ and $P(A \cdot \bar{B}, C)$ are large enough, the probability that an object which exhibits order was the product of intelligent design may still be quite low. This point was illustrated by the fictitious pearl example. In the course of the argument, Philo brings out these considerations quite explicitly.

Although it may be granted that intelligent planning often gives rise to order, it should be explicitly noted that the probability $P(A \cdot B, C)$ is not equal to unity, and moreover, it may not even be near that value. I do not find this point made explicitly in the *Dialogues*, and it is not essential to the argument, though perhaps it has some bearing. As the Vietnam war and countless other wars remind us, intelligent design may produce disorder: bombs reduce villages to rubble, defoliants destroy plant life, and many other products of human ingenuity maim and kill. Meanwhile, back home, industrial pollution and insecticides destroy many other forms of life as well.

Let us now take stock of the situation. By making plausible assessments of the probabilities which appear on the right-hand side of Bayes's theorem, we are in a position to say, quite confidently, that the probability $P(A \cdot C, B)$—that an unspecified entity, which came into being and exhibited order, was produced by intelligent design—is rather low. This conclusion can be reinforced even more directly by considering all of the entities with which we are acquainted which come into being exhibiting order. If we count the relative frequency with which such entities were the result of intelligent design, we easily see that it is rather low. This conclusion holds even if we exclude such items as galaxies and atoms on the ground that we are not very sure how they are created. There is still a vast numerical preponderance of such occurrences as animal reproduction, growth from seeds, formation of crystals, and spinning of spider webs over the relatively few instances in which watches, houses, and ships are built by people. Why does that not settle the case against the design argument without further ado? Why doesn't everyone agree that it is *improbable* that the universe, as an object exhibiting order, is a result of intelligent design? Is this mere obstinacy and prejudice on the part of upholders of "natural religion"?

4. THE UNIQUENESS OF THE UNIVERSE

There is a sound logical reason why the matter cannot be settled quite so easily. In discussing the design argument, we are attempting to assign a probability to the hypothesis that the universe was created by an intelligent designer. We are dealing with a *single case*, for the creation of the universe is a unique event, at least as far as any possible experience we may have is concerned. The problem of assessing probabilities of single events notoriously involves the problem of deciding to which class the single event is most appropriately to be assigned. If we are trying to find the probability that a particular individual, John Jones, will survive for another decade—perhaps to determine a fair life insurance premium for him to pay—we have to take into account certain relevant factors, such as age, occupation, marital status, state of health, etc. The general rule, as I prefer to formulate it, is to refer the individual case to the broadest homogeneous class available—i.e., to the broadest class that cannot be relevantly subdivided. Relevance is the key notion. I shall leave it somewhat vague in this context, even though I have tried to explicate it elsewhere.[13] But it is, I believe, clear enough intuitively for present purposes. A similar principle, incidentally, is invoked by Hempel in his inductive-statistical model of scientific explanation, namely, the *requirement of maximal specificity*.[14]

When we apply this consideration to the design argument, we see that we must give a closer specification of the particular case with which we are dealing. We must take into account the type of order which the universe exhibits, and we must also take a closer look at the nature of the intelligent creator hypothesized by the proponent of natural theology.

If we consider the sheer magnitude of the universe, all of our experience suggests that it was not constructed by a unitary being. Where human artifacts are concerned, the larger the project, the more likely it was to have been executed by a group rather than an individual. Moreover, even complicated machines are sometimes made by rather dull artisans who only copy the work of others. Philo drives the point home in the fifth dialogue with cutting wit: Taking account of the magnitude of the machine, and the imperfections in its construction, for all we know the world may have been created by a juvenile deity who had not yet learned his trade, or a stupid deity who only copies and does not do that very well, or a committee of deities, or a superannuated senile deity who had lost the knack by the time he got around to making our world. If we pay close heed to experience, it is impossible to assign a high probability to the hypothesis that the world, if created as a divine artifact, was the product of a God bearing any resemblance to the theist's conception.

Worse still is the fact that the God of traditional theism has usually been regarded as a pure spirit—a disembodied intelligence. In no instance within our experience, however, has a disembodied intellect produced any kind of artifact, whether or not it might have exhibited any order. Indeed, since disembodied intelligence has never operated in any fashion, to the best of our knowledge, we must conclude from experience that for such an intelligence, $P(A, B) = 0$, and in that case $P(A \cdot B, C)$ is simply undefined.

If we examine more closely the kind of order exhibited by the universe, says Philo in the sixth dialogue, we may find that it more closely resembles that of a vegetable or an animal than it does that of a machine. In that case, again, $P(A \cdot B, C)$ is low, while $P(A \cdot \bar{B}, C)$ must be rated high, for animals and vegetables arise from biological generation, not intelligent design. (The fact that farmers deliberately plant crops and breed animals does nothing to enhance the value of $P(A \cdot B, C)$, for the order exhibited by the organisms thus produced arises from genetic principles, not from the intelligent design of the farmer, who merely provides the occasion for their operation.)

Philo is not seriously entertaining the hypothesis that the universe arises from biological generation, but he does seem to give purely mechanical principles somewhat more credence. Later in the sixth dialogue he remarks, "And were I obliged to defend any particular system of this nature, which I never willingly should do, I esteem none more plausible than that which ascribes an eternal, inherent principle of order to the world, though attended with great and continual revolutions and alterations."[15] Philo is not, of course, assigning a high prior probability to this hypothesis—quite the contrary. When, in the eighth dialogue, he undertakes a fuller elaboration of this theme, he cautions against such a notion: "Without any great effort of thought, I believe that I could, in an instant propose other systems of cosmogony which would have some faint appearance of truth; though it is a thousand, a million to one if either yours or anyone of mine be the true system."[16]

In this eighth dialogue, Philo brings up "the old Epicurean hypothesis" which he characterizes as "the most absurd system that has yet been proposed," but which "with a few alterations . . . might . . . be brought to bear a faint appearance of probability."[17] He offers what seems to me a clear anticipation of Darwinian evolution; moreover, other aspects of this hypothesis bear a tenuous connection with more recent cosmological ideas. With the benefit of modern scientific knowledge, we are inclined to endow this sort of hypothesis with a more substantial prior probability, but Philo does not press for this conclusion. He urges only that the prior probability of the mechanical hypothesis is not less than the prior probability of the hypothesis of intelligent design. Moreover, he seems to argue that each of these hypotheses provides the same likelihood of order of the type exhibited by the universe: "But wherever matter is so poised, arranged, and adjusted, as to continue in perpetual motion, and yet preserve a constancy in the forms, its situation must, of necessity, have all the same appearance of art and contrivance which we observe at present."[18]

At the close of the eighth dialogue, we come to the end of the analysis of one form of the design argument. The conclusion is that the hypothesis of intelligent design, where no "moral attributes" are ascribed to the creator, is completely on a par with the mechanical hypothesis. Neither is very plausible, and neither is supported by compelling evidence. The prior probabilities and the likelihoods, respectively, are about the same for the two hypotheses. But because of the plethora of alternatives—mentioned, but not elaborated, at the beginning of the eighth dialogue—none can be assigned a high posterior probability. The probabilities of all of the many incompatible alternative hypotheses cannot add up to more than one, and none of the candidates stands out as commanding a very large share of the total. The hypothesis of intelligent design is quite improbable, but no other hypothesis fares any better.

According to traditional theism, the creator of the universe possesses the moral attributes of "justice, benevolence, mercy, and rectitude." Cleanthes is as anxious to attribute them to the Deity as he is to attribute wisdom and power. For religious purposes, the moral attributes are at least as important as the natural; ". . . to what purpose establish the natural attributes of Deity," he asks, "while the moral are still doubtful and uncertain?"[19] Thus, Cleanthes maintains, the universe gives evidence of a creator who is intelligent, powerful, and benevolent—analogous, but immeasurably superior, to his human counterpart. This is a different theistic hypothesis; it is not seriously discussed until the tenth dialogue.

Philo does not seem to argue that the addition of the moral attributes significantly affects the prior probability of the theistic hypothesis, but he does claim that it has a marked adverse effect upon the likelihood. Other things being equal, a lowering of the likelihood will result in a reduced posterior probability. Following this tack, he notes that the world seems utterly indifferent to values. The rain falls alike upon the just and the unjust. Evil abounds. Untold misery and suffering plague mankind. Hume's eloquence, when he speaks through Philo, creates a vivid picture. And Hume didn't even know about nuclear bombs, chemical and biological warfare, pollution, and overpopulation problems. It is crucial to realize that Philo is *not* raising the traditional theological problem of evil. That problem is the problem of reconciling the existence of an omniscient, omnipotent, and perfectly benevolent God with the existence of real or apparent evil in the world. It is resolved if you can show that there is no contradiction between asserting the existence of such Deity and the occurrence of human suffering and pain.

The problem for the design argument is rather different, as Philo emphatically insists. It is not merely a question of showing that the world as we know it is not incompatible with the existence of God. Rather the proponent of natural religion must maintain that the world as we know it is *positive evidence for* the claim that it was created by a wise, powerful, benevolent being. To test a scientific hypothesis, one derives observational consequences that would be expected to hold if the hypothesis were true, and then observes to see whether such consequences obtain. In the eleventh dialogue, Philo puts the question:

> Is the world, considered in general and as it appears to us in this life, different from what a man . . . would, *beforehand*, expect from a very powerful, wise, and benevolent Deity? It must be strange prejudice to assert the contrary. And from thence I conclude that, however consistent the world may be, allowing certain suppositions and conjectures, with the idea of such a Deity, it can never afford us an inference concerning his existence. The consistency is not absolutely denied, only the inference.[20]

Philo then proceeds to enumerate four rather obvious ways in which an all-powerful creator could have reduced the amount of evil in the world if he had wanted to:

(1) Pain need not be inflicted upon man—he need not have been endowed with the capacity for suffering. "Men pursue pleasure as eagerly as they avoid pain; at least, they might have been so constituted. It seems, therefore, plainly possible to carry on the business of life without any pain."
(2) The Deity need not have governed the world by inviolable general laws. A little tinkering with the works now and then could be quite beneficial: an extra large wave upon a warship sailing to inflict harm on helpless people; a little calming of the waters for a ship on an errand of mercy.
(3) Mankind and the other species have been so frugally endowed with capacities as to make their existence hazardous and grim. Why could not the creator have endowed them a bit more lavishly, for example, with industry, energy, and health?
(4) A further source of "misery and ill of the universe is the inaccurate workmanship of all the springs and principles of the great machine of nature . . . they are, all of them, apt, on every occasion, to run into one extreme or the other. One could imagine that this grand production had not received the last hand of the maker—so little finished is every part, and so coarse are the strokes with which it is executed." It never rains but it pours; it is always feast or famine.[21]

If Philo could so easily conceive of ways in which, for all we can tell, the world might have been vastly improved, why could not a supreme intelligence have done even better? Remember, Philo is not asking whether it is conceivable that God made the best world it was possible to make and this is it. He is asking whether this world is what we would antecedently expect of an omnipotent, omniscient, benevolent being.

> Did I show you a house or palace where there was not one apartment convenient or agreeable; where the windows, doors, fires, passages, stairs, and the whole economy of the building were the source of noise, confusion, fatigue, darkness, and the extremes of heat and cold, you would certainly blame the contrivance, without any further examination. The architect would in vain display his subtlety, and prove to you that, if this door or that window were altered, greater ills would ensue. What he says may be strictly true: The alteration of one particular, while the other parts of the building remain, may only augment the inconveniences. But still you would assert in general that, if the architect had had skill and good intentions, he might have formed such a plan of the whole, and might have adjusted the parts in such a manner as would have remedied all or most of these inconveniences. His ignorance, or even your own ignorance of such a plan, will never convince you of the impossibility of it. If you find any inconveniences and deformities in the building, you will always, without entering any detail, condemn the architect.[22]

Whereas the universe might equally be the product of mechanical causes or of an intelligence not assumed to be benevolent, the universe as we observe it can hardly be attributed to a creator who is benevolent as well as omniscient and omnipotent. Given the hypothesis that God is supremely wise, good, and powerful, there is a *very low* probability, $P(A \cdot B, C)$, that he would create a world such as this![23] Notice that Philo is not denying that the world exhibits order—one of his complaints, mentioned above, is that the world is too orderly. He is saying that the kind of order it manifests is not what would be expected as the result of creation by a wise, powerful, benevolent creator.

Hume evidently felt that the objections to the design argument which are based upon the existence of apparently gratuitous evil were far more potent than any of the other objections; at any rate, he has Philo declare at the close of the tenth dialogue,

> . . . when we argued concerning the natural attributes of intelligence and design, I needed all my skeptical and metaphysical subtlety to elude your grasp . . . But there is no view of human life or of the conditions of mankind from which, without the greatest violence, we can infer the moral attributes or learn that infinite benevolence conjoined with infinite power and infinite wisdom, which we must discover by the eyes of faith alone . . . It is your turn now to tug the laboring oar, and to support your philosophical subtleties against the dictates of plain reason and experience.[24]

Although Cleanthes is unwilling, for religious reasons, to abandon the argument concerning moral attributes, and to rest his case entirely upon the natural attributes, some defenders of "natural religion" might consider pursuing this approach.

There is, it seems to me, a logical (as well as a religious) reason why the proponent of the design argument cannot abandon consideration of the moral attributes. If one asks what sort of order the world exhibits which gives such strong evidence of intelligent design, the answer given repeatedly is "the adjustment of means to ends." It is patently impossible to bring such considerations to bear unless we have some conception of what ends the means are designed to serve. If the ends are justice, mercy, and benevolence as we conceive them in our better moments, one sort of order would count as evidence for intelligent design. If the end is to secure from mankind blind unreasoning adulation of and obedience to a Deity who says in one breath, "Thou shalt not kill," and in another, "Slay and spare not," another kind of order would be suitable. Still another kind of order would be appropriate if the creator, as revealed in the book of Job, is mainly concerned to win a bet with his old gaming companion, Satan. Thus, the moral attributes of God are inextricably bound up even in the argument directed toward his natural attributes. The author who wrote in his *A Treatise of Human Nature*, "Reason is, and ought only to be, a slave of the passions, and can pretend to no other office but to serve and obey them,"[25] could hardly have overlooked this point.

5. ORDER AND PURPOSE

We have not yet come sufficiently to grips with the nature of the order which the theist finds in the world, and which seems to him to furnish compelling evidence of intelligent design. Philo points out that the order exhibited by living organisms comes from biological generation. This is no news to Cleanthes; he was not under the impression that babies are brought by the stork from the baby-factory, where they are fashioned by artisans. This consideration does not seem to the proponent of the design argument to undermine his position; indeed, such biological wonders seem to him to reinforce his argument, for they are further evidence of ingenious design. Pursuing the example of the watch presented in the earlier quotation, William Paley addresses precisely this issue:

> Suppose, in the next place, that the person, who found the watch, should, after some time, discover, that, in addition to all the properties which he had hitherto observed in it, it possessed the unexpected property of producing, in the course of its movement, another watch like itself; (the thing is conceivable;) that it contained within it a mechanism, a system of parts, a mould for instance, or a complex adjustment of lathes, files and other tools, evidently and separately calculated for this purpose; let us inquire, what effect ought such a discovery to have upon his former conclusion?
>
> The first effect would be to increase his admiration of the contrivance, and his conviction of the consummate skill of the contriver. . . . If that construction

> *without* this property, or, which is the same thing, before this property had been noticed, proved intention and art to have been employed about it; still more strong would the proof appear, when he came to the knowledge of this further property, the crown and perfection of the rest.[26]

Paley proceeds to drive home the argument:

> The conclusion which the *first* examination of the watch, of its works, construction, and movement suggested, was, that it must have had, for the cause and author of that construction, an artificer, who understood its mechanism, and designed its use. The conclusion is invincible. A *second* examination presents us with a new discovery. The watch is found in the course of its movement, to produce another watch, similar to itself; and not only so, but we perceive in it a system of organization, separately calculated for that purpose. What effect would this discovery have, or ought it to have, upon our former inference? What, as hath already been said, but to increase, beyond measure, our admiration of the skill, which had been employed in the formation of such a machine? Or shall it, instead of this, all at once turn us round to an opposite conclusion, viz. that no art or skill whatever has been concerned in the business, although all other evidences of art and skill remain as they were, and this last supreme piece of art be now added to the rest? Can this be maintained without absurdity? Yet this is atheism.[27]

In these passages, Paley articulates what is, perhaps, the most fundamental issue concerning natural religion and the design argument. Hume addresses this issue in the *Dialogues*. For Cleanthes, the order which arises out of biological generation is only further evidence of intelligent design on the part of the creator of the universe. Philo retorts that, within our experience, all instances of intelligent design issue from biological organisms—biological generation always lies behind intelligence. We do not have experience of intelligent creation as a prior source of biological generation. Why, then, does the defender of the design argument insist, contrary to experience, that intelligent design must lie behind the operation of any other principle which generates order?

The answer lies, of course, in a teleological conception of order. In his fullest and most careful statement of the design argument, Cleanthes describes the universe as a "great machine," composed of a prolific array of "lesser machines," all of which are characterized by "the curious adapting of means to ends." This theme recurs frequently throughout the *Dialogues*, and it is conspicuous in the quotations from Paley, who confines his discussion to instances in which he believes it can be shown that the parts work together to achieve some useful end. Indeed, there is a pervasive tendency in the writings of the defenders of natural religion to equate order and design—to treat them as synonymous. But such a procedure flagrantly begs the question, as Philo is careful to point out in the seventh dialogue:

> To say that all this order in animals and vegetables proceeds ultimately from design is begging the question; nor can that great point be ascertained otherwise than by proving, a priori, both that order is, from its nature, inseparably attached to thought, and that it can never of itself or from original unknown principles belong to matter.[28]

Can such a proof be given? The universe, it is admitted on all sides, exhibits order. Is this order evidence of intelligent design? It cannot be shown by experience. Its assertion can only be as the sort of a priori pronouncement the proponent of "experimental theism" eschews. It is, in short, an anthropomorphic conceit.

As I read the eighth dialogue, it seems to me to contain a rather clear anticipation of a non-teleological theory of biological evolution. I do not know whether this reading is correct, or whether I am indulging in wishful thinking. Be that as it may, in the nineteenth century Darwin provided just such a theory. To put the matter briefly, Darwin showed how the nonpurposive factors of chance mutations and natural selection could lead to the evolution of the species, and in that evolutionary process, those species which are best adapted to compete for food and reproductive opportunities would evolve. Although evolutionary biology poses many problems, there is little reason to think that a retreat into teleology is the answer. Twentieth-century molecular biology has added to our understanding of the mechanisms of heredity by showing precisely how order is reproduced. It seems to me, indeed, that one of the chief accomplishments of Galileo and Newton was the removal of Aristotelian teleological conceptions from physics. The beautiful order of the solar system, for example, so greatly venerated by Kepler, could be reduced to mechanical principles. The next great scientific revolution was due to Darwin; its main achievement was to rid the biological sciences of their teleological elements. Order in the physical world, and in its biological realms, was shown to be independent of intelligent design. The a priori principle to which the design argument ultimately appeals was thus undermined.

6. THE CONCEPT OF ORDER

The net result of the scientific revolution, of which Newton's mechanics was the fundamental ingredient, was to present a picture of the world which exhibits a wonderful mechanical order and simplicity. The world is seen as a collection of material particles which respond to forces in accordance with Newton's three incredibly simple laws of motion. Moreover, one of the forces—gravitation—obeys another very simple law. The further development of classical mechanics, which reached its zenith at the end of the nineteenth century, revealed that other forces—electric and magnetic, in particular—also conform to simple and precisely specifiable laws. At the turn of the century, it appeared that all natural phenomena could be explained in terms of these fundamental principles of classical physics. Although Newton had entertained the idea that God might need to intervene from time to time to keep the cosmic machine in good adjustment, later authors—most notably Laplace—maintained that the universe is entirely governed by mechanical principles. The success of classical mechanics, along with the advent of Darwinian evolutionary theory, banished teleological principles from nature.

The fact that the constituents of the world behave in accordance with simple laws is a kind of order, but it is not the only kind of order nature exhibits. A random and totally disorganized system of material particles would obey the same laws as a finely constructed machine—e.g., the heaps of metal in junk yards obey the same physical laws as do the finest newly-fabricated motor cars. The universe does not, however, appear to be a cosmic heap of unorganized parts; to the eyes of many observers, it seems more like a finely constructed machine. The manifestation of this latter kind of order seemed to many deists[29] to constitute evidence of intelligent creation, even though all teleological elements had been removed from the operation of nature itself. The story is told of an astronomer, who believed in intelligent creation, and a friend who did not. One day the friend came to visit the astronomer, and he saw an elaborate model of the entire solar system which the astronomer had just acquired. The model was so constructed that when a crank was turned, the various planets and their satellites moved around a sun at the center, just as the real planets and satellites do. When asked by the friend where he had procured the model, and who had constructed it, the astronomer replied simply that no one had made it—the parts had just happened to fall together in that arrangement by chance. Thus, with irony, did he attempt to show the absurdity of his friend's atheism.

One of the severe difficulties faced by eighteenth- and nineteenth-century authors who discussed, pro and con, the design argument was their inability to characterize in any satisfactory way the kind of order they saw in the world. To say that the universe conforms to simple laws is one thing; to say that it also exhibits an orderly configuration is quite another. The best they seemed able to do was to talk in terms of the adjustment of means to ends, and the similarity of the universe—or its parts—to man-made machines. Each of these characterizations leads to problems. It is difficult to deal with the means-end relationship if we do not have some independent evidence concerning the nature of the end which is supposed to be served. The similarity of the world to a machine can easily be challenged, as Philo does in the seventh dialogue where he says, "The world plainly resembles more an animal or a vegetable than it does a watch or a knitting loom."[30]

Scientific developments since about the middle of the nineteenth century have significantly clarified the concept of order. In dealing with physical problems closely related to practical concerns about the efficiency of machines, physicists and engineers created the science of thermodynamics. They established a viable concept of energy, discovered laws relating the various forms of energy to each other, and developed the concept of *entropy*. Entropy is essentially a measure of the unavailability of energy to do mechanical work. Given two physical systems, each with the same amount of energy, the one with the lower entropy is the one from which it is possible in principle to extract the greater amount of work. All machines, in the course of their operation, tend to dissipate some of their energy in useless forms—through friction, for example. They are subject to the universal law of degradation of energy, the famous second law of thermodynamics. The discovery of this fundamental law of nature—that entropy tends to increase—has led to considerable speculation about the "heat death" of the universe. The entire universe seems to be "running down."[31]

Toward the end of the nineteenth century, thermodynamics was given a theoretical foundation in statistical mechanics, and the concept of entropy was given a statistical interpretation.[32] Low entropy was shown to be associated with non-random, highly ordered arrangements, which are relatively improbable, while high entropy is associated with random, unordered arrangements which are relatively probable. If, for example, we have a container with 80 molecules in it—40 oxygen molecules and 40 nitrogen molecules—the arrangement would be highly ordered and non-random if all of the oxygen molecules happened to be in the left half of the container and all of the nitrogen molecules happened to be in the right half. The probability, incidentally, of the molecules spontaneously sorting themselves out in this way in the course of their random motions is approximately 10^{-24}. Arrangements in which about half of the oxygen molecules are in one half of the box, and about half in the other (and similarly for the nitrogen molecules) are disordered, random, and vastly more probable.[33]

We can now restate the problem of the design argument in terms of these thermodynamic considerations. If (as is admittedly problematic) we allow ourselves to speak of the entropy of the entire universe, it appears that the order exhibited by the universe can be described by saying that the entropy of the universe is now relatively low, and it has been even lower in the past. As we have seen, to say that the entropy is low is tantamount to saying that the universe contains large stores of available energy. The question of creation can be posed again. The universe is a physical system in a relatively low entropy state; is there strong reason to claim, by virtue of this fact, that it must have been produced by intelligent design?

According to the modern statistical interpretation of the second law of thermodynamics, the entropy in a closed physical system is very probably high. It is not, however, impossible for the entropy of such a system to decrease as a result of a mere statistical fluctuation—though such occurrences are exceedingly improbable. It is also possible for a closed physical system to be in a state of low entropy as a result of a recent interaction with its environment. This means, of course, that the system has not been closed for an indefinite period in the past—it has not always been isolated, but has, instead, interacted with other parts of the world. For example, a thermos bottle containing tepid water with ice cubes floating in it is in a low entropy state. In the course of time the ice cubes will melt, the water will cool, and the whole system inside the insulated container will arrive at a uniform temperature. This is a state of higher entropy. Upon finding a thermos whose contents were in the lower of the two states, we would infer without hesitation that it had recently been put into that state by an outside agency—in this case, a person who had removed the ice cubes from a refrigerator and deliberately placed them in the thermos with the water. In this instance, the low entropy state was a result of an interaction with an intelligent planner who put the ice cubes into the water to fulfill a conscious purpose. Low entropy states which are the results of interaction with the environment do not always involve human intervention. A hail storm on a summer day may deposit pieces of ice in the lukewarm water of a swimming pool.[34]

It is, I suspect, quite desirable to reformulate the problem of intelligent design in terms of the concept of entropy, rather than the vague concept of order. There will not be as strong a temptation to beg the question by identifying low entropy with conscious design as there was to do so by identifying—almost by definition—order with purpose and "the adjustment of means to ends." We may, once more, look around the world, surveying the physical systems which come into being in low entropy states, to ascertain what percentage of them are created with conscious design. The results will be similar to those already discussed. An exceedingly small proportion of low entropy systems—i.e., systems which are highly organized and orderly—result from an interaction with the environment which involves any conscious purpose or design. There is no need to repeat the whole story.

7. MODERN COSMOLOGY

In our day, unlike Hume's, we can claim some physical knowledge about the evolution of the universe.[35] There is strong reason to believe that, sometime between

10 billion and 20 billion years ago, the universe consisted of a compact concentration of energy which exploded with incredible violence. This "Big Bang" conception of the universe is supported, not only by the observed red-shifts of light from distant galaxies, but also by the more recently discovered cosmic microwave background radiation. It seems likely that statistical fluctuations in the rapidly expanding fireball gave rise to stable inhomogeneities in the distribution of matter, and that these inhomogeneities, by gravitational attraction of neighboring matter, led to the formation of galaxies. Further concentrations, within the galaxies, led to the formation of stars. Our universe contains roughly 10 billion such galaxies, each of which is an inhomogeneous concentration of energy in the vast expanses of the universe. Each galaxy contains, on the average, perhaps 10 billion stars. These again are inhomogeneous concentrations of energy. Can we not say that we have already cited on the order of 100 billion billion systems which came into being in states of low entropy? Where in the annals of human history can we find like numbers of systems created in low entropy states by conscious human intervention? We believe, moreover, that we have some understanding of the processes by which atoms are formed in the interiors of stars. The earth alone contains on the order of 10^{50} atoms—each a highly organized low entropy system—each, to the best of our knowledge, brought into being without conscious intent. Not only do the low entropy systems created without intelligent purpose outnumber by orders of magnitude those which involve intelligent design: the orders of magnitude are greater by orders of magnitude!

But what of the universe itself—that unique system whose mode of creation is at issue? We cannot, at present, say much. It seems possible that our universe will continue to expand for many more billions of years, its rate of expansion continually declining, until eventually it begins to contract in a reverse process which will inevitably lead to a "big crunch." Perhaps it has a cyclic history of repeated expansion and contraction ad infinitum. This hypothesis seems unlikely as things now stand, for there does not seem to be enough matter in the universe to bring the expansion to a halt and induce a subsequent process of contraction. Perhaps it will simply continue expanding forever. It is difficult to draw any conclusions with much confidence. Perhaps—as Philo might say—the universe was created by a juvenile deity who, on a super-cosmic holiday, set off a super-gigantic firecracker. Or, perhaps our universe is a black hole in some incomprehensibly larger universe.

8. ASSESSMENT OF THE HYPOTHESIS

What morals should we draw from our analysis of the design argument? I think we should say that the attempt to deal with the question of God's existence as a scientific hypothesis is quite successful. We have considered the hypothesis that the universe is the product of intelligent design, and we have seen that a very rough estimate, at least, can be made of its probability by applying Bayes's theorem. The result is, of course, disappointing to the theist (or deist), for the conclusion is that the hypothesis is quite *improbable*. This conclusion can, I believe, be drawn quite unequivocally from the kinds of evidence which Philo adduces in Hume's *Dialogues*, and more recent scientific developments tend only to reinforce this result, pushing the posterior probability of intelligent design even closer to zero. If scientific evidence is relevant, it tends to disprove the existence of God as an intelligent designer of the universe.

Compare this result with a legal situation. Suppose that a suspect in a crime is defended by an attorney who can show:

(i) It is antecedently improbable that his client committed the crime, since he had no motive.
(ii) If his client had committed the crime, the clues found at the scene of the crime would very probably have been altogether different.
(iii) Someone else, who had motive and opportunity to commit the crime, would very probably have left just the sort of traces which were found at the scene of the crime, if he had committed the crime. Under these circumstances, only an egregious miscarriage of justice could lead to the conviction of the client.

Or suppose that a scientist has an explanatory hypothesis for some phenomenon. Upon investigation, it turns out that:

(i) This hypothesis is antecedently implausible because it is in direct conflict with a large body of well-established theory.
(ii) It makes the occurrence of the facts to be explained quite improbable if it is true.
(iii) There is a plausible alternative hypothesis which makes the facts to be explained highly probable.

Under these circumstances, only gross prejudice would make a scientist retain such a hypothesis.

Hume's *Dialogues* constitute, in my opinion, a logical, as well as an artistic, masterpiece. With consummate skill, he put together the diverse elements of a complex argument. It is a striking tribute to his logical acumen that he seemed intuitively aware of the structure of scientific arguments whose explicit characterization is essentially a product of the twentieth century.

9. THE RELEVANCE OF SCIENTIFIC EVIDENCE

In this essay, I have tried to carry out what I consider a legitimate philosophic enterprise. Using materials from Hume's *Dialogues*, I have tried to give a logical analysis of one of the historically and systematically important arguments for the existence of God. Although many such analyses of the ontological and cosmological arguments can be found in the philosophical literature, I am not aware that the same type of analysis of the design argument has been undertaken.[36] The reason may lie in the fact that deductive logic seems to enjoy greater popularity among philosophers than does inductive logic. Whatever the reason for the neglect of the design argument, there is a very significant difference between the outcome of its analysis and the outcomes of the analyses of the others. If an analysis of one of the a priori arguments reveals a fallacy, the most severe consequence is merely that the argument in question may have to be abandoned. Discovery of a fallacy is not apt to transform a putative argument for the existence of God into a valid argument for his nonexistence. Our analysis of the design argument, in contrast, does tend to show that there is no intelligent creator (although it is admittedly irrelevant to other theological hypotheses).

The main reaction of those who have placed some stock in the design argument—if they admit that the foregoing analysis has any validity at all—is likely to be the contention that the design argument should be abandoned, and that all such considerations are irrelevant to the existence or nonexistence of God. This position is, I believe, untenable. The result of the analysis is *not* to show that all conceivable empirical evidence is irrelevant to the theological hypothesis. Cleanthes makes this point clear in the third dialogue when he offers a new twist on the design argument:

> Suppose, therefore, that an articulate voice were heard in the clouds, much louder and more melodious than any which human art could ever reach; suppose that this voice were extended in the same instant over all nations and spoke to each nation in its own language and dialect; suppose that the words delivered not only contain a just sense and meaning, but convey some instruction altogether worthy of a benevolent Being superior to mankind—could you possibly hesitate a moment concerning the cause of this voice, and must you not instantly ascribe some design or purpose?[37]

Philo does not deny that such an inference would be appropriate in this case. If such evidence did obtain, he seems to concede, it would constitute grounds for believing in an intelligent source. Cleanthes maintains that the argument from design, as originally stated, is just as strong as this. Although Philo leaves the matter hanging there, such a view is unsupportable. The hypothetical evidence just offered involves meaningful linguistic performances of an intricate sort. In our experience, complex linguistic performances take place rather frequently, and they *invariably* arise from intelligent design. When, moreover, such a performance comes from an inanimate object, such as a radio or a phonograph, we do have overwhelmingly strong experiential evidence to support the claim that it can be traced back to an intelligent source. There is conceivable evidence which does not happen to obtain, but which, if it did obtain, would support the hypothesis of a super-human intelligence. Empirical evidence is not, ipso facto, irrelevant.[38]

Karl Popper has argued, with considerable justification, that the essence of the scientific approach is to put forth bold conjectures that can be tested—that are capable of being falsified by negative evidence. It is decidedly unscientific to frame hypotheses in a manner that makes them appear confirmable by positive evidence but which, at the same time, renders them immune to falsification by possible negative evidence. In the field of theology, this scientific approach is illustrated by a passage from Kings I:

> Elijah drew near to all the people and said, "How long will you hobble on this faith and that? If the Eternal is God, follow him; if Baal, then follow him." The people made no answer. Then Elijah said to the people, "I, I alone, am left as a prophet of the Eternal, while Baal has four hundred and fifty prophets. Let us have a couple of bullocks; they can choose one bullock for themselves and chop it up, laying the pieces on the wood, but putting no fire underneath it; I will dress the other bullock and lay it on the wood, putting no fire underneath it. You call to your god, I will call to the Eternal, and the God who answers by fire, he is the real God."
>
> "All right," said the people.
>
> So Elijah told the prophets of Baal, "Choose one bullock for yourselves, and dress it first (for you are many), calling to your god, but putting no fire underneath."
>
> They took their bullock, dressed it, and called to Baal from morn to midday, crying, "Baal, answer us!" But not a sound came, no one answered, as they danced about the altar they had reared.
>
> When it came to midday, Elijah taunted them. "Shout," he told them, "for he is a god!" So they shouted, gashing themselves with knives and lances, as was their practice, till the blood poured over their bodies. After noon they raved on till the hour of the evening sacrifice; but not a sound came, there was no one to answer them, no one to heed them.
>
> Then said Elijah to all the people, "Come close to me." All the people came close to him, and he repaired the altar of the Eternal which had been broken down, making a trench around the altar about the space of eighteen hundred square yards. He arranged the wood, chopped up the bullock, and laid the pieces on the wood. "Fill four barrels with water," he said, "and pour them over the sacrifice and over the wood."
>
> "Do it again," he added, and they did it again. "Do it a third time," he said, and they did it a third time, till the water flowed round the altar. He also filled the trench with water.

> Then at the hour for the evening sacrifice Elijah the prophet came forward. "Oh Eternal, God of Abraham and Isaac and Israel," he cried, "this day may it be known that thou art God in Israel and that I am thy servant, that I have done all this at thy bidding. Hear me, Oh Eternal, hear me, to let this people know that thou the Eternal art God and that thou has made their minds turn to thee again."
>
> Then the Eternal's lightning fell, burning up the sacrifice, the wood, the stones, and the dust, and licking up the water in the trench. At the sight of this, all the people fell on their faces, crying, "The Eternal is God, the Eternal is God!"[39]

This, I submit, is an instance in which a religious hypothesis was formulated and put to the test. Cleanthes spoke of "experimental theism," but he proposed no experiments. Elijah practiced real experimental theism. There is, alas, a "concluding unscientific postscript":

> "Seize the prophets of Baal," said Elijah, "let not a man of them escape." They seized the prophets, and Elijah, taking them down to the brook Kishon, killed them there.[40]

If a scientific approach to the propositions of theology is to be adopted, the evidence must be considered, whether it be favorable or unfavorable. Negative evidence, as Francis Bacon so forcefully reminds us, cannot be ignored.

> The human understanding when it has once adopted an opinion (either as being the received opinion or as being agreeable to itself) draws all things else to support and agree with it. And though there be a greater number and weight of instances to be found on the other side, yet these it either neglects and despises, or else by some distinction sets aside and rejects; in order that by this great and pernicious predetermination the authority of its former conclusions may remain inviolate. And therefore it was a good answer that was made by one who when they showed him hanging in a temple a picture of those who had paid their vows as having escaped shipwreck, and would have him say whether he did not now acknowledge the power of the gods,—"Aye," asked he again, "But where are they painted that were drowned after their vows?"[41,42]

NOTES

1. William Paley, *Natural Theology* (Boston: Gould and Lincoln, 1851), p. 5.
2. Ibid., p. 13. As Professor Frederick Ferré kindly pointed out to me, Paley—unlike Cleanthes—rests his version of the design argument upon the existence of particular contrivances in nature, such as the human eye, rather than appealing to the alleged machine-like character of the whole universe.

3. David Hume, *Dialogues Concerning Natural Religion*, edited by Nelson Pike (Indianapolis: Bobbs-Merrill, 1970), p. 22. For readers who do not happen to have this edition at hand, I shall indicate which dialogue any quoted passage is taken from.

4. Editors note: Salmon's postscript on "Hume's Intentions" is not included here for reasons of space. It can be found on pp. 168–76 in Salmon's original paper, "Religion and Science: A New Look at Hume's *Dialogues*," *Philosophical Studies* 33 (1978): 143–76.

5. Ibid., pp. 23–24.

6. Ibid., p. 37.

7. Wesley C. Salmon, *The Foundations of Scientific Inference* (Pittsburgh: University of Pittsburgh Press, 1967), chap. VII.

8. A comparison and critical discussion of their views can be found in the place cited in the preceding note.

9. By employing a slightly different form of Bayes's theorem, we can replace $P(A \cdot \bar{B}, C)$ by $P(A, C)$, but in either case, three distinct probabilities are required.

10. Hume, *Dialogues*, p. 32.

11. Ibid. See, especially, the seventh and eighth dialogues.

12. Ibid., p. 28.

13. Salmon, *The Foundations of Scientific Inference*, pp. 90–96.

14. Carl G. Hempel, *Aspects of Scientific Explanation* (New York: Free Press, 1965), pp. 397–403.

15. Hume, *Dialogues*, p. 59.

16. Ibid., p. 68.

17. Ibid., p. 69.

18. Ibid., p. 70.

19. Ibid., p. 89.

20. Ibid., p. 96.

21. Ibid., pp. 96–102.

22. Ibid., pp. 95–96.

23. Paley was much more careful than was Cleanthes to refrain from ever literally imputing omnipotence, omniscience, and perfect benevolence to God. He also held that natural theology must be supplemented by revealed theology in order to ascertain the attributes of God.

24. Hume, *Dialogues*, p. 92.

25. David Hume, *A Treatise of Human Nature*, edited by L. A. Selby-Bigge (London: Oxford University Press, 1965), book II, part III, sect. III.

26. Paley, *Natural Theology*, pp. 8–9.

27. Ibid., pp. 12–13.

28. Hume, *Dialogues*, p. 65.

29. The term 'deism' is often used to refer to the doctrine that there is a God who created the universe, but after the creation does not interfere with it in any way.

30. Ibid., p. 62.

31. Some of these historical developments are presented in elementary terms in Gerald Holton, *Introduction to Concepts and Theories in Physical Science*, revised edition by Stephen G. Brush (Reading, MA: Addison-Wesley, 1973), chaps. 17.7–10 and 18.

32. In the spirit of bicentennialism, which inspired the Hume Conference at which

this paper was presented, it should be noted that the fundamental work on statistical mechanics by J. Willard Gibbs dates from 1876. See *Physics Today* (March 1976): 24–25.

33. See F. Reif, *Statistical Physics* (New York: McGraw-Hill, 1965), pp. 4–14.

34. Many of these considerations are discussed with philosophical clarity in Hans Reichenbach, *The Direction of Time* (Berkeley and Los Angeles: University of California Press, 1956), chaps. 3–4.

35. See Steven Weinberg, *The First Three Minutes* (New York: Basic Books, 1977), for an accurate and reliable popular presentation of current cosmological theory. I do not mean to assert that the history of the universe is completely understood, or that there are no substantial controversies. My point is merely that such knowledge, incomplete and tentative as it may be, is not negligible. Bringing it to bear in the present context is not contrary to the spirit of Hume's discussion.

36. The one exception—hardly worth mentioning—was my early paper cited in the note at the beginning of this essay.

37. Hume, *Dialogues*, p. 34.

38. If I recall correctly, Bertrand Russell was once asked if there were any conceivable evidence which could lead him to a belief in God. He offered something similar to Cleanthes's suggestion. He was then asked what he would say if, after dying, he were transported to the presence of God; how would he justify his failure on earth to be a believer? "I'd say, 'Not enough evidence, God, not enough evidence!'" Several years ago I gave a talk on the design argument at De Pauw University. After the lecture there was a party, and this story about Russell was told. The next day we learned that he had died that very evening.

39. Kings I, 18:21–40, Moffatt translation.

40. Ibid.

41. Francis Bacon, *Nollum Organum*, aphorism xlvi.

42. This paper was written for presentation at a conference held at the University of Arizona in 1976, the bicentennial of Hume's death. On that occasion it seemed appropriate to discuss his *Dialogues Concerning Natural Religion,* for this posthumously published work is a significant part of Hume's legacy.

The composition of these dialogues was begun in 1751, and a first draft had been completed by 1756. Hume wanted to publish them at that time, but because of the controversial nature of this work, friends persuaded him to delay publication. He revised the *Dialogues* in 1761, and again in 1776. One of Hume's chief concerns during the last year of his life was that they be published shortly after his death. To this end he made elaborate provisions in his will, but the actual publication did not occur until 1779. The first edition did not carry the publisher's name or any editorial comment.

The present paper is a drastically revised version of an article, "A Modern Analysis of the Design Argument," which appeared in *Research Studies of the State College of Washington* in 1951—just 200 years after Hume began his first draft. That article was defective in many ways, and I am thankful for the obscurity it enjoyed.

I am grateful to Professor Nancy Cartwright for stimulating and penetrating comments on the version of this paper which was presented at the Hume conference. I am grateful to Professor Frederick Ferré for important information concerning William Paley's construal of the design argument.

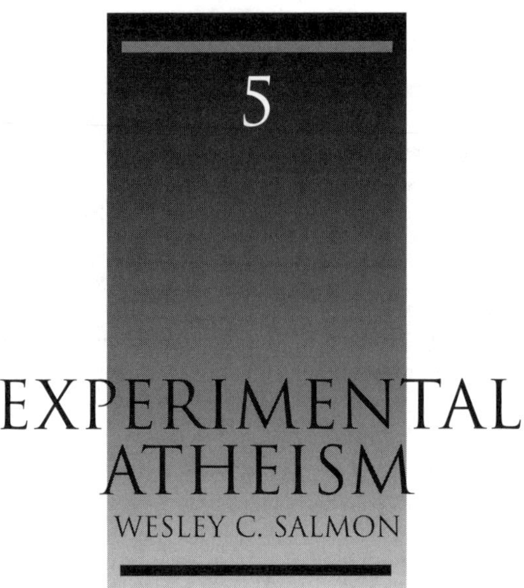

5

EXPERIMENTAL ATHEISM

WESLEY C. SALMON

In Hume's *Dialogues Concerning Natural Religion*, Cleanthes defends a view known as "experimental theism"—the thesis that the existence of an intelligent creator of the cosmos can be rendered highly probable in the light of empirical evidence. As the *Dialogues* proceed, Philo mercilessly attacks Cleanthes's version of the design argument, the chief pillar of his experimental theism. In the end—so I argued in "Science and Religion: A New Look at Hume's *Dialogues*"[1]—Philo's arguments are so powerful that they not only undermine the theistic claim, but even go so far as to render the *non*-existence of an intelligent creator highly probable. This result might be labeled "experimental atheism."

Professor Nancy Cartwright, in her comment[2] on my Bayesian analysis of the *Dialogues*, argues that my approach is too exclusively inductive and insufficiently experimental. As she points out, "it is very difficult to assess the probabilities inductively, for there are so few cases on whose origins the theist and the anti-theist can agree."[3] I urged that atoms, molecules, stars, and galaxies are instances of order arising from non-intelligent forces operating on randomly distributed constituents; the theist, obviously, denies that they constitute such instances. What are we to do in the face of an impasse of this sort? She offers a helpful and constructive suggestion, namely, that we can resort to controlled experiments:

> . . . in a controlled experiment it is possible to deliberately set things up so that the initial arrangement of parts is unplanned. We could, for instance, shake the parts in a box, or label them by a random number generator. There is no doubt what the outcome would be. The probability of getting a bunch of gears shaken together in a box to come out in a fine adjustment to any end whatever is as near zero as can be.[4]

I do not dispute this conclusion. Recognizing that the age of the universe in seconds is of the order of 10^{17}, and that the number of possible arrangements of a standard deck of cards is 52! (approximately 8×10^{67}), we see that it is overwhelmingly unlikely that such a deck, randomly shuffled each second since the beginning of time, would come out in some predesignated order (such as the standard order beginning with the ace of spades, king of spades, etc., down to the deuce of clubs). Much less do I suppose that unassembled parts of a fine watch, shaken in a box since the early history of the world, would by chance be assembled into a working timepiece. Even if, as Cartwright suggests, the parts were shaken "a million times for 12 billion years at a time,"[5] I would not expect to find a finished watch.

But I did not claim that watches result from unintelligent causes; many kinds of clearly recognizable artifacts are known to be produced only by intelligent design. I rested my case on things like atoms and molecules, stars and galaxies. Let us, therefore, contemplate the *relevant* sort of experiment. Take a container; place within it a large number of oxygen atoms, and twice as many hydrogen atoms. Shake well. Pass an electric spark through the container. Regardless of the initial situations of the atoms, a vast number of water molecules will be formed. Better still, take a plasma consisting of many protons and many electrons, at a temperature above 4000°K. Let it cool. As the kinetic energies of the particles fall below the energy of ionization of a hydrogen atom, hydrogen atoms will form. It makes little difference what the initial positions of the individual particles may be; as they move around randomly proton will repel proton, electron will repel electron, but a proton will readily attract an electron, and they will fall into the orderly configuration which constitutes a hydrogen atom. As long as the temperature remains low enough, these atoms will be stable. As the cooling continues, hydrogen molecules will be formed.

I would be inclined to suggest, on the basis of our best current cosmological knowledge, that a situation not altogether unlike the foregoing thought experiment actually obtained at an early stage in the history of the universe. Since, according to reasonable current estimates, about 80 percent of the matter in the universe consists of hydrogen atoms, the number of instances of this sort of orderly configuration arising out of conditions of disorder is prodigious to say the least.

There may, perhaps, be some temptation to dismiss such cosmological considerations as ill-grounded speculation. I think this move would be unjustified at the present time. In his excellent popular book, *The First Three Minutes*, Steven Weinberg comments as follows on the current state of cosmological knowledge:

> . . . the urge to trace the history of the universe back to its beginnings is irresistible. From the start of modern science in the sixteenth and seventeenth centuries, physicists and astronomers have returned again and again to the problem of the origin of the universe.
>
> However, an aura of the disreputable has always surrounded such research. . . . Throughout most of the history of modern physics and astronomy, there simply has not existed an adequate observational and theoretical foundation on which to build a history of the early universe.
>
> Now, in just the past decade, all this has changed. A theory of the early universe has become so widely accepted that astronomers often call it "the standard model." It is more or less the same as what is sometimes called the "Big Bang" theory, *but supplemented with a much more specific recipe for the contents of the universe.*[6]

This book by Weinberg provides a sound popular account of current cosmology. The technical details can be found in Weinberg's comprehensive treatise, *Gravitation and Cosmology*—especially Chapter 15, which contains discussions of the formation of everything from atoms to galaxies.[7]

I do not mean to suggest, of course, that cosmological theory is complete and unmodifiable; no body of scientific knowledge ever achieves that status. But I do suggest, quite seriously, that when one takes account of the cosmological knowledge which is available, it strongly supports "experimental atheism." The universe appears to be full of objects displaying high degrees of order whose existence can be adequately explained without recourse to intelligent design on the part of a creator. To be sure, cosmology is not an experimental science, but it is built upon physical disciplines, such as thermodynamics and quantum mechanics, which are extensively supported by experimental evidence.

One evening in March 1976, an astronomer friend, Dr. Frederic Chaffee of the Mt. Hopkins Harvard-Smithsonian Observatory, kindly took a small group of philosophers—which included Cartwright—on a tour of that facility (which is located a short distance from Tucson). Among the objects we saw that night was the nebula in Orion. Chaffee called particular attention to a group of stars in the nebula known as the Trapezium, and remarked that, in the opinion of astronomers, this is a site in which stars are being created. Indeed, as I later learned, that region of the nebula contains an object suspected of being a newly formed star.

The January 7, 1978, edition of the *Arizona Daily Star* has just come out with a story bearing the caption, "'Youngest' known star is verified." It reports that a team of astronomers at the Kitt Peak National Observatory (located a few miles west of Tucson) has recently established that the above-mentioned object is, indeed, a star. It is called "the Becklin-Neugebauer Star" in honor of the astronomers who first discovered the object in 1966. As the newspaper article goes on to say,

> According to the scientists, the massive clouds of interstellar dust throughout the universe are nurseries where stars are born. The dust and gases in the clouds—called nebulas—are pulled together by their own gravitational fields until the combination of heat and pressure triggers a spontaneous and self-sustaining fusion reaction—a star.

I do not know what more Cartwright could ask for. Not only have I cited substantial quantities of scientific information relating to the creation of ordered structures in staggering numbers—cases in which the explanation does not rely upon closely contrived special initial conditions. In addition, I have even arranged for her to observe the creation of stars!

This rejoinder should perhaps have been titled, "A Star is Born."

NOTES

1. Wesley C. Salmon, "Science and religion: A new look at Hume's *Dialogues*," *Philosophical Studies* 33 (1978): 143.
2. Nancy Cartwright, "Comments on Wesley Salmon's 'Science and Religion . . . ,'" *Philosophical Studies* 33 (1978): 177.
3. Ibid., p. 181.
4. Ibid., p. 182.
5. Ibid., p. 183.
6. Steven Weinberg, *The First Three Minutes* (New York: Basic Books, 1977), p. 4 (my emphasis).
7. Steven Weinberg, *Gravitation and Cosmology* (New York: John Wiley & Sons, 1972).

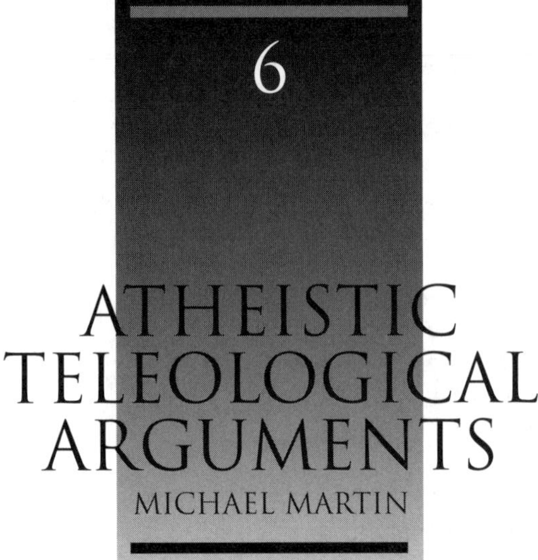

6

ATHEISTIC TELEOLOGICAL ARGUMENTS

MICHAEL MARTIN

As I showed in *Atheism: A Philosophical Justification*,[1] the traditional teleological argument and its various modern formulations are not sound arguments for the existence of God. However, what has not been fully appreciated is that the sort of criticisms of the traditional teleological argument developed by Hume can be used *against* the existence of an all-knowing, all-powerful, and all-good God. That is to say, Hume's arguments, if properly understood, can be used to support positive atheism in the narrow sense. In other words, they can be used to support disbelief in the existence of a theistic God. Here I develop and defend arguments of this sort. I call them atheistic teleological arguments.

SALMON'S ARGUMENT

Recall that Philo in Hume's *Three Dialogues Concerning Natural Religion* maintained that there is no strong argument from analogy from our experience to the conclusion that the universe was created out of nothing by an infinite disembodied being. A stronger argument from analogy, he says, is from our experience to the conclusion that the universe was created from preexisting material by a plurality of finite embodied gods. If we take Philo's argument seriously, it sug-

From *Atheism: A Philosophical Justification* (Philadelphia: Temple University Press, 1990), pp. 317–33 (slightly edited for this anthology).

gests that the *nonexistence* of a theistic God is supported by analogical arguments from experience.

A recent argument by Wesley Salmon can be understood as building upon this insight. Salmon uses probabilistic considerations derived from a reformulation of Philo's argument to show that the existence of God is improbable.[2] Salmon estimates these probabilities: (1) that an entity created by an intelligent agency exhibits order, (2) that an entity that is not created by an intelligent agency does not exhibit order, (3) that an entity is created by an intelligent agency, (4) that an entity is not so created, (5) that an entity exhibits order, and (6) that an entity does not. Given these estimates and Bayes's theorem, he argues that it is much more probable that an entity such as the universe whose origin is unknown was not created by an intelligent agency than that it was.

The argument, stated more formally and in greater detail, is this: Let D designate the class of objects created by an intelligent agency. Let O refer to the class of objects that exhibit order. Then

P(D,O) = the probability that an object created by an intelligent agency exhibits order.
P(~D,O) = the probability that an object not created by an intelligent agency exhibits order.
P(D) = the probability of an object created by an intelligent agency.
P(O) = the probability of an object exhibiting order.
P(~D) = the probability of an object not created by an intelligent agency.
P(O,D) = the probability that an object exhibiting order is created by an intelligent agency.
P(O,~D) = the probability that an object exhibiting order is not created by an intelligent agency.

According to Bayes's theorem:

$$P(O,D) = [P(D,O) \times P(D)] / P(O)$$
$$P(O,\sim D) = [P(\sim D,O) \times P(\sim D)] / P(O)$$

Salmon attempts to assess the various probabilities involved in this theorem. He maintains that given the incredibly large number of entities in our universe that are not the result of intelligence—galaxies, planets, atoms, molecules—P(D) is very low whereas P(~D) is very high. Further, he maintains that although P(D,O) is high, it may not be near unity. This is because intelligent design may in fact produce chaos such as one finds in war. He maintains that P(~D,O) is not negligible since biological generation and mechanical causation often produce order. Salmon argues that given this assessment, "we are in a position to say, quite confidently," that P(O,D) is very low for any unspecified entity.[3]

But Salmon maintains that this does not settle the matter in the case of the creation of the universe, since we are dealing with a single unique event. Where a unique event is at issue one should refer the case to the broadest homogeneous reference class—that is, to the broadest class that cannot be relevantly subdivided. When this is applied to the design argument, Salmon says, one must take into account the type of order that the universe exhibits and the sort of intelligent creator that theists believe the teleological argument proves. Following Philo's argument, he maintains that if one takes these considerations into account, far from improving the probability of the theists' conclusion, the situation is worsened.

For example, the creator of the universe is regarded as pure spirit, a disembodied intelligence. But in no instance in our experience has a disembodied intelligence produced order. Thus where D_i is the class of disembodied intelligences, $P(D_i) = 0$. Further, as far as our experience is concerned, order of a large magnitude is never produced by a single designer. Thus if D_s is the class of single designers and O_m is the class of extremely large objects, $P(D_s,O_m) = 0$. Since the universe is an entity with a large magnitude it is improbable that it was created by a single designer. Thus when one takes into account the particular attributes involved in the unique case of the creation of the universe, the probability that the universe was created by an intelligent being becomes vanishingly small.

Cartwright's Critique

Nancy Cartwright maintains that Salmon has begged the question in supposing that galaxies, planets, atoms, molecules, and so on are not the result of design.[4] Consequently, he cannot assume that P(D) is very low whereas P(~D) is very high. She argues that in fact it is very hard to assess these probabilities inductively since there are few cases on whose origin the theist and the atheist agree. Therefore, to determine the frequency at which ordered objects arise from a random process, she suggests a controlled experiment. For example, she suggests that we might put the parts of a watch in a box and shake the box. The probability of getting the watch together in this way is, according to Cartwright, "as near to zero as can be."[5] As Cartwright points out, atheists may argue that given billions of years there is a great likelihood that the watch would come together in this random way. But there is no way of knowing this with any confidence, she says, and it is best to use experimental results. On the basis of these results, and contrary to Salmon's claim, P(D,O) is much higher than P(~D,O).

Salmon's Retort

In a reply to Cartwright, Salmon maintains that the proposed experiment is irrelevant. He never supposed, he argues, that watches and other human artifacts could result from unintelligent causes: "I rested my case on things like atoms and molecules, stars and galaxies."[6] Salmon says that on the best cosmological knowledge, "everything from atoms to galaxies" was formed without intelligent design. Although cosmology is not an experimental science, Salmon adds, "it is built upon physical disciplines, such as thermodynamics and quantum mechanics, which are extensively supported by experimental evidence."[7]

Assessment of the Debate

Has Salmon answered Cartwright's charge that he has begged the question? What does it mean to beg the question? As this expression is usually understood, to beg the question is to assume what one is supposed to prove. Salmon was out to show that it is probable that the universe was not designed by an intelligent being, and he assumed in his premises that atoms, molecules, and galaxies were not the result of intelligent design. This is not what he was out to prove unless one supposes that the universe is nothing more than atoms, molecules, and galaxies. But it is not clear that Salmon assumes this. At the very least, Cartwright's criticism is mislabeled. Cartwright can be understood, however, as simply saying that some of Salmon's premises are now unjustified and could only be justified by experimental evidence that is all but impossible to acquire. But Salmon provides indirect experimental evidence from scientific cosmology to support the premises that Cartwright questioned. Unless Cartwright finds problems with this evidence it would seem not only that no question has obviously been begged but that the disputed premises have a good degree of empirical support.[8] Given these premises, it is improbable that the universe was created by an intelligent being.

Furthermore, even if Salmon has begged the question in assuming that atoms, molecules, and galaxies are not the result of an intelligent agency, or if at least he has not provided enough support for this assumption, his arguments that turn on the special properties of the universe and the alleged creator of this universe would not be affected. Recall that he maintained:

$$P(D_i) = 0$$
$$P(D_s,O_m) = 0$$

It is difficult to see that any question has been begged or why these propositions are not justified by our experience. Experience surely teaches that there are no disembodied beings. As Salmon puts it: "In no instance within our experience . . . has a disembodied intellect produced any kind of artifact, whether or not it might have exhibited any order. Indeed, since disembodied intelligence has never operated in any fashion, to the best of our knowledge, we must conclude from experience that for such an intelligence," $P(D_i) = 0$, and $P(D_i,O)$ is simply undefined.[9]

Furthermore, experience teaches that the agency of a single being does not produce extremely large objects with order; that is, $P(D_s,O_m) = 0$. Substituting in Bayes's theorem we obtain the following results: $P(O,D_i)$ is undefined and $P(O_m,D_s) = 0$. In terms of our experience, then, the probability that a unique disembodied being created the universe is "as near to zero as can be." $P(O_m,D_s) = 0$ yields this result when substituted in Bayes's theorem, and $P(D_i) = 0$ yields this directly without need of substitution.

I conclude, therefore, that unless a better refutation is offered, Salmon's argument gives good grounds for supposing that God did not create the universe.

EXPANSION OF THE ARGUMENT

If Salmon's arguments concerning the unique properties of God are restated and expanded, they provide a powerful inductive case for positive atheism in the narrow sense.[10] The theistic God is an all-powerful, all-knowing, all-good, disembodied person who created the universe out of nothing. If it can be shown that, in the light of the evidence, such a being is improbable, then disbelief that the theistic God exists is justified. Consequently, positive atheism in the narrow sense is justified.

The general form an expanded argument takes is this:

(1) In terms of our experience, created entities of kind K that have been examined are always (or almost always, or usually) created by a being (or beings) with property P.
(2) The universe is a created entity.
(2a) If the universe is a created entity, it is of kind K.

[Probably]
(3) The universe was created by a being with property P.
(4) If the theistic God exists, then the universe was not created by a being with property P.

---

(5) Therefore, the theistic God does not exist.

The first part of the argument takes the form of an acceptable inductive argument. The inference from premises (1), (2), and (2a) to the conclusion (3)—sometimes called a predictive inference—moves from a property shared by all or most of the examined members of a class to some unexamined member that has this property. Premises (1), (2), and (2a) do not entail (3), they only make (3) probable. On the other hand, (3) and (4) do entail (5). Nevertheless, since (3) is only probable and it is one of the premises used in the derivation of (5), (5) is not established with certainty. Premise (1) is established by empirical observation. That is, in all cases that we have observed, created entities of a certain kind are created by a being or beings with certain properties. Premise (2) is assumed by theists. Premise (2a) is justified unless we have independent evidence to suppose that the universe should not be classified as an entity of type K. Premise (4) is all analytic truth; given our usual understanding of 'God', it is true by definition. Let us now consider some instantiations of this argument.

The Argument from Embodiedness

As we have seen, theists believe that God is a disembodied person and that He created the universe.[11] Some people have questioned whether the concept of a disembodied person is meaningful and, if it is, whether it is coherent. In the present argument I assume that the concept is both meaningful and coherent. It maintains that it is unlikely that a being who is disembodied created the universe, and since this is unlikely, it is unlikely that God exists.

The argument proceeds as follows:

(1) In terms of our experience, all created entities of the kinds that we have so far examined are created by one or more beings with bodies. [Empirical evidence]
(2) The universe is a created entity. [Supposition]
(2a) If the universe is a created entity, then it is of the same kind as the created entities we have so far examined. [Empirical evidence]

[Probably]
(3) The universe was created by one or more beings with bodies. [From (1), (2), and (2a) by predictive inference]
(4) If the theistic God exists, then the universe was not created by a being with a body. [Analytic truth]

---

(5) Therefore, the theistic God does not exist. [From (3) and (4) by modus tollens]

Since premises (2) and (4) seem unproblematic and the deductive inference from (3) and (4) to (5) seems uncontroversial, let us concentrate on premises (1) and (2a) and the inference from (1), (2), and (2a) to (3).

Consider premise (1). What possible objections could there be to this premise? One objection that could be raised is that premise (1) begs the question against theism by assuming what needs to be proved: that if the universe was created, it was not created by a being without a body. It may be said that this is already assumed in premise (1), for it is assumed that all created entities are created by one or more beings with bodies. However, this objection is mistaken. Premise (1) does not assume that all created entities are created by one or more beings with bodies.

It simply says that, as far as we can tell from our experience, all created entities of the kinds we have so far examined are created by one or more beings with bodies.

There might be cases for which there is no evidence as to whether some entity is created by some being or beings. Perhaps in the case of living organisms we do not have this kind of evidence. Perhaps this is also true in the case of stars and atoms. Then again, taking into account Salmon's retort to Cartwright, perhaps we do. For the purpose of the argument this need not be decided. What *is* clear is that in all uncontroversial cases of created objects, these were created by one or more beings with bodies. Or to put it in a slightly different way, we know of no cases where an entity is created by one or more beings without bodies.

Our experience does not rule out the possibility of an entity created by a disembodied being. Indeed, some of the entities we see every day may be of that sort. But we have no experience to support the belief that there are such entities. We have seen created entities that are large, old, complex, and so on that are created by one or more beings with bodies. We have not seen any created entities that are large, beautiful, difficult to understand, and so on that are created by a disembodied entity or entities. The universe is large, old, complex, and so on. We cannot observe whether it is created by one or more beings with or without bodies. But from the evidence we do have, we can infer that if it was created, it was probably created by one or more beings with bodies. Thus there is no reason to suppose that the question has been begged. We do not *assume* that the universe was created by one or more beings with bodies. We *infer* this from the available evidence.

It may also be objected that premise (2a) is dubious, and therefore the argument fails. The universe, it is said, is unique; it is one of a kind. Consequently, it is a mistake to put it in the same class as other created objects. For example, the universe is infinitely larger, older, and more complex than any created object we have ever experienced. Because of these differences, we have no right to assimilate the universe to the kind of created object that we normally experience.

What reason is there to suppose that the vast size, age, or complexity of the universe is relevant? There does not seem to be any evidence supporting this view. For example, as we examine larger and larger entities that we know are created, we do *not* find that more and more of them are created by beings that are disembodied. In fact, as far as our evidence is concerned, the size of the created object is irrelevant. All created objects from the smallest (a pinhead) to the largest (a battleship or a city) are created by beings with bodies. Similar points can be made about age and complexity. As far as our experience is concerned, neither the age nor the complexity of a created object is relevant to whether it is created by a being that is disembodied. Indeed, as far as our experience is concerned, no property of a created thing is relevant to whether it is created by a disembodied entity. No matter what kinds of things known to be created we have examined, none of them is known to be created by a disembodied entity. We must conclude that this objection does not show that (2a) is a dubious premise.

Finally, it may be argued that the inductive inference from (1), (2), and (2a) to (3) is weak in that the sample on which it is based is relatively small. For most of the objects we experience in our lives, we do not know if they are created or not. For all we know, atoms, molecules, stars, living organisms, and grains of sand may be created objects. Relative to this class, the class of objects that we know to be created is small. Yet it is this latter class that our inference is based on. If, for example, we had knowledge of whether atoms, molecules, stars, living organisms, and grains of sand were created, our sample might well give us good grounds for concluding that the universe is a created object. But we do not.

As Salmon has argued, scientific theory and evidence strongly support the view that entities such as stars and molecules are not created. But let us suppose that such evidence and theory do not exist. We must base our rational beliefs on the available evidence, which indicates that in all noncontroversial cases of objects known to be created, these objects were treated by beings with a body. Our sample would be changed if new evidence came to light, and our present belief would not be rational in relation to this enlarged sample. Yet this is irrelevant to our present situation. Our sample as it stands is large and varied. It consists of literally billions of known created entities that have not been created by a disembodied being or beings and contains no known created entity that has been created by a disembodied being or beings. Furthermore, it contains evidence of all the various kinds of known created entities. It is surely irrelevant that the sample would be larger or more varied if, for example, we knew that atoms, molecules, stars, living organisms, and grains of sand were created and if these were included in it. The larger sample might give us more confidence in any inference made on its basis, but it would not show that an inference made on the basis of a smaller and less varied sample was unreliable.

Since the argument from embodiedness has the form of a strong inductive argument, the premises are well supported, and objections to it can be met, we conclude that it is a strong argument for the nonexistence of the theistic God.

The Argument from Multiple Creators

Theism is a monistic view in that God and not a plurality of supernatural beings is said to have created the universe. Yet our experience indicates that all large and complex entities are created by a group of beings working together. Although we have no direct experience of the universe's being created by a group of beings, from our experience one should infer inductively that if the universe is a created entity, it was created by a group of beings. But if so, then the existence of a theistic God is unlikely. The argument can be stated more formally as follows:

(1) In terms of our experience, all large and complex created entities of the

kinds that we have so far examined are created by a group of beings working together. [Empirical evidence]

(2) The universe is a created entity. [Supposition]

(2a) If the universe is a created entity, then it is a large and complex created entity of the same kind as some of the created large and complex entities we have so far examined. [Empirical evidence]

[Probably]

(3) The universe was created by a group of beings working together. [From (1), (2), and (2a) by predictive inference]

(4) If the theistic God exists, then the universe was not created by a group of beings working together. [Analytic truth]

---

(5) Therefore, the theistic God does not exist. [From (3) and (4) by modus tollens]

Presumably the same sort of objections that just were discussed in relation to the argument from embodiedness could be raised against this argument, and they can be disposed of in exactly the same way. For example, it may be argued that the universe is unique; it is infinitely larger and more complex than any known created object. Consequently, it cannot be classified with the known created entities that are large and complex. But why should the universe's infinitely greater size and complexity make any difference? Indeed, as far as experience is concerned, the larger and more complex a created entity becomes the greater the likelihood that it was created by a group of beings working together. The largest and most complex created entities—cities, battleships, hydroelectric plants, interstate highway systems—are in all cases created by many individuals working together. In general, the larger and more complex the entity, the more beings are involved in its creation. Thus the vastness and complexity of the universe would show not the inappropriateness of the argument from multiple creators but that its conclusion is even better supported than one might have supposed. This conclusion about the number of beings involved in the creation of large and complex entities is supported also by a large and varied sample. We have found that large and complex created objects are created by multiple beings in numerous cases and in a wide variety of circumstances—for example, the pyramids and Hoover Dam. It seems to be true no matter what the object is made of, no matter what the moral views of the participants, no matter what the technology of the creators.

We must conclude, then, that there is strong inductive reason to suppose that if the universe was created, it was created by multiple beings and, consequently, that the theistic God does not exist.

The Argument from Apparent Fallibility

In our observation of created objects we sometimes notice what appear to be mistakes and errors. It usually turns out that these are the result of the fallibility of the creator or creators. The universe also appears to have mistakes and errors. If it is a created object, chances are that any and all of its creators are fallible. But if the creator of the universe is fallible, then God does not exist, since God is infallible and the creator of the universe. The argument, stated more formally, is as follows:

(1) In terms of our experience, most seeming errors or mistakes in the kinds of created entities we have so far examined are the result of the fallibility of one or more creators of the entities. [Empirical evidence]
(2) The universe is a created entity. [Supposition]
(2a) If the universe is a created entity, then it is an entity of a kind we have so far examined, with seeming errors or mistakes. [Empirical evidence]

[Probably]
(3) The seeming errors or mistakes in the universe are the result of the actions of a fallible being or beings. [From (1), (2), and (2a) by predictive inference]
(4) If the theistic God exists, then the seeming errors or mistakes in the universe are the results of the actions of a being who is infallible. [Analytic truth]

---

(5) Therefore, the theistic God does not exist. [From (3) and (4) by modus tollens]

Consider premise (1). This is well confirmed by our experience. For example, we are told that a recently constructed building has poor ventilation; we notice that getting the spare tire out of the trunk in our new car is awkward because of the way the trunk is constructed; we read about a new city in Brazil that has been constructed with inadequate sanitation facilities for the estimated population.

Sometimes, of course, we are mistaken in our judgments about what is an error. The evidence of poor ventilation may stem from our failure to understand how the new system works. The city in Brazil may have adequate sanitation facilities despite reports. Our mistaken suppositions about errors are usually corrected as we become acquainted with the created objects. Indeed, it would be most unusual if the misapprehension persisted after a few years of acquaintance. Moreover, whatever the problems with the created entity, we usually discover that they result from the fallibility of the creator or creators. For example, the failure of the architects of the building to anticipate certain factors resulted in poor circulation of air; the automotive engineers did not foresee that building the trunk in a certain way would make it awkward to remove the spare tire; the city planners made errors in their calculations.

Sometimes, of course, we find that the problem was anticipated, yet there was a compelling reason for creating the object in that way. For example, the automotive engineers built the trunk in a certain way, knowing it would be awkward to remove a tire, because it was much cheaper to do so. If this is not so, we can usually tell. For example, we reason that if the trunk was built in this way to save money, we can expect that other design aspects of the automobile will reflect similar attempts at economy. But we may not find other attempts at economy. Moreover, there may be other reasons to suppose that economy was not an issue. For example, we may also estimate that getting a tire out of the trunk could have been made much easier without any more expense by raising one part of the trunk and lowering another. We could be wrong in our reasoning, but experience teaches that we usually are not. What appear to be mistakes because of the fallibility of the creators of objects are usually just that.

If the universe is a created entity, it contains what appear to be errors or mistakes of its creator or creators. For example, there appear to be great inefficiencies in the process of evolution: some of the organs of animals have no apparent function; some organisms seem to have no function in the ecological whole. There are apparent errors also in the genetic endowment of certain organisms: for example, because of genetic deficiencies, children are born blind and crippled. Our experience indicates that in most of the cases we have examined when a created entity seems to have some mistakes, the mistakes are due to the fallibility of the creator or creators. So it is probable that this is true of the apparent errors or mistakes found in the universe; the creator or creators of the universe are fallible. However, since God is supposed to be infallible and the creator of the universe, God does not exist.

The same sort of objections can be raised against this argument as against the argument from embodiedness and the argument from multiple creators, and they can be handled in exactly the same way. However, a new objection can be raised against this argument. It can be maintained that, to the eye of the believer, the universe does not seem as if it contains errors or mistakes. It may be said that what the nonbeliever sees as the uselessness of certain organs and organisms, a theist sees as God's mysterious but perfect handiwork.

This objection has no force, however. First, the way the universe appears to the believer is irrelevant. The question is how it appears to those who have not made up their minds and are basing their beliefs on the evidence. Second, very often the universe appears to theists to contain mistakes and errors of creation. They attempt to explain these appearances away by assumptions such as that God cannot logically create a better universe. The force of the present argument is that all these ways of explaining away the appearance of error fly in the face of the evidence. If we remain true to the evidence, we must suppose, if the universe was created at all, that what seems like an error is just that and is based on what most apparent errors are based on: the fallibility of the creator or creators.

We must therefore conclude that there is good reason to suppose that the theistic God does not exist.

The Argument from Finiteness

Our experience with entities known to be created is that they are created by beings with finite power. No matter what the object—be it small or large, old or new, simple or complex—if we know that it was created, we have found that it was created by a being or beings with finite power. If the universe is a created object, then probably it was created by a being or beings with finite power. However, since the theistic God has unlimited power and is supposed to be the creator of the universe, the theistic God does not exist. More formally, the argument can be stated in this way:

(1) In terms of our experience, all created entities of the kinds that we have so far examined were created by a being or beings with finite power. [Empirical evidence]
(2) The universe is a created entity. [Supposition]
(2a) If the universe is a created entity, then it is of the same kind as some of the created entities we have so far examined. [Empirical evidence]

[Probably]
(3) The universe was created by a being or beings with finite power. [From (1), (2), and (2a) by predictive inference]
(4) If the theistic God exists, then the universe was not created by a being with finite power. [Analytic truth]

---

(5) Therefore, the theistic God does not exist. [From (3) and (4) by modus tollens]

The same sort of objections can be raised against this argument as against the preceding ones, and they can be handled in exactly the same way. Again, however, a new objection can be raised. It can be maintained that the vast size and complexity of the universe suggest that the creator or creators of the universe would have to have infinite power. If we extrapolate to the universe from the amount of power it takes to produce the things we know are created, we can reasonably infer that the universe, if it was created, was created by a being or beings with unlimited power.

This argument is not warranted by our experience, however. Of course, one could imagine a world in which experience supports to some extent the extrapolation assumed in the argument. But even in that case it is unclear that an inference to an infinitely powerful being would be warranted. Consider a world in which the larger and more complex the entities known to have been created, the larger and more powerful the beings who created the objects. For example, in this world there might be a series of progressively larger giants. If an object of x size and complexity were found, we would discover that it was created by 20-foot-tall giants; if an object of x^2 size and complexity were found, we would discover that it was created by 200-foot-tall giants. And so on. In this world we might infer that if galaxies were created, they were created by giants of truly enormous size and power. In this world we also might infer that if the universe was created at all, then it was created by giants of even greater size and power than those that created the galaxies. However, it is unclear that we would be justified in inferring that the universe was created by giants of infinite size and power.

In any case, the world is not our world. In our world all known created objects are created by finite beings. The size of the beings seems to be roughly the same; the power of the beings is increased only through technological means. If modern creators have more power than the ancients, it is only because of advanced technology. The ancients were able to compensate for inferior technology by the use of mass labor. Given this experience we may infer that if the world was created, it was created by finite beings, perhaps with their power greatly enhanced through superadvanced technology. Any inference that goes beyond this is simply flying in the face of the evidence.

We again must conclude that if the universe was created, it was probably created by a being or beings with finite power. Consequently, the theistic God does not exist.

The Argument from Preexisting Material

In all cases of created objects that have been investigated, the created object was created on the basis of preexisting material. This is true of all the various kinds of created objects we know, small and large, old and new, complex and simple, useful and useless. We can infer then that the universe, if it was created, was probably created on the basis of preexisting material. However, although creation ex nihilo is perhaps not an essential tenet of theism, it has been claimed to be a distinctive feature of Christianity.[12] If it is, we can infer that the Christian God does not exist. The argument, stated more formally, is this:

(1) In terms of our experience, all created entities of the kinds that we have so far examined are created from preexisting material. [Empirical evidence]

(2) The universe is a created entity. [Supposition]

(2a) If the universe is a created entity, it is of the same kind as some of the created entities we have so far examined. [Empirical evidence]

[Probably]

(3) The universe was created from preexisting material. [From (1), (2), and (2a) by predictive inference]

(4) If the Christian God exists, then the universe was not created from preexisting material. [Analytic truth]

---

(5) Therefore, the Christian God does not exist. [From (3) and (4) by modus tollens]

The same sort of objections can be raised against this argument as against the preceding ones, and they can be handled in exactly the same way. So again we must conclude that there are good inductive reasons to suppose that the Christian God does not exist.

THE UNIVERSE AS A CREATED OBJECT

In all the arguments considered above I have supposed for the sake of argument that the universe is a created object. I have shown that if it is, then it probably was not created by the theistic God. But is there any reason to believe that the universe is a created entity? There is Salmon's argument against this. It may be possible, moreover, to develop an argument similar to his that does not make any assumptions about the size of the relative classes of created and noncreated objects. Wallace Matson, in a critique of the analogical version of the teleological argument, maintained that both proponents and critics of the argument assume that "the properties according to which we judge whether or not some object is an artifact, are accurate adjustments of parts and the curious adapting of means to ends."[13] However, Matson argues that this assumption is false. In actual practice an artifact is distinguished from a natural object by the evidence of machinery and the material from which the object was made.

Matson's insight can be developed in the following way. Let T be the tests that anthropologists and other scientists use to determine whether some item is a created object. We know that almost always when an object meets test T it turns out to be a created object. For example, we know almost always that when an object has certain peculiar marks on it, these have been left by a flaking tool and, consequently, that the object was created. We also know that usually when an object does not meet test T it is not a created object. As Matson points out, the tests actually used by anthropologists and other scientists are not aimed at determining whether the object serves some purpose—that is, whether it shows a fine adjustment of parts and a curious adaptation of means to ends. To illustrate his point, Matson suggests the thought experiment of separating into two piles a heap of created and noncreated objects that one has not seen before:

> Let us put in the heap a number of "gismos"—objects especially constructed for the test by common methods of manufacture, i.e., metallic, plastic, painted, machined, welded, but such that the subject of the test has never seen such things before, and they do not in fact display any "accurate adjustment of parts" or "curious adaptation of means to ends." Put into the heap also a number of natural objects which the subject has never seen. Will he have any more difficulty [in separating the objects into two piles]? He will not. The gismos go into one pile, the platypuses and tektites into the other, quite automatically.
>
> Of course one might conceivably make mistakes in this sorting procedure. And it is perhaps hazardous to predict that human visitors to another planet would be entirely and immediately successful in determining, from an inventory of random objects found on its surface, whether it was or had been the abode of intelligent beings. But space explorers would not be at a loss as to how to proceed in the investigation. They would look for evidence of machining, materials that do not exist in nature, regular markings, and the like. Presence of some of these things would be taken as evidence, though perhaps not conclusive, of artifice.[14]

Let us call the argument for the nonexistence of God developed on the basis of Matson's insight the argument from the tests of artifice and state it more formally as follows:

(1) In almost all the cases examined so far, if an object does not meet test T, it is not created. [Empirical observation]
(2) The universe does not meet test T. [Empirical observation]

[Probably]
(3) The universe is not created. [From (1) and (2) by predictive inference]
(4) If the theistic God exists, then the universe is created. [Analytic truth]

---

(5) Therefore, the theistic God does not exist. [From (3) and (4) by modus tollens]

This argument may be criticized in much the same way as the other ones considered here, and these criticisms can be just as easily answered. First, it may be maintained that it begs the question of whether the universe is created. But no question has been begged. I have not assumed that the universe is not created; I inferred this from the evidence. Second, it may be argued that premise (1) is not established. But it has been established in the same way that Salmon's assumption was established that planets, atoms, and galaxies are not created objects.

According to the best scientific theory and evidence we have, if some object is not made of certain material, does not have certain markings, and so on, it is usually not a created object. Such evidence and theory could be mistaken, but it is the best we have to go on. Third, it may be objected that the universe is unique and should not be judged by the same tests we use to judge other objects. Although it may be true that the universe is unique, there is no reason to suppose, in the light of our present evidence, that this is relevant in judging whether it is created or not. We have no reason to suppose it cannot be judged by the same criteria we use to judge whether planets, rocks, and gismos are created. Fourth, it may be urged that as our technology advances, we may be able to create objects that resemble more and more the natural objects we find in the universe. If so, then test T will no longer be a reliable method of distinguishing some created objects from noncreated objects. Whether our technology will ever advance to a stage where it would be possible to distinguish by any conceivable test, for example, a created platypus from a noncreated one seems unlikely. Of course, it is certainly likely that our technology will advance to a stage where it would be impossible to tell a created object from a noncreated one by test T. But there is every reason to suppose that our tests for an artifice will improve with our technology and that a new test will be devised that will be able to distinguish the created from the uncreated. In any case, the argument from the tests of artifice is based on our *present* evidence and may have to be given up as new evidence is gathered. This possibility does not affect the present force of the argument.

We can conclude that there is good reason to suppose that the universe is not created and, consequently, that the theistic God does not exist.

CONCLUSION

I have shown that if we take seriously the evidence at our disposal, we can infer that the theistic God does not exist. If we assume that the universe is a created object, the creator is probably not the theistic God. However, if we use the criteria for creation that are used by scientists, it is probable that the universe is not created and consequently that the theistic God does not exist.

NOTES

1. Michael Martin, *Atheism: A Philosophical Justification* (Philadelphia: Temple University Press, 1990), chap. 5.

2. Wesley C. Salmon, "Religion and Science: A New Look al Hume's *Dialogues*," *Philosophical Studies* 33 (1978): 143–76.

3. Ibid., p. 151.

4. Nancy Cartwright, "Comments on Wesley Salmon's 'Science and Religion . . . ,'" *Philosophical Studies* 33 (1978): 177–83.

5. Ibid., p. 182.

6. Wesley C. Salmon, "Experimental Atheism," *Philosophical Studies* 35 (1979): 102.

7. Ibid., p. 103.

8. Whether Salmon's arguments would be affected by recent cosmological thinking that is influenced by the anthropic principle is not clear. For a brief discussion of this principle, see Martin, *Atheism: A Philosophical Justification*, chap. 5.

9. Salmon, "Religion and Science," p. 153.

10. Students of David Hume will recognize that I do little more than expand some of the arguments in *Dialogues Concerning Natural Religion*.

11. In recent literature one theist has gone so far as to argue that God does indeed have a body. God's body is the world. See, for example, Grace Jantzen, *God's World, God's Body* (Philadelphia: Westminster Press, 1984). Apparently, this unorthodox theology is in response to arguments attempting to show that the notion of a disembodied being is incoherent. Whether Jantzen's theology succeeds we need not decide here. The problem with this position, from the perspective of the present argument, is that either the world is created or it is not. If it is created, then it is improbable that God exists, even if we grant that He has a body, since in our experience there have been no cases of beings creating their own bodies. If it is not created, then an essential aspect of theism has been given up. For a discussion of Jantzen's views, see Charles Taliaferro, "The Incorporeality of God," *Modern Theology* 3, no. 2 (1987): 179–88; Grace Jantzen, "Reply to Taliaferro," *Modern Theology* 3, no. 2 (1987): 189–92.

12. See Ronald W. Hepburn, "Religious Doctrine of Creation," *Tile Encyclopedia of Philosophy,* edited by Paul Edwards (New York and London: Macmillan and Free Press, 1967), vol. 2, p. 252.

13. Wallace I. Matson, *The Existence of God* (Ithaca: Cornell University Press, 1965), p. 129.

14. Ibid., pp. 129–30.

7

NEITHER INTELLIGENT NOR DESIGNED

BRUCE AND FRANCES MARTIN

Intelligent Design is a well-worn concept in theological argument. Since ancient times, the harmony and complexity of natural organs and systems have served as "proof" for the existence of God. In modern times before Charles Darwin (1859), William Paley (1802) was the most famous proponent of this idea. Remember the watch found on the heath? Paley supposed that, just as the discovery of such an intricate mechanical setting would be proof of a human designer, so the intricate mechanisms of the natural world, such as the human eye, prove the existence of a benevolent, divine designer. Today design has new currency in the latest anti-evolution thrust. Robert T. Pennock gives a list of its academic sponsors[1] and cites Phillip E. Johnson as "the most influential new creationist and unofficial general" of the Intelligent Design school. Johnson is a retired professor of law at the University of California at Berkeley and author of *Darwin on Trial* (1991) and *Defeating Darwinism* (1997).[2] Since the word *design* itself implies plan or purpose, it appears redundant to say "intelligent design" unless one means to imply intelligence of the highest order or divine intelligence. Despite its abstract aura, the origin of the term is undeniably religious.

By their own definition, creationists believe that the world in general, and mankind in particular, are designed and exist for a divinely ordained purpose.[3] Therefore, creationists reject the possibility that new species appear through evolution by common descent, which proceeds without a preordained purpose. They

---

From *Skeptical Inquirer* 27, no. 6 (2003): 45–49.

offer as *the* alternative Intelligent Design: the purposeful fashioning of each species by an Intelligent Designer—by implication God. Like its forerunner, creation science, this movement presumes that by undermining Darwinism they ensure Intelligent Design reigns as the sole available alternative, ignoring numerous other creation myths. A full defense of evolution is available elsewhere; our purpose in this short article is to cite some cases incompatible with Intelligent Design.

Does the real world show evidence of wise, omniscient design? To be plausible, an argument must take all the facts into account. The scientific study of biology shows us that existing species have serious flaws, belying claims of a beneficent creator. Intelligent Design spokesmen ignore vestigial organs, anatomical inefficiency, destructive mutation, the sheer wastefulness of natural processes, and the findings of molecular genetics. The constant interplay of random mutations honed by selection pressures during evolution produces many instances of poor design. What follows are a few of the less technical of the hundreds of examples of flaws noted by paleontologists and other students of evolutionary processes.

VESTIGIAL FEATURES

Darwin was not only convinced by the success of evolution in explaining numerous instances of common descent, but also by its ability to account for vestigial organs, "parts in this strange condition, bearing the stamp of inutility." These organs are of little or no current use to an organism but are probable remnants of an earlier form from which the organism evolved. Intelligent Design has no explanation for these organs. As Stephen Jay Gould has put it, "Odd arrangements and funny solutions are the proof of evolution—paths that a sensible God would never tread but that a natural process, constrained by history, follows perforce."[4] Let's look at some examples.

Cockroaches and other insects may grow an extra set of wings, as did their fossilized ancestors. Unlike most other snakes, boa constrictors possess small vestigial hind legs. Crabs possess small useless tails under their broad, flat bodies, remnants of some ancestral form. Flounders lie flat on the sea floor and in the adult both eyes are on the same side of the head, but when young the eyes are on opposite sides of the head and one moves to the other side! The earlier stage is a clue to an evolutionary path. The result is a wrenched and distorted skull.

The frigate, a non-aquatic bird, does not benefit from the webbing on its feet. In flightless birds the number of usable limbs is reduced from four to two with the presence of two non-functional limbs. Penguins possess hollow bones although they do not have the same need for minimal body weight as flying birds. Otherwise fully aquatic animals such as sea snakes, dolphins, and whales must rise to the surface to breathe air. Modern whales exhibit several non-functional vestigial traits. Fetuses of baleen whales bear teeth that are absorbed as the fetus matures; adult baleen whales do not have teeth.

Paleontologists proposed that whales had evolved from land mammals with legs, and therefore, in an example of its predictive power, the theory of evolution forecast that legs would be found on fossilized whales. In recent years the evolution of whales from now extinct land mammals has become well documented through newly found fossils from the Eocene epoch, about 50 million years ago.[5] The fossilized whales contain well-defined feet and legs. In modern adult whales, the front legs have evolved into flippers and the rear legs have shrunk so that no visible appendages appear. Hindlimbs still appear in the fetuses of some modern whales but disappear by adulthood. Externally invisible, vestigial diminished pelvic bones occur in modern adult whales. Evolution accounts for these useless vestigial elements as leftovers in the development of whales from land mammals, but they remain unaccounted for by Intelligent Design.

ANATOMICAL INEFFICIENCY

Some anatomical features that may be useful to a creature do not show efficient design one could term intelligent. They testify instead to the process of natural selection. Tails have a widely varied role in mammal bodies. They appear essential for monkeys, but the small, wispy tail in a large elephant seems useless. Tails are absent in adult apes and humans, except they appear in early embryos and are residual in the coccyx at the end of the vertebra. In some human babies a residual tail is clipped at birth.

Why should moles, bats, whales, dogs, and humans among others possess forelimbs based on the same bones that have been adapted in each case unless inherited from a common ancestor? Starting from scratch, an engineer could do a better job in each case. In pandas a normally small bone in the wrist has undergone significant enlargement and elongation so it is opposable as a thumb to the other five fingers, enabling them to strip leaves from a bamboo stalk.[6] To achieve this feat, the thumb muscles normally assigned to other functions have been rerouted. It is difficult to see how this anatomical architect would receive another commission.

The early embryos of most animals with backbones have eyes on the sides of the head. In those such as humans that develop binocular vision, during development the eyes must move forward. Sometimes this forward movement is incomplete and a baby is born with the eyes too far apart.

In mammals the recurrent laryngeal nerve does not extend directly from brain to larynx, but upon reaching the neck bypasses the larynx and drops into the chest where it loops around a lung ligament and only then retraces up to the larynx in the neck. While a one-foot length of nerve would be required for the direct route from brain to larynx in giraffes, the actual length of the doubled-back nerve from the chest of giraffes may reach twenty feet.[7]

There are many features of human anatomy we might wish were better designed. Our jaws are a little small to accept wisdom teeth that are often impacted and may need pulling. The openings of our tubes for breathing and swallowing are so close that we often choke. In humans the appendix serves no apparent purpose, but it is infection-prone, leading to inflammation and potentially fatal appendicitis. In men the testes form inside the abdomen and then drop through the abdominal wall into the scrotum, leaving two weak areas that often herniate, requiring surgery to relieve pain. Also in men the collapsible urethra passes though the prostate gland that enlarges in later life and impedes urine flow. Anatomists cite many more examples of such inefficient or useless structures, such as nipples in male primates.

Creationists often cite the human eye as a model of perfection for which Darwinism cannot account, claiming that such a complex organ could not be created by natural selection. But throughout the animal kingdom eyes have evolved many times, presumably beginning with plentiful photosensitive material followed by a stepwise incremental buildup over generations to the current organs. And the human eye is far from a model of perfection. In all vertebrate eyes the "wire" from each of three million light-sensitive retinal cells passes in front of the retina, and the collection is bundled into the optic nerve, creating a blind spot. This set-up is just the reverse of what any designer would construct: wires leading away from the backside, not light side, of the light-sensitive cells.[8] On the other hand, the wires do lead from the backside of the separately evolved eyes of the squid, octopus, and other cephalopods. Why does the designer favor squid over humans?

Instead of the efficiency and elegance one expects from Intelligent Design, we see numerous vestigial characteristics and instances of poor design. Such anomalies are both expected and accommodated by evolution. Only evolution offers a self-contained explanation of why more than 99 percent of the species that have lived on Earth are extinct. What sport does a benevolent, omniscient, and omnipotent deity receive from visiting on humans and other mammals all sorts of afflictions including parasitic bacteria, viral diseases, cancer, and genetic diseases?

These and many other examples suggest that any Intelligent Design must have been undertaken by a committee of fractious gods who could not agree. Taken at face value, invocation of Intelligent Design supports an argument for polytheism.

Of course creationists might respond to these and other examples by saying that the ways of God are mysterious and inscrutable, and that we are not wise enough to comment on the means by which he achieves his ends. If anyone offers this argument, what gives him license to propose Intelligent Design as the means by which God achieves his ends? Such a personal view is patently religious, and does not belong in any science classroom.

DESTRUCTIVE MUTATIONS

The study of molecular evolution strongly reinforces and extends the classic whole animal conclusions for evolution, while appearing whimsical at best for an Intelligent Designer. Modern evolutionary theory regards genetic mutation in the DNA of a species as the source of favorable variations that nature selects for their value in aiding the survival of an individual. But mutation occurs randomly, and in most cases the variation is harmful and results in miscarriage, deformity, or early death. Such mutations are passed from one generation to the next, sometimes lurking in recessive genes until they meet a recessive partner. One example is cystic fibrosis, which causes mucus buildup in lungs, liver, and pancreas. Sickle cell anemia results in poor blood circulation, general weakness, and when inherited from both parents, painful crises owing to sickling and clumping of the red cells. Phenylketonuria prevents infant brain development. Muscular dystrophy wastes muscles and often leaves the victim helpless. In other cases such mutations are dominant. Huntington's Disease causes gradual deterioration of brain tissue in middle age. Hypercholesterolemia causes heart disease due to cholesterol build-up. Neither intelligence nor design seems at work in producing such cruel mutations, though modern evolutionary theory fully accounts for nature's fickleness.

DISCOVERIES OF MOLECULAR GENETICS

In the genetic material, DNA, the sequence of four nucleic bases furnishes three-letter code words for the sequence of twenty amino acids that occur in proteins. Owing to similarities among the properties of some of the twenty amino acids, substitutions may occur without consequence for proper protein folding and function. For many animals it has proved possible to follow the sequences of both nucleic bases in DNA and amino acids in proteins to spot the changes that have occurred over time. One example is the blood protein hemoglobin, which is a tetramer composed of two alpha and two beta chains working in concert to bind four oxygen molecules. For the beta chain of hemoglobin, the number of amino acid differences compared to that in normal adult humans of 146 amino acids appears in parentheses after the listed animal: gorilla (1), gibbon (2), rhesus monkey (8), dog (15), horse and cow (25), mouse (27), chicken (45), frog (67), and lamprey (125).[9] Clearly, species more closely related to man have fewer differences from humans in their hemoglobin. Since each amino acid substitution requires millions of years to occur, a time scale for branching descent from a common organism according with evolutionary theory is more probable than creation by an Intelligent Designer.

The known library of DNA and protein sequences is now so huge that numerous comparisons between organisms are possible. If evolution had not already been elaborated by Darwin, we would be led to it by the more recent results of substitutions in molecular sequences. Many amino acid substitutions result in inactive mutant proteins that are not further elaborated by the organism, if it survives the mutation. On the other hand, many substitutions do not impair function and result in amino acid sequence variation of a functional protein, as in the example of the beta chain of hemoglobin above. Furthermore, in humans there are more than 100 amino acid substitutions in the 146-amino-acid beta chain of normal adult human hemoglobin that still yield a functional protein, and most carriers are unaware that they bear a hemoglobin variant. On the other hand, the substitution of only the third amino acid in the beta chain of human hemoglobin gives rise to an aberrant hemoglobin that aggregates within and produces sickling of the red cell with consequent reduced oxygen-carrying capability. This kind of trial-and-error probing involving numerous inter- and intra-species amino acid substitutions has evolution written all over it; it is very difficult to ascribe any design or anything intelligent to this process.

HUMAN NATURE

Is it any more than an overweening human ego that proposes Intelligent Design for such a poorly designed creature? In this egoism, creationists confirm in a perverse way that they have great difficulty rising above their animal origins. It is by reducing influence of ego that the nobler aspects of human nature emerge in humanistic values, values which have been appropriated by some religions.

Of course, evolutionary history fails to induce the warm and fuzzy feeling inspired by Intelligent Design. People would rather believe in a benevolent creator who cares for them. Evolution offers no mercy for the individual or species that lack the traits enabling them to compete in the struggle for food or adapt to changing environments. Fossil evidence shows the number of species that have failed these trials. An Intelligent Designer would create only successful species, but evolutionary theory can account for the many unsuccessful ones. If Intelligent

Design fails so badly to account for the real world, aside from the emotional appeal of a wise providence, is there any justification for its continued promotion?

ADDENDUM: THE LAW OF EVOLUTION

We end with a comment on the status of evolution—as fact, "just a theory," or something in between. In the physical sciences there are many observations or facts that have given rise to generalizations: two of these are the law of conservation of matter and the law of definite proportions (which states that when two or more elements combine to form a compound they do so in definite proportions by weight). The statements of facts and their convenient generalization to laws are expressed in terms of macroscopically observable and weighable quantities. The overarching explanation for these laws is achieved in atomic theory, which is expressed in terms of invisible atoms and molecules. No one thinks that atomic theory is "just a theory," for it possesses extraordinary explanatory power and provides the context in which many of the conveniences of our civilization depend. Thus we proceed from many observations or facts to their generalization in terms of laws, both levels macroscopic, to a theory expressed in terms of invisible entities.

If we now apply this scheme to biology, we see that the concept of evolution is at the law level, as it summarizes the results of a large number of observations or facts about organisms. The analogous theory is natural selection or other means by which evolution is achieved. Unknown nearly 150 years ago to Darwin, explanations of macroscopic evolution in terms of microscopic genes and molecular sequences of nucleic bases in DNA are known to us. Placing the concept of evolution at the law level clarifies its status; it is not a theory.

In contrast, the premise of Intelligent Design fails to meet even the most fundamental elements of rational inquiry. By being able to account for everything by divine edict, Intelligent Design explains nothing.

NOTES

1. R. T. Pennock, *Tower of Babel* (Cambridge, MA: MIT Press, 1999), p. 29.

2. Phillip E. Johnson, *Darwin on Trial* (Downers Grove, IL: InterVarsity Press, 1991), and *Defeating Darwinism by Opening Minds* (Downers Grove, IL: InterVarsity Press, 1997).

3. R. T. Pennock, *Intelligent Design Creationism and Its Critics* (Cambridge, MA: MIT Press, 2001).

4. S. J. Gould, *The Panda's Thumb* (New York: W. W. Norton, 1980); Gould in Pennock, *Intelligent Design*, p. 670.

5. K. Wong, "The Mammals That Conquered the Seas," *Scientific American* 286, no. 5 (May 2002): 70–79.

6. Gould, *The Panda's Thumb*; Gould in Pennock, *Intelligent Design*, p. 669.

7. K. C. Smith in Pennock, *Intelligent Design*, pp. 724–25.

8. R. Dawkins, *The Blind Watchmaker* (New York: W. W. Norton, 1987).

9. N. A. Campbell, *Biology* (Menlo Park, CA: Benjamin/Cummings, 1987).

8

THE IMPROBABILITY OF GOD

RICHARD DAWKINS

Much of what people do is done in the name of God. Irishmen blow each other up in his name. Arabs blow themselves up in his name. Imams and ayatollahs oppress women in his name. Celibate popes and priests mess up people's sex lives in his name. Jewish *shohets* cut live animals' throats in his name. The achievements of religion in past history—bloody crusades, torturing inquisitions, mass-murdering conquistadors, culture-destroying missionaries, legally enforced resistance to each new piece of scientific truth until the last possible moment—are even more impressive. And what has it all been in aid of? I believe it is becoming increasingly clear that the answer is absolutely nothing at all. There is no reason for believing that any sort of gods exist and quite good reason for believing that they do not exist and never have. It has all been a gigantic waste of time and a waste of life. It would be a joke of cosmic proportions if it weren't so tragic.

Why do people believe in God? For most people the answer is still some version of the ancient Argument from Design. We look about us at the beauty and intricacy of the world—at the aerodynamic sweep of a swallow's wing, at the delicacy of flowers and of the butterflies that fertilize them, through a microscope at the teeming life in every drop of pond water, through a telescope at the crown of a giant redwood tree. We reflect on the electronic complexity and optical perfection of our own eyes that do the looking. If we have any imagination, these things drive us to a sense of awe and reverence. Moreover, we cannot fail to be

From *Free Inquiry* 18, no. 3 (Summer 1998): 6–9.

struck by the obvious resemblance of living organs to the carefully planned designs of human engineers. The argument was most famously expressed in the watchmaker analogy of the eighteenth-century priest William Paley. Even if you didn't know what a watch was, the obviously designed character of its cogs and springs and of how they mesh together for a purpose would force you to conclude "that the watch must have had a maker: that there must have existed, at some time, and at some place or other, an artificer or artificers, who formed it for the purpose which we find it actually to answer; who comprehended its construction, and designed its use." If this is true of a comparatively simple watch, how much the more so is it true of the eye, ear, kidney, elbow joint, brain? These beautiful, complex, intricate, and obviously purpose-built structures must have had their own designer, their own watchmaker—God.

So ran Paley's argument, and it is an argument that nearly all thoughtful and sensitive people discover for themselves at some stage in their childhood. Throughout most of history it must have seemed utterly convincing, self-evidently true. And yet, as the result of one of the most astonishing intellectual revolutions in history, we now know that it is wrong, or at least superfluous. We now know that the order and apparent purposefulness of the living world has come about through an entirely different process, a process that works without the need for any designer and one that is a consequence of basically very simple laws of physics. This is the process of evolution by natural selection, discovered by Charles Darwin and, independently, by Alfred Russel Wallace.

What do all objects that look as if they must have had a designer have in common? The answer is statistical improbability. If we find a transparent pebble washed into the shape of a crude lens by the sea, we do not conclude that it must have been designed by an optician: the unaided laws of physics are capable of achieving this result; it is not too improbable to have just "happened." But if we find an elaborate compound lens, carefully corrected against spherical and chromatic aberration, coated against glare, and with "Carl Zeiss" engraved on the rim, we know that it could not have just happened by chance. If you take all the atoms of such a compound lens and throw them together at random under the jostling influence of the ordinary laws of physics in nature, it is *theoretically* possible that, by sheer luck, the atoms would just happen to fall into the pattern of a Zeiss compound lens, and even that the atoms round the rim should happen to fall in such a way that the name Carl Zeiss is etched out. But the number of other ways in which the atoms could, with equal likelihood, have fallen, is so hugely, vastly, immeasurably greater that we can completely discount the chance hypothesis. Chance is out of the question as an explanation.

This is not a circular argument, by the way. It might seem to be circular because, it could be said, *any* particular arrangement of atoms is, with hindsight, very improbable. As has been said before, when a ball lands on a particular blade of grass on the golf course, it would be foolish to exclaim: "Out of all the billions of blades of grass that it *could* have fallen on, the ball actually fell on this one. How amazingly, miraculously improbable!" The fallacy here, of course, is that the ball had to land somewhere. We can only stand amazed at the improbability of the actual event if we specify it a priori: for example, if a blindfolded man spins himself round on the tee, hits the ball at random, and achieves a hole in one. That would be truly amazing, because the target destination of the ball is specified in advance.

Of all the trillions of different ways of putting together the atoms of a telescope, only a minority would actually work in some useful way. Only a tiny minority would have Carl Zeiss engraved on them, or, indeed, *any* recognizable words of any human language. The same goes for the parts of a watch: of all the billions of possible ways of putting them together, only a tiny minority will tell the time or do anything useful. And of course the same goes, a fortiori, for the parts of a living body. Of all the trillions of trillions of ways of putting together the parts of a body, only an infinitesimal minority would live, seek food, eat, and reproduce. True, there are many different ways of being alive—at least ten million different ways if we count the number of distinct species alive today—but, however many ways there may be of being alive, it is certain that there are vastly more ways of being dead!

We can safely conclude that living bodies are billions of times too complicated—too statistically improbable—to have come into being by sheer chance. How, then, did they come into being? The answer is that chance enters into the story, but not a single, monolithic act of chance. Instead, a whole series of tiny chance steps, each one small enough to be a believable product of its predecessor, occurred one after the other in sequence. These small steps of chance are caused by genetic mutations, random changes—mistakes really—in the genetic material. They give rise to changes in the existing bodily structure. Most of these changes are deleterious and lead to death. A minority of them turn out to be slight improvements, leading to increased survival and reproduction. By this process of natural selection, those random changes that turn out to be beneficial eventually spread through the species and become the norm. The stage is now set for the next small change in the evolutionary process. After, say, a thousand of these small changes in series, each change providing the basis for the next, the end result has become, by a process of accumulation, far too complex to have come about in a single act of chance.

For instance, it is theoretically possible for an eye to spring into being, in a single lucky step, from nothing: from bare skin, let's say. It is theoretically possible in the sense that a recipe could be written out in the form of a large number of mutations. If all these mutations happened simultaneously, a complete eye could, indeed, spring from nothing. But although it is theoretically possible, it is in practice inconceivable. The quantity of luck involved is much too large. The "correct" recipe involves changes in a huge number of genes simultaneously. The correct recipe is one particular combination of changes out of trillions of equally probable combinations of chances. We can certainly rule out such a miraculous coincidence. But it *is* perfectly plausible that the modern eye could have sprung from something almost the same as the modern eye but not quite: a very slightly less elaborate eye. By the same argument, this slightly less elaborate eye sprang from a slightly less elaborate eye still, and so on. If you assume a *sufficiently large number of sufficiently small differences* between each evolutionary stage and its predecessor, you are bound to be able to derive a full, complex, working eye from bare skin. How many intermediate stages are we allowed to postulate? That depends on how much time we have to play with. Has there been enough time for eyes to evolve by little steps from nothing?

The fossils tell us that life has been evolving on Earth for more than 3,000 million years. It is almost impossible for the human mind to grasp such an immensity of time. We, naturally and mercifully, tend to see our own expected lifetime as a fairly long time, but we can't expect to live even one century. It is 2,000 years since Jesus lived, a time span long enough to blur the distinction between history and myth. Can you imagine a million such periods laid end to end? Suppose we wanted to write the whole history on a single long scroll. If we crammed all of Common Era history into one meter of scroll, how long would the pre–Common Era part of the scroll, back to the start of evolution, be? The answer is that the pre–Common Era part of the scroll would stretch from Milan to Moscow. Think of the implications of this for the quantity of evolutionary change that can be accommodated. All the domestic breeds of dogs—Pekingeses, poodles, spaniels, Saint Bernards, and Chihuahuas—have come from wolves in a time span measured in hundreds or at the most thousands of years: no more than two meters along the road from Milan to Moscow. Think of the quantity of change involved in going from a wolf to a Pekingese; now multiply that quantity of change by a million. When you look at it like that, it becomes easy to believe that an eye could have evolved from no eye by small degrees.

It remains necessary to satisfy ourselves that every one of the intermediates on the evolutionary route, say from bare skin to a modern eye, would have been favored by natural selection; would have been an improvement over its predecessor in the sequence or at least would have survived. It is no good proving to ourselves that there is theoretically a chain of almost perceptibly different intermediates leading to an eye if many of those intermediates would have died. It is sometimes argued that the parts of an eye have to be all there together or the eye won't work at all. Half an eye, the argument runs, is no better than no eye at all. You can't fly with half a wing; you can't hear with half an ear. Therefore there can't have been a series of step-by-step intermediates leading up to a modern eye, wing, or ear.

This type of argument is so naive that one can only wonder at the subconscious motives for wanting to believe it. It is obviously not true that half an eye is useless. Cataract sufferers who have had their lenses surgically removed cannot see very well without glasses, but they are still much better off than people with no eyes at all. Without a lens you can't focus a detailed image, but you can avoid bumping into obstacles and you could detect the looming shadow of a predator.

As for the argument that you can't fly with only half a wing, it is disproved by large numbers of very successful gliding animals, including mammals of many different kinds, lizards, frogs, snakes, and squids. Many different kinds of tree-dwelling animals have flaps of skin between their joints that really are fractional wings. If you fall out of a tree, any skin flap or flattening of the body that increases your surface area can save your life. And, however small or large your flaps may be, there must always be a critical height such that, if you fall from a tree of that height, your life would have been saved by just a little bit more surface area. Then, when your descendants have evolved that extra surface area, their lives would be saved by just a bit more still if they fell from trees of a slightly greater height. And so on by insensibly graded steps until, hundreds of generations later, we arrive at full wings.

Eyes and wings cannot spring into existence in a single step. That would be like having the almost infinite luck to hit upon the combination number that opens a large bank vault. But if you spun the dials of the lock at random, and every time you got a little bit closer to the lucky number the vault door creaked open another chink, you would soon have the door open! Essentially, that is the secret of how evolution by natural selection achieves what once seemed impossible. Things that cannot plausibly be derived from very different predecessors *can* plausibly be derived from only slightly different predecessors. Provided only that there is a sufficiently long series of such slightly different predecessors, you can derive anything from anything else.

Evolution, then, is theoretically *capable* of doing the job that, once upon a time, seemed to be the prerogative of God. But is there any evidence that evolution actually has happened? The answer is yes; the evidence is overwhelming. Millions of fossils are found in exactly the places and at exactly the depths that we should expect if evolution had happened. Not a single fossil has ever been found in any place where the evolution theory would not have expected it, although this *could* very easily have happened: a fossil mammal in rocks so old that fishes have not yet arrived, for instance, would be enough to disprove the evolution theory.

The patterns of distribution of living animals and plants on the continents and islands of the world is exactly what would be expected if they had evolved from common ancestors by slow, gradual degrees. The patterns of resemblance among animals and plants is exactly what we should expect if some were close cousins, and others more distant cousins to each other. The fact that the genetic code is the same in all living creatures overwhelmingly suggests that all are descended from one single ancestor. The evidence for evolution is so compelling that the only way to save the creation theory is to assume that God deliberately planted enormous quantities of evidence to make it *look* as if evolution had happened. In other words, the fossils, the geographical distribution of animals, and so on, are all one gigantic confidence trick. Does anybody want to worship a God capable of such trickery? It is surely far more reverent, as well as more scientifically sensible, to take the evidence at face value. All living creatures are cousins of one another, descended from one remote ancestor that lived more than 3,000 million years ago.

The Argument from Design, then, has been destroyed as a reason for believing in a God. Are there any other arguments? Some people believe in God because of what appears to them to be an inner revelation. Such revelations arc not always edifying but they undoubtedly feel real to the individual concerned. Many inhabitants of lunatic asylums have an unshakable inner faith that they are Napoleon or, indeed, God himself. There is no doubting the power of such convictions for those that have them, but this is no reason for the rest of us to believe them. Indeed, since such beliefs are mutually contradictory, we can't believe them all.

There is a little more that needs to be said. Evolution by natural selection explains a lot, but it couldn't start from nothing. It couldn't have started until there was some kind of rudimentary reproduction and heredity. Modern heredity is based on the DNA code, which is itself too complicated to have sprung spontaneously into being by a single act of chance. This seems to mean that there must have been some earlier hereditary system, now disappeared, which was simple enough to have arisen by chance and the laws of chemistry and which provided the medium in which a primitive form of cumulative natural selection could get started. DNA was a later product of this earlier cumulative selection. Before this original kind of natural selection, there was a period when complex chemical compounds were built up from simpler ones and before that a period when the chemical elements were built up from simpler elements, following the well-understood laws of physics. Before that, everything was ultimately built up from pure hydrogen in the immediate aftermath of the big bang, which initiated the universe.

There is a temptation to argue that, although God may not be needed to explain the evolution of complex order once the universe, with its fundamental laws of physics, had begun, we do need a God to explain the origin of all things. This idea doesn't leave God with very much to do: just set off the big bang, then sit back and wait for everything to happen. The physical chemist Peter Atkins, in his beautifully written book *The Creation*, postulates a lazy God who strove to do as little as possible in order to initiate everything. Atkins explains how each step in the history of the universe followed, by simple physical law, from its predecessor. He thus pares down the amount of work that the lazy creator would need to do and eventually concludes that he would in fact have needed to do nothing at all!

The details of the early phase of the universe belong to the realm of physics, whereas I am a biologist, more concerned with the later phases of the evolution of complexity. For me, the important point is that, even if the physicist needs to postulate an irreducible minimum that had to be present in the beginning, in order for the universe to get started, that irreducible minimum is certainly extremely simple. By definition, explanations that build on simple premises are more plausible and more satisfying than explanations that have to postulate complex and statistically improbable beginnings. And you can't get much more complex than an Almighty God!

PART 3

INDUCTIVE EVIL ARGUMENTS AGAINST THE EXISTENCE OF GOD

INTRODUCTION

This section contains new and previously published papers and a book selection presenting and defending inductive evil arguments against the existence of God. An inductive evil argument against God's existence, often called an evidential or empirical argument from evil for God's nonexistence, is an inductive argument based on the weight of the evidence relative to the widespread and horrendous evil in the world.

An inductive evil argument against God's existence takes the following general form:

1. If God exists,
   then God possesses certain attributes.
2. Based on the weight of the evidence relative to the widespread and horrendous evil in the world, God does not possess all of these attributes.
3. Therefore, God does not exist.

Here are brief summaries of the papers and the book selection contained in this section.

Quentin Smith in a 1991 paper "An Atheological Argument from Evil Natural Laws" argues that the natural law of predation, whereby some animals must savagely kill and devour other animals to survive, is probably ultimately evil and that there is a possible world, the one most similar to the actual world but lacking the law of predation, that God, if God existed, could and would have actualized. Since that possible world was not actualized, God probably does not exist. Smith then criticizes a number of possible objections, such as Richard Swinburne's theodicy that natural evils are necessary to provide the knowledge required to make moral decisions, John Hick's contention that natural evils help to establish God's epistemic distance so that faith can be freely chosen, and Alvin Plantinga's defense that natural evils are the result of and outweighed by the good of fallen angels exercising their free will.

William L. Rowe in a classic 1979 paper "The Problem of Evil and Some Varieties of Atheism" presents an evidential argument from evil for the nonexistence of God based on an instance of intense suffering in nature—a fawn burned in a forest fire that experiences a slow, agonizing death. Rowe argues that since *so far as we can see* there does not appear to be any greater good that would justify God in permitting such an instance of intense suffering, let alone a daily profusion of similar instances worldwide, there probably is no greater good that would provide such a justification, and therefore God probably does not exist.

In a 1988 paper "Evil and Theodicy," Rowe considers a case of natural evil E1 (a fawn burned in a forest fire that experiences a slow, agonizing death) and a case of moral evil E2 (a young child who is raped and brutally murdered) and investigates whether there are any goods that might justify God in permitting E1 and E2. Rowe argues that there are no goods *we know of* whose value both compensates for the disvalue of E1 and E2 and can be obtained only by permitting E1 and E2, and therefore, given this result and the fact that there is a profusion of similarly intense suffering daily in our world, it is reasonable to conclude that God probably does not exist. Finally, Rowe critically examines John Hick's soul-making theodicy to determine whether it diminishes the force of the argument and concludes that it does not.

In a 1996 paper "The Evidential Argument from Evil: A Second Look," Rowe begins by explicitly assuming that God's existence is as likely as not, employs Bayes's theorem to formulate a simpler and yet stronger version of the evidential argument, and then responds to objections raised by Stephen Wykstra and William Alston. For example, Wykstra objects to the inductive inference from "No good we know of justifies God in permitting E1 and E2" to "God does not exist" on the grounds that, just as the decisions and actions of a good parent are often beyond a child's understanding, it is as likely as not that the goods that justify God in permitting E1 and E2 are beyond human understanding. Rowe responds by drawing further on the parent analogy to argue that if the goods that justify God in permitting horrendous evils are indeed beyond human understanding then, just like a good parent with a suffering child, God would not simply remain silent but rather would make the suffering victims of horrendous evil consciously aware of God's comforting presence, love, and concern. Since many who suffer do not become consciously aware of God's comforting presence, love, and concern, the evidential argument from evil retains its force, and therefore God probably does not exist.

In a 1998 paper "Reply to Plantinga," Rowe responds to three objections raised by Alvin Plantinga to the 1996 evidential argument from evil for the nonexistence of God. The principal objection, that the evidential argument from evil is really "an argument from degenerate evidence" that employs a logical technique to misleadingly lower the probability of God, is shown by Rowe to be based on a faulty analogy.

In a 2001 paper "Skeptical Theism: A Response to Bergmann," Rowe takes on Michael Bergmann's objection to the 1996 evidential argument from evil that the use of the parent analogy to infer "No good justifies God in permitting divine silence" from "No good *we know of* justifies God in permitting divine silence" presupposes a prior rejection of the skeptical thesis "We have no good reason for thinking that the possible goods we know of are representative of the possible goods there are." Denying that the 1996 argument rejects any skeptical theses, Rowe argues that the claim that God exists and is silent in the face of all of the horrendous evil that occurs implies an inherently implausible infinite series of inabilities on the part of an omniscient, omnipotent, and omnibenevolent God, from which it still follows that God probably does not exist.

Michael Martin in a selection "An Indirect Argument from Evil" from *Atheism: A Philosophical Justification* (1990) presents an argument against the existence of God based on the general failure of all known theodicies throughout history. Since no known theodicy has been successful, probably no theodicy *will be* successful; and since probably no theodicy *will be* successful, there is *probably no justification* for God in permitting evil. Since there must be such a justification if God exists, God probably does not exist. Considering the objection that no known theodicy has been successful because God's justification for permitting widespread and horrendous evil might be beyond human understanding, Martin concedes this possibility but points out that there is no reasonable independent evidence that there *actually is* a justification beyond human understanding, and so the indirect argument from evil stands.

Thomas Metcalf in "An Argument from Non-Gratuitous Evil," a paper written in 2004 for this anthology, presents the case that, even if it is assumed that God is justified in permitting evil, an evidential argument from *justified* evil for the nonexistence of God can be formulated. Assuming that God exists and is justified in permitting all the evil that occurs, Metcalf argues that there are several good reasons to hold that God has a moral obligation to inform the victims of horrendous evil that their suffering is justified and, although it is possible that there are even better reasons unknown to us for God to remain silent, none has been presented. Given that many victims of horrendous evil do not know that their suffering is justified and that God, according to the weight of the reasons known to us, should have made this known to them, it is reasonable to conclude that God probably does not exist.

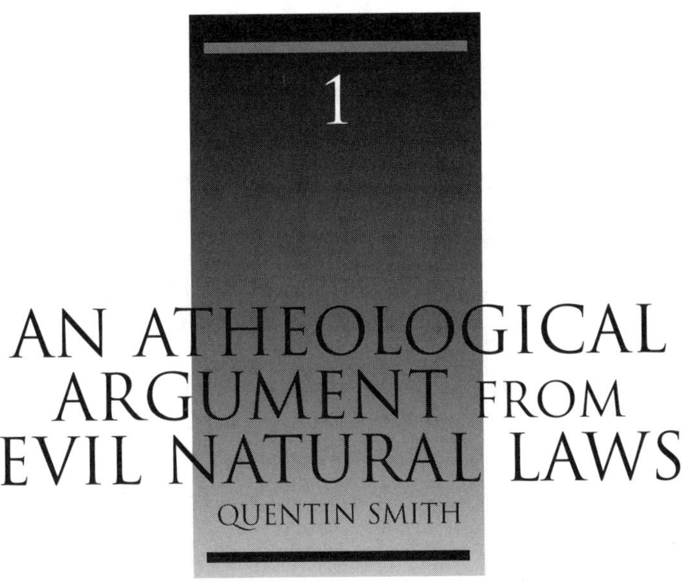

1

AN ATHEOLOGICAL ARGUMENT FROM EVIL NATURAL LAWS

QUENTIN SMITH

1. PROLOGUE

Not long ago I was sleeping in a cabin in the woods and was awoken in the middle of the night by the sounds of a struggle between two animals. Cries of terror and extreme agony rent the night, intermingled with the sounds of jaws snapping bones and flesh being torn from limbs. One animal was being savagely attacked, killed and then devoured by another.

A clearer case of a horrible event in nature, a natural evil, has never been presented to me. It seemed to me self-evident that the natural law that *animals must savagely kill and devour each other in order to survive* was an evil natural law and that the obtaining of this law was sufficient evidence that God did not exist. If I held a certain epistemological theory about "basic beliefs," I might conclude from this experience that my intuition that *there is no God co-existing with this horror* was a "basic belief" and thus that I am epistemically entitled to be an atheist without needing to justify this intuition. But I do not hold such an epistemological theory and believe that intuitive atheological beliefs, such as the one I experienced (and the corresponding intuitive theological beliefs, such as that *God is providentially watching over this gruesome event*), require justification if they are to be epistemically warranted. The following sections of this article present a justification for the atheological intuition I experienced on that dark

From *International Journal for Philosophy of Religion* 29 (1991): 159–74.

night. My justification will consist mostly in providing reasons to believe premise (3) in the following probabilistic argument:

1. God is omnipotent, omniscient, and omnibenevolent.
2. If God exists, then there exist no instances of an ultimately evil natural law.
3. It is probable that the law of predation is ultimately evil.
4. It is probable that there exist instances of the law of predation.
   Therefore, it is probable that
5. God does not exist.

2. THE DEFINITION OF AN ULTIMATELY EVIL LAW

I shall assume the Armstrong–Tooley Dretskc[1] theory that laws are relations among universals and have the form, in the simplest cases, of

(L) N(F,G),

where N stands for nomic necessitation and F and G are universals that are related by the relation of nomic necessity. (L) states that *being F* nomologically necessitates *being G*. I shall assume with Tooley (and against Armstrong) that there are uninstantiated universals. But I shall assume, in opposition to Armstrong, Tooley and Dretske, and with Kripke and Putnam,[2] that some laws are logically necessary (in Plantinga's sense of broadly logical necessity[3]; hereafter by 'logically necessary' I mean "broadly logically necessary"). Examples of logically necessary laws are the laws that water is H_2O and that tigers are animals. All the laws I discuss in this paper are cases of laws that (some) essentialists would regard as logically necessary, so I shall henceforth talk of the necessity of laws as logical. Accordingly, the laws I shall discuss have the form, in the simplest cases, of

(L′) □ (N(F,G)) (In every logically possible world, *being F* nomically necessitates *being G*.)

I shall assume, thirdly, that there is a distinction between the holding (obtaining) of a law and its instantiation. If a law □ (N(F,G)) holds but is not instantiated, then it is true both that there is nothing that is F and that for any merely possible world W and for anything x, if x is F in W, then x is G in W. Assuming Newtonian physics, the first law of motion holds but is uninstantiated; there are no bodies uninfluenced by external forces and therefore no uninfluenced bodies that continue in a state of rest or uniform motion; but if there were such bodies, they would continue in such a state.

Let us consider the law of predation. I shall call this law E, such that

(E) $\Box$ (N(F,G)),

where F is the relational property of *obtaining nourishment*, and G the relational property of *savagely killing and devouring another animal*.[4] Each possible instance of this law is an event which (assuming J. Kim's definition[5] of events) contains constituent substances and relational properties and times of the sort contained in the set

(S) {the animals x_1 and x_2, the relational property of *savagely killing*, the relational property of *obtaining nourishment*, the time t}.

The event-schema (S) is a schema of a complex event that consists of other events as proper parts. One such proper part is an event-type of the form *x_1's being nourished at t*. An event of this sort may be a tiger as exemplifying the relational property of *obtaining nourishment at time t*. Now this event, I concede, is intrinsically good; that is, this event, considered by itself (apart from its relations to other events that are good or evil) is good. And another part of an event of the sort schematized in (S) may be the less complex event consisting of a certain zebra as exemplifying the relational property of *being savagely killed at the time t*. This event, considered by itself, is evil. When I say 'considered by itself', I mean this strictly, so that the statement "the zebra's being savagely killed is good since the zebra was suffering severe agony from a broken leg and it is good that the zebra be put out of its misery" counts as considering the event *the zebra's being savagely killed at t* in relation to another event that has negative value, namely, *the zebra's suffering agony from a broken leg at t*.

Now all events of the type schematized by (S) consist of two events of the above-illustrated sorts, such that we have the true premise

6. Each possible instance of E, considered by itself, is partly good and partly evil.

Given the ethical premise

7. For any complex event A, if A is partly intrinsically good and partly intrinsically evil, then A is *as a whole* intrinsically evil if and only if its evil part outweighs its good part,

it follows that each instance of E is as a whole intrinsically evil if the negative value of the prey's being savagely killed outweighs the positive value of the predator's being nourished. But I shall not make this assumption.[6] That is, I shall not assume that each or even any instance of E is overall intrinsically evil. The argument that E is ultimately evil can be made even if it is assumed that each possible instance of E is as a whole intrinsically good.

The key notion is that of being intrinsically good but ultimately evil, which may be partially defined for laws as follows. A law L′ is overall intrinsically good but ultimately evil if the following three conditions obtain:

i. Each possible instance of L′ is overall intrinsically good.
ii. In each possible world in which L′ is instantiated, the intrinsic evil of the aggregate of the immediate and remote causes and effects of the instances of L′ outweighs the intrinsic good of the aggregate of the instances of the law in that world. (God or God's creative activity is meant to be excluded from the mentioned aggregate of causes.)
iii. In each world in which L′ is instantiated, L′'s instantiation is not necessary to prevent the occurrence of an evil whose negative value is greater than the negative value of the aggregate composed of the instances of L′ and their causes and effects.

However, I shall not assume that the law of predation meets this three-part sufficient condition of being ultimately evil. For example, I shall not assume that the aggregate of the actual instances of the law of predation is such that its overall positive value is outweighed by the negative value of the aggregate of the actual causes and effects of these instances. Indeed, I shall concede that it is actually the case that the aggregate of the causes and effects of the instances of E has an overall positive value. This concession is not far-fetched, since some of the members of this aggregate include events in human life, for any event in human life that has a cause is caused, at least remotely, by some instance of E. (A necessary causal condition of the evolution of human beings is the operation of E, assuming the necessity of origins.)

The argument that the law of predation is ultimately evil is based on a different sufficient condition of ultimate evil, a condition that has not been discussed in the literature on the problem of evil but that is nonetheless crucial to the problem. This condition has a complicated definition but it shall become clearer once I provide an illustration of it. A law L′ is overall intrinsically good but ultimately evil if the following eightfold condition is met:

i. Each possible instance of L′ is overall intrinsically good.
iii. In each world in which L′ is instantiated, L′'s instantiation is not nec-

essary to prevent the occurrence of an evil whose negative value is greater than the negative value of the aggregate composed of the instances of L′ and their causes and effects.

iv. In some or all possible worlds in which L′ is instantiated, the aggregate of the immediate and remote causes and effects of the instances of L′ is overall intrinsically good.

v. Each possible instance of L′ is partly intrinsically evil.

vi. For each intrinsically good part g of each instance of L′ (in any world W′ in which L′ is instantiated), there is a counterpart g_c of g in another world W″, such that g_c is at least as intrinsically good as g and is a part of an instance of a different law L″.

vii. Necessarily, no intrinsically evil part of e of any instance of L′ has a counterpart e_c that is a part of an instance of the mentioned law L″.

viii. Necessarily, the part of each instance of L″ other than the counterpart g_c is either intrinsically good or significantly less intrinsically evil than the evil part e of any instance of L′.

ix. There are two possible worlds W′ and W″ that satisfy (vi) and the following four conditions:
    (a) L′ is instantiated in W′ but not in W″,
    (b) L″ is instantiated in W″ and W′,
    (c) of all the worlds in which L″ but not L' is instantiated, W″ is the most similar to W', and
    (d) the positive value of the aggregate of all the causes and effects of the instances of L″ in W″ is greater than or equal to the positive value of the aggregate of all the causes and effects of the instances of L′ and L″ in W′.

I include (iv) to emphasize the distinction between the eightfold sufficient condition (i) and (iii)–(ix) and the threefold sufficient condition (i)–(iii).

The complex condition (i) and (iii)–(ix) involves the notion of a counterpart. An event x is a counterpart of an event y if the constituent substance of the event x is a counterpart of the constituent substance of the event y, and x exemplifies a property that is a counterpart of the property y exemplifies. A substance S_1 is a counterpart of a substance S_2 if S_1 has similar macroscopic properties to S_2 but some different microscopic properties, e.g., DNA structure. A property F_1 of S_1 is a counterpart of a property F_2 of S_2 if F_1 (a) is a species of the same genus of properties as F_2 and (b) F_1's exemplification by S_1 serves the same role or function in S_1's existence as F_2's exemplification by S_2 has in S_2's existence. (I do not claim this is the only way to define partially ‘counterpart’, merely that it is the only way needed for my argument.) Take the event consisting of the nourishment of a certain tiger at time t. There is some possible counterpart to the tiger that looks just like a tiger (same shape and size, striped, etc.) but which has different DNA than the tiger, such that the tiger-counterpart's DNA programs the tiger-counterpart to be nourished by vegetables rather than by meat. Given that a tiger's DNA is essential to it, these counterparts are not tigers but some other species. The tiger's property of *being nourished by meat* has its counterpart in the tiger-counterpart's property of *being nourished by vegetables*; these two properties are species of the genus *being nourished by some food* and their exemplification serves the same function or role in the lives of the tiger and tiger-counterpart (namely, that of providing chemical fuel needed to go on living).

3. THE ATHEOLOGICAL ARGUMENT

We may now proceed to the crucial premises of our atheological argument. There is some merely possible world W such that

8. For each predator that exists in the actual world, there is a vegetarian counterpart in W.
9. For each actual event g of a predator being nourished, there is an event g_c of its counterpart being nourished in W, such that g_c is at least as intrinsically good as g.
10. For each actual instance of the law E of predation, there is an instance in W of the law V of vegetation-nourishment (being nourished by a vegetable).
11. E is instantiated in the actual world but not in W and V is instantiated in both worlds; W is the world most similar to the actual world, consistent with this nomological difference.
12. Each instance of V also contains an event involving an animal *taking hold of and eating a vegetable*, and each such event is either intrinsically good or significantly less intrinsically evil than any event of a predator *savagely killing and devouring another animal.*
13. The aggregate of all causes and effects of the instances of E and V in the actual world is equal or inferior in positive value to the aggregate of all causes and effects of the instances of V in W.
14. In each world in which E is instantiated, E's instantiation is not necessary to prevent the occurrence of an evil whose negative value is greater than the negative value of the aggregate composed of the instances of E and their causes and effects.

Intuitively, (8)–(14) say that W is exactly like the actual world except that all (and not just some) animals or animal-like creatures are vegetarians. For example, in W there are counterparts to humans that are exactly like humans except that their DNA includes a strictly vegetarian blueprint. The Florence Nightingale counterpart performs her medical deeds and the Beethoven counterpart composes his symphonies, but they eat soybeans instead of pork.

But conditions (9) and (10) conceal ambiguities, since it is not clear-cut what is to count as the counterpart of any given act of nourishment. For example, is eating 5 potatoes the counterpart of eating a part of a shank of a zebra, or is perhaps eating 9 carrots the counterpart? Definitions could be provided here, e.g., in terms of a set of all properties of a given genus and function exemplified by the relevant sort of animal or animal-like creature, but a precision of this sort is not necessary for our purposes.[7]

Now, if theses (8)–(14) are true, it follows that the law of predation E is ultimately evil. For if (8)–(14) are true, then E satisfies the above-mentioned eightfold sufficient condition of being an ultimately evil law. If E is ultimately evil and is actually instantiated, then there is actually no being that is omnibenevolent, omnipotent, and omniscient. Or so it might be argued. But if this is to be argued successfully, some additional defense is needed for the theses (8)–(14). This is particularly the case for (13), which is the claim most vulnerable to attack. In the following section I shall consider and respond to some familiar objections to claims of this sort.

4. SWINBURNE, HICK, SCHLESINGER, REICHENBACH AND PLANTINGA

4.1 Richard Swinburne

It is arguable that it is implicit in Swinburne's theodicy in *The Existence of God* that it is false that

> 13. The aggregate of all causes and effects of the instances of E and V in the actual world is equal or inferior in positive value to the aggregate of all causes and effects of the instances of V in W.

Swinburne's theodicy arguably implies that instances of the law of predation causally contribute to the provision of moral agents with the knowledge necessary for morally significant action, whereas instances of a law V of vegetation-nourishment would not. Since the aggregate of all events of morally significant actions (and all other causes and effects of instances of E) outweighs in positive value the aggregate of causes and effects of the instances of V in the closest pure V-world (i.e., a world in which V but not E is instantiated), it follows that (13) is false and therefore that the law of predation is not ultimately evil. But let us examine some of the particulars in Swinburne's argument.

According to Swinburne, natural evil is morally justified by the "need for knowledge"; natural evils are logically "necessary if agents are to have the *knowledge* of how to bring about evil or prevent its occurrence"[8] and opportunities for such knowledge are outweighing goods relative to the evils. This argument, however, breaks down when it comes to instances of E, for there are no plausible candidates for "opportunities for ethically relevant knowledge" that both logically require instances of E and outweigh them in positive value. Swinburne mentions as one candidate the opportunities to learn about the potentially disastrous consequences to animals of our choices to change the environment and mutate genes; he explains that

> . . . the story of pre-human nature "red in tooth and claw" already provides some very general information crucially relevant to our possible choices. For suppose that animals had come into existence at the same time as man (e.g. 4004 B.C.) always in situations where men could save them from any suffering. Naturally it would then seem a well-confirmed theory that (either through act of God or nature) suffering never happens to animals except such as men can prevent. So men would seem not to have the opportunity to do actions which would cause suffering to later generations of animals of a subsequently unpreventable kind, or the opportunity to prevent such suffering. The story of evolution tells us that this is not so—the causation or prevention of long-term suffering is indeed within our power; such suffering can happen because it has happened. The story of pre-human evolution reveals to man just how much the subsequent fate of animals is in his hands—for it will depend on the environment which he causes for them and their genes which he may cause to mutate.[9]

The invalidity of this argument clearly appears if we isolate the relevant inferences. Swinburne infers from

15. Animals exist only in situations in which humans can prevent them from suffering.

to

16. It would seem to humans a well-confirmed theory that suffering never happens to animals except such as humans can prevent.

and from (16) to

17. It would seem to humans that they do not have the opportunity to do

actions which could cause or prevent subsequently unpreventable suffering to later generations of animals.

But (17) does not follow from (16). Imagine that the only animals that ever have existed are pets and farm animals. It would then be a well-confirmed theory that suffering never (or rarely) happens to animals except such as humans can prevent. But would it then seem that we do not have the opportunity to engage in actions that would cause or prevent subsequently unpreventable suffering to future generations of animals? Of course not. Suppose some pesticides are used in a limited area and blind all pets and farm animals in that area and cause all generations of offspring of these animals to be blind. This would provide us with knowledge of an action (use of this pesticide everywhere) that would cause unpreventable suffering (blindness) to all future generations of animals.

Swinburne also suggests that instances of E provide humans with helpful knowledge pertinent to themselves: ". . . seeing the fate of sheep, men have learnt of the presence of dangerous tigers."[10] It is also suggested that instances of E provide the higher animals with helpful knowledge about survival: "Seeing the suffering, disease, and death of others in certain circumstances, they learn to avoid those circumstances."[11] To narrow our focus to the law E let us consider only the helpful knowledge provided by instances of E; let us call this helpful knowledge *self-preservation E-knowledge*. Swinburne's remarks might suggest the following argument about self-preservation E-knowledge:

18. Self-preservation E-knowledge is an outweighing good relative to the instances of E.
19. The overall positive value of the aggregate of self-preservation E-knowledge and the instances of E (and all other causes and effects of these instances) is greater than the positive value of the aggregate of the instances of V and their causes and effects in the closest pure V-world.

Therefore

20. Premise (13) of the atheological argument is false and consequently E is not ultimately evil.

Although both (18) and (19) seem false, I shall content myself with showing that (18) is false. The idea that self-preservation knowledge gained from instances of E is an outweighing good relative to instances of E is based on the fallacious assumption that it is good that an evil of a certain type exists since its existence provides an opportunity to learn how to prevent future instances of the evil. In particular, the assumption is that "It is good that animals savagely attack, kill and devour each other and occasionally humans, so that animals and humans can learn to avoid being savagely attacked, killed and devoured on some occasions in the future." If the assumption underlying this argument were true, then it would be a sound argument that "It is good that millions of humans die agonizing deaths of cancer, since this provides humans with opportunities to learn how to prevent some people from dying of cancer in the future." This assumption is false since the opportunity to learn to prevent some evils of a certain type does not outweigh in positive value the negative value of the extant evils of this type. If it did outweigh them, we should be rejoicing in the AIDS epidemic since the instances of AIDS combined with the opportunities to learn how to prevent AIDS would result in an overall increase in the positive value in the universe.[12]

4.2 John Hick

John Hick's account of instances of E is also based in part on counterintuitive moral principles. Hick suggests that seemingly unjustified natural evils are necessary if humans are to have a natural environment that does not automatically incite faith and love of God but requires this faith and love to be freely chosen from an epistemic "distance." In Hick's words, ". . . in order for man to be endowed with the freedom in relation to God that is essential if he is to come to his Creator in uncompelled faith and love, he must be initially set at an epistemic 'distance' from that Creator. This entails his immersion in an apparently autonomous environment which presents itself to him etsi deus non daretur, 'as if there were no God.'"[13] This might suggest an argument to the effect that an environment of Hick's "soul-making" sort requires E to be instantiated, and therefore that the actual world is superior in value in the relevant respects to the closest pure V-world. But this argument fails since the instantiation of E is not necessary for the existence of an environment that seems morally ambiguous or theologically doubtful to humans. The occurrence of natural disasters that befall humans, such as plagues, wheat famines, floods, and tornadoes, is sufficient by itself to create a questionable natural environment. We are at an epistemic "distance" from God due to the sufferings and horrible deaths nature sometimes inflicts upon us, and the hundreds of millions of years of animals preying on each other before we even evolved are not needed for this "distancing."

But there is a second and more fundamental problem with Hick's theodicy; it ascribes to God the morally pernicious attitude of "speciesism," to borrow a term from Peter Singer.[14] No omnibenevolent creator would use animals as a mere means to the end of human welfare, treating them as if they had no value or rights by themselves and could be tortured with complacency on a mass scale for the sake of "spiritual benefits" to the human species. Animals are sentient creatures capable of suffering and as such are moral ends in themselves; the failure to treat them as such is a sign of selective benevolence and callousness and is inconsistent with the definition of God. If God intended to create a questionable natural environment for the human species, he could and would have done so without violating the rights of animals. (For those who hold, contra Regan,[15] that animals have no rights but that their welfare is of value, this point may be put by saying that an omnibenevolent creator could and would have created a questionable environment without callously neglecting the welfare of animals.)[16]

4.3 George Schlesinger

The "no best possible world defense" of natural evil, most thoroughly developed by Schlesinger,[17] is also inadequate since the alleged fact that there is no best possible world does not license God to create just any world. Schlesinger's argument does not show that every world creatable by God contains instances of ultimately evil natural laws, or that every creatable world without such instances is inferior in overall positive value to worlds with such instances, and thus his argument is open to the objection that a perfectly good, wise, and powerful being would have created one of the worlds devoid of such instances. Furthermore, the fact that there is no best possible world does not show that it is morally permissible to create our E-world with its massive amount of gratuitous animal evil rather than the closest pure V-world W with no E-evil but similar goods to the actual world. (By analogy, the fact that there is no best possible political system does not morally permit politicians to choose Nazism rather than some version of constitutional democracy as the actual political system.) In fact a much stronger case can be made against Schlesinger's argument, as Keith Chrzan[18] has recently demonstrated. Schlesinger's "no best possible world defense" shows only that there is no world with a maximal positive value and not that there is no world *without any natural and moral evil*; consequently, this defense fails to demonstrate that natural and moral evil is a necessary implication of creation and thus fails to explain how God's existence is compatible with the actual world.

4.4 Bruce Reichenbach

Reichenbach's argument[19] is that the possibility of natural evil is necessary for the outweighing good of rational agents making moral choices. But we can admit this consistently with maintaining that E's instantiation counts as evidence that God does not exist. It may be granted that the *possibility of natural evils of some sort* is necessary for moral choices, but denied that *instances of E* are necessary for such choices. The proposition

21. The possibility of natural evil of some sort is a necessary condition of rational agents making moral choices.

does not even entail

22. The possibility of E-evil is a necessary condition of rational agents making moral choices.

let alone

23. E-evil is a necessary condition of rational agents making moral choices.

I have argued that instances of E are not necessary for such choices in response to Swinburne and Hick. But an even stronger argument is that some initial conditions which make it *impossible* for E to be instantiated are perfectly compatible with rational agents making moral choices, and thus that (22) is also false. For example, in W, the closest pure V-world, the only living creatures are vegetarians and thus no E-evil can occur in W. Of course, a human counterpart could madly kill and then devour a rabbit in W, but he would not be nourished by it, since his DNA allows him only vegetarian nourishment, and thus this act would not be an instance of E. Thus, Reichenbach's argument fails to impugn the thesis that E is ultimately evil.[20]

4.5 Alvin Plantinga

Plantinga does not offer a theodicy but a defense. He argues that it is possible that all natural evil is due to the free activity of non-human creatures; that there is a balance of good over evil with respect to the actions of these creatures; and that there is no world God could have created which contains a more favorable balance of good over evil with respect to the free activity of these creatures. Now it may be granted that this is possible, consistently with the soundness of my atheological argument. That is, it may be granted that it is possible that all instances of E are effects of free decisions of fallen angels and that the positive value of the free activity of these angels outweighs the negative value of the instances of E, but at the same time insisted that this is not actually the case. And this insistence is consistent with Plantinga's free will defense.

But how do I "know" this is not actually the case? If this question is motivated by skeptical considerations (e.g., how do I "know" that the universe did not begin to exist five minutes ago?) then it may be rejected for the same reasons that philosophers reject skepticism in general. But if this question is motivated by non-skeptical epistemological considerations, I would explain that I have probabilistic knowledge that there are no fallen angels who cause the instances of E. *There is no evidence* that there are free non-human creatures who cause the instances of E and this fact justifies the belief that there probably are no such creatures. As P. J. McGrath[21] has recently shown in some detail, if there is no evidence for a positive existence claim then that justifies belief in the nonexistence of the entities claimed to exist.[22]

This principle also deflates the more general theistic argument that "we do not know enough to make any rational judgment about the truth-value of (13); therefore we do not know if the atheological argument based on (8)–(14) is sound." I think we are warranted in believing (13) since *there is no evidence* for the positive existence claim that there are goods that are causes or effects of the instances of E that render the actual aggregate of all the causes and effects of the instances of E and V greater in positive value than the aggregate of all the causes and effects of the instances of V in the closest pure V-world. For example, there is no evidence that there are angels that cause the instances of E or that the chain of effects of E will eventually result in some Great Glorious Good in the distant future. Of course, it is possible that there is some such Great Good but mere possibility does not suffice to impugn a probabilistic argument. The only evidence we possess about the causes and effects of the instances of E supports the view that these causes and effects are similar or inferior in value to the causes and effects of the instances of V in the closest pure V-world. For example, we know that some effects of the instances of E are humans (or the coming into existence of humans) and humans are similar in positive value to the human counterparts that are effects of instances of V in the closest pure V-world. (Or else humans are inferior in value, simply by virtue of being carnivores.) Furthermore, the known causes of the instances of E (the causal chain leading to the evolution of carnivores, including the big bang, the formation of galaxies and planets, chemical reactions taking place in the oceans, etc.) are of a sort similar to the events that cause vegetarian animals to evolve in the closest pure V-world. There is no extraordinary difference between causal chains leading to carnivores and those leading to vegetarians, as far as we know. Since events of a similar sort are of similar value, all else being equal, it is reasonable to assume that the causal chains in both worlds are of similar value. (Or else the causal chain leading to carnivores is of inferior value simply by virtue of the fact that it leads to carnivores.) But we can make a stronger statement than this. Some of the later carnivores are causal outcomes of earlier carnivorous events and by virtue of this fact the causal chain that produces carnivores is inferior in positive value to the causal chain that produces only vegetarians. Thus, it is probable that (13) is true, that the positive value of the aggregate of the causes and effects of the instances of E and V is equal or inferior to the positive value of the aggregate of the causes and effects of the instances of V in the closest pure V-world.

A defender of Plantinga's line of thinking might respond to the foregoing by rejecting the force of my probabilistic claims about the causes and effects of the instances of E. He may allege, for instance, that my claim that *the instances of E are probably not effects of the free decisions of fallen angels and therefore instances of E make it probable that God does not exist* presupposes some particular theory of probability and there is no non-question-begging application of a theory of probability to the issue at hand.[23] To this allegation, I shall permit myself only the brief retort that Plantinga's criticism of the probabilistic argument from evil is based on a number of technical and substantive fallacies, as has been recently demonstrated by Keith Chrzan.[24]

Further defenses of my argument are possible and there are probably still further objections that need to be considered. But I believe the considerations I have presented put the ball in the theist's court and at the very least make it prima facie reasonable to believe that the law E is ultimately evil and that God does not exist.

Thus, it seems to me that I am entitled to believe that the horror I experienced on that dark night in the woods was a veridical insight. What I experienced was a brief and terrifying glimpse into the ultimately evil dimension of a godless world.[25]

NOTES

1. See D. M. Armstrong, *What Is a Law of Nature?* (Cambridge: Cambridge University Press, 1983); Michael Tooley, "The Nature of Laws," *Canadian Journal of Philosophy* 7 (1977): 667–98; Fred Dretske, "Laws of Nature," *Philosophy of Science* 44 (1977): 248–68.

2. See Saul Kripke, *Naming and Necessity* (Cambridge, MA: Harvard University Press, 1980), and Hilary Putnam, "The Meaning of 'Meaning,'" in *Philosophical Papers*, Vol. II (Cambridge: Cambridge University Press, 1975).

3. See Alvin Plantinga, *The Nature of Necessity* (Oxford: Oxford University Press, 1974), pp. 1–2.

4. The phrase 'obtaining nourishment' is an abbreviation of some more complex expression that expresses a property that involves the peculiarities of predators. Obviously not all nourishment is predatory. Furthermore, 'obtaining nourishment' should be understood as meaning "obtaining nourishment in its natural environment," for in some artificial environments, e.g., zoos, predators obtain nourishment without killing anything.

5. Jaegwon Kim, "Events as Property Exemplifications," in *Action Theory*, edited by M. Brand and D. Walton (Dordrecht: Reidel, 1976), pp. 159–77.

6. One reason for denying the assumption is Moore's principle of organic unities, which implies that "the evil part of the whole w outweighs the good part" is consistent with "w as a whole is good." See G. E. Moore, *Principia Ethica* (Cambridge: Cambridge University Press, 1971), chap. 1.

7. The same should be said of element (vi) of the eightfold sufficient condition (i) and (iii)–(ix) of an ultimately evil law.

8. Richard Swinburne, *The Existence of God* (Oxford: Clarendon Press, 1979), p. 202.

9. Ibid., p. 210.

10. Ibid., p. 209.

11. Ibid., p. 208.

12. For additional and sound criticisms of Swinburne's theodicy, see David O'Connor, "Swinburne on Natural Evil," *Religious Studies* 19 (1983): 65–74; Eleonore Stump, "Knowledge, Freedom, and the Problem of Evil," *International Journal for the Philosophy of Religion* 14 (1983): 49–58; Bruce Russell, "The Persistent Problem of Evil," *Faith and Philosophy* 6 (1989): 121–39.

13. John Hick, *Evil and the God of Love* (New York: Harper and Row, 1978), p. 323.

14. Peter Singer, *Animal Liberation* (New York: Avon Books, 1977), p. 7.

15. Tom Regan, *The Case for Animal Rights* (Berkeley: University of California Press, 1983).

16. For additional and sound criticisms of Hick's theodicy, see G. Stanley Kane, "The Failure of Soul-Making Theodicy," *International Journal for the Philosophy of Religion* 6 (1975): 1–22, and Bruce Russell, "The Persistent Problem of Evil," *Faith and Philosophy* 6 (1989): 121–39.

17. George Schlesinger, *Religion and the Scientific Method* (Dordrecht: Reidel, 1977).

18. Keith Chrzan, "The Irrelevance of the No Best Possible World Defense," *Philosophia* 17 (1987): 161–67.

19. Bruch Reichenbach, *Evil and a Good God* (New York: Fordham University Press, 1986).

20. For further sound criticisms of Reichenbach's theory, see Michael Martin, "Reichenbach on Natural Evil," *Religious Studies* 24 (1988): 91–99.

21. P. J. McGrath, "Atheism or Agnosticism," *Analysis* 47 (1987): 54–57.

22. Further defense of principles of epistemic justification of the relevant sort can be found in William Rowe's excellent article "Evil and Theodicy," *Philosophical Topics* 16 (1988): 119–32, and Quentin Smith's *The Felt Meanings of the World: A Metaphysics of Feeling* (West Lafayette, IN: Purdue University Press, 1986), pp. 131–34, 140–42.

23. See Alvin Plantinga, "The Probabilistic Argument from Evil," *Philosophical Studies* 35 (1979): 1–53.

24. Keith Chrzan, "Plantinga and Probabilistic Atheism," *International Journal for Philosophy of Religion* 30 (1991): 21–27.

25. Considerations about the origin and evolution of the natural universe also suggest there is a *cosmological* argument for God's nonexistence. See Quentin Smith, "A Big Bang Cosmological Argument for God's Nonexistence," *Faith and Philosophy* 9 (1992): 217–37; "Atheism, Theism and Big Bang Cosmology," *Australasian Journal of Philosophy* 69 (March 1991): 48–66; and "The Uncaused Beginning of the Universe," *Philosophy of Science* 55 (1988): 39–57.

I should like to thank Keith Chrzan, P. G. McGrath, Susan Ament Smith, and an anonymous referee for this journal for helpful comments on an earlier version of this paper. I should also like to thank two anonymous referees for *Philosophy and Phenomenological Research* for extensive and brilliant criticisms of an earlier and very different version of this paper; many of the improvements in the present version were motivated by their criticisms.

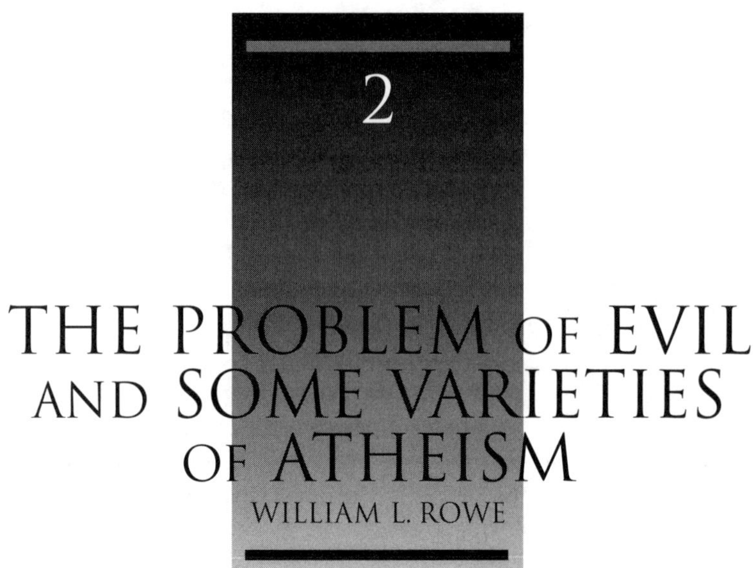

2

THE PROBLEM OF EVIL AND SOME VARIETIES OF ATHEISM

WILLIAM L. ROWE

This paper is concerned with three interrelated questions. The first is: Is there an argument for atheism based on the existence of evil that may rationally justify someone in being an atheist? To this first question I give an affirmative answer and try to support that answer by setting forth a strong argument for atheism based on the existence of evil.[1] The second question is: How can the theist best defend his position against the argument for atheism based on the existence of evil? In response to this question I try to describe what may be an adequate rational defense for theism against any argument for atheism based on the existence of evil. The final question is: What position should the informed atheist take concerning the rationality of theistic belief? Three different answers an atheist may give to this question serve to distinguish three varieties of atheism: unfriendly atheism, indifferent atheism, and friendly atheism. In the final part of the paper I discuss and defend the position of friendly atheism.

Before we consider the argument from evil, we need to distinguish a narrow and a broad sense of the terms 'theist', 'atheist', and 'agnostic'. By a 'theist' in the narrow sense I mean someone who believes in the existence of an omnipotent, omniscient, eternal, supremely good being who created the world. By a 'theist' in the broad sense I mean someone who believes in the existence of some sort of divine being or divine reality. To be a theist in the narrow sense is also to be a theist in the broad sense, but one may be a theist in the broad sense—as was

---

From *American Philosophical Quarterly* 16 (1979): 335–41.

Paul Tillich—without believing that there is a supremely good, omnipotent, omniscient, eternal being who created the world. Similar distinctions must be made between a narrow and a broad sense of the terms 'atheist' and 'agnostic'. To be an atheist in the broad sense is to deny the existence of any sort of divine being or divine reality. Tillich was not an atheist in the broad sense. But he was an atheist in the narrow sense, for he denied that there exists a divine being that is all-knowing, all-powerful, and perfectly good. In this paper I will be using the terms 'theism', 'theist', 'atheism', 'atheist', 'agnosticism', and 'agnostic' in the narrow sense, not in the broad sense.

I

In developing the argument for atheism based on the existence of evil, it will be useful to focus on some particular evil that our world contains in considerable abundance. Intense human and animal suffering, for example, occurs daily and in great plenitude in our world. Such intense suffering is a clear case of evil. Of course, if the intense suffering leads to some greater good, a good we could not have obtained without undergoing the suffering in question, we might conclude that the suffering is justified, but it remains an evil nevertheless. For we must not confuse the intense suffering in and of itself with the good things to which it sometimes leads or of which it may be a necessary part. Intense human or animal suffering is in itself bad, an evil, even though it may sometimes be justified by virtue of being a part of, or leading to, some good which is unobtainable without it. What is evil in itself may sometimes be good as a means because it leads to something that is good in itself. In such a case, while remaining an evil in itself, the intense human or animal suffering is, nevertheless, an evil which someone might be morally justified in permitting.

Taking human and animal suffering as a clear instance of evil which occurs with great frequency in our world, the argument for atheism based on evil can be stated as follows:

1. There exist instances of intense suffering which an omnipotent, omniscient being could have prevented without thereby losing some greater good or permitting some evil equally bad or worse.[2]
2. An omniscient, wholly good being would prevent the occurrence of any intense suffering it could, unless it could not do so without thereby losing some greater good or permitting some evil equally bad or worse.

---

3. There does not exist an omnipotent, omniscient, wholly good being.

What are we to say about this argument for atheism, an argument based on the profusion of one sort of evil in our world? The argument is valid; therefore, if we have rational grounds for accepting its premises, to that extent we have rational grounds for accepting atheism. Do we, however, have rational grounds for accepting the premises of this argument?

Let's begin with the second premise. Let s_1 be an instance of intense human or animal suffering which an omniscient, wholly good being could prevent. We will also suppose that things are such that s_1 will occur unless prevented by the omniscient, wholly good (*OG*) being. We might be interested in determining what would be a *sufficient* condition of *OG* failing to prevent s_1. But, for our purpose here, we need only try to state a *necessary* condition for *OG* failing to prevent s_1. That condition, so it seems to me, is this:

Either (i) there is some greater good, *G*, such that *G* is obtainable by *OG* only if *OG* permits s_1,[3]

or (ii) there is some greater good, *G*, such that *G* is obtainable by *OG* only if *OG* permits either s_1 or some evil equally bad or worse,

or (iii) s_1 is such that it is preventable by *OG* only if *OG* permits some evil equally bad or worse.

It is important to recognize that (iii) is not included in (i). For losing a good greater than s_1 is not the same as permitting an evil greater than s_1. And this because the *absence* of a good state of affairs need not itself be an evil state of affairs. It is also important to recognize that s_1 might be such that it is preventable by *OG without* losing *G* (so condition (i) is not satisfied) but also such that if *OG* did prevent it, *G* would be lost *unless OG* permitted some evil equal to or worse than s_1. If this were so, it does not seem correct to require that *OG* prevent s_1. Thus, condition (ii) takes into account an important possibility not encompassed in condition (i).

Is it true that if an omniscient, wholly good being permits the occurrence of some intense suffering it could have prevented, then either (i) or (ii) or (iii) obtains? It seems to me that it is true. But if it is true then so is premise (2) of the argument for atheism. For that premise merely states in more compact form what we have suggested must be true if an omniscient, wholly good being fails to prevent some intense suffering it could prevent. Premise (2) says that an omniscient, wholly good being would prevent the occurrence of any intense suffering it could, unless it could not do so without thereby losing some greater good or permitting some evil equally bad or worse. This premise (or something not too distant from it) is, I think, held in common by many atheists and nontheists. Of course, there may be disagreement about whether something is good, and whether, if it is good, one would be morally justified in permitting some intense suffering to occur in order to obtain it. Someone might hold, for example, that no good is great enough to justify permitting an innocent child to suffer terribly.[4] Again, someone might hold that the mere fact that a given good outweighs some suffering and would be lost if the suffering were prevented, is not a morally sufficient reason for permitting the suffering. But to hold either of these views is not to deny (2). For (2) claims only that *if* an omniscient, wholly good being permits intense suffering *then* either there is some greater good that would have been lost, or some equally bad or worse evil that would have occurred, had the intense suffering been prevented. (2) does not purport to describe what might be a *sufficient* condition for an omniscient, wholly good being to permit intense suffering, only what is a *necessary* condition. So stated, (2) seems to express a belief that accords with our basic moral principles, principles shared by both theists and nontheists. If we are to fault the argument for atheism, therefore, it seems we must find some fault with its first premise.

Suppose in some distant forest lightning strikes a dead tree, resulting in a forest fire. In the fire a fawn is trapped, horribly burned, and lies in terrible agony for several days before death relieves its suffering. So far as we can see, the fawn's intense suffering is pointless. For there does not appear to be any greater good such that the prevention of the fawn's suffering would require either the loss of that good or the occurrence of an evil equally bad or worse. Nor does there seem to be any equally bad or worse evil so connected to the fawn's suffering that it would have had to occur had the fawn's suffering been prevented. Could an omnipotent, omniscient being have prevented the fawn's apparently pointless suffering? The answer is obvious, as even the theist will insist. An omnipotent, omniscient being could have easily prevented the fawn from being horribly burned, or, given the burning, could have spared the fawn the intense suffering by quickly ending its life, rather than allowing the fawn to lie in terrible agony for several days. Since the fawn's intense suffering was preventable and, so far as we can see, pointless, doesn't it appear that premise (1) of the argument is true, that there do exist instances of intense suffering which an omnipotent, omniscient being could have prevented without thereby losing some greater good or permitting some evil equally bad or worse?

It must be acknowledged that the case of the fawn's apparently pointless suffering does not *prove* that (1) is true. For even though we cannot see how the fawn's suffering is required to obtain some greater good (or to prevent some equally bad or worse evil), it hardly follows that it is not so required. After all, we are often surprised by how things we thought to be unconnected turn out to be intimately connected. Perhaps, for all we know, there is some familiar good outweighing the fawn's suffering to which that suffering is connected in a way we do not see. Furthermore, there may well be unfamiliar goods, goods we haven't dreamed of, to which the fawn's suffering is inextricably connected. Indeed, it would seem to require something like omniscience on our part before we could lay claim to *knowing* that there is no greater good connected to the fawn's suffering in such a manner that an omnipotent, omniscient being could not have achieved that good without permitting that suffering or some evil equally bad or worse. So the case of the fawn's suffering surely does not enable us to *establish* the truth of (1).

The truth is that we are not in a position to prove that (1) is true. We cannot know with certainty that instances of suffering of the sort described in (1) do occur in our world. But it is one thing to *know* or *prove* that (1) is true and quite another thing to have *rational grounds* for believing (1) to be true. We are often in the position where in the light of our experience and knowledge it is rational to believe that a certain statement is true, even though we are not in a position to prove or to know with certainty that the statement is true. In the light of our past experience and knowledge it is, for example, very reasonable to believe that neither Goldwater nor McGovern will ever be elected President, but we are scarcely in the position of knowing with certainty that neither will ever be elected President. So, too, with (1), although we cannot know with certainty that it is true, it perhaps can be rationally supported, shown to be a rational belief.

Consider again the case of the fawn's suffering. Is it reasonable to believe that there is some greater good so intimately connected to that suffering that even an omnipotent, omniscient being could not have obtained that good without permitting that suffering or some evil at least as bad? It certainly does not appear reasonable to believe this. Nor does it seem reasonable to believe that there is some evil at least as bad as the fawn's suffering such that an omnipotent being simply could not have prevented it without permitting the fawn's suffering. But even if it should somehow be reasonable to believe either of these things of the fawn's suffering, we must then ask whether it is reasonable to believe either of these things of *all* the instances of seemingly pointless human and animal suffering that occur daily in our world. And surely the answer to this more general question must be no. It seems quite unlikely that *all* the instances of intense suffering occurring daily in our world are intimately related to the occurrence of greater goods or the prevention of evils at least as bad; and even more unlikely, should they somehow all be so related, that an omnipotent, omniscient being could not have achieved at least some of those goods (or prevented some of those evils) without permitting the instances of intense suffering that are supposedly related to them. In the light of our experience and knowledge of the variety and scale of human and animal suffering in our world, the idea that none of this suffering could have been prevented by an omnipotent being without thereby losing a greater good or permitting an evil at least as bad seems an extraordinary absurd idea, quite beyond our belief. It seems then that although we cannot *prove* that

(1) is true, it is, nevertheless, altogether *reasonable* to believe that (1) is true, that (1) is a *rational* belief.[5]

Returning now to our argument for atheism, we've seen that the second premise expresses a basic belief common to many theists and nontheists. We've also seen that our experience and knowledge of the variety and profusion of suffering in our world provides *rational support* for the first premise. Seeing that the conclusion, "There does not exist an omnipotent, omniscient, wholly good being" follows from these two premises, it does seem that we have *rational support* for atheism, that it is reasonable for us to believe that the theistic God does not exist.

II

Can theism be rationally defended against the argument for atheism we have just examined? If it can, how might the theist best respond to that argument? Since the argument from (1) and (2) to (3) is valid, and since the theist, no less than the nontheist, is more than likely committed to (2), it's clear that the theist can reject this atheistic argument only by rejecting its first premise, the premise that states that there are instances of intense suffering which an omnipotent, omniscient being could have prevented without thereby losing some greater good or permitting some evil equally bad or worse. How, then, can the theist best respond to this premise and the considerations advanced in its support?

There are basically three responses a theist can make. First, he might argue not that (1) is false or probably false, but only that the reasoning given in support of it is in some way *defective*. He may do this either by arguing that the reasons given in support of (1) are *in themselves* insufficient to justify accepting (1), or by arguing that there are other things we know which, when taken in conjunction with these reasons, do not justify us in accepting (1). I suppose some theists would be content with this rather modest response to the basic argument for atheism. But given the validity of the basic argument and the theist's likely acceptance of (2), he is thereby committed to the view that (1) is false, not just that we have no good reasons for accepting (1) as true. The second two responses are aimed at showing that it is reasonable to believe that (1) is false. Since the theist is committed to this view I shall focus the discussion on these two attempts, attempts which we can distinguish as "the direct attack" and "the indirect attack."

By a direct attack, I mean an attempt to reject (1) by pointing out goods, for example, to which suffering may well be connected, goods which an omnipotent, omniscient being could not achieve without permitting suffering. It is doubtful, however, that the direct attack can succeed. The theist may point out that some suffering leads to moral and spiritual development impossible without suffering.

But it's reasonably clear that suffering often occurs in a degree far beyond what is required for character development. The theist may say that some suffering results from free choices of human beings and might be preventable only by preventing some measure of human freedom. But, again, it's clear that much intense suffering occurs not as a result of human free choices. The general difficulty with this direct attack on premise (1) is twofold. First, it cannot succeed, for the theist does not know what greater goods might be served, or evils prevented, by each instance of intense human or animal suffering. Second, the theist's own religious tradition usually maintains that in this life it is not given to us to know God's purpose in allowing particular instances of suffering. Hence, the direct attack against premise (1) cannot succeed and violates basic beliefs associated with theism.

The best procedure for the theist to follow in rejecting premise (1) is the indirect procedure. This procedure I shall call "the G. E. Moore shift," so called in honor of the twentieth-century philosopher G. E. Moore, who used it to great effect in dealing with the arguments of the skeptics. Skeptical philosophers such as David Hume have advanced ingenious arguments to prove that no one can know of the existence of any material object. The premises of their arguments employ plausible principles, principles which many philosophers have tried to reject directly, but only with questionable success. Moore's procedure was altogether different. Instead of arguing directly against the premises of the skeptic's arguments, he simply noted that the premises implied, for example, that he (Moore) did not know of the existence of a pencil. Moore then proceeded indirectly against the skeptic's premises by arguing:

I do know that this pencil exists.

If the skeptic's principles are correct I cannot know of the existence of this pencil.

∴ The skeptic's principles (at least one) must be incorrect.

Moore then noted that his argument is just as valid as the skeptic's, that both of their arguments contain the premise "If the skeptic's principles are correct Moore cannot know of the existence of this pencil," and concluded that the only way to choose between the two arguments (Moore's and the skeptic's) is by deciding which of the first premises it is more rational to believe—Moore's premise "I do know that this pencil exists" or the skeptic's premise asserting that his skeptical principles are correct. Moore concluded that his own first premise was the more rational of the two.[6]

Before we see how the theist may apply the G. E. Moore shift to the basic argument for atheism, we should note the general strategy of the shift. We're given an argument: *p*, *q*, therefore, *r*. Instead of arguing directly against *p*, another argument is constructed—not-*r*, *q*, therefore, not-*p*—which begins with the denial of the conclusion of the first argument, keeps its second premise, and ends with the denial of the first premise as its conclusion. Compare, for example, these two:

I.		II.	
	p		not-*r*
	q		*q*
	r		not-*p*

It is a truth of logic that if I is valid II must be valid as well. Since the arguments are the same so far as the second premise is concerned, any choice between them must concern their respective first premises. To argue against the first premise (*p*) by constructing the counter argument II is to employ the G. E. Moore shift.

Applying the G. E. Moore shift against the first premise of the basic argument for atheism, the theist can argue as follows:

not-3. There exists an omnipotent, omniscient, wholly good being.

2. An omniscient, wholly good being would prevent the occurrence of any intense suffering it could, unless it could not do so without thereby losing some greater good or permitting some evil equally bad or worse.

Therefore,

not-1. It is not the case that there exist instances of intense suffering which an omnipotent, omniscient being could have prevented without thereby losing some greater good or permitting some evil equally bad or worse.

We now have two arguments: the basic argument for atheism from (1) and (2) to (3), and the theist's best response, the argument from (not-3) and (2) to (not-1). What the theist then says about (1) is that he has rational grounds for believing in the existence of the theistic God (not-3), accepts (2) as true, and sees that (not-1) follows from (not-3) and (2). He concludes, therefore, that he has rational grounds for rejecting (1). Having rational grounds for rejecting (1), the theist concludes that the basic argument for atheism is mistaken.

III

We've had a look at a forceful argument for atheism and what seems to be the theist's best response to that argument. If one is persuaded by the argument for atheism, as I find myself to be, how might one best view the position of the theist? Of course, he will view the theist as having a false belief, just as the theist will view the atheist as having a false belief. But what position should the atheist take concerning the *rationality* of the theist's belief? There are three major positions an atheist might take, positions which we may think of as some varieties of atheism. First, the atheist may believe that no one is rationally justified in believing that the theistic God exists. Let us call this position "unfriendly atheism." Second, the atheist may hold no belief concerning whether any theist is or isn't rationally justified in believing that the theistic God exists. Let us call this view "indifferent atheism." Finally, the atheist may believe that some theists are rationally justified in believing that the theistic God exists. This view we shall call "friendly atheism." In this final part of the paper I propose to discuss and defend the position of friendly atheism.

If no one can be rationally justified in believing a false proposition then friendly atheism is a paradoxical, if not incoherent position. But surely the truth of a belief is not a necessary condition of someone's being rationally justified in having that belief. So in holding that someone is rationally justified in believing that the theistic God exists, the friendly atheist is not committed to thinking that the theist has a true belief. What he is committed to is that the theist has rational grounds for his belief, a belief the atheist rejects and is convinced he is rationally justified in rejecting. But is this possible? Can someone, like our friendly atheist, hold a belief, be convinced that he is rationally justified in holding that belief, and yet believe that someone else is equally justified in believing the opposite? Surely this is possible. Suppose your friends see you off on a flight to Hawaii. Hours after take-off they learn that your plane has gone down at sea. After a twenty-four hour search, no survivors have been found. Under these circumstances they are rationally justified in believing that you have perished. But it is hardly rational for you to believe this, as you bob up and down in your life vest, wondering why the search planes have failed to spot you. Indeed, to amuse yourself while awaiting your fate, you might very well reflect on the fact that your friends are rationally justified in believing that you are now dead, a proposition you disbelieve and are rationally justified in disbelieving. So, too, perhaps an atheist may be rationally justified in his atheistic belief and yet hold that some theists are rationally justified in believing just the opposite of what he believes.

What sort of grounds might a theist have for believing that God exists? Well, he might endeavor to justify his belief by appealing to one or more of the traditional arguments: Ontological, Cosmological, Teleological, Moral, etc. Second, he might appeal to certain aspects of religious experience, perhaps even his own religious experience. Third, he might try to justify theism as a plausible theory in terms of which we can account for a variety of phenomena. Although an atheist must hold that the theistic God does not exist, can he not also believe, and be justified in so believing, that some of these "justifications of theism" do actually rationally justify some theists in their belief that there exists a supremely good, omnipotent, omniscient being? It seems to me that he can.

If we think of the long history of theistic belief and the special situations in which people are sometimes placed, it is perhaps as absurd to think that no one was ever rationally justified in believing that the theistic God exists as it is to think that no one was ever justified in believing that human beings would never walk on the moon. But in suggesting that friendly atheism is preferable to unfriendly atheism, I don't mean to rest the case on what some human beings might reasonably have believed in the eleventh or thirteenth century. The more interesting question is whether some people in modern society, people who are aware of the usual grounds for belief and disbelief and are acquainted to some degree with modern science, are yet rationally justified in accepting theism. Friendly atheism is a significant position only if it answers this question in the affirmative.

It is not difficult for an atheist to be friendly when he has reason to believe that the theist could not reasonably be expected to be acquainted with the grounds for disbelief that he (the atheist) possesses. For then the atheist may take the view that some theists are rationally justified in holding to theism, but would not be so were they to be acquainted with the grounds for disbelief—those grounds being sufficient to tip the scale in favor of atheism when balanced against the reasons the theist has in support of his belief.

Friendly atheism becomes paradoxical, however, when the atheist contemplates believing that the theist has all the grounds for atheism that he, the atheist, has, and yet is rationally justified in maintaining his theistic belief. But even so excessively friendly a view as this perhaps can be held by the atheist if he also has some reason to think that the grounds for theism are not as telling as the theist is justified in taking them to be.[7]

In this paper I've presented what I take to be a strong argument for atheism, pointed out what I think is the theist's best response to that argument, distinguished three positions an atheist might take concerning the rationality of theistic belief, and made some remarks in defense of the position called "friendly atheism." I'm aware that the central points of the paper are not likely to be warmly received by many philosophers. Philosophers who are atheists tend to be tough minded—holding that there are no good reasons for supposing that theism is true. And theists tend either to reject the view that the existence of evil provides rational grounds for atheism or to hold that religious belief has nothing to do with reason and evidence at all. But such is the way of philosophy.[8]

NOTES

1. Some philosophers have contended that the existence of evil is *logically inconsistent* with the existence of the theistic God. No one, I think, has succeeded in establishing such an extravagant claim. Indeed, granted incompatibilism, there is a fairly compelling argument for the view that the existence of evil is logically consistent with the existence of the theistic God. (For a lucid statement of this argument, see Alvin Plantinga, *God, Freedom, and Evil* [New York: Harper & Row, 1974], pp. 29–59.) There remains, however, what we may call the *evidential* form—as opposed to the *logical* form—of the problem of evil: the view that the variety and profusion of evil in our world, although perhaps not logically inconsistent with the existence of the theistic God, provides, nevertheless, *rational support* for atheism. In this paper I shall be concerned solely with the evidential form of the problem, the form of the problem which, I think, presents a rather severe difficulty for theism.

2. If there is some good, *G*, greater than any evil, (1) will be false for the trivial reason that no matter what evil, *E*, we pick the conjunctive good state of affairs consisting of *G* and *E* will outweigh *E* and be such that an omnipotent being could not obtain it without permitting *E*. (See Alvin Plantinga, *God and Other Minds* [Ithaca: Cornell University Press, 1967], p. 167.) To avoid this objection we may insert "unreplaceable" into our premises (1) and (2) between "some" and "greater." If *E* isn't required for *G*, and *G* is better than *G* plus *E*, then the good conjunctive state of affairs composed of *G* and *E* would be *replaceable* by the greater good of *G* alone. For the sake of simplicity, however, I will ignore this complication both in the formulation and discussion of premises (1) and (2).

3. Three clarifying points need to be made in connection with (i). First, by 'good' I don't mean to exclude the fulfillment of certain moral principles. Perhaps preventing s_1 would preclude certain actions prescribed by the principles of justice. I shall allow that the satisfaction of certain principles of justice may be a good that outweighs the evil of s_1. Second, even though (i) may suggest it, I don't mean to limit the good in question to something that would *follow in time* the occurrence of s_1. And, finally, we should perhaps not fault *OG* if the good *G*, that would be lost were s_1 prevented, is not actually greater than s_1, but merely such that allowing s_1 and *G*, as opposed to preventing s_1 and thereby losing *G*, would not alter the balance between good and evil. For reasons of simplicity, I have left this point out in stating (i), with the result that (i) is perhaps a bit stronger than it should be.

4. See Ivan's speech in book V, chap. IV of *The Brothers Karamazov*.

5. One might object that the conclusion of this paragraph is stronger than the reasons given warrant. For it is one thing to argue that it is unreasonable to think that (1) is false and another thing to conclude that we are therefore justified in accepting (1) as true. There are propositions such that believing them is much more reasonable than disbelieving them, and yet are such that *withholding judgment* about them is more reasonable than believing them. To take an example of Chisholm's: it is more reasonable to believe that the Pope will be in Rome (on some arbitrarily picked future date) than to believe that he won't; but it is perhaps more reasonable to suspend judgment on the question of the Pope's whereabouts on that particular date, than to believe that he will be in Rome. Thus,

it might be objected, that while we've shown that believing (1) is more reasonable than disbelieving (1), we haven't shown that believing (1) is more reasonable than withholding belief. My answer to this objection is that there are things we know which render (1) probable to the degree that it is more reasonable to believe (1) than to suspend judgment on (1). What are these things we know? First, I think, is the fact that there is an enormous variety and profusion of intense human and animal suffering in our world. Second is the fact that much of this suffering seems quite unrelated to any greater goods (or the absence of equal or greater evils) that might justify it. And, finally, there is the fact that such suffering as is related to greater goods (or the absence of equal or greater evils) does not, in many cases, seem so intimately related as to require its permission by an omnipotent being bent on securing those goods (the absence of those evils). These facts, I am claiming, make it more reasonable to accept (1) than to withhold judgment on (1).

6. See, for example, the two chapters on Hume in G. E. Moore, *Some Main Problems of Philosophy* (London, 1953).

7. Suppose that I add a long sum of numbers three times and get result *x*. I inform you of this so that you have pretty much the same evidence I have for the claim that the sum of the numbers is *x*. You then use your calculator twice over and arrive at result *y*. You, then, are justified in believing that the sum of the numbers is *not x*. However, knowing that your calculator has been damaged and is therefore unreliable, and that you have no reason to think that it is damaged, *I* may reasonably believe not only that the sum of the numbers is *x*, but also that you are justified in believing that the sum is not *x*. Here is a case, then, where you have all of my evidence for *p*, and yet I can reasonably believe that you are justified in believing not-*p*—for I have reason to believe that your grounds for not-*p* are not as telling as you are justified in taking them to be.

8. I am indebted to my colleagues at Purdue University, particularly to Ted Ulrich and Lilly Russow, and to philosophers at the University of Nebraska, Indiana State University, and the University of Wisconsin at Milwaukee for helpful criticisms of earlier versions of this paper.

3

EVIL AND THEODICY

WILLIAM L. ROWE

Many people feel that some of the human and animal suffering going on in our world makes it difficult to believe in the existence of an omnipotent, omniscient, wholly good being (hereafter referred to as 'O'). Why, for example, would such a being permit the awful suffering and near extermination of the Jews in Europe? Clearly, it is very difficult to understand why an omnipotent, omniscient, perfectly good being would permit this evil. But if our awareness of such evils does make it difficult to believe that O exists, what sort of difficulty is it? It might be a psychological difficulty. We might be so disposed that when we view films of the victims being herded into box cars, being forced into gas chambers, etc., we simply find ourselves inclined to doubt the existence of O, or inclined to abandon our belief in O. On the other hand, the difficulty may be epistemological. We may think that disbelief is somehow rationally justified by our awareness of these terrible evils. It is this latter topic that I want to discuss.

I. THE STRUCTURE OF THE PROBLEM

I will begin with two instances of evil that have been mentioned in the literature. The first is a case of animal suffering due to natural forces, what would be called a *natural evil*. The second is a case of human suffering and death due to the inten-

From *Philosophical Topics* 16, no. 2 (1998): 119–32.

tional action of a human agent, what would be called a *moral evil.* The first case, although I made it up, is surely a familiar sort of tragedy, played not infrequently on the stage of nature.

> In some distant forest lightning strikes a dead tree, resulting in a forest fire. In the fire a fawn is trapped, horribly burned, and lies in terrible agony for several days before death relieves its suffering.

I turn now to a second case, an actual case reported in the *Detroit Free Press* of January 3, 1986. The case involves a little girl in Flint, Michigan, who was severely beaten, raped, and then strangled early on New Year's Day of 1986. Here is Bruce Russell's account of the case, which I take from his paper, "The Persistent Problem of Evil."[1]

> The girl's mother was living with her boyfriend, another man who was unemployed, her two children, and her 9-month-old infant fathered by the boyfriend. On New Year's Eve all three adults were drinking at a bar near the woman's home. The boyfriend had been taking drugs and drinking heavily. He was asked to leave the bar at 8:00 p.m. After several reappearances he finally stayed away for good at about 9:30 p.m. The woman and the unemployed man remained at the bar until 2:00 a.m. at which time the woman went home and the man to a party at a neighbor's home. Perhaps out of jealousy, the boyfriend attacked the woman when she walked into the house. Her brother was there and broke up the fight by hitting the boyfriend who was passed out and slumped over a table when the brother left. Later the boyfriend attacked the woman again, this time she knocked him unconscious. After checking the children, she went to bed. Later the woman's 5-year-old girl went downstairs to go to the bathroom. The unemployed man returned from the party at 3:45 a.m., and found the 5-year-old dead. She had been raped, severely beaten over most of her body, and strangled to death by the boyfriend.

Let's refer to these two cases as E1 (for the fawn's case) and E2 (for the little girl's case). Now about E1 and E2, I want to make the following initial judgment.

> P. No good state of affairs we know of is such that an omnipotent, omniscient being's obtaining it would morally justify that being's permitting E1 or E2.

What am I implying in making this assertion? I am implying that we have *good reason* to believe that no good state of affairs we know of would justify an omnipotent, omniscient being in permitting either E1 or E2. I don't mean simply that we can't see how some good we know about (say, my enjoyment on smelling a good cigar) would justify an omnipotent being's permitting E1 or E2. I mean that we can see how such a good would *not* justify an omnipotent being's permitting E1 or E2. For we can see that an omnipotent being wouldn't have to permit E1 or E2 in order to obtain the good of my enjoyment on smelling a good cigar. And we can see that even were that not so, obtaining such a good wouldn't justify any being in permitting E1 or E2. Is there some other good state of affairs we know of that would justify an omnipotent being in permitting E1 or E2? I don't believe there is. The good states of affairs I know of, when I reflect on them, meet one or both of the following conditions: either an omnipotent being could obtain them without having to permit E1 or E2, or obtaining them wouldn't morally justify that being in permitting E1 or E2. And if this is so, I have reason to conclude that:

> Q. No good state of affairs is such that an omnipotent, omniscient being's obtaining it would morally justify that being in permitting E1 or E2.

II. THREE RESPONSES

I propose now to describe three general ways of responding to the line of reasoning that moves from consideration of E1 and E2 to the conclusion Q.

A. One response would be to argue that the reasoning is in some way faulty. Either it makes some untenable or unsupported claim or engages in some faulty inference. For example, one might challenge the claim that among the goods we know about none is such that obtaining it would justify an omnipotent, omniscient being in permitting E1 or E2. Alternatively, one might argue that the reasoning is fallacious, engaging in an inference from "we don't know of any such good" to the conclusion that there aren't any, or in an inference from "no goods we know about would justify such a being in permitting E1 or E2" to the conclusion that no goods we don't know about would justify such a being in permitting E1 or E2.

B. A second response might acknowledge that the considerations I've mentioned do tend to support Q. But it might be argued that we have good reasons to believe that O exists. And surely, if O exists then there is some good state that O brings about that justifies O in permitting E1, and some good state O brings about that justifies O in permitting E2.[2] So, since if O exists Q is false, it might be contended that our reasons to believe that O exists *outweigh* the tendency of the considerations mentioned to support Q. In brief, this response contends that although the considerations mentioned do support Q, when we take into account our reasons for thinking that O exists we see that on balance we have more reason to think Q false than to think it true.

C. A third response, like the second, may acknowledge that the considerations mentioned support Q. Again, like the second this response contends that there is something we know or have good reason to believe that, when conjoined with the considerations mentioned, gives us something that on balance does not support Q. Unlike the second response, however, the thing we know or have good reason to believe is neutral with respect to Q. For example, one might have good reason to believe that if there are good states of affairs the obtaining of which would justify an omnipotent, omniscient being in permitting E1 or E2, all would be goods we know nothing about. Now this information by itself does not make Q unlikely, but when we conjoin this information with our initial judgment P (no good we know of is such that obtaining it would justify an omnipotent, omniscient being's permitting E1 or E2), the conjunction does not support Q. So here, instead of saying that the tendency of these considerations to support Q is outweighed, we shall say that it is *defeated*.

My chief interest here is to discuss the first and third of these responses. To evaluate the strength of the second response would require an evaluation of our reasons for believing that O exists, a topic far too large to take up here.

According to the first response, the attempt we have made to reason from the existence of certain evils, such as E1 and E2, to the nonexistence of O is flawed in one of two ways, if not both. First, it may be flawed in its implicit claim to have good reason to make the initial judgment P (no good we know of is such that obtaining it would justify an omnipotent, omniscient being in permitting E1 or E2). Second, it may be flawed in concluding from this initial judgment that Q (no good is such that obtaining it would justify an omnipotent, omniscient being in permitting E1 or E2). Let's now consider whether this first sort of response is successful.

To simplify our discussion, I will use the letter 'J' to stand for the property a good has just in case obtaining that good would justify an omnipotent, omniscient being in permitting E1 or E2. If a good is such that obtaining it would justify an omnipotent, omniscient being in permitting E1 or E2, then that good has J; and if not, the good lacks J. The first question, then, that this response raises is whether we are really able to judge with any assurance that P: all the goods we know of lack J. And the second question this response raises is whether from our initial judgment, P, we can reasonably infer that Q: all goods (including those we don't know of) lack J.

Before turning to these questions, however, it's worth noting that both questions imply that the class of goods can be divided into those we know of and those we don't know of. What is it to know of an intrinsically good state of affairs?[3] Well, as a start, I'm sure we would all be able to list some states that are intrinsically good, some that are intrinsically bad, and some that are neutral, neither intrinsically good nor bad. On our good list we would have pleasure, happiness, love, the exercise of virtue, good intentions, etc. On our bad list we would have pain, unhappiness, hatred, the exercise of vice, bad intentions, etc. Other states, the existence of a stone, say, we would judge to be neither intrinsically good nor intrinsically bad. Now if we could imagine the list of intrinsic goods as *completed*, I think the completed list would include some states of affairs we would recognize as intrinsically good, even though they did not come to mind when we first started composing the list. We might, for example, find *knowledge* on the list, and respond with the recognition that it too is intrinsically good. But the *complete* list might well include states that are enormously complex, so complex as to tax our powers of comprehension. Determining that such a state is intrinsically good may be as difficult for us as it would be for a child of three to determine whether Bayes's theorem is true. Goods of this sort are what I have in mind when I speak of goods we don't know of.[4]

Among the goods we know of, is any such that it has J? It is obvious that many of these goods lack J. For when we contemplate them we see that their value is not high enough (e.g., my enjoyment on smelling a good cigar) to offset the evils in question. Other goods we know of may have a great deal of intrinsic value, perhaps even more value than E1 or E2 have disvalue. But here we readily see that an omnipotent, omniscient being could obtain them without permitting E1 or E2.[5] Reflections of this sort justify us, I believe, in making our initial judgment, P, that the goods we know about lack J.

Suppose we accept P. What about the inference to Q? Are we justified in believing that no goods (including those we don't know of) have J on the basis of our justified premise that no goods we know of have J? Perhaps any such inference commits some fallacy. After all, if we don't know of these goods, how can we be justified in concluding either that they do or do not have J? My answer is that we are justified in making this inference in the same way we are justified in making the many inferences we constantly make from the known to the unknown. All of us are constantly inferring from the A's we know of to the A's we don't know of. If we observe many A's and all of them are B's we are justified in believing that the A's we haven't observed are also B's. If I encounter a fair number of pit bulls and all of them are vicious, I have reason to believe that all pit bulls are vicious. Of course, there are all sorts of considerations that may defeat this inference. I may discover that all the pit bulls I've encountered have been trained for dog-fighting, a training that engenders viciousness. I may also come to know that there are many pit bulls that are not so trained. If so, then this additional information, along with my initial information, may *not justify* me in believing that the pit bulls I haven't encountered are also vicious. So, too, with my inference from P to Q. But considerations of this sort (defeaters) properly belong to the third response, not the first. The first response, I believe, is not successful.[6]

The third response holds greater hope for discrediting the argument from evil here being considered. Before seeing how it proceeds, we should look a bit more carefully at the notion of *defeat*. Let's do this with an example. Suppose it is true that

1. The wall appears red.

From (1) we infer that

2. The wall is not white.

The inference is undoubtedly justified. If (1) were all we knew relative to the truth of (2), we would be justified in believing (2). How might the tendency of (1) to support (2) be defeated? Well, suppose we knew the following proposition:

3. If the wall were white, the wall would appear red anyway.

Clearly, although (1) tends to support (2), this tendency would be defeated if (3) were added to our knowledge. That is, the *conjunction* of (1) and (3) does *not support* (2). (Note that (3) by itself does not support the denial of (2). So this is not a case in which our new knowledge *outweighs* the support we have for (2).) How might we come to know or rationally believe (3)? Well, suppose we learn that

4. There are red lights shining on the wall and when red lights shine on a white wall the wall will appear red.

(4) gives us a good reason for accepting (3), and, as we've seen, when we conjoin (3) with (1) we no longer are justified in believing (2)—the tendency of (1) to support (2) is *defeated*.

Although it is risky to generalize from a single example, let's note the following pattern. From A we infer B. Instead of having evidence against B itself, as in attempting to *outweigh* A's tendency to support B, we have reason to believe that *If not-B, A would be (or would likely be) true anyway*. When we conjoin this hypothetical with A, we have a conjunction that does not support B. With this pattern in mind, let's return to our original inference to Q (no goods have J) from P (no goods we know of have J). To defeat P's tendency to support Q we need some good reason to believe that if not-Q (some good has J), P would be (or likely be) true anyway. Do we have any good reason to believe that if not-Q, P would be true anyway?

In considering our question it is important to note that our hypothetical refers to omniscience and omnipotence, as opposed to something akin to human knowledge and power. If a human being permits some great evil to occur, we would have some reason to think that if the obtaining of some good does justify the permission, we would likely know of the good; for another human being's knowledge and power resembles quite closely our own. For this reason we generally would have reason to reject the hypothetical that if the obtaining of some good would justify this person in permitting the evil, it would still be true that it is a good we do not know. But omniscience would view all goods, including the ones we don't know of. So, unlike the hypothetical referring to human knowledge and power, we have no similar reason to think that if some good is such that obtaining it would justify an omnipotent, omniscient being in permitting E1 or E2, it would likely be one we know of.

But all that we have seen, thus far, is that when we replace omniscience by human knowledge and power we have good reason to think that the hypothetical that would correspond to If not-Q, P anyway (i.e., the hypothetical concerning human knowledge and power), is *false.* The question before us, however, is whether we have some reason to think the original hypothetical (If not-Q, P anyway) is *true.* And I must confess that I cannot think of any special reason to think that this hypothetical is true. Given the high degree of intrinsic badness of E1 and E2, we do know that the justifying goods would be very significant goods. But this, by itself, is no good reason to think that the goods would be ones we don't know of. For we do know of very significant goods. Consider, for example, the state consisting of a vast number of conscious beings deeply enjoying the admirable qualities exhibited by one another. This is a very significant good we know of. So the mere fact that the goods must be significant is not, of itself, good reason to think that the goods that might justify an omnipotent, omniscient being in permitting E1 or E2 would be goods we do not know. Perhaps there is some fact such that if we knew it we would have a good reason to think that the hypothetical is true. We certainly cannot rule out there being such a fact. But until we learn of it we have no good reason to think that if Q were false, P would be true anyway. And lacking such a reason, we are unable to defeat P's tendency to support Q.[7]

Let's look back, briefly, at the path along which we have come. Our original question was whether certain facts about evil provide rational support for the view that O does not exist. In considering this question, we noted two particular instances of evil, E1 and E2, and noted that P (no good we know of would justify an omnipotent, omniscient being in permitting E1 or E2). From P we inferred Q (no good at all would justify an omnipotent, omniscient being in permitting E1 or E2). Suppose we are justified in believing Q on the basis of our belief that P. If so, then, since we see that Q would be false if O existed, we are justified in believing that O does not exist. In response to this line of argument, I suggested that there are three responses worthy of consideration, only two of which (the first and third responses) I would take up in this paper. Against the first response,

I argued that we are justified in believing P and in inferring Q from P. Against the third response, I argued that although having a good reason for believing the hypothetical (If not-Q, P anyway) would *defeat* our acceptance of Q on the basis of P, we do not in fact have a good reason to accept this hypothetical. In short, unless we have good reasons to think that O exists (or some other reason to reject Q), we are justified in believing that O does not exist.

III. THEODICY AND THE PROBLEM OF EVIL

Thus far we've taken no account of the various theodicies that have been mounted to reconcile our belief in theism with the difficulty raised by some of the human and animal suffering that goes on in our world. What I propose to do in this section is to look briefly at one of the more promising theodicies to determine just where it impinges on the difficulty, as we have developed it. In addition, we will need to consider the extent to which the theodicy reduces the difficulty.

The theodicy I have in mind is the one developed and defended by John Hick, and referred to as a theodicy of "soul-making."[8] Before giving a synopsis of this theodicy, it will be helpful to reflect on the general bearing of theodicies on the difficulty we have developed. Just what does a theodicy endeavor to do? Does it propose to tell us in some detail just what good state it is that justifies O, if O exists, in permitting E1 and E2? No. Such an account would presume a knowledge of O's specific purposes, a knowledge that it would be unreasonable to expect we would have without some detailed revelation to us from O. What a theodicy does endeavor to do is to fasten on some good state of affairs and argue that it would justify O in permitting evils like E1 and E2. Whether obtaining the good in question is O's actual reason for permitting evils like E1 and E2 is not really part of what a theodicy tries to establish. It only hopes to show that *if* obtaining the good in question were O's aim in permitting evils like E1 and E2, then (given what we know) O would be justified in permitting such evils. In addition, it is important to the success of the theodicy that the good in question not be a good we have reason to believe does not obtain. It would not be helpful, for example, to argue that the good in question is every human being turning to Christ before that person experiences bodily death. For we have very good reason to think that such a good does not obtain. The theodicist doesn't have to establish that the good in question does obtain, but she must at least argue that we do not have any really strong reasons to think that it doesn't obtain. In terms of our presentation of the difficulty, then, we should see the theodicist as denying P. What the theodicist claims, so it seems to me, is that *some good we know of* is such that obtaining it would justify O in permitting E1 and E2. Need a theist be a theodicist? I don't think so. A theist *must* reject Q. But she need not reject P. Someone could hold that her reasons for thinking O exists *outweigh* P's support of Q, so that it is rational on balance for the theist to believe that Q is false. Such a theist might hold that the good that would justify O in permitting E1 and E2 is a good that is totally beyond our ken in this life. Such a position is not inconsistent with theism, although it does abandon the project of providing a theodicy.[9]

Some theodicies depend on having very strong reasons for believing that O exists. Leibniz's theodicy, as I read it, is a case in point. Having established to his satisfaction that O exists, Leibniz claimed to deduce that the good in question is this being the best of all possible worlds. Now if this is the best of all possible worlds then clearly such a good would justify an omnipotent, omniscient being in permitting E1, E2, and all the other evils our world contains.[10] Other theodicies need not depend for their success on proving the existence of O. Hick's theodicy, as I read it, does not depend on such a proof. With these preliminary remarks out of the way, we can now consider the basic structure of Hick's "soul-making" theodicy.

There are two good states that figure in Hick's theodicy. The first is the state in which all human beings develop themselves through their free choices into moral and spiritual beings. The second good state is that in which all such beings enter into an eternal life of bliss and joy in fellowship with O. The second of these good states (and probably the first) obtains only if O exists. But, as I've suggested, in order to be successful a theodicy need not *establish* that the good in question obtains. Let's begin our synopsis by considering the first of these states, the state in which all human beings develop themselves through their free choices into moral and spiritual beings. How might the obtaining of such a good justify an omnipotent, omniscient being in permitting evils like E1 or E2?

Since E1 and E2 are instances of natural and moral evil, different answers may be required. Let's begin with horrendous moral evils like E2. Hick's first step is to argue that if moral and spiritual development through free choices is the good in question then an environment in which there is no significant suffering, no occasion for significant moral choices, would not be one in which moral and spiritual growth would be possible. In particular, a world in which no one can harm another, in which no pain or suffering results from any action, would not be a world in which such moral and spiritual growth could occur.

I think we can concede to Hick that a pain-free paradise, a world in which no one could be injured and no one could do harm, would be a world devoid of significant moral and spiritual development. But what are we to make of the fact that the world we live in is so often inimical to such moral and spiritual development? For clearly, as Hick is careful to note, much of the pain and suffering in our world frustrates such development.

> The overall situation is thus that, so far as we can tell, suffering occurs haphazardly, uselessly, and therefore unjustly. It appears to be only randomly related either to past desert or to future soul-making. Instead of serving a constructive purpose, pain and misery seem to fall upon men patternlessly and meaninglessly, with the result that suffering is often undeserved and often occurs in amounts exceeding anything that could have been morally planned.[11]

Hick's response to this point is to ask us what would happen were our world one in which suffering occurred ". . . not haphazardly and therefore unjustly, but on the contrary justly and therefore non-haphazardly."[12] In such a world, Hick, following Kant, reasons that people would avoid wrongdoing out of fear rather than from a sense of duty. Moreover, once we saw that suffering was always for the good of the sufferer, human misery would no longer ". . . evoke deep personal sympathy or call forth organized relief and sacrificial help and service. For it is presupposed in those compassionate reactions both that the suffering is not deserved and that it is *bad* for the sufferer."[13] Hick then concludes:

> It seems, then, that in a world that is to be the scene of compassionate love and self-giving for others, suffering must fall upon mankind with something of the haphazardness and inequity that we now experience. It must be apparently unmerited, pointless, and incapable of being morally rationalized. For it is precisely this feature of our common human lot that creates sympathy between man and man and evokes the unselfishness, kindness, and goodwill which are among the highest values of personal life.[14]

Let's assume with Hick that an environment fit for human beings to develop the highest qualities of moral and spiritual life must be one that includes real suffering, hardships, disappointments, failure, and defeat. For moral and spiritual growth presuppose these. Let's also assume that such an environment must operate, at least for the most part, according to general and dependable laws, for only on the basis of such general laws can a person engage in the purposeful decision-making essential to rational and moral life.[15] And given these two assumptions it is, I think, understandable how an omniscient, omnipotent being may be morally justified in permitting the occurrence of evils, both moral and natural.

Our excursion into John Hick's theodicy has shown us, perhaps, how a theodicy may succeed in justifying O's permission of both natural and moral evil. But so far we haven't been given any justification for O's permission of E1 or E2. In the case of E1 we can say that *given* the existence of the animals in our world and the operation of the world according to natural laws, it is unavoidable that instances of intense and prolonged animal suffering would occur. In the case of E2 we can say that on their way toward moral and spiritual development it is perhaps unavoidable that human beings will sometimes seriously harm others through a bad use of freedom. But neither of these points will morally justify an omnipotent, omniscient being in permitting E1 and E2. In the case of E2, it is simply unreasonable to believe that if the boyfriend acted freely in brutally beating and raping the little girl, his moral and spiritual development would have been permanently frustrated had he been prevented from doing what he did. And it is also unreasonable to believe that permitting such an act is morally justified even if preventing it would somehow diminish the boyfriend's moral and spiritual odyssey.[16] And in the case of E1, it is simply unreasonable to believe that preventing the fawn's being severely burned, or mercifully ending its life so that it does not suffer intensely for several days, would so shake our confidence in the orderliness of nature that we would forsake our moral and spiritual development. I think Hick is not unaware of this limitation to his theodicy, at least with respect to natural evils. With respect to human pain due to sources independent of the human will, he remarks:

> In response to it, theodicy, if it is wisely conducted, follows a negative path. It is not possible to show positively that each item of human pain serves God's purpose of good; on the other hand, it does seem possible to show that the divine purpose, [. . .] could not be forwarded in a world that was designed as a permanent hedonistic paradise.[17]

What Hick says here is, I believe, right, with one minor modification. The minor modification is this. In Hick's theodicy some evils themselves are necessary to the attainment of the good of moral and spiritual development. But many evils, particularly those resulting from the operation of the laws of nature, will not themselves serve moral and spiritual development. They may even hinder it. Nevertheless, as the by-product of the general operation of the laws of nature, something that is essential to rational decision making and moral living, an omnipotent, omniscient being would have reason to permit even these evils, at least to the extent that further intervention on its part would diminish our expectation that the world operates on general laws.

What we've seen is that Hick's theodicy fails if it is intended to provide a good that would justify an omnipotent, omniscient being in permitting E1 or E2. The best that Hick can do is to argue that a world *utterly devoid* of natural or moral evil would preclude the realization of the goods he postulates as justifying an omnipotent, omniscient being in permitting evil. However, since the prevention of E1 or E2 would not leave our world utterly devoid of natural or moral evil, his all-or-nothing argument provides no answer to our question. Nor will it do to say that if an omnipotent, omniscient being were to be morally obligated to prevent E1 or E2 it would thereby be obligated to prevent all such evils. For were it to do so it may well be that we would cease to engage in very significant soul-making. The problem Hick's theodicy leaves us is that it is altogether reasonable to believe that some of the evils that occur (E1 and E2, for example) could have been prevented without either diminishing our moral and spiritual development or undermining our confidence that the world operates according to natural laws. Hick's theodicy, therefore, does not succeed in showing that we have no good reason to accept P. Nor does his theodicy show that we aren't justified in inferring Q from P. In short, Hick's theodicy does little to diminish the claim that the existence of certain evils provides rational grounds for atheism.

Some may feel that I have criticized Hick's theodicy for failing to do what it was never meant to do: to show us the good the obtaining of which would justify an omnipotent, omniscient being in permitting E1 or E2. Theodicies, one might argue, are not intended to provide a justification for *particular evils.* I acknowledge the merit of this criticism. There are, I think, four different things a theodicy might aim at doing, each more difficult than its predecessor. First, a theodicy might seek to explain why O would permit *any evil* at all. Second, a theodicy might endeavor to explain why there are instances of the various *kinds* of evil we find in our world—animal pain, human suffering, wickedness, etc. Third, a theodicy might endeavor to explain why there is the *amount* of evil (of these kinds) that we find in our world. And, finally, a theodicy might endeavor to explain certain *particular evils* that obtain. I think Hick's theodicy may be successful on the first level, and perhaps the second. In so far, therefore, as we argue against the existence of O solely by appealing to the fact that our world contains evil, or to the fact that our world contains certain kinds of evil, Hick's theodicy may show that the relevant P-like premise can be reasonably rejected. But arguments based on the third and fourth levels, so far as I can see, remain undiminished by Hick's theodicy. If his theodicy is not intended to diminish the strength of these arguments—by giving grounds for rejecting their P-like premises—then it is a mistake to charge that the theodicy fails to accomplish *its end.* But the point will remain that the theodicy does little or nothing to diminish the force of the strongest arguments from evil.

NOTES

1. Bruce Russell, "The Persistent Problem of Evil," *Faith and Philosophy* 6 (1989): 121–39.

2. For sake of simplicity, I shall ignore the possibility that O permits E1 or E2 in order to prevent some equal or worse state from obtaining. I shall also ignore the possibility that there are two evils equally bad such that either could be prevented without loss of the justifying good, but one or the other must be permitted to obtain the good.

3. Roughly, to know of a good state of affairs is to (a) conceive of that state of affairs, and (b) recognize that it is intrinsically good.

4. In addition, there may be simple properties we have never thought of, properties whose presence in a state of affairs might render that state a great intrinsic good.

5. Of course, the *conjunction* of one of these great goods, G, with E1, say, will be unobtainable by omnipotence without permitting E1. But since we have reason to think that G can be obtained by omnipotence without permitting E1, obtaining the conjunction of G and E1 won't justify this being in permitting E1. The conjunction of G and E1, like G itself, will lack J.

6. The first response in effect claims that if P were all we knew relative to the truth or falsity of Q, we would not be rationally justified in believing Q. It is this claim that I am rejecting as false.

7. Stephen Wykstra has pointed out to me that it may suffice to defeat P's support of Q to show that if not-Q, P would be no less likely than not-P. We should, therefore, distinguish a stronger and more modest defeater. To give a reason for believing *If not-Q, P would be true anyway* is to provide a strong defeater. To give a reason for believing *If not-Q, P would be no less likely than not-P* is to provide a modest defeater. In the text I discuss only the strong defeater. A more comprehensive discussion would need to consider the more modest defeater as well.

8. See John Hick, *Evil and the God of Love* (New York: Harper and Row, 1966), particularly chap. 17 of the revised edition, published in 1978, *God and the Universe of Faiths* (New York: St. Martin's Press, 1973), and chap. 4 of *Philosophy of Religion*, 3rd edition (Englewood Cliffs: Prentice-Hall, 1983).

9. The account I've given of the aim of a theodicy takes it to be providing a plausible justification for O's permitting *particular evils*. Perhaps this is too ambitious. Perhaps the aim of a theodicy is only to provide a plausible justification for O's permitting *some instances of various types of evil*. One might succeed at the latter and yet fail at the former. If we do take the second account, we need to revise my judgment of Hick's theodicy. One might then conclude that although Hick's theodicy is successful, it is largely irrelevant to the question of whether the existence of particular evils provides rational grounds for atheism. (See the final paragraph of this essay.)

10. Is *this being the best of all possible worlds* a good we know of? I'm not sure of the proper answer to this question. If it isn't, then my suggestion that theodicies are committed to denying P needs to be qualified. But apart from good reasons to believe that O exists, I would argue that we have reason to think that this is not the best of all possible worlds.

11. Hick, *God and the Universe of Faiths*, p. 58.

12. Ibid.

13. Ibid., p. 60.

14. Ibid.

15. This point is forcefully argued by William Hasker in "Suffering, Soul-Making and Salvation," *International Philosophical Quarterly* 28 (1988): 3–19.

16. See Bruce Russell's paper for further argument on this point.

17. Hick, *Philosophy of Religion*, p. 46.

4

THE EVIDENTIAL ARGUMENT FROM EVIL

A SECOND LOOK

WILLIAM L. ROWE

I

It is as misleading to speak of *the* evidential argument from evil as it is to speak of *the* cosmological argument. Just as there are distinct arguments that qualify as cosmological arguments, there are distinct arguments that qualify as evidential arguments from evil.[1] My purpose here is to look again at an evidential argument from evil that I first presented in 1979.[2] Since that time I have made several changes in that argument in an effort to make it clearer and to patch up weaknesses in earlier statements of it. Starting with the latest published account of the argument, I will discuss some important criticisms of it and will continue my efforts to clarify, simplify, and strengthen the argument.

The latest formulation I have given of the evidential problem of evil goes something like this.[3] (E1 is the case of a fawn trapped in a forest fire and undergoing several days of terrible agony before dying. E2 is the case of the rape, beating, and murder by strangulation of a five-year-old girl.)[4]

P: No good we know of justifies an omnipotent, omniscient, perfectly good being in permitting E1 and E2;
therefore,

Q: No good at all justifies an omnipotent, omniscient, perfectly good being in permitting E1 and E2;

From *The Evidential Argument from Evil*, edited by Daniel Howard-Snyder (Bloomington: Indiana University Press, 1996), pp. 262–85.

therefore,
not-G: there is no omnipotent, omniscient, perfectly good being,

The first inference, from P to Q, is, of course, an inductive inference. My claim was that P makes Q probable. The second inference, from Q to not-G, is deductive.

Against this argument from evil a variety of criticisms are possible. One might claim (1) that none of us is in a position to be justified in believing P. One might claim (2) that the inference from P to Q is not a good inductive inference, that P does not make Q more probable than not. So, one cannot be justified in believing Q on the basis of P. One might claim (3) that even though the inference from P to Q is a good inductive inference, we have reasons (defeaters) on the basis of which it is rational to refrain from accepting Q on the basis of P. Finally, one might claim (4) that not-G does not deductively follow from Q because two possibilities are not excluded. First, (4a) it could be that the prevention of some worse evils is what justifies God in permitting E1 and E2.[5] Second, (4b) it could be that in a world with free, morally responsible creatures God needs to permit the occurrence of unjustified evil (gratuitous evil).[6]

Criticisms that have been advanced against this version of the evidential argument from evil have focused mainly on (1) and (2). Although several important papers have developed such criticisms, special mention should be made of William Alston's essay "The Inductive Problem of Evil and the Human Cognitive Condition" and several papers by Stephen Wykstra.[7] Obviously, the whole issue of whether what we know about evil in our world makes it likely that the theistic God does not exist is quite complex and cannot be satisfactorily addressed in any single essay. But I will undertake here to answer some serious objections concerning the inference from P to Q (raised by Alston, Wykstra, and others) and some serious objections concerning P itself (mostly raised by Alston). After discussing two preliminary matters, I will take up the objections to the inference from P to Q, later turning to some issues concerning P itself.

II

Initially, we need to do two things. First, we need to specify just what P and Q assert. Although I have endeavored to do this in earlier writings on this topic, I don't think I have been as clear as is necessary. So I want to begin with this task, departing somewhat from earlier formulations. Second, we need to settle on our background information, connecting it to the question of God's existence in a way that will make our discussion relevant to the dispute between theists and nontheists over the problem of evil.

As we've already noted, at least initially our discussion revolves around two particular evils, E1 (Bambi) and E2 (Sue). What is it that P affirms about E1 and E2? P says *no good we know of* justifies an omnipotent, omniscient, perfectly good being in permitting E1 and E2. What then does P entail? P entails that among the good states of affairs that we know of (however dimly or through a glass darkly) none is such that it justifies an omnipotent, omniscient, perfectly good being in permitting E1 and E2. So long as we keep in mind the features of the being in question, we can abbreviate our formulation of P as follows:

P: No good we know of justifies God in permitting E1 and E2.

Since we are talking about a good that justifies God in permitting E1 *and* E2, we should allow, if not expect, that the good in question would be a *conjunctive* good. Perhaps there is a good we know of that justifies God in permitting E1. Perhaps there is some other good we know of that justifies God in permitting E2. If so, then we will allow that it is true that some good we know of (a conjunction of the goods in question) justifies God in permitting E1 and E2. It should be obvious that I am trying to pose a serious difficulty for the theist by picking a difficult case of natural evil, E1 (Bambi), and a difficult case of moral evil, E2 (Sue). Should no good we know of justify God in permitting either of these two evils, P is true.

What counts as a "good we know of"? I do not mean to limit us to goods that we know to have occurred. Nor do I mean to limit us to those goods and goods that we know will occur in the future. I mean to include goods that we have some grasp of, even though we have no knowledge at all that they have occurred or ever will occur. For example, consider the good of Sue's experiencing complete felicity in the everlasting presence of God. Theists consider this an enormous personal good. I have no doubt that it is. So, even though we don't have a very clear grasp of what this great good involves, and even though we don't know that such a good state of affairs will ever obtain, we do mean to include the good of Sue's experiencing complete felicity in the everlasting presence of God as among *the goods we know of*. Of course, if the good in question never does occur, then it is not a good that justifies God in permitting E1 or E2. So if some good state of affairs we know of does justify God in permitting E1 or E2, that good state of affairs must become actual at some point in the future, if it is not already actual.

Under what conditions would P be true? P says that there is no good we know of that justifies God in permitting E1 and E2. One condition that would render P true is the nonoccurrence of the known good (supposing there is just one) whose occurrence would justify God in permitting E1 or E2. Suppose that among all known goods only Sue's experiencing eternal felicity in the presence of God is such that its occurrence would justify God in permitting E2 (Sue's suffering on being brutally beaten, raped, and strangled). If this good never occurs, P is true. As I indicated earlier, a good state of affairs justifies God in permitting some actual evil only if that good state of affairs occurs. Second, we should note that the nonexistence of God is also a sufficient condition of the truth of P. For the realization of a known good justifies God in permitting E1 or E2 only if God exists. To see this, consider the *negation* of P. The negation of P asserts that God exists and that some good known to us justifies him in permitting E1 and E2. Since the negation of P is false if God does not exist, P will be true if God does not exist.[8]

Having spent some time clarifying P, we can be brief with Q.

> Q: No good at all justifies an omnipotent, omniscient, perfectly good being in permitting E1 and E2.

So long as we keep in mind the features of the being in question, we can abbreviate our formulation as follows:

> Q: No good justifies God in permitting E1 and E2.

As with P, we should note that if God does not exist, Q is true. For given that E1 and E2 exist, if God does not exist then it is not the case that there is an omnipotent, omniscient, perfectly good being who is justified in permitting E1 and E2 by virtue of realizing some good. Another way of seeing this point is to note that the *negation* of Q asserts that God exists and that there is a good that justifies God in permitting E1 and E2. Since the negation of Q is false if God does not exist, Q is true if God does not exist.

I turn now to the background information k on which we will rely in forming judgments about how likely P, Q, and G (God exists) are. What will k include? I take it as important here that k be restricted almost entirely to information that is shared by most theists and nontheists who have given some thought to the issues raised by the problem of evil.[9] To this end, we will want to include in k our common knowledge of the occurrence of various evils in our world, including E1 and E2, as well as our knowledge that the world contains a good deal of evil. k will also include our common understanding of the way the world works, the sorts of things we know to exist in the world, along with our knowledge of many of the goods that occur and many of the goods that do not occur. Of course, k will not include the information that God exists or the information that God does not exist.

If we conceive of k in the way just suggested, what assignment should be given to the probability that God exists, given k, Pr(G/k)? Many nontheists hold that the enormous amount of evil in our world, particularly instances of horrendous human or animal suffering such as E1 and E2, make the existence of the theistic God unlikely. Many theists and some nontheists, however, will disagree with this assessment. On the other hand, many theists will argue that the mere existence of a world (or the order in the world) makes the existence of God likely. But some theists and many nontheists will disagree with this assessment. In order not to beg any of these questions, I will assign a probability of 0.5 to Pr(G/k), and, of course, 0.5 to Pr(~G/k). We will say that k by itself makes neither God's existence nor his nonexistence more likely than not. This need not be understood as denying what some nontheists hold concerning the possible negative evidential impact of the existence and multitude of horrendous evils in the world. Nor need it be understood as denying what some theists hold about the possible positive evidential impact of the existence of a world exhibiting order, etc. What it does indicate is that these different aspects of k—if they do impact positively or negatively on the likelihood of God's existence—in some way balance out so that the totality of k leaves the probability of the existence of God at 0.5.[10]

Will k include the information that ordinary religious experiences and mystical religious experiences occur? Insofar as the inclusion of such information raises the probability of G on k above 0.5 we will have to exclude it. This may seem arbitrary and harmful to the theist's position. But it need not be construed in that way. If it should turn out that we have reason to believe that P is true and that P lowers the probability of God's existence, it is open to the theist to reply that the addition to k of our information concerning the occurrence of ordinary and mystical religious experiences restores the balance or even tips the scales in favor of theism. As I endeavored to make clear in "The Problem of Evil and Some Varieties of Atheism," I have *not* argued that no matter what other evidence a person has, the argument from evil will still make it unreasonable for that person (who understands the argument from evil and accepts the grounds for its premises) to believe in God. For one might have stronger evidence for the existence of God than is provided by the problem of evil for the nonexistence of God.[11]

k will not, of course, include either P or Q. Moreover, so that we do not beg an important question central to the criticism that P is not a good reason for Q, k will not include any explicit claim as to whether the goods we know are representative of all the goods there are.

III

We want to discover the answer to four questions:

1. Does P make Q more likely than it would otherwise be? That is, is Pr(Q/P&k) > Pr(Q/k)?

2. Does P make Q more likely than not? That is, is Pr(Q/P&k) > 0.5?[12]
3. Does P make G less likely than it would otherwise be? That is, is Pr(G/P&k) < Pr(G/k)?
4. Does P make G less likely than not? That is, is Pr(G/P&k) < 0.5?[13]

In this section we will give reasons for an affirmative answer to the first question and note a difficulty in one attempt to provide an affirmative answer to the second question.

To begin our investigation, let's consider what Bayes's Theorem tells us about Pr(Q/P&k), the probability of Q given P and k. According to Bayes's Theorem,

$$\Pr(Q/P\&k) = \Pr(Q/k) \times \Pr(P/Q\&k) \,/\, \Pr(P/k).$$

By reflecting on this equation, can we make any progress toward answering either of our first two questions? I believe we can. First, all of us will certainly agree that Pr(Q/P&k) < 1. Indeed, according to Alston and others, we have no reason at all to think that Pr(Q/P&k) isn't less than 0.5. Moreover, since Q entails P, Pr(P/Q&k) = 1. Now, since Pr(Q/P&k) < 1 and Pr(P/Q&k) = 1, it follows that

Pr(Q/k) < Pr(P/k).[14]

It is also clear that our background information k does not entail P, so Pr(P/k) does not equal 1. And from the conjunction of Pr(P/Q&k) = 1, Pr(Q/k) < Pr(P/k), and Pr(P/k) < 1, it follows that

Pr(Q/P&k) > Pr(Q/k).

So, we have reached a definitive answer to our first question. P does make Q more likely than it would otherwise be.

But what of our second question? Does P make Q more likely than not? In an earlier paper[15] I gave an affirmative answer to this question and endeavored to support that answer with an argument I've since come to believe is inadequate. I noted first that the inference from P to Q is like an inference from "All the A's we've observed are B's" to "All A's are B's." I then argued that if we have observed many A's and found all of them to be B's, we have a prima facie good reason to believe that the A's we haven't observed will likely be B's as well. Thus we have a prima facie good reason to believe that all A's are B's.

I now think this argument is, at best, a weak argument.[16] To shore it up we would need some reason to think it likely that the goods we know of (the A's we've observed) are representative of the goods there are (the A's there are).

Noting the variety of goods we know of would be relevant to this task. Having a good argument to think that most goods are known to us would also be relevant.[17] But I now propose to abandon this argument altogether and give what I believe is a better argument for thinking that P makes Q more likely than not. Consideration of this new argument, however, must be postponed until we have discovered the answers to questions 3 and 4, the questions that are of ultimate interest to us.

IV

If we substitute G (God exists) for Q (No good justifies God in permitting E1 and E2) in our earlier representation of Pr(Q/P&k) according to Bayes's Theorem, we get the following:

$$Pr(G/P\&k) = Pr(G/k) \times Pr(P/G\&k) \,/\, Pr(P/k).$$

Recall that from our earlier discussion of k, Pr(G/k) = 0.5. Also note that *if* Pr(P/k) > Pr(P/G&k) *then* Pr(G/P&k) < Pr(G/k). (The general point here is that G makes P less likely than it would otherwise be if and only if P makes G less likely than it would otherwise be.) So, *if* we can succeed in showing Pr(P/k) > Pr(P/G&k) *then* we will have established an important point about what can be inferred from P. For we will have shown, first, that given k, P makes G less likely than it would otherwise be, Pr(G/P&k) < Pr(G/k), and, second, that given k, P makes G less likely than not, Pr(G/P&k) < 0.5. (This part follows from the first part and the fact that Pr(G/k) = 0.5.)[18] But can we establish that Pr(P/k) > Pr(P/G&k)? I believe we can.

Let's begin by considering Pr(P/G&k). In the end we shall discover that it will not matter much what value is assigned to Pr(P/G&k), so long as it is less than 1.[19] But for the moment it will be instructive to assign it a value of 0.5. Theodicists who believe that there are goods that we know of that could justify God in permitting E1 and E2 may think that Pr(P/G&k) < 0.5. Other theists who find themselves quite incapable of thinking of any good whose realization might be God's reason for permitting E1 and E2 would undoubtedly be sympathetic to the assignment of 0.5, and may even think that it should be somewhat higher than that.[20] But for instructive purposes, let's assume that Pr(P/G&k) = 0.5. If so, can we determine Pr(P/k)? Or, if we cannot determine Pr(P/k), can we at least determine that it is > 0.5? The truth is that given that Pr(G/k) = 0.5 and given that Pr(P/G&k) is 0.5, we can determine exactly what Pr(P/k) is. To see this, let's first establish that Pr(P/k) must lie somewhere between a low of 0.25 and a high of 0.75. We establish this by using the rule of elimination to determine the value of Pr(P/k):

Pr(P/k) = [Pr(G/k) × Pr(P/G&k)] + [Pr(~G/k) × Pr(P/~G&k)].

Since Pr(G/k) and Pr(P/G&k) are both 0.5, we have 0.25 on the left side of the plus sign. And since Pr(~G/k) = 0.5 and Pr(P/~G&k) must lie somewhere between zero and 1, it follows that on the right side of the plus sign the number must be somewhere between zero and 0.5. Therefore, Pr(P/k) is somewhere between 0.25 and 0.75.

Now if we could go no further toward establishing Pr(P/k), very little of interest could be established concerning Pr(G/P&k). But we can go further. In fact, we can establish that if both Pr(G/k) and Pr(P/G&k) = 0.5, then Pr(G/P&k) = 0.333.[21] This can be shown once we note that Pr(P/~G&k) = 1. For, as we earlier noted, P is entailed by ~G. So, since P is entailed by ~G, Pr(P/~G&k) = 1.

If both Pr(G/k) and Pr(P/G&k) = 0.5, Pr(P/k) = 0.75, with the result that Pr(G/P&k) = 0.333. And this shows us a general truth: given that Pr(G/k) = 0.5 and Pr(P/G&k) < 1, P not only lowers the probability of G, it also makes G lower than 0.5. But we need to distinguish these two results. The first, that P lowers the probability of G, makes G less likely than it would otherwise be, is bound to be true provided that Pr(P/G&k) < 1. For given that Pr(P/G&k) < 1 (as almost all would agree), it must be that Pr(P/k) > Pr(P/G&k). And, if Pr(P/k) > Pr(P/G&k) then Pr(G/P&k) < Pr(G/k)—no matter what Pr(G/k) happens to be. The second, that P makes G lower than 0.5, does depend to some degree on our original assignment of 0.5 to Pr(G/k). If we sufficiently increase Pr(G/k), then although Pr(G/P&k) will always be lower than Pr(G/k), it will rise above 0.5. And this is what we should expect. For if the existence of God is sufficiently probable apart from the negative impact of P, then the existence of God may still be more probable than not even when the negative impact of P is taken into account. No one should disagree with this result.

To sum up then: Since Pr(Q/P&k) < 1 and Pr(P/k) < 1, it follows that

1. Pr(Q/P&k) > Pr(Q/k).

And given that Pr(G/k) = 0.5 and that Pr(P/G&k) < 1, we have established two other important points.

2. Pr(G/P&k) < Pr(G/k).
3. Pr(G/P&k) < 0.5.

What we have yet to establish is

4. Pr(Q/P&k) > 0.5.

Let's return to our first formula concerning Pr(Q/P&k):

$$Pr(Q/P\&k) = Pr(Q/k) \times Pr(P/Q\&k) \,/\, Pr(P/k).$$

Since Pr(P/Q&k) = 1, we can eliminate it from the formula with the following result:

$$Pr(Q/P\&k) = Pr(Q/k) \,/\, Pr(P/k).$$

Relying on our earlier stipulation that Pr(G/k) = 0.5 and Pr(~G/k) = 0.5, we can use the rule of elimination to determine the value of Pr(Q/k). We have the following:

$$Pr(Q/k) = [Pr(G/k) \times Pr(Q/G\&k)] + [Pr({\sim}G/k) \times Pr(Q/{\sim}G\&k)].$$

On the left side of the plus sign, we have 0.5×0, for the conjunction (G&k) entails that Q is false.[22] On the right side of the plus sign we have 0.5×1, for Q is entailed by ~G. So Pr(Q/k) = 0.5. If we accept the earlier assignment of 0.5 to Pr(P/G&k), then Pr(P/k) = 0.75, with the result that Pr(Q/P&k) = 0.666. But aside from this argument, it is evident that Pr(P/k) > Pr(Q/k).[23] So, given that Pr(P/k) < 1, if Pr(Q/k) = 0.5, it follows that Pr(Q/P&k) > 0.5. In fact, if our argument is correct, Pr(Q/P&k) = 1 – Pr(G/P&k), and this will be true no matter what non-zero assignments less than 1 are made to Pr(P/k), Pr(G/k), and Pr(Q/k).

Returning to our summing up, we can now add

4. Pr(Q/P&k) > 0.5

to our list of propositions we have established given that Pr(G/k) = 0.5 and that Pr(P/G&k) < 1. This is the better argument I mentioned earlier for the view that P not only makes Q more likely than it otherwise would be but also makes it more likely than not.[24]

Return now to the formulation of the argument at the beginning of this paper. The argument proceeds inductively from P to Q and deductively from Q to ~G. Given the discussion in sections II and III, it is clear that we can simplify the argument considerably by bypassing Q altogether and proceeding directly from P to ~G. And that is what I now propose to do. Our evidential argument from evil, therefore, can now be stated more succinctly as

P: No good we know of justifies God in permitting E1 and E2;
therefore, it is probable that
~G: There is no omnipotent, omniscient, perfectly good being.

So far, we have not considered what justification we might have for the initial premise P. As I noted earlier, we need to consider this issue in the light of objections raised by Alston in "The Inductive Problem of Evil and the Human Cognitive Condition." What we have been considering is the justification we have for the claim that P makes ~G probable. And what we have seen is that given that the probability of G on our background information k is 0.5, there is a compelling argument that P makes ~G more probable than G. So it does seem that we are justified in holding not only that P makes G less likely than it would otherwise be, but also justified in holding that P makes G less likely than ~G. But we need to look more deeply into the degree of support P provides for ~G, particularly in light of Wykstra's penetrating discussions of this point.

V

I refer the reader to Wykstra's new essay, "Rowe's Noseeum Arguments from Evil," for a full explication of CORNEA (Condition of Reasonable Epistemic Access) and his current understanding of its application to my inference from P to ~G.[25] But in brief it comes to this: Wykstra's CORNEA, as he now explains it, tells us that we are entitled to believe Q (or ~G) on the basis of P only if it is reasonable for us to believe that

> If P is true, it is likely that Q (~G) is true.

As he puts it: "So all CORNEA really says is that premise P justifies our believing conclusion Q only if it is reasonable for us to believe that if P is true, then Q is likely true." Since we have deleted Q from our statement of the evidential argument, we can take the proposition in question to be:

> If P (No good we know of justifies God in permitting E1 and E2), it is likely that ~G (There is no omnipotent, omniscient, perfectly good being).

In his 1984 paper, to which I responded, Wykstra argued that given God's omniscience and that he is the creator of all that is, it is *quite likely* that the goods for the sake of which he permits many sufferings would be altogether *beyond our ken*. Noting my claim that in a great many cases of evil the justifying goods are nowhere within our ken, he remarked:

> The linchpin of my critique has been that if theism is true, this is *just what one would expect*; for if we think carefully about the sort of being theism proposes for our belief, it is *entirely expectable*—given what we know of our cognitive

limits—that the goods by virtue of which this Being allows known suffering should very often be beyond our ken.[26]

In his new essay he argues that it is not necessary for him to take such a strong position. He now holds that it would be sufficient to take a more "modest" approach, arguing that *it is just as likely as not* that these goods should be beyond our ken. So, instead of arguing that it is *quite likely* that the goods for the sake of which God permits many sufferings would be *beyond our ken*, Wykstra now opts for the more modest claim that it is *as likely as not* that these goods would be *beyond our ken*. He also argues that I cannot simply take the inference from P to ~G as a good inference, one we are entitled to make unless someone shows that we are not. Finally, he finishes his new essay by reworking and defending his analogy between God and the good parent who often acts in ways the child cannot understand.

Let's first consider his point that for my argument to work *it must be reasonable to believe* that if P is true then it is likely that ~G, that it is not sufficient just to claim that we are entitled to believe it unless we have a good reason not to believe it, thus throwing all the burden on the theist to argue that P's being true does not make it likely that God does not exist. I agree with Wykstra that it must be reasonable to believe that if P is true then it is likely that ~G. And I hope that the first several sections of this paper show that relative to background information k, on which G is as likely as not, P does make it likely that ~G. But this is a somewhat complicated matter and we need to look at it a bit more fully.

Given the level playing field assumption that the probability of God's existence is 0.5 relative to the theist's and nontheist's shared background information k, we raised the question of whether P makes G unlikely. We saw that *whatever probability (less than 1) we assign to G on k*, it will be the case that Pr(G/P&k) is lower than Pr(G/k).[27] We then saw, of course, that Pr(G/P&k) < 0.5. Have we then satisfied Wykstra's requirement that it be reasonable to believe that if P is true then it is likely that ~G? This depends on how we understand Wykstra's requirement. We've shown that it is reasonable to believe that P lowers the probability of G. We've shown that on our background information k, it is reasonable to believe that if P is true ~G is more likely than not. But have we shown that relative to background information k it is reasonable to *believe* that if P is true G is unlikely? Well, it might seem that we have. But suppose we put Wykstra's requirement like this. It must be reasonable to believe that *P is a good reason to believe that G is false*. Have we shown that the conjunction P&k is a good reason to believe ~G? If we have, then we may conclude that it is reasonable to believe that P is a good prima facie reason to believe that G is false. But what we have shown is that the conjunction P&k is a good reason to believe that G is *less likely than not*. And to have a good reason to believe that G is less likely than not is not the same as having a good reason to believe that G is false. For suppose we establish that Pr(G/P&k) = 0.45. If we do *establish* this, then we may agree that P is a good reason to believe that G is less likely than not. But we would require something more than this for P to be a good reason to believe that G is false. 0.45 is so close to 0.5 that the rational thing to do would be to suspend judgment about the truth or falsity of G. And I think what Wykstra requires of me is some reason to think that the probability of G on P&k is low enough for P to be a good reason to believe that G is false. Have I provided any such reason?

We've taken note of two major points in Wykstra's essay. First, we've seen that he holds that my evidential argument succeeds only if it is reasonable for me to believe that if P is true it is likely that ~G. Second, we've seen that he thinks that if the considerations he brings forth (the parent-child analogy, the moral depth line, etc.) suffice to show that if G is true P is *just as likely as not* (the "modest" attack), this will render it *unreasonable* for me to believe that if P is true it is likely that ~G. Concerning the first point, I've responded by noting (a) that P lowers the probability of G, and (b) that given k, P makes G less probable than not. The remaining issue is *how low* G must be on P&k for P&k to be a good reason to believe ~G. On this last point, we might settle on something like ~G being twice as likely as G. If so, then given our level playing field assumption, Pr(G/k) = 0.5, I believe I can satisfy Wykstra's requirement. For I think we have reason to believe that Pr(P/G&k) is no greater than 0.5. And given that Pr(G/k) = 0.5 and that Pr(P/G&k) is no greater than 0.5, it follows that Pr(G/P&k) is no greater than 0.333.

It is clear, however, that Wykstra thinks that a probability of 1/3 is not low enough to justify disbelief. He holds, I believe, that if the initial probability of G on k is 0.5 and the probability of P on G&k is 0.5, then, although P lowers G's likelihood to 1/3 and increases ~G's likelihood to 2/3, thus making ~G twice as likely as G, P does not sufficiently lower G's probability to justify abandoning agnosticism and taking up atheism. I have some sympathy for this view. Using some concepts employed by Chisholm, so long as we had only k to go on we might say that believing theism was not more reasonable than believing atheism, and believing atheism was not more reasonable than believing theism. Adding P to k, however, shifts things in favor of atheism. It is now more reasonable to believe atheism than it is to believe theism. But this may be true without it being true that it is now more reasonable to believe atheism than it is to withhold judgment on the matter of God's existence (agnosticism). How much must P lower G's probability in order for Wykstra to think that we are justified in moving from agnosticism to atheism, assuming that our initial position was one of agnosticism? It may well be that there is no sharp cut-off point here. But even if there is, Wykstra's view is that the cut-off point is less than 1/3. In the penultimate version of his paper he suggested that if the initial probability of a hypothesis is 0.5

and some evidence lowers its probability to 0.2, this entitles a shift from "square agnosticism" to "semi-square atheism"; whereas if the evidence lowers its probability to 0.17, this entitles a shift from "square agnosticism" to "square atheism."[28] But in the final version he suggests that "levering evidence," evidence sufficient to lever a belief-state from square agnosticism to square atheism, must lower the probability of theism virtually to 0, "to something under .05." In support of this rather strict view of what constitutes "levering evidence," Wykstra remarks: "In ordinary contexts, the things we typically squarely believe each day (say, that one is wearing shoes and socks, that it is cloudy outside, etc.) are, in effect, rated so near to 1 as to make no practical difference."[29] I think Wykstra's examples here are typically cases of knowledge, rather than belief in the absence of knowledge. Typically, I know that I'm wearing socks and shoes. Typically, when outdoors I'm in the position to know that it is cloudy (when it is). But when clouds are dark and I hear what sounds like thunder, I may form the belief that it will rain soon. Is my belief that it will rain soon rated something well above .95? I don't think so. But this is a minor point. The important point here is Wykstra's observation that evidence that lowers an initial probability from 0.5 to 1/3 falls somewhat short of "levering evidence." I believe Wykstra is right about this point. Given our judgments about the probability of G on k and the probability of P on G&k, P is evidence for atheism. But it is not "levering evidence"; it does not justify a shift from square agnosticism to square atheism.

In reply to this interesting criticism, I have two points to make. First, it must be acknowledged that P does lower the probability of G. (Theists have been rather reluctant to acknowledge that the evils in our world, or what we have reason to believe about some of them, render God's existence less likely than it would otherwise be.) And if we start with our judgments about the probability of G on k and the probability of P on G&k, P lowers G's probability *significantly*, making ~G twice as likely as G. Although it does not lower G's probability sufficiently to move one from square agnosticism to square atheism, it does make it more rational to believe atheism than to believe theism. Second, we should remember that we are here considering one *particular argument* from evil, an argument based on the claim that no good we know of provides sufficient justification for God to permit two instances of evil, E1 and E2. As I suggested in an earlier essay,[30] there are two basic types of arguments from evil, one beginning from the fact that there exist evils "that seem to us to serve no good whatever, let alone one that is otherwise unobtainable by omnipotence," and the other that starts "from the somewhat less complex fact that the world contains vast amounts of intense human and animal suffering." In reaching any *overall conclusion* as to the force of the evidential argument from evil on the rationality of belief in God, we need to consider arguments of the second type as well. And the important point for our purposes here is that unlike the argument I've presented—resting as it does on a statement, P, that is not a part of k—arguments based simply on the existence of evils we know to occur are based on statements already contained in k. For k includes information about the kinds, amounts, and distribution of evils and goods in the world. Since I do think arguments based on our shared information about the kinds, amounts, and distribution of evils and goods in the world do have merit, I earlier noted in an endnote that my own view is that Pr(G/k) < 0.5. Suppose that after a thorough investigation of arguments of this sort we were to come to the conclusion that Pr(G/k) < 0.5. What bearing would this have on the argument that I have given in this paper? It would mean that Pr(G/P&k) < 0.333. How much less would depend on how low the probability of G on k is and how low the probability of P given G and k is. If Pr(G/k) = 0.2 and Pr(P/G&k) = 0.25, Pr(G/P&k) would be < .06. Of course, even if we were to agree to all this, we would not have answered Wykstra's point that my argument from P to ~G does not suffice to *leverage* us from square agnosticism to square atheism. For, since we are no longer taking Pr(G/k) to be 0.5, we are not beginning with square agnosticism. But if we were then to introduce k' as k *minus* the information about the kinds, amounts, and distribution of evils and goods in the world, we could then say that given Pr(G/k') as 0.5, the *combination* of the two sorts of arguments from evil may suffice to move us from square agnosticism to square atheism.

Wykstra's second point, his "modest" attack, turns out to be too modest to do much good. If all Wykstra does is establish that if God exists it is just as likely as not that P, we will be left with the result that Pr(G/P&k) = 0.333. Of course, since we've agreed that a probability of 0.333 is not sufficiently low to warrant belief in atheism, as opposed to belief that atheism is epistemically preferable to theism, Wykstra can rest content that my argument is insufficient to justify a move from square agnosticism to square atheism. But, as I've pointed out, the argument would still show that P *significantly lowers* the probability of G and makes belief in atheism more reasonable than belief in theism. To do anything more, Wykstra needs to revert to his *strong* attack and argue that Pr(P/G&k) is *very high*. Even if he is entirely successful in doing so, however, so long as Pr(P/G&k) < 1, it will still be true that Pr(G/P&k) < 0.5, that atheism is more probable than not. But if Wykstra succeeds in showing that Pr(P/G&k) is *very high*, Pr(G/P&k) will be quite close to 0.5. And this, of course, is not unimportant. For it would show that P does not *significantly lower* the probability of G.

Two questions remain:

> Are there good reasons for believing that Pr(P/G&k) is very high?
> Are there good reasons for believing that P is true?

In the next two sections I will take up these questions.

VI

Wykstra believes that if God exists it is quite likely that the goods for the sake of which he permits many instances of suffering (including Bambi's and Sue's) are beyond our ken. He argues from what he calls "the parent analogy." In his 1984 essay he claimed that our discerning most of these goods is "about as likely as that a one-month-old should discern most of his parents' purposes for those pains they allow him to suffer—which is to say, it is not likely at all."[31] In his new essay, he further develops and defends this argument from analogy.[32]

Before examining Wykstra's analogical argument for the view that Pr(P/G&k) is quite high, it will be helpful to see the bearing of this point on our evidential argument from evil. If God exists then some good justifies him in permitting Sue's horrendous suffering on being beaten, raped, and strangled. Either that good is a good we know of or it is not. Suppose that P is true, that *no good we know of* justifies God in permitting the sufferings of Bambi and Sue. Would this fact be a good reason for thinking it likely that God does not exist? As we've seen, this depends to a considerable extent on the degree to which P lowers the probability of G. Of course, P *does* lower the probability of G. But our question is whether it *significantly lowers* the probability of G. And the importance of Wykstra's parent analogy argument is that if it is correct we have a reason to think that P does not significantly lower the probability of G. So, much hangs on whether it can be successfully shown that if G is true, P is just what one would expect, that G makes P quite likely. We must now explore Wykstra's argument to this effect.

Is our intellectual grasp of goods for the sake of which God (if he exists) permits horrendous human and animal suffering *analogous* to a one-month-old infant's intellectual grasp of his parents' purposes for those pains they allow him to suffer? It hardly seems so. For a one-month-old infant hasn't developed the *concepts* necessary for even contemplating the proposition that good purposes may justify parents in permitting pains.[33] Adult human beings, on the other hand, have the intellectual equipment to distinguish intrinsic goods from extrinsic goods, to distinguish different kinds of intrinsic goods, to recognize certain intrinsic goods as superior to others, to form an idea of goods that have never been experienced by living human beings on earth (e.g., total felicity in the eternal presence of God), and to make some reasonable judgments about what goods an omnipotent being would (or would not) be able to bring about without permitting various instances of horrendous suffering. Of course, we have to allow that there may be kinds of intrinsic goods we have not thought of. But we do have reason to believe both that every intrinsic good necessarily involves conscious experience and that the highest intrinsic good human beings are capable of involves conscious experience of God. So, we know of many goods and we know of some of the very highest goods that human beings can experience. Why then does Wykstra believe that the parent analogy provides a strong argument for the view that the goods that justify God in permitting much horrendous suffering will be goods of which we have no knowledge?

Wykstra argues that the greater the degree of the parents' intelligence, care for the future life of the child, and ability, the more likely it is that their permitting present sufferings of the child serves goods in the *distant future*. Since God has unlimited intelligence, cares infinitely about the totality of each creature's life, and is unlimited in power, the argument from analogy implies that the goods justifying God in permitting horrendous human and animal suffering are often likely to be realized in the distant future.

What are we to make of this argument? Well, I don't think we should dismiss it out of hand simply because a parent's intelligence, loving concern for her children, and ability to provide are finite, whereas these features in God are infinite. But we should note that these differences make for significant disanalogies between the loving parent and God. The following are *often true* of the loving parent but are very likely *never true* of God:

A. The parent does not prevent the child's suffering (due to disease, etc.) simply because the parent is *unaware* of the cause of the suffering or *unable* to prevent the suffering.
B. The parent does not prevent the child's suffering because the parent has other duties to fulfill that preclude her from being in a position to prevent the suffering. Unlike God, parents cannot be everywhere at once.
C. The parent permits present sufferings for distant goods not because these goods are incapable of existing sooner, or better for being distant, but because of insufficient intelligence and ability to realize the goods in the present or near future.

But let's put aside these disanalogies and focus on what is, I believe, the major weakness of the argument based on the analogy between God and the loving parent. What happens when a loving parent intentionally permits her child to suffer intensely for the sake of a distant good that cannot otherwise be realized? In such instances the parent attends directly to the child throughout its period of suffering, comforts the child to the best of her ability, expresses her concern and love for the child in ways that are unmistakably clear to the child, assures the child that the suffering will end, and tries to explain, as best she can, why it is necessary for her to permit the suffering even though it is in her power to prevent it. In short, during these periods of intentionally permitted intense suffering, the child is *consciously aware* of the direct presence, love, and concern of the parent, and receives *special assurances* from the parent that, if not why, the suffering (or the parent's permission of it) is necessary for some distant good.

If we do apply the parent analogy, the conclusion about God that we should draw is something like the following: When God permits horrendous suffering for the sake of some good, if that good is *beyond our ken*, God will make every effort to be consciously present to us during our period of suffering, will do his best to explain to us why he is permitting us to suffer, and will give us special assurances of his love and concern during the period of the suffering.[34] Since enormous numbers of human beings undergo prolonged, horrendous suffering without being consciously aware of any such divine presence, concern, and explanations, we may conclude that if there is a God, the goods for the sake of which he permits horrendous human suffering are more often than not goods we know of. In any case, I think we are justified in concluding that we've been given no good reason to think that if God exists the goods that justify him in permitting much human and animal suffering are quite likely to be beyond our ken.[35]

VII

At long last we come to the question of P itself. What reason do we have to believe that *no good we know of justifies God in permitting E1 and E2*? The main reason to believe P is this: When we reflect on some good we know of we can see that it is very likely, if not certain, that the good in question *either* is not good enough to justify God in permitting E1 or E2 *or* is such that an omnipotent, omniscient being could realize it (or some greater good) without having to permit E1 or E2. Consider, for example, Sue's pleasure upon receiving some toys on her fourth birthday. Clearly that pleasure is not good enough to justify the permission by God of what we can only suppose to be her terror and pain on being brutally beaten, raped, and strangled when she was five years old. And if we begin to reflect on the various kinds of goods we know of, we will come to the sound judgment that many of them are not good enough to justify anyone in permitting E2. Similar remarks can be made concerning various kinds and degrees of goods relative to the terrible pain Bambi endures for several days upon being badly burned in the forest fire. In short, we can see that various kinds of goods we know of simply aren't good enough to justify permitting horrendous evils such as E1 and E2. On the other hand, for those goods we know of that do seem to *outweigh* either E1 or E2, reflection on them leads us to the judgment that it is very likely, if not certain, that an omnipotent being could have realized the goods in question (or some better goods) without having to permit E1 or E2. Consider, for example, Sue's experiencing complete felicity in the eternal presence of God. While this good may justly be held to outweigh almost any horrendous evil that may befall Sue in her earthly life, it strains credulity to think that it is beyond the power of God to realize this good without having to permit Sue's being brutally beaten, raped, and strangled at the age of five years. It might be suggested that had Sue continued to live out her life she would have freely chosen to harden her heart against God with the result that she would have precluded herself from experiencing complete felicity in the eternal presence of God. Let this be so. If God knows this, he might then have some reason to permit her death at the age of five. On the other hand, it hardly makes sense for God to give us the freedom to develop into beings who have hardened our hearts against him and his eternal kingdom and then act to prevent us from having the chance to exercise that freedom. Moreover, we might expect that God could have brought about circumstances in which Sue would have freely refrained from hardening her heart against God. But suppose that God does have reason to permit Sue's death at an early age. Does God then have a sufficient reason to permit her to die by being brutally beaten, raped, and strangled? Clearly, given his omnipotence he could have realized her early death by more humane means. So, even when we consider some good we know of that does seem to outweigh E2, we have good reason to believe that if God could realize that good, he could realize it without permitting E2. And what of Bambi's terrible suffering? What good do we know of that outweighs it and is such that God could not have realized it without permitting E1? When we reflect on any good we know of and consider Bambi's excruciating suffering, reason cries out that it is very likely, if not certain, that either the good is not good enough or God could have realized it without having to permit E1 (or something else as bad or worse).

In "The Inductive Argument from Evil and the Human Cognitive Condition" Alston does a masterful job of surveying the terrain of goods we know of in search of some good whose realization might justify God in permitting E1 or E2. Although the overall purpose of his essay is to establish that none of us is or can be justified in believing that no good justifies God in permitting E1 or E2, my interest here concerns only that part of his essay that focuses on P (No good we *know of* justifies God in permitting E1 and E2).[36] In pursuing our question of whether we are justified in believing that P is true, we can do no better than to critically examine Alston's discussion of this issue.

A major part of Alston's project is to consider familiar Christian theodicies and to explore their possible application to Bambi and Sue. These theodicies divide into those proposing divine reasons for suffering that are concerned with possible goods to those who endure the suffering and those proposing divine reasons for suffering concerned with possible goods not restricted to the sufferers. Examples he gives of the first sort are punishment for sin, soul-making, and having a vision of the inner life of God. Examples he gives of the second sort are the value of free will, benefits to those who cause or witness the suffering, and the value generated by a lawlike, natural order.

Alston emphasizes that he is considering Christian theodicies only as *live possibilities* for divine reasons for permitting evil. He is not undertaking to show that any of these theodicies is correct. Since he does not spell out what he means by a live possibility in this context, I shall take a live possibility here to be something that we have no good reason to believe would not wholly or partially justify an omniscient, omnipotent, wholly good being in permitting some evil. The question then becomes whether any or all of the theodicies are live possibilities *for Bambi and Sue*. If they are not live possibilities, if they are implausible suggestions as to what might justify an omnipotent, omniscient being in permitting Bambi and Sue, then, insofar as his use of Christian theodicies is concerned, Alston will not have shown that no one is justified in believing P to be true.

So far as goods for the sufferer are concerned, Alston believes that the prominent Christian theodicies *fail* to provide live possibilities for the cases of Bambi and Sue. But he thinks that he can establish that some goods we are familiar with (for example, the supreme fulfillment of one's nature) are such that we've no good reason to think that an omnipotent, omniscient being can obtain them without having to permit Bambi's and Sue's sufferings. But apart from noting that it is logically possible that Bambi's and Sue's sufferings are required for the fulfillment of their natures, Alston does little or nothing by way of "establishing" that we are not justified in precluding familiar goods like the supreme fulfillment of Bambi's nature or Bambi's having a vision of God from providing an omnipotent, omniscient being with a morally sufficient reason to permit Bambi's excruciating torment and death.

The major theodicy concerned with a good that extends beyond the sufferer is the free will theodicy. I will here consider Alston's efforts to use this theodicy to establish that we cannot be justified in believing P.[37] According to this theodicy, God is justified in permitting evil actions and their consequences because he has bestowed on some of his creatures genuine freedom in a range of actions, and it is a conceptual impossibility for God to create a free agent with respect to some action and also determine the agent to choose (not choose) to perform the action. So, according to this theodicy, God permits certain horrors to occur because to prevent them would be to prevent a certain degree of freedom in his creatures. Against this theodicy, Alston notes that it has been argued (1) that God could have created free creatures who always choose to do what is right, and (2) that permitting free will with respect to certain actions at certain times isn't worth the horrendous evils (for example, Sue's suffering) that result from the use of that freedom. Concerning the first objection, Alston points out that if we set aside middle knowledge, as he does in his essay, God would not be able to create beings with genuine freedom and "guarantee" that they will always choose to do what is right. And he further notes that even if we grant middle knowledge, Plantinga "has established the *possibility* that God could not actualize a world containing free creatures that always do the right thing."

Before considering his response to the second objection, we should note two points here. First, to conduct his case on the *assumption* that there is no middle knowledge considerably weakens Alston's argument. For there is no consensus on whether middle knowledge is possible. And if middle knowledge is possible, then we have reason to think that an omnipotent, omniscient being could have created a world with less evil, but as much good, as our world contains.[38] Nor will it do to emphasize that Plantinga has established the *possibility* that even with middle knowledge God could not have created a world with free creatures that always do the right thing. For Alston needs to show that even with middle knowledge it remains a *live possibility* that God could not have created a world with free creatures who always do what is right. But all that Plantinga has shown is that it is a *logical possibility* that such would be the case. And here again, I'm afraid, we have a slide on Alston's part from what is a logical possibility to what is a live possibility, from what is broadly logically possible to what we have no good reason for thinking isn't so. Indeed, that such a slide has occurred is indicated by the sentence with which Alston begins his very next paragraph: "Thus we may take it to be a *live possibility* that the maintenance of creaturely free will is at least part of God's reason for permitting wrongdoing and its consequences" (emphasis mine).

Suppose we endeavor to apply the free will theodicy to the case of Sue's suffering on being beaten, raped, and strangled. The first question we need to ask is whether the possession of free will is something that is *in itself* of such great value as to merit God's permission of the horrendous moral evils in the world. I think the answer must be no. We should distinguish the intrinsic value of possessing free will from its extrinsic value. The mere possession of free will does not strike me as itself having much in the way of intrinsic value.[39] But the possession of free will does seem necessary to attaining states that are of great intrinsic value. Thus, if we can agree that free will is necessary for the existence of things of great intrinsic value, we can agree that an omnipotent, omniscient, perfectly good being would likely endow his creatures (or some of them) with free will, provided that it does result to a sufficient degree in the things of great intrinsic value for which its possession was intended. But, of course, it is sometimes right to curtail a particular exercise of free will when one foresees or predicts that its exercise is evil and/or will result in considerable suffering. Since curtailing a particular exercise of free will does not significantly diminish a person's overall degree of freedom, the question at hand is whether it is rational to believe that an omnipotent, omniscient, perfectly good being would have prevented the particular exercise of free will (if that is what it was) Sue's attacker engaged in when he brutally beat, raped, and strangled the five-year-old child. As Alston puts the issue:

> presumably a tiny additional constriction such as would be involved in God's preventing Sue's attacker from committing that atrocity would not render things radically different, free-will-wise, from what they would have been without that. So God could have prevented this without losing the good emphasized by this theodicy. Hence we can be sure that this does not constitute a sufficient reason for His not preventing it.[40]

Alston, however, thinks that the preservation of Sue's attacker's free will is a *live possibility* for at least part of God's reason for permitting the suffering Sue undergoes at the hands of her attacker. For he reasons that the value of free will is such that God can intervene in only a small proportion of cases.

> Rowe's claim would then have to be that Sue's murder was so horrible that it would qualify for the class of exceptions. But that is precisely where the critic's claims far outrun his justification. How can we tell that Sue falls within the most damaging n percent of what would be cases of human wrongdoing apart from divine intervention? To be in a position to make such a judgment we would have to survey the full range of such cases and make reliable assessments of the deleterious consequences of each. Both tasks are far beyond our powers.[41]

Alston's point seems to be this: God cannot intervene in all cases of the use of free will in doing evil that results in suffering, for this would severely limit human capacity to choose between good and evil. God, then, would intervene only in a certain percentage (n) of such cases. The cases in which God intervenes would be selected so as to minimize human suffering overall or to maximize human welfare. And we simply don't know enough about what would be cases of human wickedness (past, present, and future) apart from divine intervention to determine whether or not Sue's case would be included among the percentage of cases God would select to eliminate. Alston states:

> Hence, by the nature of the case, we are simply not in a position to make a warranted judgment that Sue's case is among the n percent worst cases of wrongdoing in the history of the universe. No doubt it strikes us as incomparably horrible on hearing about it, but so would innumerable others. Therefore, the critic is not in a position to set aside the value of free will as at least part of God's reason for permitting Sue's murder.[42]

Does this argument *establish* that we aren't justified in excluding the value of human free will as part of God's reason for permitting Sue's suffering? Well, if the basic premise of Alston's argument is correct, the argument does establish just that. For to be so justified, Alston requires that we compare the episode involving Sue with the whole range of cases of human wrongdoing in the universe (past, present, and future) that would occur apart from divine intervention in order to determine whether Sue's case is sufficiently bad to warrant God in setting aside the value of free will in that case. And, of course, no human being knows enough to engage in such a comparison. But I do not think this knowledge is required. The free will theodicy is built around the idea that the possession of freedom to do good and evil is a good in *each person* that God creates. What is important, therefore, is that each person have some measure of freedom to do good and evil. Now, as Alston will readily admit, (1) we don't possess unlimited freedom, and (2) it is sometimes right to curtail someone's freedom in order to prevent some horrendous evil act that results in considerable suffering to an innocent person. But if God were to select some person and effectively prevent that person from ever choosing to do an evil deed that results in suffering to an innocent person, we can agree that this might severely diminish the value of that person's freedom to do good and evil. So God has a reason to permit each person to effectively engage in doing good and evil acts. Of course, God would be able to intervene in some of those acts without significantly diminishing the person's general freedom to do good and evil. What, then, do we have to make a judgment about in order to determine whether the prevention of Sue's attacker's freedom to brutally beat, rape, and strangle Sue would have severely diminished the value of that person's freedom to do good and evil? Do we have to compare it with all the cases of human wrongdoing, past, present, and future, as Alston claims? Clearly not. What is at issue here is not some sort of amount of freedom to do good and evil in the entire universe, past, present, and future. What is at issue here is the degree and value of Sue's attacker's freedom to do good and evil. Would this particular intervention severely diminish the value of that individual's overall degree of freedom to do good and evil? And if it would, is the value of that individual's overall degree of freedom to do good and evil worth the price of permitting the act in question? Perhaps some rational judgments are required about these questions in order for us to be justified in taking Sue's suffering as an instance of gratuitous suffering. But this is a far cry from having to do a survey of all human acts of wickedness in the universe, past, present, and future.[43]

We've had a look at Alston's efforts to single out *among goods we know of* some live possibilities for a sufficient reason for God to permit Bambi's or Sue's suffering. Concerning goods we know of that are restricted to the sufferer, Alston concedes that "none of the sufferer-centered reasons I considered could be any part of God's reasons for permitting the Bambi and Sue cases." And because it would be wrong for God to permit horrendous suffering *solely* for the benefit of others, Alston concludes "that nonsufferer-centered reasons could not be the whole of God's reasons for allowing any case of suffering." So, Alston's final conclusion is that he must appeal to goods *beyond our ken* in order to argue that we cannot be justified in believing that God has no sufficient reason to permit E1 or E2. Thus, quite apart from the specific criticisms I have presented against his attempts to provide live possibilities for God's reasons to permit E1 and E2, Alston concedes that he hasn't shown that we cannot be justified in believing that no good we *know of* justifies God in permitting E1 and E2.

Of course, it's one thing for the most talented philosophers and theologians to fail to show that we aren't justified in believing P, and another thing for us to be justified in believing P, and still another thing for us to *show* that we are justified in believing P. And I must confess that I know of no way to *prove* that P is true. What we do have is genuine knowledge that many goods we know of are insufficient to justify God in permitting E1 or E2. In addition we have very good reason to believe that many other goods we know of could be realized by an omnipotent, omniscient being without his having to permit E1 and E2 (or something just as bad). And, finally, we have the failure of theodicists to show how any of the goods we know of can plausibly be held, separately or collectively, to constitute a sufficient reason for God to permit E1 or E2. All this, I believe, gives us good reason to believe that P is true.

VIII

The evidential problem of evil derives its strength from our almost inescapable conviction that among the goods that fall within our intellectual grasp none can reasonably be thought to constitute God's justifying reason for permitting such horrendous evils as E1 and E2. For if we divide the possible justifying goods into those that fall within our intellectual grasp and those utterly beyond our ken, and then discover that none of the goods in the first category are justifying for God with respect to such horrendous evils, we significantly lower the likelihood of God's existence. This is particularly so if our antecedent expectations are that the justifying goods are as likely to fall in the first category as in the second.

Tough-minded theists have held that the facts about evil in our world do not render God's existence less likely than not. Indeed, some have held that the facts about evil do not even make God's existence less likely than it would otherwise be. In this paper I have argued that these views are seriously mistaken. Given our common knowledge of the evils and goods in our world and our reasons for believing that P is true, it is *irrational* to believe in theism unless we possess or discover strong evidence in its behalf. I conclude, therefore, that the evidential argument from evil is alive and well.[44]

NOTES

1. See Bruce Russell, "Defenseless," in *The Evidential Argument from Evil*, edited by Daniel Howard-Snyder (Bloomington: Indiana University Press, 1996), pp. 193–205, for a classification of several kinds of evidential arguments from evil.

2. William L. Rowe, "The Problem of Evil and Some Varieties of Atheism," *American Philosophical Quarterly* 16 (1979): 335–41.

3. See William L. Rowe, "Evil and Theodicy," *Philosophical Topics* 16 (1988): 119–32, and "Ruminations about Evil," *Philosophical Perspectives* 5 (1991): 69–88.

4. William Alston uses 'Bambi' to refer to E1 and 'Sue' to refer to E2. See Alston, "The Inductive Argument from Evil and the Human Cognitive Condition," in *The Evidential Argument from Evil*, pp. 97–125.

5. This objection can be remedied by complicating P and Q so that they include some clause concerning the prevention of some equal or worse evils. For sake of simplicity, I ignore this complication. See note 2 of my "Evil and Theodicy."

6. For an interesting development of this objection, see William Hasker, "The Necessity of Gratuitous Evil," *Faith and Philosophy* 9 (1992): 23–44. I discuss Hasker's view in "Ruminations about Evil."

7. Alston, "The Inductive Argument from Evil." Stephen Wykstra, "The Humean Obstacle to Evidential Arguments from Suffering: On Avoiding the Evils of 'Appearance,'" *International Journal for Philosophy of Religion* 16 (1984): 73–93. Wykstra's essay, along with my reply, is reprinted in *The Problem of Evil*, edited by M. M. Adams and R. M. Adams (Oxford University Press, 1990). Also see Wykstra's co-authored piece (with Bruce Russell), "The 'Inductive' Argument from Evil: A Dialogue," *Philosophical Topics* 16 (1988): 133–60, as well as his "Rowe's Noseeum Arguments from Evil," in *The Evidential Argument from Evil*, pp. 126–50. Also see Terry Christlieb, "Which Theisms Face an Evidential Problem of Evil?" *Faith and Philosophy* 9 (1992): 45–64; Paul Draper, "Probabilistic Arguments from Evil," *Religious Studies* 28 (1992): 303–17; and James Sennett, "The Inscrutable Evil Defense," *Faith and Philosophy* 10 (1993): 220–29.

8. It is important not to confuse P with

> P*: No good we know of *would* justify God (*if he exists*) in permitting E1 and E2.

> While P must be true if God does not exist, P* may be false if God does not exist. For even though God does not exist, it could still be true that if he did exist some good we know of would justify him in permitting E1 and E2. To avoid any confusion of P with P*, it will be helpful to keep in mind that the sentence "No good we know of justifies God in permitting E1 and E2" is here being used to express the negation of the following proposition:

> God exists & there exists a good we know of & that good justifies him in permitting E1 and E2.

9. The information that *I exist near the earth's surface* is not shared by most the-

ists and nontheists. But we may well include such information in k, since most of us (at some time) know a proposition that corresponds to the one I know. It is also understood here that k includes certain stipulated information. In particular, k includes our information concerning E1 (the case of Bambi) and E2 (the case of Sue).

10. My own view is that $Pr(G/k) < 0.5$. For I think the information we possess concerning the abundance of various evils in the world renders G unlikely. And I do not think the other information in k manages to counterbalance the weight of our information about the abundance of evils in the world. But for purposes of finding a starting point for the "theist-nontheist dialogue" I am here putting this view aside, although I will return to it later.

11. In "The Problem of Evil and Some Varieties of Atheism," I made use of what I called "the G. E. Moore shift" to show how belief in God can be sustained as rational by having stronger evidence for God's existence than the evidence from evil constitutes for God's nonexistence.

12. Alternatively, is $Pr(Q/P\&k) < Pr(\text{not-}Q/P\&k)$?

13. Alternatively, is $Pr(G/P\&k) < Pr(\text{not-}G/P\&k)$?

14. If $Pr(Q/k) = Pr(P/k)$ then $Pr(Q/P\&k)$ would be 1, which we know it not to be. If $Pr(Q/k) > Pr(P/k)$ then $Pr(Q/P\&k)$ would be > 1, which is impossible.

15. Rowe, "Evil and Theodicy," pp. 123–24.

16. If we have observed many A's and all of them are B's, this fact will make the proposition "All A's are B's" more likely than it would otherwise be. But one proposition may make another more likely than it would otherwise be without making it more likely than not.

17. Michael Tooley advances such an argument in "The Argument from Evil," *Philosophical Perspectives* 5 (1991): 114–15.

18. This point is important, in part, because its first part has been denied by some in writing on the problem of evil. For example, Wykstra in "The Humean Obstacle" argued that propositions like P do not even "weakly disconfirm" G. A proposition weakly disconfirms a second proposition if, given the first, the second proposition is less likely than it otherwise would be.

19. That is, it won't matter if all we are trying to show is that $Pr(G/P\&k) < 0.5$. As we shall see later, for the resolution of other important issues it matters a great deal what value is assigned to $Pr(P/G\&k)$.

20. Some theists hold that although $Pr(P/G\&k)$ is at least 0.5, for all we know $Pr(P/G\&k) = 1$. See, for example, Daniel Howard-Snyder, "Inscrutable Evil and the Silence of God," doctoral dissertation, Syracuse University, 1992. Assuming these theists will agree to an assignment of 0.5 to $Pr(G/k)$, we can characterize this view as holding the following propositions: (1) unless the conjunction of G and k *entails* P, P lowers the probability of G, (2) if $Pr(P/G\&k) < 0.5$ then P lowers the probability of G anywhere from 0.333 to 0, (3) we have a sufficient reason to believe that $Pr(P/G\&k)$ is not less than 0.5, (4) we are completely in the dark as to what assignment between 0.5 and 1 belongs to $Pr(P/G\&k)$, and therefore, (5) we can be *confident* that if P lowers the probability of G, it does not lower it beyond 0.333.This view clearly merits consideration. Here I will only note that it is somewhat odd to suggest that human reason is *fully adequate* to determine that $Pr(P/G\&k)$ cannot be a decimal point below 0.5, but *utterly inadequate* to judge whether it is closer to 0.5 than it is to 1.

21. Strictly speaking, this isn't exactly right. Pr(G/P&k) = 1/3. But for reasons of uniformity I will continue to use the approximate decimal equivalent.

22. Common to most theists and nontheists is a principle (a necessary truth) to the effect that if God exists and some horrendous evil exists then there is some good whose realization justifies God in permitting that evil. Given G&k, it follows that God exists and that E1 and E2 exist. And given the principle just noted, it will follow that there is some good that justifies God in permitting E1 and E2. But if this is so, Q is false. For Q says that no good justifies God in permitting E1 and E2.

23. Rowe, "Evil and Theodicy," pp. 123–24.

24. As with our conclusion that Pr(G/P&k) < 0.5, our conclusion that Pr(Q/P&k) > 0.5 depends to some degree on our original assignment of 0.5 to Pr(G/k).

25. Wykstra, "Rowe's Noseeum Arguments from Evil." Actually, Wykstra applies CORNEA to my inference from P to Q. But his point remains the same when extended to my more succinct statement of the argument which bypasses Q with a direct inference from P to ~G. For some important criticisms of Wykstra's CORNEA, see Daniel Howard-Snyder, "Seeing through CORNEA," *International Journal for Philosophy of Religion* 32 (1992): 25–49.

26. Italics mine. I have taken this remark from Wykstra, "The Humean Obstacle," in *The Problem of Evil*, p. 159.

27. It is taken for granted here that Pr(P/G&k) < 1.

28. See note 7 of Wykstra, "Rowe's Noseeum Arguments from Evil."

29. Ibid.

30. William L. Rowe, "The Empirical Argument from Evil," in *Rationality, Religious Belief, and Moral Commitment*, edited by Robert Audi and William J. Wainwright (Ithaca: Cornell University Press, 1986), pp. 245–47.

31. Quoted in Wykstra, "Rowe's Noseeum Arguments from Evil."

32. Wykstra, "Rowe's Noseeum Arguments from Evil."

33. We should note that Wykstra invites us to adjust the infant's age beyond his one-month suggestion. But it is striking, nevertheless, that he thinks the one-month age is appropriate for his analogy.

34. If the good is one we know of, then we have some chance of recognizing that good as one that may well be God's reason for permitting the suffering in question, thus reducing the need for God to attend to us directly, providing us with special assurances and explanations of why the suffering (or his permission of it) is necessary for some good.

35. Theists may say that there are special reasons applying to God, but not to loving parents, that prevent him from making his loving concern for our sufferings apparent to us, thus adding a further epicycle to the theistic response to evil. Tough-minded theists may insist that it is human perversity itself that prevents God from responding to human suffering in the way the loving parent responds to her child's suffering. Tender-minded theists may say that our freedom in relation to God would be destroyed if he were not to remain hidden during our times of apparently pointless travail and suffering. For helpful discussions of questions concerning the hiddenness of God, see Daniel Howard-Snyder, "The Argument from Divine Hiddenness," and J. L. Schellenberg, *Divine Hiddenness and Human Reason* (Ithaca: Cornell University Press, 1993).

36. I have critically discussed Alston's essay in Rowe, "William Alston on the

Problem of Evil," in *The Rationality of Belief and the Plurality of Faiths*, edited by Thomas D. Senor (Ithaca: Cornell University Press, 1994). A good bit of my discussion here is taken from that paper.

37. For an examination of his discussion of other theodicies that emphasize a good not restricted to the sufferer, see my essay "William Alston on the Problem of Evil."

38. For a brief discussion of this point, see my essay "Ruminations about Evil," pp. 74–76.

39. Thus, it seems to me that the free will theodicy needs to be included within something like Hick's soul-making theodicy, a theodicy that stresses some intrinsic goods for which free will is a necessary condition.

40. Alston, "The Inductive Argument from Evil," p. 113.

41. Ibid.

42. Ibid., p. 114.

43. One might argue that were God to intervene in Sue's case he would have to intervene in every similar case, with the result that no human being would be free to do evil acts of the kind represented by Sue. I respond to an argument of this sort in connection with Alston's discussion of the theodicy that rests on the need for the world to operate in accordance with relatively stable laws of nature. See "William Alston on the Problem of Evil."

44. For comments on earlier drafts of this paper, I am grateful to Martin Curd, Paul Draper, William Gustason, Bruce Russell, Dan Howard-Snyder, Eleonore Stump, William Wainwright, and David Widerker.

5

REPLY TO PLANTINGA

WILLIAM L. ROWE

Consider two instances of evil.

E1: a five-year-old girl's being brutally beaten, raped, and strangled in Flint, Michigan, on New Year's Eve a few years ago.
E2: a fawn's dying a lingering and painful death due to being horribly burned in a forest fire occasioned by lightning.

Theists believe that God exists and is justified in permitting E1 and E2. Since evil is intrinsically bad, what justifies God in permitting E1 and E2 is something else. To simplify matters we will suppose here that the something else is a good state of affairs (perhaps a conjunctive state of affairs) that God brings about and could bring about only by permitting these evils. Now that good is either a good we know of or a good beyond our ken. (Goods we know of will include both actual and nonactual goods, and goods that can be actual only if God exists—for example, the little girl's enjoying eternal felicity in the presence of God.) The theist, then, believes the following proposition.

> God exists and (some known good justifies him in permitting E1 and E2 or some unknown good justifies him in permitting E1 and E2).

From *Noûs* 32 (1998): 545–52.

This proposition is equivalent to a disjunction whose first disjunct is: God exists and some known good justifies him in permitting E1 and E2. I argue that this first disjunct is false.[1] That is, I argue that

~(God exists and some known good justifies him in permitting E1 and E2).

Given that necessarily there is at most one God, this proposition is equivalent to

P: God does not exist or (God exists and no known good justifies him in permitting E1 and E2).

I try to convince the theist that P is true, or at least that it is quite likely that P is true. Of course, I could hardly persuade the theist of this by suggesting that the first disjunct of P is true. And, as a nontheist, I'm not prepared to assert the truth of its second disjunct. But we can know that a disjunction is true without knowing which disjunct is true.[2] Suppose that Smith was killed in his home under circumstances that make it clear that either he took his own life, but made it look like murder, or he was in fact murdered. Of course, if he was murdered, he was murdered by an acquaintance or a stranger. Consider, then, the proposition: Some acquaintance murdered Smith. Suppose we learn that this proposition is false. We learn that

A: Smith was not murdered or he was murdered but no acquaintance murdered him.[3]

We learn that A is true by discovering, say, that each of Smith's acquaintances was somewhere else at the time Smith was killed in his home. So, we know that the disjunction A is true. But we don't know which disjunct is true. Similarly, we may have grounds for believing P to be true without having grounds for a particular one of the two disjuncts.

Suppose that *prior* to learning the whereabouts of Smith's acquaintances at the time Smith was killed, and thereby learning that A is true, it was equally likely, given our information, that Smith was murdered as that he was not (having committed suicide instead). Now that we have learned that A is true, how is the likelihood that Smith was murdered affected? It is now more likely that he was not murdered than that he was. For, since A is entailed by *Smith was not murdered*, A is more likely given that Smith was not murdered than it is given that he was murdered. So, if we learn that A is true, it becomes more likely than before that Smith was not murdered.

And the same holds for God's existence and our learning that P is true. Suppose that prior to learning that P is true, our information made it equally likely that God exists as that God does not exist. Now that we have learned that P is true (supposing that we have learned this), how is the likelihood that God exists affected? It is now more likely that God does not exist than that he does exist. For, since P is entailed by *God does not exist*, P is more likely given that God does not exist than it is given that he does exist. So, if we learn that P is true it becomes more likely than before that God does not exist.[4]

Alvin Plantinga believes that there is something dreadfully wrong with my argument from P to it being more likely than not that God does not exist.[5] First, he thinks that my efforts to persuade the theist that P is true are doomed to failure. For he thinks that "a theist is committed to denying that no known good justifies a perfect being in permitting E1 and E2." Second, he thinks there are other arguments that counterbalance my argument from P. Third, he thinks my argument from P is what he calls "an argument from degenerative evidence." And on the basis of these three objections, he concludes that the argument has no tendency at all to show "that it is more rational to accept atheism than to accept theism." I will reply to each of these objections.

I

Plantinga gives two reasons for holding that a theist is committed to denying P. First, recognizing that apart from appealing to the existence of God we have little reason to think that the actual world, α, is itself a good state of affairs, Plantinga fastens on Γ, "the conjunction of all the goods, g1, g2, . . . , α includes or contains." He then takes it that Γ is a "known good"; and concludes that if God exists, then Γ justifies him in permitting E1 and E2.

When I endeavored to distinguish between goods we know of and goods unknown to us (goods beyond our comprehension), I never imagined that someone would think that the conjunction of a known good with a good beyond our comprehension is somehow itself a *known* good.[6] Nor did I imagine that someone would think that the conjunction of all the goods we know of with all the goods beyond our comprehension, would itself be a good we know of. By 'goods we know of' I mean good states of affairs we know of in the sense that we are *acquainted* with them in some significant way beyond merely knowing that they (the states of affairs in question) are good. To merely know that Γ is a good state of affairs is insufficient for us to be acquainted with Γ. Γ is not a good we know of. A case can be made for saying that the conjunction of all the known goods in Γ is itself a *known* good. But the latter will not serve Plantinga's purpose. For if God exists, it may be that it is some unknown good that justifies him in permitting E1 and E2.

Plantinga's second point in support of the view that some known good justifies a perfect being in permitting E1 and E2 consists of an example. He suggests that the good of enjoying God's gratitude in eternal felicity may be what justifies God in permitting E1. I think there are good reasons for rejecting this suggestion.[7] But since the issue is to provide some known good that is a live possibility for justifying God in permitting E1 *and E2*, we need not pause over the only example Plantinga provides.[8] Although Plantinga may be unconvinced that there are good reasons to accept P, or to think it more likely than its denial, I don't think he has provided any good reasons for his view.[9] So, I will continue to present my argument in terms of P itself, rather than in terms of Plantinga's proposed revision of P.[10]

II

Plantinga proposes to counterbalance my P with the claim that

> P*: Neither E1 nor E2 is such that we know that no known good justifies a perfect being in permitting it.

Just as my P is entailed by ~G (God does not exist), P*, Plantinga claims, is entailed by G (God exists). But this is a mistake. For it could be that it is some *unknown* good that justifies a perfect being in permitting E1 or E2. So, God's existence is compatible with our knowing that no *known* good justifies him in permitting either E1 or E2.[11] Nevertheless, Plantinga's example is easily repaired.

> P*′: Neither E1 nor E2 is such that we know that *no good* justifies a perfect being in permitting it.

P*′ is entailed by G. But there is a proposition that is patterned after P*′ that is entailed by ~G, and forms what I take to be the *natural counterbalance* to P*′.

> P**′: Neither E1 nor E2 is such that we know that some good justifies a perfect being in permitting it.

These two effectively counterbalance each other. So, Plantinga's argument has its own natural counterbalancer.[12] What would be very relevant to my argument from P is to find a proposition that is a natural counterbalancer to it, that is entailed by the proposition that God exists, and that we (theists and nontheists) are able to show to be true, or at least to be very likely true, independent of any appeal to the proposition that God exits.[13] We could try: *Some good we know of justifies God in permitting E*. But clearly we could not justify that proposition independent of an appeal to the existence of God. We could try something like: *No evil we know (to have occurred) is such that God wouldn't be justified in permitting it, if he were to exist.*[14] This proposition is entailed by *God exists* and, therefore, increases the likelihood that God exists. But it would be exceedingly difficult to reason our way to its being true apart from appealing to the proposition that God exists.

III

Plantinga's third objection, his main challenge to my argument from P, has three steps. First he claims that P is logically equivalent to the following disjunction:

> P*: Either God does not exist or no known good stands in J to E.[15]

Second, he holds that what I reason toward is solely the second disjunct of P*. And, finally, he thinks that the way I arrive at P* is by using addition to disjoin *God does not exist* with *no known good stands in J to E*. Because he thinks these three things, Plantinga thinks my argument parallels "precisely" the reasoning in his barefoot argument.[16] For we can just as easily disjoin *no known good stands in J to E* with *God exists* as we can with *God does not exist*. And these two disjunctions will counterbalance one another with respect to lowering the probability of God exists/God does not exist. But is Plantinga right in claiming that my argument parallels "precisely" the reasoning in his barefoot argument?

Before we can answer this question we need to consider what conditions must exist if it is to be true that some good g justifies God in permitting E1 and E2. Plantinga provides two different accounts, accounts that are not equivalent. For his first account implies that a good g justifies an evil e *only if* g is actual; whereas, the second allows that a good g may justify an evil e *even if* g is not actual. According to his second account, a good g justifies e provided that if there were a perfect being b, and g and e were actual, b would be justified by g in permitting e. Clearly, if God doesn't exist, e is actual, and g is *not* actual, it still may be true that if God were to exist and g and e were actual, he would be justified by g in permitting e.

My own approach to this matter is not to try to provide a set of conditions specifying relations between some good g and some evil e such that if all those conditions are met and God exists, God will be justified by g in permitting e. I don't think we are in any position to know the limits of such a set. What we do know, I believe, are some conditions that must hold between a good g and an evil e if it is to be true both that God exists and that g justifies God in permitting e. And I think Plantinga has elegantly set forth several such conditions. We know, for example, that if God exists and some evil e is actual, then g justifies God in permitting e only if (1) g is actual, (2) g outweighs e, (3) g cannot exist unless e is permitted to exist by a perfect being, and (4) no better world can be brought about if g and e are prevented by a perfect being. Let us, then, following Plantinga, say that if any one of these conditions fails to hold between a good g and an evil e, g fails to stand in J to e. However, departing from Plantinga, because we don't know that there aren't other conditions that must obtain for a good to justify God in permitting e, we won't say that if God exists and some good g satisfies (1)–(4) in relation to some evil e, then g justifies God in permitting e. I don't mean to positively deny that this is so. I mean only to point out that God may have requirements that we don't know to be requirements.[17] At best, then, we can only state some conditions that are necessary for a good g to justify God in permitting an evil e.

We can now return to the question of whether my argument parallels "precisely" the reasoning in his barefoot argument. As a start, we should note that what one comes to learn initially in the barefoot argument is something (B: I am now barefoot) that is *evidentially irrelevant* to whether God exists or does not exist. We can see that this is so by noting that k, our background information for the barefoot argument, contains the information that I am barefoot about one-half of the time.[18] So, given k, it is just as likely that I am now barefoot as that I am not. Since God presumably has little interest in whether I am or am not now barefoot, the probability of (B/G and k) is 1/2, just as the probability of (B/~G and k) is 1/2. What happens next is that the nontheist uses addition so as to infer (~G or B) from B, thus producing a statement that lowers the probability of God's existence; while the theist returns the favor by using addition to infer (G or B) from B, thus producing a statement that lowers the probability of God's nonexistence. Compare now what we learn in my argument. Upon reflecting both on the goods we know of and E1 and E2, we come to see that none of these goods satisfies the four conditions that must be satisfied if one of these goods has J to E1 and E2. Suppose I am right about this. Suppose both that no known good g satisfies conditions (1)–(4) relative to E1 and E2 and we have very good reason to believe that this is so. We thus have very good reason to believe that

X: No known good has J to E1 and E2.

From this result (X) we directly infer

No good we know of justifies God in permitting E1 and E2.[19]

Since this proposition is logically equivalent to P, it is entailed by ~G, and thus lowers the probability of G.

It should be clear that the above reasoning does not proceed "precisely" as the barefoot argument proceeds. For unlike B (I am now barefoot), what we learn initially in this reasoning is something (X) that is *evidentially very relevant* to the question of whether God exists. As we saw in the barefoot argument, B (I am now barefoot) is as likely on (~G and k) as it is on (G and k), and for that reason it itself is *evidentially irrelevant* to the question of God's existence. But (X) itself makes ~G more likely than G. For X is more likely given ~G than it is given G. If God does not exist, it is quite likely that no known good g satisfies each of the four conditions necessary for g to have J to E1 and E2. That is, it is very likely that no known good is actual, outweighs E1 and E2, cannot possibly be realized by a perfect being without its permitting E1 and E2, etc. One reason this is so is that no good *involving* God, such as the little girl's enjoying eternal felicity in the presence of God or (Plantinga's suggestion) the little girl's enjoying God's gratitude in eternal felicity, is even a candidate for consideration, since such a good is *actual* only if God does exist. But if God does exist, these goods are at least candidates for the job of justifying him in permitting the little girl's suffering. So, for this reason and others, X is much more likely if God does not exist than it is if God does exist. However, B (I am now barefoot) is no more likely if God does not exist than it is if God does exist.

But what if Plantinga takes (X), from which we directly inferred P, and uses the rule of addition so as to produce the disjunction, G or X? Won't he then have counterbalanced my argument? For just as ~G entails P, so does G entail (G or X). The answer is no. For, as we've just seen, X itself is a reason to think that ~G (God does not exist) is more likely than G (God exists). Of course, nothing I have noted prevents one from using X in the fashion that Plantinga describes as "an argument from degenerate evidence." Someone may learn X as new evidence, add ~G so as to produce ~G or X, and then claim that what has been arrived at lowers the probability of G. But, of course, what is sauce for the goose is sauce for the gander. The theist may accept X, use addition to arrive at G or X, and then claim that what has been arrived at lowers the probability of ~G.[20] But my argument is not "an argument from degenerate evidence." It can be taken as an argument from X alone. For X itself, given our background information k, is sufficient to render God's existence less likely than it was before we acquired X.[21] And that is sufficient to establish that my argument is not "an argument from degenerate evidence." For Plantinga stresses that in an argument from degenerate evidence a part of your evidence (e.g., B or G) makes a certain proposition (G) probable when there is "an isomorphic part of your evidence" (B or ~G) with respect to which (~G) is at least "*equally probable*." But, as we've seen, neither (P) nor (X), from which we directly inferred (P), is such that it makes G anywhere near as probable as ~G. For, unlike B, which leaves G as probable as ~G, X makes ~G more likely than G.

I conclude that none of the three main points Plantinga advances to show that my argument "has no tendency at all to show that it is more rational to accept atheism than to accept theism" is successful.[22]

NOTES

1. See William L. Rowe, "The Evidential Argument from Evil: A Second Look," in *The Evidential Argument from Evil*, edited by Daniel Howard-Snyder (Bloomington: Indiana University Press, 1996), pp. 262–85.

2. Given that we don't know the truth value of p, the obvious case is a proposition of the form p ∨ ~p.

3. I assume here for purposes of illustration that necessarily at most one person murdered Smith.

4. See Rowe, "The Evidential Argument," for proof of this point.

5. Alvin Plantinga, "Degenerate Evidence and Rowe's New Evidential Argument from Evil," *Noûs* 32 (1998): 531–44.

6. Suppose a man who is *known to me* is put into a room with some other man who is *unknown to me*. I am then told that these two men (the one known to me and the one unknown to me) are in that room. Is it true that the two men in that room are *known* to me? I do know *that* two men are in the room. But the two men are not *known to me*.

7. Is it, for example, clear that it makes any sense at all for God to be *grateful* to the little girl for enduring suffering that she had no opportunity to avoid or not endure? Saint John of the Cross prayed to God to be allowed to suffer as Christ suffered. It would be absurd to think that the little girl freely sought to suffer in this way.

8. For a discussion of various proposals of *known goods* that might be thought to justify God in permitting E1 and E2, see William Alston's illuminating essay, "The Inductive Argument from Evil and the Human Cognitive Condition," in *The Evidential Argument from Evil*, pp. 97–125. Also see William L. Rowe, "William Alston on the Problem of Evil," *The Rationality of Belief and the Plurality of Faith,* edited by Thomas Senor (Ithaca: Cornell University Press, 1996), pp. 71–93.

9. Moreover, it is evident, I believe, that the theist is not committed to *denying* that the good that justifies God in permitting E1 and E2 is an *unknown* good (a good beyond our comprehension).

10. See Rowe, "The Evidential Argument," for a discussion of P and the reasons in favor of accepting it.

11. I assume that Plantinga is here still thinking that Γ is a known good.

12. A further difficulty with P*′ is that its probability is very high, given k. For k clearly allows that there are unknown goods. And so long as there are unknown goods, we cannot know that no good justifies God in permitting E1 and E2.

13. An important feature of P is that we may reason our way to accepting it without any appeal to the claim that God does not exist.

14. This example surfaced in an email discussion with Plantinga.

15. I've made some slight changes in Plantinga's formulation here so as to render it

closer to my actual formulation of P. These changes do not affect the point Plantinga is making.

16. In the barefoot argument what one initially learns, B (I am barefoot), does not lower the probability of G (God exists). But by using addition to infer (~G or B), one can then use (~G or B) as a basis for increasing the probability of ~G. For ~G entails (~G or B). Unfortunately for the nontheist, nothing prevents the theist from using addition to infer (G or B) and using it to show that G is more likely than ~G.

17. For example, for all we know God may require that any good for which he is prepared to permit E1 (the little girl's suffering upon being brutally beaten, raped, and murdered) must involve some good for the little girl.

18. Unless k is understood to contain this information, we won't be able to hold that Pr(B/G&k) = 1/2.

19. Given the uniqueness of God, this proposition is logically equivalent to P: God does not exist or (God exists and no known good justifies him in permitting E1 and E2).

20. It is worth noting, however, that even here the parallel with the barefoot argument is not exact. For, unlike B (I am barefoot), X is not *neutral* with respect to what is derived by adding G (i.e., G or X); for, as we've seen, X itself, given what we already know, makes it less likely that G is true.

21. It should be noted, however, that if ~G does not logically imply X, then even though X reduces the likelihood that God exists, it won't reduce it to quite the degree that P does. For P is logically implied by ~G.

22. I'm grateful to Jan Cover, Jeff Jordan, Alvin Plantinga, Stephen Wykstra, and especially Mike Bergmann for helpful comments on some of the issues discussed in this paper.

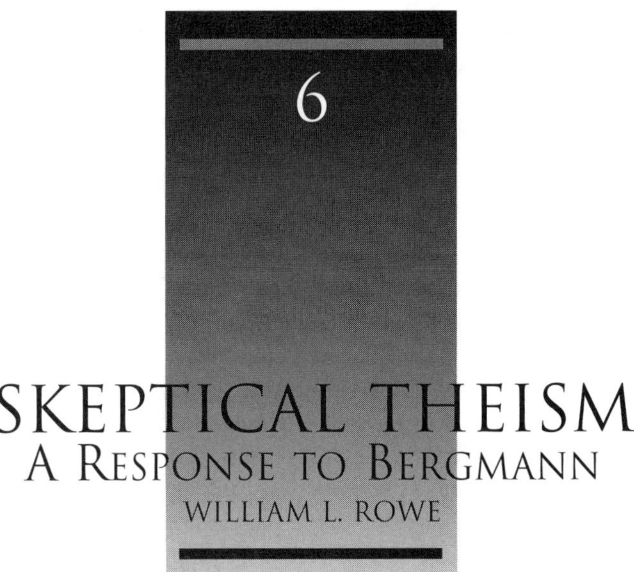

6

SKEPTICAL THEISM
A RESPONSE TO BERGMANN

WILLIAM L. ROWE

In his essay "Skeptical Theism and Rowe's New Evidential Argument from Evil"[1] Michael Bergmann argues that my 1996 effort to strengthen the evidential argument from evil[2] fails because it presupposes the falsity of one or more plausible skeptical theses. The skeptical thesis that he cites most frequently is

ST1: We have no good reason for thinking that the possible goods we know of are representative of the possible goods there are.

Bergmann suggests that ST1 is reasonable—or at least not unreasonable—owing to our "awareness of our cognitive limitations and the vastness and complexity of reality." And he notes that I seem to have some sympathy with ST1. He then considers my "new evidential argument from evil" and argues that it *depends* on "a rejection of this skeptical thesis and, therefore, suffers from the same problem that afflicts his [Rowe's] original argument." In what follows, after a preliminary comment, I will respond to Bergmann's discussion of my 1996 argument from evil.

The constant theme in my discussions of the problem of evil is our awareness that no good *within our ken* can reasonably be thought to justify an all-powerful, all-knowing, perfectly good being in permitting any particular instance of the vast number of instances of horrific suffering (both animal and human) that occurs daily in our world. Skeptical theists like Bergmann do not

From *Noûs* 35 (2001): 297–303.

directly dispute this point, although they think my claim exceeds what we are fully justified in asserting.[3] Rather, they contend that given the disparity between our knowledge of goods and the conditions of their realization and the knowledge of these matters possessed by God, if he exists, we simply aren't epistemically qualified to make *any reasonable judgments whatever* about the amount of seemingly pointless, horrific evil such a being would need to allow in the world. For all we know, they say, the world could contain a great deal more seemingly pointless evil and still be reasonably (or, at least, not unreasonably) believed to be under the care and control of an infinitely powerful, all-knowing, perfectly loving being. For, to repeat their constant refrain, since we don't know that the goods we know of are representative of the goods there are, we cannot know that it is even likely that there are no goods that justify God in permitting whatever amount of apparently pointless, horrific evil there might occur in our world. Indeed, if human life were *nothing more than a series of agonizing moments from birth to death*, their position would still require them to say that we cannot reasonably infer that it is even likely that God does not exist.[4] But surely such a view is unreasonable, if not absurd. Surely there must be some point at which the appalling agony of human and animal existence as we know it would render it unlikely that God exists. And this must be so even though we all agree that God's knowledge would far exceed our own. I believe my theistic friends have gone considerably beyond that point when in light of the enormous proliferation of horrendous evil in this world they continue to insist that we are unjustified in concluding that it is even the least bit unlikely that God exists.

But the issue to be addressed here is whether my 1996 version of the evidential argument from evil really *depends* on rejecting the skeptical thesis (ST1) stated above. In the essay in question, instead of focusing on the seemingly limitless amount of horrific evils that serve no good within our ken, I developed the argument in terms of two particular examples of such evils, E1 and E2.[5] How does Bergmann endeavor to show that my 1996 argument depends on my rejecting ST1? First, he correctly notes that my argument is successful only if we are justified in believing that in relation to our background information and the claim that God exists, the likelihood that the goods that justify God in permitting E1 and E2 are beyond our comprehension is not high.[6] That is, my argument will work only if we are justified in believing it likely, or as likely as not, that the good that justifies God, if he exists, in permitting E1 and E2 will be a good we know of, a good within our ken. For then, if we discover that none of the known goods is such that it justifies God in permitting E1 and E2 we will be justified in concluding that it is unlikely that God exists. Second, he claims that the *only way* I have of justifying the claim that it is likely, or at least not unlikely, that the God-justifying goods for E1 and E2 will be goods known to us is by *assuming as a premise* the denial of ST1. It is Bergmann's justification for this second point that I wish to discuss.

He arrives at this second point in the course of considering my discussion of the good parent analogy, an analogy favored by theists as a way of explaining our cognitive limits in terms of understanding the goods for the sake of which God permits all this horrendous human and animal suffering. The trouble with the analogy between the good parent and God is that it leads to a conclusion inimical to theism. Bergmann quotes the relevant passage from my 1996 essay.

> If we do apply the parent analogy, the conclusion about God that we should draw is something like the following. When God permits horrendous suffering for the sake of some good, if that good is *beyond our ken*, God will make every effort to be consciously present to us during our period of suffering, will do his best to explain to us why he is permitting us to suffer, and will give us special assurances of his love and concern during the period of the suffering. Since enormous numbers of human beings undergo prolonged, horrendous suffering without being consciously aware of any such divine presence, concern, and explanations, we may conclude that if there is a God, the goods for the sake of which he permits horrendous human suffering are more often than not goods we know of.[7]

He then suggests that the relevant premise at work here is the following.

(1) If God exists and the goods that justify God in permitting E1 and E2 are beyond our ken, then it is likely that we would not have divine silence (i.e., it is likely that we would at least have assurances of God's love and of the fact that there *is* a good that justifies God in permitting such horrendous evils even though we don't know what that good is).

But why should we accept (1)? Well, as seems clear from the context of my discussion, the plausibility of (1) derives from the widely accepted analogy of God to the good, loving parent. When a good, loving parent permits her child to suffer for a good the child cannot comprehend, that parent makes every effort to be consciously present to the suffering child, giving special assurances of her love and concern during the period the child is suffering. Accordingly, Bergmann remarks, "As Rowe points out, the plausibility of (1) has to do with an analogy theists like to employ—the analogy between God and human parents."

But immediately after noting that premise (1) finds its plausibility in the generally accepted good parent analogy between God and the loving parent, Bergmann tells us that "premise (1) depends on a *prior rejection* of ST1." That is, he tells us that the only way we can be justified in accepting (1) is by first being justified in rejecting ST1. Why so? Why couldn't someone just rely on the good parent analogy, so widely accepted in theistic religions, and justifiably conclude that (1)? Bergmann is silent on this question. Instead, he offers his own account of the reasoning process by which people accept (1). He says:

> It begins with a recognition of the plausibility of:
>
> (2) If God exists and the goods that justify God in permitting E1 and E2 are beyond our ken, then either
> (a) we wouldn't have divine silence
> or
> (b) there is some good that justifies God in permitting divine silence.

Next Bergmann tells us that the advocate of (1) "assumes" that (2a) is much more likely than (2b). We then learn that in order to assume that (2a) is much more likely than (2b), we must think it *likely* that

> (3) No good justifies God in permitting divine silence.

Bergmann then asks: "But how could a proponent of (1) come to any reasonable conclusion about how likely it is that there is no such good?" Well, let me make a suggestion. If someone who accepts (1) *were* to reason in the way in which Bergmann suggests we all do (if we accept (1)), she might say (3) is likely because God is to us as the good loving parent is to her child whom she must permit to undergo suffering (e.g., from a painful medical procedure) for a good the child greatly needs but cannot understand. In situations where the child must suffer for a good the child cannot understand the loving parent justifiably believes it is *best* to be consciously present to her child, expressing her love and concern.[8] Failure to be consciously present to the child she loves while the child is suffering for reasons the child cannot understand is almost always due to human limitations of power and/or knowledge. Thus, again, the good parent analogy itself provides the grounds for thinking that (3) is likely. But Bergmann needs to convince us that our acceptance of (1) "depends" on the rejection of ST1. So, instead of considering the support given by the good parent analogy, Bergmann responds to his question ("But how could a proponent of (1) come to any reasonable conclusion about how likely it is that there is no such good?") by saying: "She *could* rely on (4) 'No good we know of justifies God in permitting divine silence.'"[9] But, of course, to infer (3) from (4) presupposes a rejection of ST1. And from this Bergmann concludes that this way of supporting the conclusion (the probability that no known good justifies God in permitting E1 and E2, given our background knowledge and the claim that God exists, is not high) "doesn't avoid what Rowe seems to want to avoid—namely, reliance on a rejection of the skeptical theses of the skeptical theist."

I think we can credit Bergmann with showing that *one* way of trying to justify

(1) If God exists and the goods that justify God in permitting E1 and E2 are beyond our ken, then it is likely that we would not have divine silence (i.e., it is likely that we would at least have assurances of God's love and of the fact that there *is* a good that justifies God in permitting such horrendous evils even though we don't know what that good is)

is to rely on (4) "No good we know of justifies God in permitting divine silence." But, of course, relying on (4) in order to support (1) does presuppose a rejection of ST1. And that is not uninteresting. But what Bergmann set out to establish is that this argument of mine, an argument that can be thought of as supporting the conclusion that Pr(P/G&k) is not high, *depends* for its success "on a rejection of one or more of the skeptical theist's skeptical theses." What he does show, at best, is that *one way* of supporting (1) involves a rejection of ST1. What he needs to show is that the *only way* of supporting (1) involves a rejection of ST1. For only the latter will suffice to show that the argument *depends* for its success on rejecting ST1. It is as though Bergmann has discovered a road that starts out in the direction of Rome but doesn't in fact lead to Rome. This is not uninteresting. But to conclude from this that there is no road that leads to Rome is not quite right. One can conclude the latter only by showing that if this road doesn't lead to Rome, none other does. Similarly, he shows that one way of trying to justify (1) involves a rejection of ST1. What he needs to show is that there is no way of justifying (1) that doesn't involve a rejection of ST1. And we may justifiably be skeptical that Bergmann is in any position to show that.

Let's now consider more carefully Bergmann's proposition (2).

(2) If God exists and the goods that justify God in permitting E1 and E2 are beyond our ken, then either
(a) we wouldn't have divine silence
or
(b) there is some good that justifies God in permitting divine silence.

Bergmann's challenge is to provide a reason for thinking that (a) is more likely than (b).[10] Can we do this? I believe we can. But to do so we need to keep before our minds just what is implied by the idea of divine silence, given that God exists and permits seemingly countless instances of horrendous evil such as a five-year-old girl's being savagely beaten, raped, and strangled. To suppose that God exists and *divine silence* is what occurs in response to the seemingly countless instances of horrendous suffering in our world is to suppose all of the following:

1. A being of infinite wisdom and power is *unable* to prevent any of those

instances of horrendous suffering without thereby forfeiting a good1 so great that the world would be worse without good1, even given the instance of horrendous suffering that must be permitted by the infinitely powerful being if that being is to realize good1.

2. A being of infinite wisdom and power is *unable* to enable those who undergo such horrendous suffering to understand just what the good1 is for which this infinitely powerful being is required to permit that horrendous suffering without this being thereby forfeiting a good2 so great that the world would be worse without good2, even given the additional suffering occasioned by the sufferers being unable to understand what the good1 is for which an infinitely powerful being permits them to undergo their horrendous suffering.[11]

3. A being of infinite wisdom and power is *unable* to be consciously present to those who suffer horrendously, expressing his love and concern during their period of horrendous suffering for a good1 that is beyond their ken, without thereby forfeiting still another good, good3, such that the world would be worse without good3, even given the despair and loneliness of those who undergo seemingly pointless horrendous suffering without any conscious sense of God's being present, expressing his love and concern during their period of seemingly pointless horrendous suffering for a good1 that is beyond their ken.

4. A being of infinite wisdom and power is *unable* to enable those who undergo horrendous suffering without any sense of God being consciously present expressing his love for them to have any understanding of just what the good3 is for which this being is required to permit them to suffer without any conscious awareness of his love and concern without thereby forfeiting still another good, good4, such that the world would be worse without good4, even given the additional suffering occasioned by the sufferers and their loved ones being unable to understand what the good3 is for which an infinitely powerful being permits them to undergo their horrendous suffering.[12]

Now my position is that anyone who seriously reflects on (1)–(4) will *see* the *inherent implausibility* in the idea that (1)–(4) is the way things are. For the idea that outweighing good states of affairs are so related to the vast array of horrendous evils like E1 and E2 that an infinitely powerful, infinitely loving being is unable to prevent any of those horrendous evils without (a) forfeiting a greater good1, (b) forfeiting a greater good2 if he enables the sufferers to understand good1, (c) forfeiting a greater good3 if he is even consciously present, expressing his love and concern to those who suffer horrendously for a good1 they cannot understand, and (d) forfeiting a greater good4 if he enables the sufferers to understand good3, etc., etc., etc., is an *inherently implausible* idea. The skeptical theist, however, may agree with me about the implausibility of this idea. But she will say that its implausibility is derivative, not inherent. And she will argue that we take the idea to be implausible only because we are *assuming* that the way the goods we know of are known to be related to the evils we know of is representative of the way the goods there are are related to the evils there are. And she will then, following Bergmann's lead, construct an argument for the implausibility of the idea that (1)–(4) is the way things are that employs as a premise the claim that the way the goods we know of are known to be related to the evils we know of is representative of the way the goods there are are related to the evils there are. "See," she will say, "I've shown a way in which you can get to that conclusion by assuming the falsity of a plausible skeptical thesis." My reply is that the idea that (1)–(4) is the way things are is an *inherently* implausible idea, not dependent for its implausibility on a *prior rejection* of one or more skeptical theses.

It is worth noting that an idea may be inherently implausible and yet be justifiably believed. If, for example, we have quite strong evidence for the existence of God we can reasonably believe that (1)–(4) is the way things are. But if, as I assumed in my 1996 essay, our situation at the start is one in which God's existence is *no more likely than not*, and we then become aware that no good we know of justifies God in permitting E1 and E2, we will be in a position to conclude that God's existence is less likely than not. For, as I've argued here, to suppose otherwise is to embrace an inherently implausible idea in the absence of a justifying reason to do so.

NOTES

1. Michael Bergmann, "Skeptical Theism and Rowe's New Evidential Argument from Evil," *Noûs* 35 (2001): 278–96.

2. William L. Rowe, "The Evidential Argument from Evil: A Second Look," in *The Evidential Argument from Evil*, edited by Daniel Howard-Snyder (Bloomington: Indiana University Press, 1996), pp. 262–85.

3. See Bergmann, "Skeptical Theism," note 9.

4. In discussions with Bergmann he has indicated that his position is not as extreme as the view I here ascribe to skeptical theists. He allows that there may be some point at which the amount of seemingly pointless evil in the world would justify someone in believing that God does not exist. But this justification, Bergmann believes, would not depend on any principle to the effect that the goods we know of are representative of the goods there are.

5. E1 is a fawn's being trapped in a forest fire and undergoing several days of terrible agony before dying; E2 is a five-year-old girl's being savagely beaten, raped, and strangled.

6. I am indebted to Bergmann for pointing out to me that in my 1996 paper "The Evidential Argument from Evil" I did not give any argument for the claim that Pr(P/G&k) is not high. All I did was to show the weaknesses of arguments for the claim that Pr(P/G&k) is high. But, of course, as Bergmann notes, to show that there is no good argu-

ment for the claim that Pr(P/G&k) is high does not suffice to show that Pr(P/G&k) is not high.

7. Rowe, "The Evidential Argument from Evil," p. 276.

8. Of course, even here we can think of desert island cases. A mother comes down with a contagious disease that the child may contract in its present state. So, all things considered, that loving mother must stay away from her child while he suffers for a good he cannot understand.

9. See Bergmann, "Skeptical Theism," p. 283. (Italics mine.)

10. I think Bergmann is right to challenge me to provide such a reason. For providing such a reason seems to be an important step to establishing that Pr(P/G&k) is not high.

11. Of course, it also follows that God is unable to enable the sufferers to understand good2 without thereby having to forfeit some other yet greater good, and so on, and so on.

12. Of course, it also follows that God is unable to enable the sufferers to understand good4 without thereby having to forfeit some other yet greater good, and so on, and so on.

7

AN INDIRECT INDUCTIVE ARGUMENT FROM EVIL

MICHAEL MARTIN

THE ARGUMENT STATED

Although William Rowe does not develop the inductive argument from evil in terms of the failure of known theodicies to solve the problem of evil, it is possible to do so. The general strategy would be to maintain that since no known theodicy is successful, probably no theodicy will be successful. And since probably no theodicy will be successful, there is probably no explanation for evil. However, there must be such an explanation if God exists. So it is likely that He does not exist. I call such an argument *an indirect inductive argument from evil.*

Suppose all attempts down through the ages have failed to specify a sufficient moral reason for God to allow the existence of what seems like pointless evil; that is, suppose they have failed to explain away the appearances by showing that there is in fact a sufficient moral reason for such evil. Furthermore, suppose all attempts have failed to show that what seems like pointless evil is really not pointless but rather logically necessary. If this failure did occur, it should give us some confidence that there is no morally sufficient reason for the existence of apparently pointless evil and that the existence of such evil is not logically necessary. For if every attempt to specify a needed explanation fails over a long period of time, this gives us good grounds for supposing that an explanation is impossible.

From *Atheism: A Philosophical Justification* (Philadelphia: Temple University Press, 1990), pp. 341–49, 361 (slightly edited).

In the present case this means, if theodicies have failed, we would have good reason to suppose that evil that seems pointless *is* in fact pointless.

Even if this failure would provide indirect support for holding that there is no morally sufficient reason for the existence of apparently pointless evil and that the existence of such evil is not logically necessary, and consequently provide indirect evidence for the nonexistence of God, this evidence would not necessarily outweigh evidence for the existence of God. Given some positive evidence, disbelief in God would on balance not be rational. However, as I have shown in *Atheism: A Philosophical Justification*,[1] the traditional arguments for the existence of God are bankrupt and the nontraditional arguments are no better. Thus there is no positive reason for belief in God that could outweigh any possible negative evidence. A more formal statement of the argument is this:

(1) If (i) there is no positive evidence that P; and
(ii) unless one makes assumption A, evidence E would falsify that P; and
(iii) despite repeated attempts, no good reason has been given for believing A;
then on rational grounds one should believe that P is false.
(2) There is no positive reason that God exists.
(3) The existence of apparently pointless evil would falsify the existence of God unless one assumes either that God has morally sufficient reason for allowing the existence of such evil or that it is logically necessary.
(4) Despite repeated attempts to do so, no one has provided a good reason to believe either that God has morally sufficient reasons to allow such evil to exist or that it is logically necessary.

(C) Therefore, on rational grounds one should believe that God does not exist.

Although this is formulated as a deductive argument, it is not a demonstrative argument that God does not exist; it only purports to show that on rational grounds one ought not to believe that God exists. The argument can in fact be recast as a straightforward inductive argument rather than a deductive argument with a conclusion about what one should believe. The general form of the indirect inductive argument from evil is:

(a) Evidence E falsifies hypothesis H unless assumption A.
(b) Repeated attempts to establish A have failed.
(c) There is no positive evidence that H.

(d) Probably ~H.

~H is not established by but is made probable relative to (a), (b), and (c). The atheist argument from evil is achieved by substituting in the obvious variables.

THE ARGUMENT DEFENDED

This argument has been criticized by Robert Pargetter in the following ways. First, he argues that, unlike deductive arguments, inductive arguments must meet the requirement of total evidence.[2] An inductive argument establishes nothing if a known piece of evidence is not included. Pargetter claims that the above argument does not include a relevant piece of evidence, namely:

> (5) If God exists, then necessary evil exists, and necessarily God has sufficient reason for the evil or it is logically necessary, and necessarily any attempt to show that God didn't have such reasons would fail.

One assumes that the evil specified in (5) includes all apparently pointless evil, since even an atheist can admit that if God exists, then *some* evil may well be necessary. One problem with this objection is that either (5) is a necessary truth or it is not. If it is a necessary truth, as Pargetter seems to assume, its addition as a premise to an inductively strong argument should make no difference to the strength of support that the premises give the conclusion. Adding a necessary truth to the premises of an inductive argument no more affects the support the premises give the conclusion than it affects the support the premises give a deductive argument. On the other hand, if (5) is not a necessary truth, one must ask what justification there is for assuming it to be true. If it is not a necessary truth, its inclusion as a premise in the above argument is simply gratuitous. Indeed, if one interpreted evil in (5) to include apparently pointless evil, then (5) would be unacceptable even to many thoughtful theists, for it entails that

> (5') If God exists, then necessarily apparently pointless evil exists.

However, many theists have been puzzled about why there is such evil if God exists. Their puzzlement would be completely unintelligible if (5') were true.

In addition, Pargetter seems to be confused on what I attempt to show. His objections seem to assume that since if God exists, He necessarily has sufficient reasons for allowing apparently pointless evil, my inductive argument attempting to show that there are no sufficient moral reasons must fail. However, the argument does not attempt to show that God, assuming He exists, has no sufficient reason for apparently pointless evil. This would indeed be impossible. It shows that probably there are no such reasons; and since, if God exists, there must be such reasons, God probably does not exist.

A related objection raised by Pargetter is based on the same confusion. He maintains that the statement that God has a morally sufficient reason for evil or that evil is logically necessary "is not a simple empirical statement" and "we do not usually regard" failure to establish the truth of such a statement as evidence for its falsehood. He argues further that the argument begs the question in assuming that repeated failure to establish the truth of such a statement is evidence against the statement in a situation "where it is agreed that there *could* be such a reason, a reason for God not only allowing abundant evil but also for the world being exactly as it is."[3]

However, consider

(6) If God exists, then either there is sufficient moral reason for the existence of apparently pointless evil, or such evil is logically necessary.

Although this may not be a simple empirical statement, and the failure to establish the truth of (6) should not be taken as establishing its falsehood, this is irrelevant to the argument. No attempt is made to argue that failure to establish (6) tends to establish its falsehood. Indeed, the argument *assumes* that (6) is true. The argument is that there are inductive reasons to suppose that the *consequence* of (6) is false—that the failure to establish the truth of this consequence tends to establish the falsehood of the consequence of (6), not of (6) itself. But if this consequence is probably false and (6) is true, then the antecedent of (6) is probably false.

Obviously, theists would want to claim that the above argument does not apply to theism. However, those like Pargetter who would reject this argument must have reasons for their rejection that are not ad hoc and arbitrary. It is easy enough to treat statements about God differently from analogous statements without providing any reason for this different treatment. Consider the following hypothetical case.

Jones is dead, and some of his friends suspect foul play. Let us suppose that the available evidence E would falsify the foul play hypothesis H unless the police are involved in a cover-up R. However, although Jones's friends are skillful and dedicated, they try without success to establish R. Furthermore, there is no independent evidence for H. Surely in this case the above inductive argument applies; it would constitute an inductive argument for ~H. No question has been begged. It is irrelevant that there *could have been* a cover-up. Obviously there could have been, but the question is, was there? Clearly this is an empirical issue, and the failure to establish any cover-up after diligent and skillful effort does provide good, although not conclusive, evidence that there is no cover-up. Furthermore, the lack of positive evidence for the foul play hypothesis reinforces this conclusion. For if there was positive evidence of foul play, this might indirectly support the cover-up theory given certain background knowledge, such as that foul play is often associated with a police cover-up.

Countless other examples of the same mode of inference can be found in everyday life and in science. Critics of our argument may be correct that when this mode of inference is applied to the existence of God, religious people reject it. The crucial question, however, is whether there is any *good* reason for treating this mode of inference differently in the context of religion. So far, no reasons have been supplied. Are there any?

One reason that might be given is that, in the context of religion, one knows or has justification for believing that there must be a reason for evil in the world since God is all-good and all-powerful. Of course, if one had independent reason to suppose that God does exist, then this would indeed provide justification for believing that there was a reason. But this evidence is precisely what one does not have. As the argument is stated above, there is no independent reason for supposing that God exists, since there is no positive reason for His existence. The situation is no different in ordinary life and in science. In the case of Jones, if one had independent reason for supposing that Jones's death was the result of foul play, one might have reason to suppose that despite the failure to turn up a police cover-up, there was one. But in this example there was no such evidence.

Another reason that might be given is that the reasons God might have for creating a world with so much evil are so profound and difficult that they cannot be understood by mere mortals. Small wonder, then, that no reason for the existence of apparently pointless evil has ever been satisfactorily stated. However, what is the independent evidence that this is true? If one had independent reason to suppose that God exists and works in strange and deep ways, there might be justification for believing that there is some reason for the existence of apparently pointless evil that humans have not thought of or even never will think of. But there is no positive evidence to suggest that God exists, let alone that the reasons for evil are beyond human comprehension. Indeed, the idea that God's reasons for evil are comprehensible has been widely accepted by theologians from St. Augustine to Hick, who have attempted to specify what those reasons might be. Every attempt to formulate a systematic theodicy confirms the view that it is commonly accepted that it is possible to understand why, if God exists, there is evil. Naturally, the failure of all such attempts might have driven theists to claim that the reasons are beyond human comprehension. But without independent support, such a claim rings hollow. For example, Jones's friends could claim that despite their repeated failures to expose a police cover-up, there is one nonetheless. They could say the police are so clever and cunning that exposing such a cover-up is all but impossible. But without independent evidence, this charge is ad hoc and arbitrary. The same is true in the context of the problem of evil.

But does not the mere fact that God is omniscient create a presumption that He has knowledge about certain goods and evils as well as about certain connections between goods that humans do not have? It does create such a presumption, and if God exists, it is quite certain that God has such knowledge. The question is whether this admission by itself makes the existence of evil less surprising than it is on rival accounts—for example, than on the hypothesis that God does not exist. Why should we suppose that if God has such knowledge, this does not make it more likely that evil exists than if He does not exist? Although God might have reasons that are unknown or even unknowable to us for permitting evil, He might have reasons that are unknown or unknowable to us for preventing such evil. Further, since He is omnipotent, He may know means that we cannot understand to obtain certain goods without the evils that we find in the world. Thus the mere fact that, if God exists, He has knowledge we cannot have does not explain the existence of evil as well as rival hypotheses do. For example, the hypothesis that God exists and has knowledge of good and evil that we cannot have does not enable us to predict that there will be seemingly pointless evil as well as the rival hypothesis that neither the nature nor the condition of sentient beings on earth is the result of actions performed by benevolent or malevolent nonhuman persons.[4]

At least two further considerations strengthen the claim that failure to find a morally sufficient reason for evil is evidence that there is no reason. First, the various unsuccessful attempts down through the ages have not basically changed. As Hare and Madden point out: "The repeated failure, the recurrence and clustering of criticisms, the permutations of basic moves which have been found wanting, and the slight variations of old favorites is evidence that counts heavily against the likelihood of eventual success."[5] One might understand these philosophers to be saying there is inductive evidence that, if an inquiry results in variations of past unsuccessful explanations, it is unlikely to produce a satisfactory explanation. This claim is well supported in the history of science and in the history of many fields of inquiry.

It might be objected that this may be a strong inductive inference for the conclusion that success in finding a satisfactory explanation is unlikely, but this inference does not inductively support the conclusion that no correct theistic explanation is to be had. However, Hare and Madden's argument can be expanded and strengthened. The first thing to note is that there are successful explanations of apparently pointless evil from a naturalistic viewpoint. Indeed, naturalism has no general problem in explaining apparently pointless evil. Natural evil can be explained in terms of certain natural laws. For example, the birth of a defective baby can be explained in terms of genetics. Moral evil can be explained in terms of certain psychological or sociological theories. For example, the murder of an innocent bystander can be explained in terms of the motives and beliefs of the police. There might of course be a problem with some naturalistic explanations. Some might be inadequate. But there is no general problem like that of reconciling apparently pointless evil with belief in God.[6]

Hare and Madden's claim can be seen against the above background. There is inductive evidence that if explanations of a particular phenomenon P made from a particular theoretical perspective T_1 not only continue to be unsuccessful but are simply variants of earlier ones, and if there is another theoretical perspective T_2 that generates successful explanations, then it is unlikely that there are successful explanations from T_1. Such an inductive inference becomes even stronger when there is no positive evidence for T_1. This sort of inference is used frequently both in everyday life and in science, and it would be arbitrary and ad hoc not to use it in the context of religion.

To illustrate, let us suppose that various advocates of the occult have put forth unsuccessful explanations of Uri Geller's feats and that these explanations are simply variants of past occult explanations. Suppose further that non-occult explanations have been successful, and there is no positive evidence for the occult theoretical framework that the unsuccessful explanations assume. Surely, in this case one would be justified in inductively inferring not only that explanations will be no more successful in the future than they have been in the past, but also that there are no correct occult explanations of Geller's success. This situation is precisely analogous to the situation concerning the argument from evil. If one accepts the argument as it is used in this example, it would be arbitrary and ad hoc to reject it when it is applied to the problem of evil.

Another point that strengthens Hare and Madden's claim is "the fact that the riddle of God and evil involves the ordinary meaning of moral terms and that the structure of deliberate argumentation about God and evil has never been shown to be dissimilar to arguments in ordinary contexts about excusing or defeating evil."[7] Hare and Madden are here saying that, had the meaning of moral terms or the structure of argumentation been different from the ordinary, the failure to find sufficient moral reason for evil might not provide evidence that there is none to be found. But the meaning of the terms and the structure of the argumentation are the same.

Once again to illustrate, suppose there are fragmentary historical data concerning a group of people living in Central Africa who in the second century experienced great suffering. Some scholars who study the data postulate that there was a king named X who had a morally sufficient reason for inflicting great suffering on his subjects. Let us suppose that although many explanations of the data have been suggested through the years, none provides a satisfactory, morally sufficient reason why King X made his people suffer. Surely, in such a case one would have inductive justification for supposing that there is no morally sufficient reason for the king's action. This conclusion would be strengthened if the explanations offered over the years were simply variants of ones previously given and if there were no independent reason to believe that this king even existed or, if he did exist, that he was a moral person.

This argument and the indirect argument from evil to the nonexistence of God are closely analogous. There are some differences, of course. In the case of God, if there were independent evidence for His existence, then there would be evidence that He was moral, since God is by definition completely good. But since there is no independent reason for the existence of either God or the king, the arguments are strengthened. Furthermore, when we examine some of the proposed solutions to the problem of evil, in the argument from evil we shall see that certain explanations are ruled out a priori. One may be able to justify the actions of the postulated King X by his lack of knowledge or his lack of power, but this option is not open with respect to God. Thus in some respects it would seem easier to justify X's action than God's. In short, there are no significant differences between the structure of the argument from evil and the structure of prima facie arguments whereby relevant inductive evidence would lessen the force of the argument from evil.

It may be claimed that although the indirect inductive argument from evil is very similar to arguments in ordinary life, the meaning of the terms is different. For example, God is not good in the same sense as human beings are and consequently cannot be held to the same standards. But if this were true, it would completely change believers' view of God. God is supposed to be an object of worship and a moral ideal. Why would anyone worship God or consider Him to be a moral ideal unless He were good in *our* sense of the term?

CONCLUSION

Although I have argued that an indirect version of the inductive argument from evil is sound in the sense that it has the form of a strong inductive argument, more needs to be done. In particular, this argument assumes that theodicies produced today and in the past do not work and that there is no positive evidence for the existence of God. In *Atheism: A Philosophical Justification* I show that there is none and I critically consider all major and most minor theodicies produced by theists, concentrating on those theodicies that play the most important role in current debates. This strategy is justified. In the first place, because excellent critical reviews of past theodicies are already available, they need not be repeated here.[8] Moreover, although the latest is not always the best, theistic philosophers, like everyone else, learn from their mistakes. Thus there is a presumption that recent work constitutes the most sophisticated and best effort to date to justify God's ways to humans and to demonstrate His existence. If the most recent versions of theodicies produced by the best philosophical minds of our time in response to the problems of earlier versions can be refuted, one can have confidence that earlier versions fail as well. In addition, each refutation of a new theodicy or of a new version of an old theodicy increases support for the conclusion. The greater the number of theodicies that are refuted, the more confidence one should have that none will be successful and that none can be successful.

NOTES

1. Michael Martin, *Atheism: A Philosophical Justification* (Philadelphia: Temple University Press, 1990), Part I.

2. Robert Pargetter, "Evil as Evidence," *Sophia* 21 (1982): 14–15.

3. Ibid., p. 13.

4. Paul Draper, "An Evidential Problem of Evil," unpublished.

5. Peter H. Hare and Edward H. Madden, "Evil and Inconclusiveness," *Sophia* 11 (1975): 9.

6. In "An Evidential Problem of Evil" Draper argues that the hypothesis that neither the nature nor the conditions of sentient human beings result from actions performed by benevolent or malevolent nonhuman persons has more explanatory value than theism. Draper's hypothesis is compatible with naturalism but not identical with it, since it is compatible with the existence of supernatural beings that have no concern with humans or other sentient creatures.

7. Hare and Madden, "Evil and Inconclusiveness," p. 9.

8. For a long critical survey of arguments for the existence of God, including many of the minor arguments, see Michael Scriven, *Primary Philosophy* (New York: McGraw-Hill, 1966), chap. 4. For another standard survey of some of the problems with traditional arguments and rationales, see Wallace I. Matson, *The Existence of God* (Ithaca and London: Cornell University Press, 1965). For the critique of particular arguments for the existence of God, see the articles on each of these arguments in *The Encyclopedia of Philosophy*, edited by Paul Edwards (New York and London: Macmillan and Free Press, 1967), and *The Encyclopedia of Unbelief*, edited by Gordon Stein (Amherst, NY: Prometheus, 1985). For two recent critiques of the standard arguments and some nonstandard ones, see J. L. Mackie, *The Miracle of Theism: Arguments For and Against the Existence of God* (Oxford: Clarendon Press, 1982), and Anthony O'Hear, *Experience, Explanation and Faith* (London: Routledge and Kegan Paul, 1984). For an extended survey and critique of theodicies old and new, see Edward H. Madden and Peter H. Hare, *Evil and the Concept of God* (Springfield, IL: Charles C. Thomas, 1968).

8

An Argument from Non-Gratuitous Evil

THOMAS METCALF

This argument proceeds from the premise that some of the evil (that is, inscrutable intense suffering and premature death) in the world is non-gratuitous, that is, that some of it has a justifying or morally sufficient reason to exist. I present a dilemma for the defender of theism: either gratuitous evil exists or it does not. The first of these horns leads to a sound deductive argument against the apologists' God, and the second leads to a strong evidential argument against that God. Thus, a new argument from evil is presented, one that takes a rather different strategy from other arguments from evil.

I. GOD'S EXISTENCE AND GRATUITOUS EVIL ARE INCOMPATIBLE

Traditional evidential arguments from evil are concerned with showing, in various ways and not always explicitly, that gratuitous (or pointless or unjustified) intense suffering and premature death probably exist. For example, William Rowe's classic evidential argument from evil urges the reader to conclude that there is probably no good reason for the suffering of a fawn burned in a forest fire; this is a conclusion that the fawn's suffering is probably gratuitous.[1] Paul Draper's argument is intended to advance the same conclusion, but the argument is framed rather differently.[2] And Theodore M. Drange presents another eviden-

Written in 2004 for this anthology.

tial argument from evil that also attempts to confirm the existence of gratuitous evil, though not stated in those terms.[3] All of these evidential arguments, and indeed almost every evidential argument from evil, take as a tacit premise that gratuitous evil is inconsistent with the existence of God. (In fact, it seems that most theistic philosophers accept this as well.)[4] So the problem for the atheologian has commonly been to demonstrate that gratuitous evil probably exists. If gratuitous evil is indeed logically incompatible with God's existence, then the probability that God does not exist is at least as great as the probability that gratuitous evil exists. My purpose in the present paper, however, is not to provide an argument that gratuitous evil probably exists. Instead, I will explore the consequences if the atheologian grants to the defender of theism that gratuitous evil does *not* exist. I will argue that even if gratuitous evil does not exist, then there is nonetheless strong evidence against God's existence. But in this initial section I am concerned with demonstrating that gratuitous evil really is inconsistent with God's existence, in order to make sure that this horn of the dilemma is closed to the defender of theism.

It seems widely recognized that if God exists, God will prevent any evil that he could not prevent without thereby sacrificing a greater good. This is supposed to be a consequence of God's moral perfection; it is morally better to prevent gratuitous suffering than to allow it, so God will prevent any gratuitous suffering. But there have been at least three interesting defenses of the position that gratuitous evil and God's existence are logically compatible. The first I will consider is William Hasker's, the second is Michael Peterson's, and the third is Peter van Inwagen's. In answering the first two, I will follow an important paper of Daniel and Frances Howard-Snyder. In answering the third, I will utilize a paper of Jeff Jordan's.

William Hasker argues that some gratuitous evil is consistent with God's existence: the evil required for morality itself to be significant.[5] But the following is probably the best response to Hasker's argument, a response that the Howard-Snyders use.[6] The alleged gratuitous evil that Hasker has identified is actually not gratuitous evil, for it is necessary for a greater good: the greater good, simply, of morality's being significant. This should not be surprising; any justification for God's allowing of some evil seems likely indeed to constitute a greater good for which that evil is necessary. On the other hand, Michael Peterson has argued that humans must have the ability to create completely meaningless evils if they are to have significant free will.[7] But as the Howard-Snyders note, one can simply define gratuitous evil, following Rowe, as evils such that "God could have prevented them without thereby losing some greater good or permitting some evil equally bad or worse."[8] So this would not truly be gratuitous evil, by the prevailing definition.

Peter van Inwagen has written an interesting piece in which he argues that the "incompatibility claim," the claim that God and gratuitous evil are logically incompatible, depends upon the denial of a very plausible thesis that has come to be called the No Minimum Claim, essentially that there is no minimum amount of suffering that would accomplish God's purposes.[9] Now, this is a very interesting argument and probably more convincing than Hasker's and Peterson's, as the Howard-Snyders have noted.[10] Yet it does not succeed. For, as Jeff Jordan points out in a paper called "Evil and Van Inwagen," all plausible interpretations of the No Minimum Claim lead to the conclusion that either no evil at all is necessary for God's purposes or else humans must be able to notice infinitesimally small variations in the amount of suffering they're experiencing. Jordan concludes, rightly, that the No Minimum Claim must be denied.[11]

These are the only remotely common strategies to argue that God and gratuitous evil are compatible. But the responses I note above suffice in showing that those strategies are unsuccessful. The consistent defender of theism must maintain that no gratuitous evil exists at all. Otherwise, it would be possible to formulate a sound deductive argument against God's existence based on the incompatibility of gratuitous evil and God's existence. In the next section, however, I will argue that the position according to which there is no gratuitous evil will lead to a new argument from evil, a strong evidential argument against God's existence.

II. JUSTIFIED EVIL PROVIDES EVIDENCE AGAINST GOD'S EXISTENCE

To say that no gratuitous evil exists is to say that all evil is non-gratuitous. (I have referred to this evil as 'non-gratuitous' to make the contrast with traditional arguments from evil obvious, but calling it 'justified evil' will be more perspicuous, so I will do so henceforth. I still mean intense suffering and premature death such that God could not have prevented it without thereby sacrificing an equal or greater good.) The empirical fact that *some inscrutable evil exists*, conjoined with the proposition that *if God exists, all evil is justified evil*, yields the conclusion that *if God exists, some justified evil exists*. And because humans, in part, are the ones suffering this inscrutable evil, we must conclude that *if God exists, all the evil that befalls us is justified*. This much is quite undeniable.

Now we are in a position to see the motivation for the argument in this section. If God exists, all the evil we suffer is justified, so if God exists, either God has informed us that our suffering is justified, or he hasn't. Now consider this hypothetical situation:

(S) More people who suffer intensely know that their intense suffering is justified.

Situation (S) is by definition not actual; it is a *possible* situation in which more humans know that their suffering is justified than know now, in the world we all live in today. If I can successfully argue that if God exists, (S) would probably obtain, I will have a strong evidential argument against God's existence. To proceed with the argument, I must introduce a moral principle—the Principle of Assurance—that seems widely accepted, if sometimes only implicitly:

> (PA) If a person S is suffering intensely, and S's suffering is justified, it is morally better to inform S that her suffering is justified than to withhold that information.

The basic structure of my argument is now obvious. The apologists' God knows that our suffering is justified and has the power to bring about (S), and (PA) would require that God bring about (S), unless he has some good reason not to bring about (S). Therefore, if God existed, we would expect that (S) would obtain. But of course (S) has not obtained, so either God does not exist, or God has some good reason not to bring about (S) that outweighs the force of (PA). It is my position, to be elaborated further below, that we can reasonably rule out the second of these disjuncts, thereby leaving us with the conclusion that God probably does not exist.

I continue now to my defense of (PA). Daniel Howard-Snyder in "The Argument from Inscrutable Evil" notes that if God loves us, we have good reason to expect him to reveal himself and comfort us so horrific evils in the world won't be quite so psychologically damaging.[12] Howard-Snyder is surely correct about this, although I would point out that God wouldn't need to reveal himself, exactly, but rather, simply cause us to know that our suffering is justified. But overall, it is a feature of most people's moral systems that one ought to inform a victim of suffering why her suffering is justified, if one is indeed in possession of such information. If one is unable to explain to the victim why that victim is suffering, one ought at least to inform her *that* her suffering is justified. One way to provoke these intuitions is what can be called the Vaccine Analogy:

> Suppose there is an important vaccine that, while useful in preventing a horrible disease, is itself quite painful, if only temporarily. It is certainly justified to administer this vaccine to someone if she requests it, despite the pain it causes. But suppose there were a group of vigilante doctors who took it upon themselves to rove around the countryside, administering the vaccine and escaping before the authorities could be called. The doctors refuse to explain to their "patients" what the purpose of this painful vaccine is.

The intended conclusion is that these doctors are acting wrongly, that they would be acting morally better if they would explain the point of the pain. Of course, they would be better still if they would wait for consent from their "patients,"[13] but at least explaining the point of the vaccine would both reduce the psychological suffering of their victims and in addition would constitute better treating their victims as persons, ends in themselves who wish to know why they are being made to suffer.

In fact, Daniel Howard-Snyder offers a similar analogy in a paper called "The Argument from Inscrutable Evil," although he is there concerned with discussing a "skeptical theist" response to the evidential argument from evil. Howard-Snyder writes of the hypothetical situation in which parents are putting their child through a painful operation that nonetheless serves a greater good; Howard-Snyder concludes that the parents ought to inform their child why the child suffers.[14] I trust that many people agree with Howard-Snyder that it would simply be better to tell the child in the analogy why she must suffer, or, if that's not possible, merely to tell her that her suffering has a point. There is a considerable intuitive plausibility to (PA), and I trust we would look askance upon someone who kept the justification for a person's suffering secret from her. If we thought the person who failed to inform the sufferer was generally a morally good person, we would be surprised if she withheld that information and there didn't seem to be any good reason to withhold that information. It may be possible to describe more explicitly the moral beliefs that lead us to the above mentioned moral response to someone who keeps the justification for a person's suffering a secret from her; the present paper is not chiefly concerned with justifying (PA) on its own, but I have the space to sketch briefly how four normative ethical theories might justify (PA).

(1) Utilitarian ethical theories typically state that the consequences of a permissible action or moral principle must maximize happiness or satisfied preferences for a maximum number of salient agents. It is fairly easy to see that if utilitarianism is true, (PA) is correct. For we all certainly prefer that we know that our suffering has a purpose, and preferably, that we know what that purpose is—unless, of course, our possessing the knowledge in question would actually lead to *more* suffering. Reassuring a victim that her suffering is necessary for a greater good would generally tend to increase that person's happiness, or at least, to decrease that person's unhappiness. Simply recall the Vaccine Analogy and Howard-Snyder's similar analogy; the point of informing the child under a utilitarian view is to cause the child to suffer less. And we all are more ready to accept suffering if we know that such suffering is required for some sort of beneficial medical procedure. The knowledge in question provides some reassurance that our suffering is justified, and the reassurance makes the suffering easier to endure.

(2) A deontological ethical theory would identify certain rules by which we should behave toward other people. It seems eminently plausible that part of

respecting other persons as Kantian ends in themselves, and treating them as autonomous beings, is to inform them of why the suffering they endure is necessary. Autonomous, informed choices require knowledge of what befalls oneself and *why* it befalls oneself. And certainly, it seems somewhat deceptive to know some piece of information that someone else wants to know, and not to tell her that piece of information, when telling her that information wouldn't compromise any of one's own interests; it seems as if we have a right to know if that knowledge wouldn't compromise other rights.

(3) A contractarian ethical theory, roughly, would ask what rational members of a society would choose as rules to govern that society. There is no reason that rational persons wouldn't want to have the best information they could about why they are suffering, and no reason why they wouldn't wish for others to be required or obligated to provide that information, especially if such a provision of information didn't sacrifice those others' own interests.

(4) Finally, a virtue ethical theory tries to identify virtues that make someone a good person or a person living a good life. Good persons, I submit, are open with their fellow humans, telling them the information the latter want to know if telling them this information doesn't sacrifice the formers' interests. Good persons try to alleviate others' suffering, and as is argued earlier in this section, informing someone of why she is suffering is likely to reduce at least the emotional pain of her suffering.

Of course, these treatments are necessarily brief, but (PA) seems so obvious and widely accepted that it would only serve to distract if I were to continue in more detail. So in the end, (PA) seems undeniable. What is left is to try to think of a good reason for God *not* to actualize (S). If there is no such reason, then our preponderance of evidence indicates that God would have actualized (S) if he existed. It is a mechanical process to render the rest of the argument: (S) is not actual, so our preponderance of evidence indicates that God does not exist.[15]

III. WHY NOT ACTUALIZE (S)?

If God has a good reason not to actualize (S), one that outweighs the reasons *to* actualize (S) described in the foregoing section, then my conclusion is incorrect. What follow are some possible reasons not to actualize (S), along with why I don't think they are *good* reasons. (One crucial point to note at the outset is that the project of theodicy itself *presupposes* that it would be good for (S) to obtain, so any objection to humans knowing that their suffering is justified is rationally inconsistent with the propounding of a theodicy.)

(1) "For God to actualize (S) would mean God revealing himself, which would preclude free will decisions to believe in him and to follow his laws." But

it would not mean this; God might simply send a vivid dream to a prominent apologist in which a decisive theodicy is explained. He might bestow upon humans a faculty akin to rational insight by which humans could realize that their suffering is justified. He might make it an intuitively inescapable belief that our suffering has a purpose; this would not constitute any form of deception. All that would result from (S) is that arguments from evil would be rendered unsound. In a similar way to how "*lack of evidence* is not *evidence of lack*," one might say, albeit awkwardly, "*lack of evidence of lack* is not *evidence*." So God's revealing himself would be sufficient but not necessary for (S).

(2) "If we believed that our suffering is justified, we would cease fighting evil, because we would know our suffering is justified." But perhaps the good in question is simply that humans are fighting evil at all. If that's so, then we would have no reason to stop fighting evil, despite knowing that our suffering is justified. On the other hand, if there is some *other* reason that our suffering is justified, it is not clear precisely why it would be *bad* for humans to stop fighting evil. If it's simply a sort of moral brute fact that fighting evil is obligatory, then we would have a reason to fight evil even if we knew our suffering is justified. (And again, it is important to note that if this is a good reason not to actualize (S), then the project of theodicy is not only misguided but in fact highly inadvisable.)

(3) "God wants us to figure things out for ourselves, such as that our suffering is justified, because that process of discovery would provide the opportunity for mental, emotional, and spiritual growth." One might draw an analogy with a parent who wants her child to work out a mathematical problem herself. But it is unclear how the process in question would benefit humans in a way that God could not achieve on his own. The point of letting a child work out a mathematical problem herself is for the child to get better at mathematics, and perhaps, to gain self-confidence; yet God can bestow these traits upon humans directly. And humans don't need practice formulating theodicies, because one alone would suffice. Further, if a successful theodicy were discovered, it seems as if this information would be disseminated rapidly enough that this discovery would immediately obviate others' attempting to formulate one; would the proponent of this objection have the discovery of a successful theodicy remain a secret? And in the end, there seem to be plenty of other opportunities for growth, such as the processes of figuring out God's particular characteristics, desires, plan for humanity, etc. Recall the Vaccine Analogy; it seems wrong for parents to let their child suffer, ignorant of the reasons for her pain, until much later when the child can finally understand vaccines. The analogy is potent, at the very least, for the most psychologically troubling evils in the world.

(4) "For all we know, God has an unknown purpose for failing to bring about (S), a purpose that he can't explain to us." Readers will likely recognize this as an analogue of skeptical theist responses to arguments from evil.[16] My response

is that I have already adduced some good reasons for God to actualize (S), and the mere identification of the possibility that God has good reasons not to actualize (S) is in no way an indication that God is *likely* to have such reasons. The present objection is simply a claim that *maybe* God has a good reason not to actualize (S), but this would only suffice if my argument were a deductive argument, a claim that God and the failure of (S) to obtain were *logically* incompatible. If "maybe God has a good reason not to actualize (S)" is enough to reject the present argument, then "maybe this argument is unsound" is enough to reject *any* argument.

One alternate way to try to employ a skeptical theist response to my argument is the following. "You are concluding from the fact that you can't think of a reason for God not to actualize (S) that there really isn't a reason for God to actualize (S), but you have no reason to believe you're in a good position to know of this reason if it existed." In response, I say that what I have done is simply to have adduced some evidence that God would bring about (S) if he existed. If the defender of theism cannot adduce some "rival" evidence that God would *not* bring about (S) if he existed, then the balance of evidence favors my position. Another way to think about this matter is to appeal to something like this: there are lots of instances of inscrutable evil in the world, and the more of those instances there are, the less likely it is that *all* of them are such that to reveal their purpose would be to sacrifice some greater good for which our ignorance is necessary. And in terms of our experience, we humans can inform people of the reason for their suffering all the time without thereby sacrificing greater goods.

One further way to respond to a skeptical worry such as this is presented by William L. Rowe.[17] It would simply be very surprising, prima facie, if God, an *omnipotent* being, were unable to inform us of the reason for merely *one more* instance of evil in the world without thereby sacrificing some greater good. God's omnipotence, I would suggest (following Rowe), provides extremely strong prima facie reason to think that for any particular piece of information, God can inform us of that information without thereby sacrificing a greater good. So again, in this case, we can think of no reason for God not to actualize (S), and we have good prima facie reason to think he *would* actualize (S).

Because these possible reasons for God not to actualize (S) all fail to be *good* reasons, we are entitled to conclude that probably, if God existed, he would actualize (S). But (S) has not obtained. Therefore, probably, God does not exist. The dilemma's results are now obvious: to respond to any argument from evil, the defender of theism must maintain that all evil is justified. But this opens the defender of theism up to a strong evidential argument from evil, one that does not seem answerable. The intended conclusion is that God probably does not exist.[18]

NOTES

1. William L. Rowe, "The Problem of Evil and Some Varieties of Atheism," *American Philosophical Quarterly* 16 (1979): 335–41.

2. Paul Draper, "Pain and Pleasure: An Evidential Problem for Theists," *Noûs* 23 (1989): 331–50.

3. Theodore M. Drange, *Nonbelief & Evil: Two Arguments for the Nonexistence of God* (Amherst, NY: Prometheus Books, 1998), pp. 53–59.

4. But there are a few exceptions. See especially William Hasker, "The Necessity of Gratuitous Evil," *Faith and Philosophy* 9 (1992): 23–44; and Peter van Inwagen, "The Magnitude, Duration, and Distribution of Evil: A Theodicy," *Philosophical Topics* 16, no. 2 (1988): 161–87.

5. Hasker, "The Necessity of Gratuitious Evil," p. 30.

6. Daniel and Frances Howard-Snyder, "Is Theism Compatible with Gratuitous Evil?" *American Philosophical Quarterly* 36 (1999): 119–27.

7. Michael Peterson, "The Problem of Evil: The Case against God's Existence," chap. 6 in *Reason and Religious Belief*, 2nd ed. (New York: Oxford University Press, 1998), pp. 126–27.

8. Howard-Snyder, "Is Theism Compatible with Gratuitous Evil?" p. 118.

9. van Inwagen, pp. 161–87.

10 Jeff Jordan, "Evil and van Inwagen," *Faith and Philosophy* 20 (2003): 236–39.

11. Ibid.

12. Daniel Howard-Snyder, "The Argument from Inscrutable Evil," in *The Evidential Argument from Evil*, edited by Daniel Howard-Snyder (Bloomington: Indiana University Press, 1996), pp. 305–307.

13. Of course, God doesn't seem to have asked many of the sufferers in the world for their consent in his purposes, either. Some major theodicies argue that some people's suffering and premature death is instrumentally necessary for other people's moral development, but it is not at all obvious that the former have had any say in the matter. Rather, they seem to have been used as means to ends rather than treated as ends in themselves. See, especially, Richard Swinburne, "Some Major Strands of Theodicy," in *The Evidential Argument from Evil*, pp. 30–48.

14. Howard-Snyder, "The Argument from Inscrutable Evil," pp. 305–306.

15. It is important to ask whether this would truly count as non-gratuitous evil. I say it is not 'evil' at all by our usual sense, but rather, simply a moral failing on God's part. Evil, as it is used in the present paper (and in much of the rest of the debate), is intense suffering and premature death.

16. Some representative skeptical theist arguments appear in Howard-Snyder's *The Evidential Argument from Evil*. See especially William P. Alston, "The Inductive Argument from Evil and the Human Cognitive Condition," pp. 97–125; and Stephen John Wykstra, "Rowe's Noseeum Arguments from Evil," pp. 126–50.

17. William L. Rowe, "Skeptical Theism: A Response to Bergmann," *Noûs* 35 (2001): 297–303.

18. I am grateful to Kenneth Clatterbaugh and to Angela Smith for helpful comments on previous versions of this essay.

PART 4

NONBELIEF ARGUMENTS AGAINST THE EXISTENCE OF GOD

INTRODUCTION

This section contains new and previously published papers and a book selection presenting and defending nonbelief arguments against the existence of God. A nonbelief argument against God's existence is an inductive argument based on the weight of the evidence relative to the widespread nonbelief or the reasonable nonbelief in the world.

A nonbelief argument against God's existence takes the following general form:

1. If God exists,
   then God possesses certain attributes.
2. Based on the weight of the evidence relative to the widespread nonbelief or the reasonable nonbelief in the world, God does not possess all of these attributes.
3. Therefore, God does not exist.

Here are brief summaries of the papers and the book selection contained in this section.

Theodore M. Drange in a 1993 paper "The Argument from Nonbelief" presents an argument from widespread nonbelief for the nonexistence of the God of evangelical Christianity. It is argued that the evangelical Christian God wants and has the power to bring about a world in which nearly all humans since the time of

Jesus come to believe before their physical deaths that God exists and Jesus is savior, but even after two thousand years such a world does not obtain, as evidenced by the fact that a large majority of the world's present population is non-Christian, and therefore the evangelical Christian God probably does not exist. Drange then defends the argument from a number of possible objections, including the free will and unknown purpose defenses, and speculates about how it might be turned into an argument for the nonexistence of the God of Orthodox Judaism.

In a 2002 paper "McHugh's Expectations Dashed," Drange sharply criticizes an objection raised by Christopher McHugh to a crucial premise in the argument from widespread nonbelief for the nonexistence of the evangelical Christian God. That premise, which has indirect but compelling biblical support, states that God does not want anything more strongly than for nearly all humans to believe that God exists and Jesus is savior. McHugh denies this premise on the grounds that some biblical passages describe God as not only allowing but causing widespread nonbelief, which suggests that God indeed does want something more strongly. Drange concedes that there are such passages but criticizes McHugh for neither identifying what it is God wants more strongly nor reconciling these passages with more important ones suggesting that God does *not* want anything more strongly, such as God's Great Commission to bring the gospel message to the world and God's commands about loving God maximally and believing in Jesus.

Victor Cosculluela in a 1996 paper "Bolstering the Argument from Nonbelief" presents a deductive argument to strengthen the crucial premise in Drange's argument from widespread nonbelief for the nonexistence of the evangelical Christian God. This premise states that God does not want anything more strongly than for nearly all humans to believe that God exists and Jesus is savior. Cosculluela argues that if God has *any* desire for a particular situation among competing situations then, because God would never have any desire for less than the best, that situation is necessarily both the best and only one desired. Since there is indirect but compelling biblical evidence that God wants nearly all humans to believe that God exists and Jesus is savior, God cannot have any competing desire. This strengthens the crucial premise, and thus also the conclusion that the evangelical Christian God probably does not exist.

Theodore M. Drange in a paper "The Arguments from Confusion and Biblical Defects," written in 2004 for this anthology, presents two more arguments from widespread nonbelief for the nonexistence of the evangelical Christian God. According to the argument from confusion, since the evangelical Christian God loves humans and wants a personal relationship with them, this God would want them to know, and would probably prevent widespread confusion about, what is needed to have this relationship. However, the history of Christianity is replete with disagreements, disputes, and even wars about what is needed to have a personal relationship with God, and thus the evangelical Christian God probably does not exist. Drange defends the argument from three possible objections, including the unknown purpose defense. Finally, according to the argument from biblical defects, if the Bible is a divine revelation, as evangelical Christians claim, then it would probably be clear, inerrant, and consistent. Since the Bible contains numerous ambiguities, factual mistakes, and contradictions, the evangelical Christian God probably does not exist.

Walter Sinnott-Armstrong in a selection "The Argument from Ignorance" from *God?* (2004), a debate with William Lane Craig, argues that if God exists then God would provide strong evidence of God's existence because the benefits of providing such evidence far outweigh the costs. For instance, strong evidence of God's existence would bring assurance and solace to those in deep pain or sorrow without undermining any valuable kind of freedom. However, as Sinnott-Armstrong demonstrates, putative arguments for God's existence, religious experiences, and alleged miracles all fail to provide strong evidence for God's existence. Since such kinds of evidence would be available if God exists, but in fact are not, God probably does not exist.

In "The Real Argument from Ignorance," also a selection from *God?*, Sinnott-Armstrong defends the argument in the face of several objections raised by William Lane Craig. For example, Craig claims that God, while interested in building a loving relationship with people, is relatively indifferent to whether they "(merely) believe" in God's existence. Sinnott-Armstrong replies by pointing out that "mere belief" in God's existence, even if not sufficient for a loving relationship with God, is nevertheless necessary, and thus an important potential benefit of God's providing strong evidence.

J. L. Schellenberg in "An Argument for Atheism from the Reasonableness of Nonbelief," a paper written in 2004 for this anthology and based on excerpts from *Divine Hiddenness and Human Reason* (1993), presents an argument from reasonable nonbelief for the nonexistence of God. It is argued that a perfectly loving God would seek a personal relationship with every human based on reciprocity and mutuality, a logically necessary condition of which is human belief in God's existence. But this requires that God, while allowing the freedom not to believe, provide to humans sufficient evidence that God exists so that reasonable (inculpable) nonbelief does not occur. However, reasonable nonbelief *does* occur, and therefore God probably does not exist.

In the first half of a 1996 paper "Response to Howard-Snyder," Schellenberg demonstrates the inadequacy of Daniel Howard-Snyder's attempt to reformulate the argument from reasonable nonbelief for the nonexistence of God as a Rowe-type evidential argument. In the second half, three possible reasons that Howard-Snyder thinks God might have for allowing the occurrence of reasonable nonbelief are critically examined and rejected.

In a 2004 paper "Divine Hiddenness Justifies Atheism," Schellenberg presents two arguments from reasonable nonbelief for the nonexistence of God. In the Analogy Argument it is argued that just as loving parents would, if they could, make themselves present when their child is searching for them, especially in circumstances where their child is lost, afraid, or in pain, even more so God, who is perfectly loving, would not remain hidden but could and would provide each human who is searching, especially in similar circumstances, with sufficient evidence to believe in God's existence and comforting presence. Yet such evidence is absent, and therefore God probably does not exist. Schellenberg criticizes several possible objections, including the objection that God remains hidden for some greater good beyond human understanding. In the Conceptual Argument it is argued that God, who is perfectly loving, could and would provide sufficient evidence to everyone capable of a personal relationship with God and not inclined to resist such evidence. Everyone here includes not only seekers, as in the Analogy Argument, but also those who are not aware of any need to seek God. Again, since such evidence is absent, God probably does not exist.

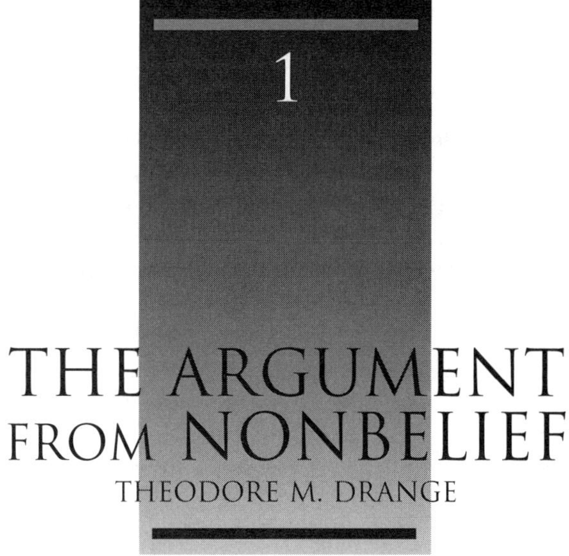

1

THE ARGUMENT FROM NONBELIEF

THEODORE M. DRANGE

Attempts have been made to prove God's nonexistence. Often this takes the form of an appeal to the so-called Argument from Evil: if God were to exist, then he would not permit as much suffering in the world as there actually is. Hence the fact that there is so much suffering constitutes evidence for God's nonexistence. In this essay I propose a variation which I shall call "The Argument from Nonbelief." Its basic idea is that if God were to exist, then he would not permit as much *nonbelief* in the world as there actually is. Hence the fact that there is so much nonbelief constitutes evidence for God's nonexistence.

Obviously not all gods will succumb to this line of reasoning. Gods who care little about humanity's belief or nonbelief will be immune to it. The argument needs to be directed specifically against gods who place great value upon love and worship from humans. In this essay, it will be directed specifically against the God of evangelical Biblical Christianity, that form of Christianity which is based strongly on the Bible, especially the New Testament, which emphasizes the doctrine of salvation by faith in Jesus Christ and which seeks to help people obtain such salvation. In what follows, I shall use the term 'God' to refer specifically to the God of evangelical Biblical Christianity. The Argument from Nonbelief, then, very roughly, is the argument that God, thus construed, does not exist, for if he were to exist, then he would not permit there to be as many non-

From *Religious Studies* 29 (1993): 417–32.

believers in the world as there actually are. Here the term 'nonbelievers' does not refer just to atheists and agnostics, but to anyone who does not believe specifically in God, conceived in the given way, and in his son, Jesus Christ. Possibly the nonexistence of other gods, or God conceived of in other ways, might also be established by a similar line of reasoning, and I shall comment briefly on that matter at the end.

To formulate the Argument from Nonbelief more precisely, I put forward, first, these definitions:

Set P = the following three propositions:

- (*a*) There exists a being who rules the entire universe.
- (*b*) That ruler of the universe has a son.
- (*c*) The ruler of the universe sent his (or her or its) son to be the savior of humanity.

Situation S = the situation of all, or almost all, humans since the time of Jesus of Nazareth coming to believe *all three* propositions of set P by the time of their physical death.

Using the above definitions, the argument may be formulated as follows:

- (A) If God were to exist, then he would possess all of the following four properties (among others):
  - (1) *Being able* to bring about situation S, all things considered.
  - (2) *Wanting* situation S, i.e., having it among his desires.
  - (3) *Not wanting* anything that conflicts with his desire for situation S as strongly as it.
  - (4) *Not being irrational*, which entails that he would never refrain from acting in accord with his own highest purposes.
- (B) If a being which has all four properties listed above were to exist, then situation S would have to obtain.
- (C) But situation S does *not* obtain. It is *not* the case that all, or almost all, humans since the time of Jesus of Nazareth have come to believe all three propositions of set P by the time of their physical death.
- (D) Therefore [from (B) & (C)], there does not exist a being who possesses all four properties listed in premise (A).
- (E) Hence [from (A) & (D)], God does not exist.

I. SOME COMMENTS ON THE ARGUMENT

Note, at the outset, that situation S does not call for *every* person, without exception, to believe set P. It allows the possibility that in some cases special circumstances may prevent such belief. That qualification in itself helps make premise (A) of the Argument from Nonbelief true.

Dividing (A) into four premises, we should inquire of each of them whether it receives Biblical support. Premise (A1) is supported by the Bible's repeated claim[1] that God is all-powerful. There are various ways by which God might have brought about situation S. One way would be direct implantation of the given beliefs into people's minds. (A possible Biblical example of belief-implantation would be the case of Adam and Eve.) Another way would be the performance of spectacular miracles. For example, God could speak to people in a thunderous voice from the sky or use skywriting to proclaim the gospel message worldwide. In addition, back in the days of Jesus, events could have occurred differently. Instead of appearing only to his followers, the resurrected Christ could have appeared to millions of people, including Pontius Pilate and even Emperor Tiberius and others in Rome. He could thereby have made such a definite place for himself in history that it would have enlightened billions of people coming later about the truth of set P. Finally, God might have brought about situation S through non-spectacular, behind-the-scenes actions. For example, he could have sent out millions of angels, disguised as humans, to preach to people in all nations in such a persuasive manner as to get them to believe set P. Another useful action would have been to protect the Bible itself from defects. The writing, copying, and translating of Scripture could have been so carefully guided (say, by angels) that it would contain no vagueness or ambiguity and no errors of any sort. Also, it could have contained a large number of clear and precise prophecies that become amazingly fulfilled, with that information widely disseminated. Then people reading it would have been much more likely to infer that everything in it is true, including the propositions of set P. If all that had been done, then situation S would probably now obtain. Certainly the way God is depicted in the Bible, he has the *power* to accomplish all such things, which makes premise (A1) of the argument true.

Premise (A2) states that if God were to exist then he would *want* situation S, where that is to be understood in a kind of minimal way, meaning only that situation S is *among* God's desires. So, it is a desire that might be overridden by some other desire, which creates a need for premise (A3). When premise (A2) is understood in this weak sense, it is clear that it, too, is supported by the Bible. There are at least five different arguments to show that. Let us label them Arguments (1)–(5).

Argument (1). The Bible says that God has commanded people to "believe on the name of his son Jesus Christ" (I John 3:23). The way that is usually interpreted, it calls for at least belief in the truth of the propositions of set P. It follows that God must want people to believe those propositions, which makes premise (A2) true.

Argument (2). There is another Biblical commandment to the effect that people love God maximally (Matt. 22:37–38; Mark 12:30). But loving God maximally (i.e., to an extent that could not possibly be increased) requires that one be aware of *all* that God has done for humanity, which, in turn, calls for belief in the propositions of set P. Hence, again, God must want people to believe those propositions, which makes premise (A2) true.

Argument (3). A third argument for (A2) is based on the Great Commission, according to which God (via his son) directed missionaries to preach the gospel to all nations (Matt. 28:19–20) and to every creature (Mark 16:15–16). Since set P is part of the gospel, he must have wanted people to believe the propositions of set P. Furthermore, according to the Book of Acts,[2] God went so far as to empower some of the missionaries to perform miracles which would help convince listeners of the truth of their message. So, getting people to believe that message must have been a high priority for him. This is good evidence that premise (A2) is true.

Argument (4). According to the Bible, God "wants all men to be saved and to come to a knowledge of the truth" (I Tim. 2:4, NIV). The 'truth' here referred to includes the gospel and, thereby, the propositions of set P. Interpreting it that way, the verse is in effect telling us that God wants (among other things) situation S. And that makes premise (A2) true. The support for (A2) is here very direct.

Argument (5). The final argument for (A2) is more controversial. One of its premises is the claim that, according to the Bible, God wants all humans to be saved. There are indeed verses, like the one quoted in Argument (4), above, that either state it directly or else point in that direction.[3] But in order for a person to be saved he/she must believe in God's son.[4] Hence, God must want people to believe in his son, which entails believing the propositions of set P. It follows that (A2) must be true.

There are two main objections to this argument. One is that some verses in the Bible indicate that God does *not* want all humans to be saved.[5] The other is that the Bible is not perfectly clear about the requirements for salvation and some verses suggest that charitable behavior might be sufficient,[6] in which case belief in God's son would *not* be a necessary condition, after all. It appears, then, that the premises of this last argument for (A2) leave some room for doubt.

In defense of Argument (5), it could be pointed out that there are conflicting interpretations of the relevant verses among Biblical scholars, and some of them favor Argument (5). Furthermore, evangelical Christianity supports such interpretations. It regards God as a loving and merciful being who wants *all* to be saved, at least in the minimal sense of having that as one of his desires. In addition, evangelical Christianity accepts the doctrine that belief in God's son is an absolute requirement for salvation. Thus, although there are other forms of Biblical Christianity based on other interpretations of the relevant verses, that form which fosters belief in the God of evangelical Christianity, the being referred to in the Argument from Nonbelief, would accept the premises of Argument (5). That then allows Argument (5) to provide further Biblical support for premise (A2) of the Argument from Nonbelief.

Even if Argument (5) were rejected, the other four arguments would suffice to establish premise (A2). It might be said, then, that, like premise (A1), premise (A2) receives good Biblical support.

When it comes to the argument's next premise, (A3), the situation is different. There are no Biblical verses that support it directly. If (A3) is to receive any support at all from the Bible, it would need to be of an indirect nature. One possible argument for premise (A3) is the following. Let us call it "Argument (6)." The way the verb 'conflicts' is used in (A3), in order for God to have two conflicting wants, it would have to be *impossible* for him to satisfy both of them simultaneously. But for God, nothing is impossible.[7] Therefore, he cannot have conflicting wants, which makes premise (A3) automatically true.

One defect in this argument is that it paradoxically claims both that God cannot have conflicting wants and that for God nothing is impossible, which seems to be a contradiction. But the more basic defect in Argument (6) is that it interprets "for God, nothing is impossible" in an unrestricted way. Most theologians and philosophers of religion recognize that omnipotence needs to be restricted to what is logically possible and to what is consistent with God's other defining properties.[8] God might have two desires that *logically* conflict. Since it is *logically* impossible for both desires to be satisfied, even a being who is omnipotent (defined in the appropriate way) would be unable to satisfy both of them. And that is how 'conflicts' in premise (A3) is to be taken. The word 'logically' could be inserted just before it. Thus, Argument (6) is a failure.

Another argument for premise (A3), to be labeled "Argument (7)," appeals to the *force* of earlier arguments, especially Arguments (1)–(3). Looking back at Argument (1), we note that, according to the Bible, God has *commanded* people to believe in his son, which is quite forceful. Although that may not prove it, it does *suggest* that God's desire for situation S is not overridden by any other desire. As for Argument (2), according to the Bible, God's commandment that people love him maximally is described as the *greatest* of all the commandments (Matt. 22:38, NIV). That too *suggests* that God wants people to be aware of what he has done for them and so to believe set P, and that this is not a matter overridden by other considerations. Finally, as was already pointed out in Argument

(3), according to the Bible, God not only sent out missionaries to spread the gospel worldwide, but also empowered some of them with the ability to perform miracles to help get their listeners to accept the message. That *suggests* that situation S must have been such a *high priority* in God's mind as not to be overridden by anything else. Argument (7), then, is the argument that premise (A3), though not directly expressed in the Bible, is nevertheless *suggested* by several Biblical passages, particularly in the *forceful* way that premise (A2) is Scripturally supported.

Argument (7) is admittedly inconclusive, for it only appeals to "suggestions" that are hinted at in certain Biblical verses. It concedes the point that premise (A3) receives no explicit support from Scripture. On the other hand, this weakness may not be fatal, first of all because any support, even of an indirect nature, is better than none, and secondly because (A3) is put forward not just as a claim but also as a challenge. It says that if God were to exist, then he would *not* have a certain type of desire, one which both logically conflicts with and also equals or even overrides his desire for situation S. It is certainly a challenge to even conceive of possible candidates for such a specialized desire, for it is hard to understand what God might want from humans as much as their belief (on which depends their love and worship). There is absolutely nothing in the Bible to imply that God might have such a desire. To deny its existence, then, appears not to be such a terribly bold claim. It should be taken as a *challenge* by anyone who wishes to try to refute premise (A3) of the Argument from Nonbelief to describe a plausible candidate for the specialized desire called for. To do so would attack (A3) and thereby the argument itself. This issue will be taken up further on in the essay.

Premise (A4) denies that God is irrational. The point here is that God would not simply abandon one of his goals for no reason. Rather, he would perform whatever actions are called for by a goal that is not overridden by any other goal. The idea that God is not irrational in this sense is implied throughout Scripture. It is implied by those Biblical verses that declare him to have infinite understanding (Psalm 147:5) and to have created the universe through his wisdom and understanding (Prov. 3:19). It is also implied by verses that say of God that he does what he wants and nothing ever prevents from happening those things that he wants to happen (Isa. 46:9–11; Eph. 1:11). The Bible is largely the story of a Supreme Being who is eminently rational in having goals and performing actions to bring them about. Premise (A4) therefore receives excellent Biblical support.

Let us consider now the other steps of the argument. Premise (B) should not be controversial. It is based on the idea that if there is no reason whatever for situation S to not obtain then S must obtain. This appears to be a corollary of the Principle of Sufficient Reason. It might be objected that sometimes things fail to happen even when there is no reason for them to fail. For example, an electron may fail to make a quantum leap to a higher orbit even when there is no reason for that to not happen. But in that case there *is* a reason for the electron to not make the leap: no rational being exists who wants the electron to make the leap as one of his top priorities and who has the power to bring it about. That may not be a very illuminating explanation for the electron's failure to make the quantum leap, but it *does* provide *some* reason. In the case of situation S, however, there would not even be that sort of reason if there were to exist a being who possesses all four properties listed in premise (A). In that case, it appears, situation S would *have to* obtain. Whoever doubts premise (B) is probably not understanding it properly.

Premise (C) is an empirical fact about our world. Christianity may be the most widespread religion, but it still claims a *minority* of the earth's people, which suffices to make (C) true. Premise (C) is the proposition from which the Argument *from* Nonbelief derives its name.

Note that the Argument from Nonbelief is also an argument *for* nonbelief in that it aims to prove the nonexistence of God. Thus, it is both "from nonbelief" and also "for nonbelief," which implies circularity. However, the circularity is avoided when the two different types of "nonbelief" are specified. The argument proceeds *from* the fact of widespread nonbelief in *set P*, as one of its premises, *to* a proposition which expresses nonbelief in *God*, as its conclusion.

Step (D) is the first conclusion in the argument. It follows logically from premises (B) and (C) by modus tollens. The final conclusion, step (E), also follows logically, from steps (A) and (D), though it is not a direct inference. Premise (A) entails the proposition that if God exists, then there would exist a being who has all four properties (1)–(4). And *that* proposition, together with (D), logically entails the final conclusion, (E), by modus tollens.

Since the conclusions of the Argument from Nonbelief follow logically from its premises, the only way to attack it would be at one or more of the premises. Dividing (A) into four, there are a total of six premises to be considered: (A1), (A2), (A3), (A4), (B), and (C). Of these, I hope to have shown above that only (A2) and (A3) leave room for debate. The other four, as I see them at least, are not controversial. And of the two premises about which there may be some debate, (A2) strikes me as the one that is more clearly true, being well supported within the Bible. Nevertheless, there may still be some opposition to it. There may be people not convinced by the alleged Biblical support who wish to attack the idea that God wants situation S. I shall begin my defense of the Argument from Nonbelief by considering an objection to its premise (A2).

II. THE FUTURE-KINGDOM DEFENSE

There is a time reference built into the Argument from Nonbelief because situation S refers explicitly to the period from the time of Jesus of Nazareth to the present. Since the present keeps changing, the argument's time reference keeps changing. Every time the argument is expressed, it refers to a slightly longer span of time. And new humans keep getting born, thereby continually enlarging the set of humans referred to in situation S. What we have, then, is a temporal series of situations, S_1, S_2, S_3, . . , S_n, where the 'situation S' referred to each time the argument is expressed is a new one further along in the series. The advocate of the Argument from Nonbelief concedes this point, but insists that it does not affect the truth of any of the premises. It may not be exactly the same situation S from one moment to the next, but the difference is quite minor, and God still wants the new situation S anyway, so premise (A2) remains true.

The objection to be considered here is that premise (A2) is *false*, after all, because God is really not interested in any of the situation S's, whether past, present, or future, but rather, a future situation somewhat like S. It is a situation in which everyone will believe the propositions of set P, but most of the people will have come to believe those propositions in an *afterlife* rather than prior to their physical death, as specified in situation S. Since it is this other situation that God wants, and not situation S, the argument's premise (A2) is false. Let us call this objection to the Argument from Nonbelief "The Future-Kingdom Defense." It is a defense of God's existence which appeals to the idea of a future society in which God, or his son, reigns as king and in which everyone believes all three propositions of set P (or *knows* them, as an advocate would put it). People who died without having been sufficiently enlightened about the gospel will be resurrected at the time of the future kingdom and given another opportunity "to come to the knowledge of the truth." Because of this, God does not want situation S, which relates only to belief prior to physical death. And so, premise (A2) of the Argument from Nonbelief is false.

There are several objections to the Future-Kingdom Defense. First of all, there are conceptual problems with the idea of a general resurrection of the dead in which people somehow come back to life in new bodies and can nevertheless be identified as the people they were prior to death. This is a large topic in itself, and we need not pursue it here. It should just be noted that many are not convinced that such an afterlife is even conceptually possible.

A second objection is that the Future-Kingdom Defense has no basis in Scripture and may even conflict with it regarding the doctrine of salvation. The argument claims that some people will not attain salvation by what they do or believe in *this* life, but rather, by what they do and believe in the *next* life. It is only in the afterlife that they will come to believe in God's son and thereby meet that important requirement for salvation. But the Bible does not say anything about such a possibility, and, in fact, some verses seem to conflict with it. The Bible says, "Now is the day of salvation" (II Cor. 6:2) and "It is appointed for men to die once, and after that comes judgment" (Heb. 9:27). This seems to require that the criteria for salvation be satisfied in this life and leaves no room for anyone coming to satisfy them *after* having been resurrected into the next life.

The third objection is clearly related to the second one. If the Future-Kingdom Defense were correct, then just about everyone will eventually attain salvation. People who are aware of having become resurrected and who are at that time preached to by angels and given the opportunity for salvation are not likely to let such an opportunity slip by. Yet, according to the Bible, Jesus himself said that very few people will be saved (Matt. 7:14; Luke 13:23–24). So, here is still another place where the argument seems to conflict with Scripture.

The fourth objection to the Future-Kingdom Defense is that it seems to be incompatible with the Great Commission. Why should it be important to God to have missionaries go forth to spread the gospel to all nations, beginning at the time of Jesus of Nazareth, if people will receive another chance at such education in the afterlife? Presumably they would learn the truth of the gospel much more readily than under past or present conditions, for they would presumably be aware that they are in an afterlife, which in itself would make an enormous difference. Why should missionaries struggle to convince people of the gospel message in this life when the same job could be accomplished effortlessly (say, by angels) in the next life? The Future-Kingdom Defense has no good answer. Until some answer is given, the argument appears incompatible with the Great Commission.

The fifth objection is similar to the fourth one. There is a great mystery surrounding the Future-Kingdom Defense. Why should God set up the world in such a way that there is a prior period when people are pretty much left on their own, followed by a kingdom-period in which God or his son reigns? What is the purpose of it all, especially if people can become resurrected from the one period to the other and have the more important portion of their existence, including satisfaction of the criteria for salvation, during the second period? Why even bother with the earlier period? The argument leaves all this unanswered, and that is still another reason to regard it unsatisfactory.

Finally, there is excellent Biblical support for premise (A2) of the Argument from Nonbelief, as shown above in Arguments (1)–(5). The Future-Kingdom Defense has done nothing to undermine that support. For that reason alone, it ought to be rejected, but the above objections to the argument also render it untenable.

It appears that the only way to attack the Argument from Nonbelief is through its premise (A3). Let us turn, then, to a consideration of two objections to the argument that accept its premise (A2) but reject its premise (A3).

III. THE FREE-WILL DEFENSE

According to this objection, which may be called "the Free-Will Defense," premise (A3) of the Argument from Nonbelief is false because there is something that God wants even more strongly than situation S and that is the *free* formation of proper theistic belief. God wants people to come to believe in his son *freely* and not as the result of any sort of coercion. He knows that people would indeed believe the propositions of set P if he were to directly implant that belief in their minds or else perform spectacular miracles before them. But for him to do that would interfere with their free will, which he definitely does not want to happen. Since God's desire that humans retain their free will outweighs his desire for situation S, it follows that premise (A3) is false, which makes the Argument from Nonbelief unsound.

There are many objections to the Free-Will Defense. First and foremost, assuming that God wants to avoid interfering with people's free will, it is *not* clear that that desire actually *conflicts with* his desire for situation S. Why should showing things to people interfere with their free will? People *want* to know the truth. It would seem, then, that to show them things would not interfere with their will, but would conform to it. Even direct implantation of belief into a person's mind need not interfere with his/her free will. If that person were to *want* true beliefs and not care how the beliefs are obtained, then for God to directly implant true beliefs into his/her mind would *not* interfere with, but would rather comply with, the person's free will. An analogy would be God making a large unexpected direct deposit into someone's bank account. It would make the person quite pleased and would not at all interfere with his/her free will. Furthermore, as was explained previously in Section I, there are many different ways by which God might bring about situation S. It is not necessary for him to use either direct implantation or spectacular miracles. He could accomplish it through relatively ordinary means. It would be ludicrous to claim that free will has to be interfered with whenever anyone is shown anything. People have their beliefs affected every day by what they read and hear, and their free will remains intact. Finally, even the performance of spectacular miracles need not cause such interference. People *want* to know the truth. They *want* to be shown how the world is really set up. To perform miracles for them would only conform to or comply with that desire. It would therefore *not* interfere with their free will. Hence, the Free-Will Defense fails to attack premise (A3) of the Argument from Nonbelief because it fails to present a desire on God's part that *conflicts with* his desire for situation S. That failure makes the Free-Will Defense actually irrelevant to premise (A3).

There is another objection to the Free-Will Defense that also aims to show its irrelevance. Let us ask: how are beliefs formed and to what extent is a person's will involved in that process? Philosophers have argued, plausibly, that people do not have direct control over their own beliefs.[9] However, it is usually conceded that the will does play an indirect role in the process of belief formation. We make choices regarding which propositions to try to verify or falsify, and how strenuously such attempts are to be pursued. And those choices indirectly affect what beliefs we end up with. This view, that the will plays, not a direct, but an indirect role in belief formation, may be called "weak doxastic voluntarism." Whether or not it is correct is a large topic in itself, which I shall not pursue here. But I do want to propose that there is a kind of irrationality inherent in willfully controlling one's own beliefs, even when that is done only indirectly. Beliefs are like "a road map through the pathways of life," where the more closely the map matches the actual roads, the better. To interject *will* into the process of belief formation, even indirectly, would go counter to that function of belief, for it would interject something additional to experience and thereby prevent the belief from representing reality exactly as experienced. It would be like capriciously altering a road map. It seems more reasonable to relegate the will to its proper role, the performance of actions, and keep it as far away as possible from the process of belief formation. People who interject their own will when forming beliefs are being to some extent irrational and "losing touch with reality." If I were to fully explore this issue, I would argue that normal people do not do that. Thus, if God were to show things to normal people, and thereby cause them to acquire beliefs, then he could not be interfering with their free will for the simple reason that the wills of normal people are not involved in belief formation. But most of the billions of nonbelievers in the world *are* normal people, not irrational. Hence, the Free-Will Defense is a great failure with regard to *them*. God could certainly show them things without interfering with their free will.

Even if there were irrational people whose free will would be interfered with by God showing them things, it would seem that such people would be *benefited* by coming to know how things really are. So, the Free-Will Defense does not even work well for such people, if there are any, for it has not made clear why God should refrain from showing them things of which they *ought* to be aware. Such "interference with free will" seems to be just what such people need to get "straightened out."

There is a further objection concerning God's motivation. The Free-Will Defense seems to claim that God wants people to believe the propositions of set P in an irrational way, without good evidence. But *why* would he want *that*? Why would a rational being create people in his own image and then hope that they become irrational? Furthermore, it is not clear just *how* people are supposed to arrive at the propositions of set P in the absence of good evidence. Is picking the right religion just a matter of lucky guesswork? Is salvation a kind of cosmic lottery? Why would God want to be involved in such an operation?

Sometimes the claim is made that, according to the Bible, God really *does* want people to believe things without evidence. Usually cited for this are the words of the resurrected Christ to no-longer-doubting Thomas: "because you have seen me, you have believed; blessed are those who have not seen and yet have believed" (John 20:29). Also, Peter praises those who believe in Jesus without seeing him (I Peter 1:8). But the message here may not be that God wants people to believe things without any evidence whatever. It may be, rather, that there are other forms of evidence than seeing, such as, for example, the testimony of friends. Perhaps God is simply indicating that he approves of belief based on the testimony of others. Note that, earlier, the resurrected Christ had upbraided some of his disciples for not trusting the testimony of other disciples (Mark 16:14). His words to Thomas may have been just a continuation of that theme. Thus, it is not clear that God desires irrational belief on the part of humans, nor is it clear *why* he should want that, if indeed he does.

As another objection to the Free-Will Defense, even if it were true that showing people things interferes with their free will, that seems not to have been a very important consideration for God. According to the Bible, he did many things, some of them quite spectacular, in order to cause observers to have certain beliefs.[10] An advocate of the argument needs to explain why God was willing to do such things in the past but is no longer willing to do them in the present.

Finally, the claim that God has non-interference with human free will as a very high priority is not well supported in Scripture. According to the Bible, God killed millions of people.[11] Surely that interfered with their free will, considering that they did not want to die. Furthermore, the Bible suggests that God knows the future and predestines people's fates.[12] That, too, may interfere with human free will. In addition, there are many obstacles to free will in our present world (famine, mental retardation, grave diseases, premature death, etc.) and God does little or nothing to prevent them. This is not conclusive proof that God does not have human free will as a high priority, but it does count against it. It is at least another difficulty for the Free-Will Defense. Considering these many objections, the argument seems not to work very well. So let us turn to a different sort of defense against the Argument from Nonbelief.

IV. THE UNKNOWN-PURPOSE DEFENSE

The Free-Will Defense failed to identify a purpose that both outweighs God's desire for situation S and also logically conflicts with it. And yet, that failure does not prove that a purpose of the requisite sort does not exist. This leads to what might be called "the Unknown-Purpose Defense." It simply and boldly states that God has *some* purpose which logically conflicts with his desire for situation S and which he wants fulfilled even more strongly than it, and that makes premise (A3) of the Argument from Nonbelief false. When asked what the additional overriding purpose might be, the advocate of the Unknown-Purpose Defense declares, disappointingly, that it has not as yet been revealed to humanity. This argument, unlike the Free-Will Defense, clearly does attack premise (A3), being, in effect, not much more than a bare denial of it. The issue becomes that of which argument, the Argument from Nonbelief or the Unknown-Purpose Defense, if either, is the sound one.

Both arguments carry a burden of proof. The advocate of the Argument from Nonbelief claims to establish God's nonexistence, so he has a definite burden of proof there. On the other hand, the advocate of the Unknown-Purpose Defense claims the existence of a certain purpose on the part of God, and so he, too, has a burden of proof: to show that that purpose does exist. It might be claimed that, because of the paucity of support for premise (A3) of the Argument from Nonbelief, neither advocate has fulfilled his burden of proof, which creates a kind of "Mexican standoff" between them on this score. However, there is *some* Biblical support for premise (A3), as presented in Argument (7) of Section I above. Although the support is only indirect, it does apply specifically to that premise. In contrast, the only support for the Unknown-Purpose Defense consists of very general intimations of unknown purposes on the part of God. For example, at Isa. 55:9, God says, "as the heavens are higher than the earth, so are my ways higher than your ways, and my thoughts than your thoughts." This is too general to specifically support the argument's attack on premise (A3). For this reason, although neither side can be said to have proven its case, they are not on a par here. The Argument from Nonbelief side has the stronger position.

The question might be raised why God has not revealed to people his purpose for permitting nonbelief in set P. It would be in his interest to reveal that, for doing so would immediately destroy one main obstacle to people's belief in him and his son, namely, the Argument from Nonbelief itself. Thus, for God to keep his purpose secret is clearly counter-productive. Presumably, according to the Unknown-Purpose Defense, God has some further purpose for all the secrecy, but that further purpose is also kept secret. All that secrecy is clearly a barrier between God and mankind. It undercuts the relationship between them that is the main theme of evangelical Christianity. Some find Christianity preferable to both Judaism and Islam because it depicts God as less remote from humanity and more concerned with its problems. But the Unknown-Purpose Defense makes God remote again, which counts against it from a religious perspective. It is probably for this reason that Christians appeal to the "unknown-purpose" idea only as a last resort.

The Unknown-Purpose Defense cannot be conclusively refuted. Barring some other proof of God's nonexistence, obviously it is *possible* that he exists and has the sort of unknown purpose that the argument attributes to him. The Biblical support for premise (A3) of the Argument from Nonbelief, though worth mentioning, is in the end inconclusive. Nevertheless, there are at least two additional reasons for preferring the Argument from Nonbelief to the Unknown-Purpose Defense. Each of the arguments presents us with a kind of worldview. The worldview presented by the Argument from Nonbelief (call it "W-N") is that the God of evangelical Biblical Christianity does not exist, which leaves open many alternatives. Among them are the following four: (1) there is no god at all; (2) there are many gods; (3) there is one god but it lacks the power to bring about situation S; and (4) there is one god but it does not want situation S. In contrast, the worldview presupposed by the Unknown-Purpose Defense (call it "W-U") is that, specifically, the God of evangelical Biblical Christianity, who wants a close relationship with humanity and who possesses properties (A1), (A2), and (A4) of the Argument from Nonbelief, among others, *does* exist but is very mysterious concerning his motivations, despite the apparently counter-productive character of that.

One reason for preferring W-N to W-U is that W-U is a relatively definite and narrow outlook, trying to specify what the exact state of affairs is, whereas W-N puts forward many different alternatives, any one of which *might* be true. We could infer that, given the data available to us, the a priori probability of W-N is greater than that of W-U. An analogy would be the example of ten boxes, numbered 1–10, and a marble which is in one of the boxes. One hypothesis simply states that the marble is *not* in box 8, whereas another hypothesis states that it *is* in box 8. Without any further information on the matter, the first hypothesis is more likely true than the second. In a similar way, because of the "open" character of W-N and the "closed" character of W-U, it is more reasonable to accept the former than the latter.

It might be objected that the marble analogy fails because we do not know the initial probabilities regarding God's existence and properties. It is like the case where some boxes may be too small to hold the marble, so we cannot assume that the initial probability for each of them is 1/10. However, even given that the initial probability for each box is *not 1/10*, there is nothing to favor box 8. Thus, the "not box 8" hypothesis is still more likely true than the "box 8" hypothesis, for we have no data to suggest otherwise. The mere structure of the hypotheses entails that result. In a similar way, without any further data, W-N is more probable than W-U, just in virtue of its "open" character.

Another point in favor of W-N is that it does not leave important matters unexplained, as does W-U. W-U conceives of God as being mysterious and leaves unexplained not only why he has refrained from bringing about situation S but also why he keeps his motivation on this matter secret from humanity. As pointed out, that seems counter-productive. Why should God, who clearly wants situation S and made a start towards it with the Great Commission, decide to back off and in the end forgo it? W-N contains no such mysteries but easily explains why situation S does not obtain: it is not something that would emerge in the natural course of events, nor is there any being who wants it and is able to bring it about. In choosing a worldview, people seek illumination, not mystery, and for that reason alone they should prefer W-N to W-U.

Premise (A3) of the Argument from Nonbelief was put forward as a challenge: find a purpose on God's part that would explain why he has not brought about situation S. The Unknown-Purpose Defense has not met that challenge. It only claims that there *is* such a purpose and that the challenge *could* be met, but it does not actually meet the challenge or even tell us when that might happen. As long as the challenge remains unmet, it is reasonable to accept the Argument from Nonbelief as *good grounds* for denying God's existence.

V. OTHER GODS

It might be possible to modify the Argument from Nonbelief so as to make it applicable to God in general, for example, by dropping propositions (*b*) and (*c*) from set P. Or perhaps the argument might be applied to, say, the God of liberal Christianity or the God of Orthodox Judaism, or even the God of Islam.

Consider, for example, the God of Orthodox Judaism. Suppose propositions (*b*) and (*c*) of set P were replaced by the following propositions (call the new set 'P′'):

(*b*)′ The ruler of the universe has a "chosen people," namely, the Israelites of the Hebrew Bible.

(*c*)′ He gave them a set of laws which he wants them to follow, namely, the Torah.

And suppose situation S were to be replaced by the following:

Situation S′: the situation of all, or almost all, descendants of the Israelites since the time of Moses believing *all* the propositions of set P′.

A corresponding change would be made in the new premise (C). And the term 'God' would be understood to refer, not to any Christian God, but to the God of Orthodox Judaism. The rest of the argument would remain unchanged.

Would the new Argument from Nonbelief be sound? There would be great problems with its premises (A2) and (A3). None of the arguments formulated above in Section I to support the original premises (A2) and (A3) would be relevant to Judaism. And it is unclear whether any analogous support for the new (A2) and (A3) could be gathered from the Hebrew Scriptures. No other religion emphasizes evangelization as much as does evangelical Biblical Christianity, for which the original Argument from Nonbelief seems tailor-made, so it seems unlikely that as strong a case could be made for the Argument from Nonbelief in the context of any other religion. Nevertheless, it does not seem impossible. Perhaps, constructed in the right way, the Argument from Nonbelief may pose a threat to belief in God in general or to religions other than evangelical Biblical Christianity. Exploration of this issue is a project for the future.

NOTES

1. Gen. 17:1, 35:11; Jer. 32:17, 27; Matt. 19:26; Mark 10:27; Luke 1:37; Rev. 1:8, 19:6.

2. Acts 3:6–18, 5:12–16, 9:33–42, 13:7–12, 14:1–11, 28:3–6.

3. Matt. 18:12–14; John 12:32; Rom. 5:18, 11:32; I Cor. 15:22; Col. 1:20; I Tim. 2:4, 6; II Peter 3:9.

4. Mark 16:5–16; John 3.18, 36, 8:21–25, 14:6; Acts 4:10–12; I John 5:12.

5. Prov. 16:4; John 12:40; Rom. 9:18; II Thess. 2:11–12. Also, Jesus spoke in parables so that not everyone would understand and thereby get saved. See Matt. 13:10–15; Mark 4:11–12; Luke 8:10.

6. Matt. 25:34–40, 46; Luke 10:25–37, 18:18–22; John 5:28–9; Rom. 2.5–7, 10; James 2:24–6.

7. See the references for note 1, above.

8. For example, according to Titus 1:2 and Heb. 6:18, it is impossible for God to lie.

9. H. H. Price, "Belief and Will," *Proceedings of the Aristotelian Society, Supplementary Volume* 28 (1954): 1–26; Bernard Williams, *Problems of the Self*; chap. 9 (Cambridge University Press, 1973); Louis Pojman, "Belief and Will," *Religious Studies* 14 (1978): 1–14; H. G. Classen, "Will, Belief and Knowledge," *Dialogue* 18 (1979): 64–72.

10. Exod. 6:6–7, 7:5, 17, 8:10, 22, 9:14, 29, 10:1–2, 14:4, 17–18, 16:12; I Kings 18:1–39; John 20:24–8. See also the references in note 2, above.

11. Gen. 7:23, 19:24–25; Exod. 12:29, 14:28; Num. 16:31–35; Isa. 37:36. There are also dozens of other verses that could be cited here.

12. Prov. 16:9, 20:24; Isa. 46:9–11; Jer. 10:23; John 6:64–65; Acts 15:18; Rom. 8:28–30; Eph. 1:4–5, 11; II Thess. 2:13; Rev. 13:8, 17:8. Also, if our hearts are ever hardened, then it is God who has hardened them. See Exod. 4:21, 7:3, 9:12, 10:1, 20, 27, 11:10, 14:8, 17; Deut. 2:30; Josh. 11:20; Isa. 63:17; John 12:40; Rom. 9:18.

2

McHUGH'S EXPECTATIONS DASHED

THEODORE M. DRANGE

In my book, I apply two atheological arguments, the Argument from Evil (AE) and the Argument from Nonbelief (ANB),[1] to all of the following: the God of evangelical Christianity, the God of Orthodox Judaism, the God of liberal Christianity, and God in general. In his recent essay,[2] Christopher McHugh focuses just on the arguments applied to evangelical Christianity. He constructs a defense against both arguments, which he calls "the Expectations Defense." Let us abbreviate it as "ED." The gist of AE and ANB within this context is that if the God of evangelical Christianity (GC) were to exist, then we would not expect to find as much evil (i.e., suffering and premature death) and nonbelief (i.e., nonbelief in the gospel message) as there is; so the fact that there is so much evil and nonbelief constitutes evidence for the nonexistence of that deity. And the gist of ED is that if GC were to exist, then we *should* expect to find just as much evil and nonbelief as there actually is, which implies that AE and ANB are unsound. In what follows, I shall aim to show that ED is a complete failure.

ED AS APPLIED TO AE

McHugh's ED is based on a confusion between the God of evangelical Christianity (GC) and God exactly as described in the Bible. Let us call the latter deity "GB." Strictly speaking, there is no such thing as *the* God of the Bible (and I used the expression in a loose way in my book only for convenience). Different religious groups ascribe different properties to God, based on their own individual interpretations of the Bible. (Actually, there isn't even at present any such thing as *the* Bible, since all that has survived is a large set of disparate, and even conflicting, ancient manuscripts, but let us overlook that here.) Each of the groups refers to its own construction as "the God of the Bible," and it is hard to say who is right and who is wrong. To be precise, we should take "GB" to refer to "God exactly as described in the Bible, interpreted in a neutral way." Whether or not such a notion is ultimately intelligible is a deep question, which I shall bypass for the purposes of this essay. At any rate, although GC and GB are closely related, they are *not* identical. And that in itself refutes McHugh's ED, in which it is assumed throughout (both applied to AE and to ANB) that GC and GB are one and the same deity.[3] . . .

[A]lthough ED may have some merit as a defense against AE applied to GB (a possibly unloving deity), it has no merit whatever as a defense against AE applied to GC, which is a specifically all-loving deity. As I said, I do not try to prove the nonexistence of GB in my book. (If I were to do so, I would not employ AE but one or more incompatible-properties arguments.) As for McHugh's stated rejection of my AE's premise (A3), all I could do is ask him why he rejects that step. He does not supply any reason for doing so within his essay and thus does not supply there any refutation of AE. Simply to reject is not to refute.

ED AS APPLIED TO ANB

McHugh's application of his ED to ANB is in even worse shape. He claims that there are passages in the Bible, referenced in his notes 17 and 18, which describe God as permitting, and even causing, widespread nonbelief in the gospel message of the sort relevant to ANB. But none of the passages given in his notes actually do that. They do indicate that some groups of people in first-century Palestine were nonbelievers, but they do not at all address the sort of worldwide situation of nonbelief 2000 years later that is referred to within ANB. Furthermore, it seems to be predicted in the Bible (at Luke 24:47, Acts 1:8, 13:47) that the gospel message will actually be preached to "all nations" and "to the ends of the earth," this being connected with "bringing salvation to the ends of the earth." The authors of those predictions seemed to have the expectation that at some time in the future there would eventually be universal (or near-universal) belief in the gospel message. Thus, even if ANB were applied to GB instead of GC, McHugh's ED would not refute it.

But this is a moot point, since ANB is to be applied, not to GB, but to GC, a deity who, among other things, wants all humans to be saved and come to a knowledge of the truth (I Tim. 2:4), and who, furthermore, initiated the Great Commission, which aims to spread the gospel message to all non-Christians. How could such a deity permit there to be as much nonbelief in the gospel message as there is (with 2/3 of the present world population being non-Christian)? Some explanation is needed, and McHugh supplies none.

As with AE, McHugh attacks ANB's premise (A3),[4] according to which GC (were he to exist) would not have any desire that conflicts with, and overrides, his desire to bring about universal (or near-universal) belief in the gospel message. In denying that premise, McHugh is affirming that GC does indeed have just such an overriding desire. Well, what might the given desire be? Again, McHugh gives no answer, which leaves his attack on ANB totally baseless and incomplete. As I said above, simply to reject is not to refute. McHugh argues that God is described in the Bible as permitting, and even causing, nonbelief. That is true (to a limited extent), but it is irrelevant to GC, since evangelical Christians overlook or play down the given point. It is obviously not a point that would go over well in missionary work, which is the hallmark of evangelical Christianity. McHugh seems to imply that GC is quite satisfied to have the gospel message spread at the very slow rate that (unaided) missionary work produces, and so the fact that there are still many nonbelievers is compatible with GC's plans, whatever they may be. However, as pointed out in my book, this theory is fraught with difficulty.[5] For one thing, the worldwide missionary effort is so ineffectual that it seems hopeless for it ever to succeed without divine assistance. In addition, it is left unexplained (and highly problematic) what is the eternal fate of those many people who live and die without ever properly hearing the gospel message. Many other objections could also be raised.

As with AE, there is the possibility of appealing to the Unknown-Purpose Defense (UPD) in order to support one's rejection of premise (A3), but, again, McHugh would have none of it. (Presumably his rejection of UPD in note 13 is intended to apply to ANB as well as to AE.) It is just as well, for my attack on UPD in connection with ANB is even more severe than in the case of AE.[6] One difference is that there is good biblical support for ANB's premise (A3),[7] whereas there isn't any for the corresponding premise within AE. Although the support is of an indirect sort, it is quite compelling, and poses a challenge to anyone who is not convinced by the argument.

In my book, I pose four questions for anyone (like McHugh) in the position of denying ANB's premise (A3) and thereby claiming that GC, in the final analysis (taking into account all of his desires), does not want universal (or near-universal) belief in the gospel message.[8] The questions are as follows:

1. Why did GC issue to people a command to "believe in the name of his son Jesus Christ" (1 John 3:23), a command which, if universally obeyed, would produce universal belief in the gospel message?

2. Why did GC issue to people a command, referring to it as his "greatest commandment," to love him maximally (Matt. 22:37–38; Mark 12:29–30), which, again, if universally obeyed, would produce universal belief in the gospel message (since, arguably, only those who believe the gospel message could love GC maximally)?
3. Why did GC send his son Jesus and also John the Baptist to (among other things) "testify to the truth" (John 18:37; John 17:18; 21; 23; John 1:6–7), where the "truth" includes the gospel message, an action which aims at, and helps produce, universal belief in the gospel message?
4. Why did GC (through Jesus) issue the Great Commission,[9] even empowering some missionaries to perform miracles as an aid to convincing their listeners, which, in effect, is the beginning of a process leading to universal belief in the gospel message?

None of these actions would make any sense if GC, in the final analysis, did not and does not want universal (or near-universal) belief in the gospel message. Thus, all those (like McHugh) who deny ANB's premise (A3) owe us answers to the four questions above.

My conclusion regarding McHugh's ED as applied to ANB is that it is a dual failure. Not only is it impotent against ANB applied to GC, but it is also a failure against ANB applied to GB. The situation here is the reverse of what it was in the case of AE. There, the biblical verses pointing to a "mean" God overwhelmed the few verses implying an all-loving deity, and, for that reason, GB seems pretty invulnerable to versions of AE. But when it comes to the issue of whether God strongly wants universal (or near-universal) belief in the gospel message, verses supporting that idea have the upper hand, and tend to overwhelm the few contrary verses that point in a different direction. So, although I did not in my book specifically apply ANB to GB, it does not seem to be a hopeless quest. But, more importantly, McHugh's ED is a failure against ANB applied to GC. GC is the omnipotent deity who sent his son to testify to the truth and who initiated Christian missionary work, etc. If *that* deity were to exist, then it would be unreasonable to expect there to be as much nonbelief in the gospel message as there is. So, the fact that there is so much nonbelief constitutes good evidence for the nonexistence of said deity. If there is to be any strong attack against this version of ANB, it will need to be something other than McHugh's ED.

NOTES

1. Theodore M. Drange, *Nonbelief & Evil: Two Arguments for the Nonexistence of God* (Amherst, NY: Prometheus Books, 1998).

Editors' note: Drange's version of ANB in *Nonbelief & Evil* (pp. 59–60) is very close to, but not exactly the same as, the version in "The Argument from Nonbelief," *Religious Studies* 29 (1993): 417–32. The main difference lies in the formulation of premise (A2): "*wanting* to bring about situation S, i.e., having it among his desires" (in the book); "*wanting* situation S, i.e., having it among his desires" (in the paper).

2. Christopher McHugh, "A Refutation of Drange's Arguments from Evil and Nonbelief," *Philo* 5 (2002): 94–102.

3. It is actually GC that McHugh says the Bible describes, but of course that is an error. GC is (by definition) the deity of the Bible as specifically interpreted by evangelical Christians, particularly those of the twentieth and twenty-first centuries. The biblical authors had no awareness of such a conception of God.

Editors' note: Much of Drange's discussion of AE in this section is omitted in order to focus on the defense of ANB.

4. McHugh, "A Refutation of Drange's Arguments," p. 100.

5. Drange, *Nonbelief & Evil*, pp. 136–39.

6. Ibid., chap. 11.

7. Ibid., pp. 67–68. Near the end of his essay, McHugh claims that (A3) of ANB "receives *no* support," and that I "admit" it. That is a twofold error. First, I only admitted that it receives no *direct* support. And, second, (A3) of ANB is very strongly supported by the Bible, albeit in an indirect way, and I point that out in the pages indicated.

8. Ibid., p. 69.

9. Matt. 28:19–20; Mark 13:10, 16:15–16; Acts 3:6–18, 5:12–16, 9:33–42, 13:7–12, 14:1–11, 28:3–6.

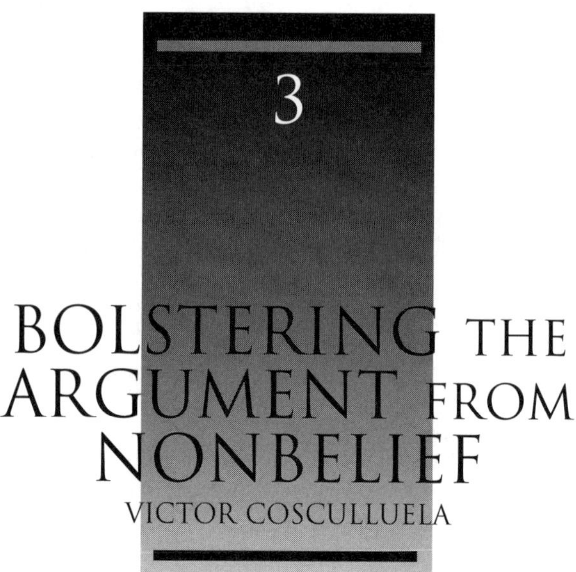

3

BOLSTERING THE ARGUMENT FROM NONBELIEF

VICTOR COSCULLUELA

Does widespread non-acceptance of Christianity constitute evidence for the nonexistence of God? Theodore M. Drange has recently claimed that this question requires an affirmative answer if certain widely held views about God are presupposed; if God is construed in a certain way, an "Argument from Nonbelief" can be developed for the nonexistence of God.[1] I hope to show that a crucial premise of Drange's argument, one for which he provides only weak Biblical evidence, can be defended by means of an a priori argument.

Drange's Argument from Nonbelief addresses the view of God proposed by evangelical Biblical Christianity, a form of Christianity which, according to Drange, (a) relies heavily on the Bible, especially the New Testament; (b) emphasizes the doctrine of salvation through faith in Jesus; and (c) seeks to help people obtain this salvation. (Although Drange suggests that perhaps alternative versions of the Argument from Nonbelief can be developed to counter varieties of theism other than evangelical Biblical Christianity, he does not develop such arguments in detail.[2]) The Argument from Nonbelief refers to a set of propositions (set P) and a possible state of affairs (situation S):

Set P = the following three propositions:

(a) There exists a being who rules the entire universe.
(b) That ruler of the universe has a son.

From *Religious Studies* 32 (1996): 507–12.

(c) The ruler of the universe sent his (or her or its) son to be the savior of humanity.

Situation S = the situation of all, or almost all, humans since the time of Jesus of Nazareth coming to believe all three propositions of set P by the time of their physical death.

Given these definitions, Drange presents his argument for the nonexistence of the evangelical Biblical Christian God as follows:[3]

(A) If [the evangelical Biblical Christian] God were to exist, then he would possess all of the following four properties (among others):
  (1) Being able to bring about situation S, all things considered.
  (2) Wanting situation S, i.e., having it among his desires.
  (3) Not wanting anything that conflicts with his desire for situation S as strongly as it.
  (4) Not being irrational, which entails that he would never refrain from acting in accord with his own highest purposes.

(B) If a being which has all four properties listed above were to exist, then situation S would have to obtain.

(C) But situation S does not obtain. It is not the case that all, or almost all, humans since the time of Jesus of Nazareth have come to believe all three propositions of set P by the time of their physical death.

(D) Therefore [from (B) and (C)], there does not exist a being who has all four properties listed in premise (A).

(E) Hence [from (A) and (D)], [the evangelical Biblical Christian] God does not exist.

The premises of this argument entail the nonexistence of the evangelical Biblical Christian God. Further, Drange provides supporting evidence for each of the argument's premises. For example, he provides a great deal of Biblical evidence to justify part (2) of premise (A);[4] although not all theists need accept Biblical arguments, the evangelical Biblical Christian, as construed by Drange, relies heavily on the Bible and cannot consistently ignore powerful Biblical support for a claim. However, he admits that the weakest point in the argument is part (3) of premise (A), hereafter referred to as (A3). According to (A3), the evangelical Biblical Christian view of God entails that God does not have a desire which both conflicts with, and is at least as strong as, his desire for situation S.

Drange accepts two arguments for (A3):[5]

(I) Several of the Bible's claims suggest (A3). (a) According to the Bible,

God commands people to believe in his son, which suggests that God's desire for situation S is not overridden. (b) According to the Bible, God's commandment that people love him maximally is the greatest of all commandments, which suggests that God wants people to realize what he has done for them and, therefore, to believe set P, and that this desire is not overridden by any other desire. (c) According to the Bible, God sent out missionaries to spread the gospel worldwide and provided some of them with the ability to perform miracles to help convince their listeners, which suggests that situation S is such a high priority in God's mind that no other desire overrides it.

(II) (A3) presents a challenge to those who would deny it: provide a plausible candidate for a divine desire that would overturn (A3). It is hard to see what God might want from people as much as their belief (without which they would neither love nor worship him). Nothing in the Bible suggests that God has such a desire.

Neither of these arguments is conclusive. First, that some passages of the Bible suggest (A3) is hardly compelling since, as Drange admits,[6] they do not assert (A3). Secondly, can we really be completely confident that nothing in the Bible even suggests that (A3) is not the case? Although Drange asserts that nothing in the Bible even suggests that (A3) is not the case, this is extremely difficult to show. Perhaps the evangelical Biblical Christian can produce Bible passages which may plausibly be taken to suggest that (A3) is not the case. If we do not rule out the notion that God has conflicting desires—and Drange does not rule it out—it may be possible for a determined evangelical Biblical Christian to provide some Biblical evidence which suggests that God has a desire which is stronger than his desire for situation S and which conflicts with that desire.

However, if it turns out that God does not have conflicting desires, and if, as Drange seems to show, there is compelling Biblical support (i.e., compelling for the evangelical Biblical Christian) for the claim that God, as conceived by evangelical Biblical Christians, wants situation S to obtain, then premise (A3) of Drange's Argument from Nonbelief has been vindicated; if the God proposed by evangelical Biblical Christianity does not have conflicting desires, and if he desires situation S (as Drange seems to show), then he has no desire that conflicts with his desire for situation S, in which case (A3) is justified.

In what follows I will defend an argument for the claim that God does not have conflicting desires. Premise (1) of this argument runs as follows:

(1) If God has *any* desire that a state of affairs X obtain, then the obtaining of X is *better* than the obtaining of any other state of affairs Y which is incompatible with X.

If there is a state of affairs Y which is incompatible with X and whose obtaining would be better than the obtaining of X, then, if God has any desire at all for X to obtain, then either God's omniscience or God's moral perfection must be questioned; an omniscient, morally perfect being would not have any desire for the obtaining of X if the obtaining of Y would be better than the obtaining of X. An omniscient being would know that the obtaining of Y is better than the obtaining of X, and a morally perfect being would not have any desire for the obtaining of X if it knew that the obtaining of Y would be better.

Suppose that the obtaining of Y is not better than the obtaining of X but as good as the obtaining of X. If the obtaining of Y and the obtaining of X have equal value, then there would be nothing about X which would give an omniscient, morally perfect being reason to desire the obtaining of X. This point can be made clearer by supposing that the obtaining of any other competing state of affairs would be much worse than the obtaining of either X or Y. In that case, if the obtaining of X and the obtaining of Y have equal value, then it appears that an omniscient, morally perfect being would desire the obtaining of (X or Y); such a being would not desire the obtaining of X, and it would not desire the obtaining of Y, but it would desire the obtaining of one or the other (X or Y). It would not desire each one independently, for it would have no reason for having such a desire.

If the reasoning contained in the last two paragraphs is sound, then, if God has any desire at all for the obtaining of X, then the obtaining of X is better than the obtaining of any state of affairs Y which is incompatible with X. However, the arguments just presented presuppose the traditional conception of God as a being who is both omniscient and morally perfect. If evangelical Biblical Christians are prepared to deny either God's omniscience or his moral perfection, then they can dismiss the arguments just presented as irrelevant to their beliefs. However, these attributes can be given strong Biblical support.

First, the Bible implies that God is morally perfect. It tells us that God's way is "perfect," and God's law is "perfect."[7] The Bible claims that God is "righteous in all his ways." "[A]ll his ways are just. A faithful God who does no wrong, upright and just is he."[8] In the Sermon on the Mount, Jesus exhorts his audience: "Be perfect, therefore, as your heavenly Father is perfect." The Bible refers to God's will as a "perfect will."[9] To this passage, the conservative commentators of *The NIV Study Bible*, who would almost certainly count as evangelical Biblical Christians,[10] add, "No improvement can be made on the will of God."[11]

Secondly, various Bible passages suggest that God is omniscient. The Bible informs us that God's "understanding has no limit." In fact, "his understanding no one can fathom." His knowledge is "too wonderful" for human comprehension.[12] "By wisdom the Lord laid the earth's foundations, by understanding he set the heavens in place; by his knowledge the deeps were divided, and the clouds let drop the dew."[13] No action is hidden from God: "The eyes of the Lord are everywhere, keeping watch on the wicked and the good."[14] The claim that God is omniscient seems inescapable for an evangelical Biblical Christian since the Bible claims that Jesus did in fact "know all things"; his disciples claimed, "this makes us believe that you come from God."[15]

If the evangelical Biblical Christian believes that God is omniscient and morally perfect, the arguments presented for premise (1), and premise (1) itself, will have to be disposed of in some other way. If the evangelical Biblical Christian denies either God's omniscience or his moral perfection, the Biblical passages just pointed out, and others which could be pointed out, must be interpreted in ways which do not suggest God's omniscience or moral perfection. It seems doubtful that this can be done for every Biblical passage which appears to suggest that God has these attributes.

The remaining steps of the argument for the claim that God does not have conflicting desires rest heavily on premise (1). Consider situation S and some other state of affairs T which is incompatible with S:

> (2) If God desires that situation S obtain (as Drange seems to show) and God desires that T obtain, and S and T are incompatible, then the obtaining of S is better than the obtaining of T and the obtaining of T is better than the obtaining of S.

(2) follows from (1). The antecedent of (2) specifies what would be the case if God has conflicting desires. However,

> (3) It is not the case that: the obtaining of situation S is better than the obtaining of T and the obtaining of T is better than the obtaining of S. (The consequent of (2) is false).

Since we are discussing overall value, we must accept (3); although situation S may be better than T in one way while T is better than situation S in another way, it cannot be the case that the situation S is better than T on the whole or all things considered while T is better than situation S on the whole or all things considered.

> (4) So, it is not the case that: God desires that situation S obtain and God desires that T obtain, and S and T are incompatible. (The antecedent of (2) is false.)

Since nothing in this argument appeals to the special nature of S or T, the argument, if sound, proves that, if God exists (and is omniscient and morally perfect), God does not have conflicting desires of any kind. The implication of this for the Argument from Nonbelief is that a proponent of the argument need not rely on flimsy Biblical evidence to justify premise (A3) of the Argument from Nonbelief. If the evangelical Biblical Christian view of God implies that God desires that situation S obtain (as Drange seems to establish), then, given the soundness of the argument just developed, God does not have any desire which conflicts with his desire that situation S obtain. In that case, (A3) is justified.

Earlier it was admitted that perhaps some Biblical passages can be produced which suggest that (A3) is not the case and that this possibility undercuts the force of Drange's Biblical defense of (A3). Suppose the evangelical Biblical Christian produces such Biblical evidence. If he presents and accepts Biblical evidence against (A3), then, if he accepts Drange's case for the claim that God desires S and the argument presented above, he will be contradicting himself; he will be claiming that God has conflicting desires and that he does not have conflicting desires. He must either undermine Drange's Biblical case for the claim that God wants situation S or undermine the argument presented above for the claim that God does not have conflicting desires. Since Drange presents what appears to be a compelling case for claiming that the evangelical Biblical Christian must accept that God desires situation S, it appears that the evangelical Biblical Christian must undermine the argument presented above for the claim that God does not have conflicting desires, even if he can present Biblical evidence against (A3).

I conclude that Drange's Argument from Nonbelief for the nonexistence of the evangelical Biblical Christian God can be strengthened at the very point where it seemed weakest. Since the rest of his argument seems justified by his evidence, it appears that, given the supporting argument developed in this article, the Argument from Nonbelief is sound.

NOTES

1. Theodore M. Drange, "The Argument from Nonbelief," *Religious Studies* 29 (1993): 417–32.
2. Ibid., pp. 431–32.
3. Ibid., p. 418.
4. Ibid., pp. 419–20.
5. Ibid., pp. 421–22.
6. Ibid., p. 420.
7. *The NIV Study Bible*, 10th Anniversary Edition, edited by Kenneth Barker (Grand Rapids: Zondervan Publishing House, 1995), 2 Sam. 22:31, Psalms 18:30, Psalms 19:7.
8. Ibid., Psalms 145:17, Deut. 32:4.
9. Ibid., Matt. 5:48, Rom. 12:2.
10. Ibid., p. xv.

11. Ibid., p. 1727.
12. Ibid., Psalms 147:5, Isa. 40:28, Psalms 139:6.
13. Ibid., Prov. 3:19–20.
14. Ibid., Prov. 15:3.
15. Ibid., John 16:30.

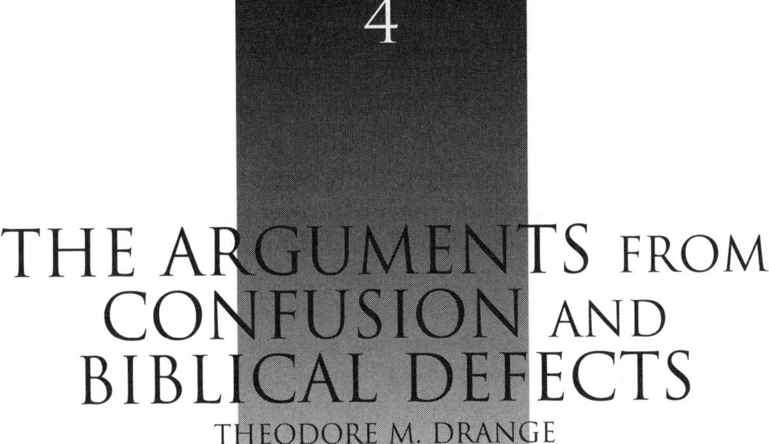

4 THE ARGUMENTS FROM CONFUSION AND BIBLICAL DEFECTS

THEODORE M. DRANGE

Many have said that God is hidden. This alleged hiddenness is particularly troublesome for evangelical Christianity, much more so than generally recognized, for it would render certain facts about the world and about the Bible very hard to explain on the hypothesis that the God of evangelical Christianity exists. Those facts would be best explained by appeal to the alternate hypothesis that that deity does not exist. Three evidential, epistemic, atheological arguments emerge from this consideration. One of them is the Argument from Nonbelief, which focuses on the fact that there is widespread nonbelief in the given deity.[1] The other two are the Argument from Confusion (to be labeled AC) and the Argument from Biblical Defects (ABD). AC focuses on the fact that there is widespread confusion among Christians regarding important doctrinal issues, including morality and salvation. ABD focuses on the fact that there are various defects in the Bible. The present essay is devoted to the latter two arguments.[2]

I. THE ARGUMENT FROM CONFUSION (AC)

According to evangelical Christianity, there are matters about which it would be very beneficial for people on earth to be knowledgeable. Included among them would be God's nature, God's laws, the nature of the afterlife, the requirements

---

Written in 2004 for this anthology.

for salvation, God's church and sacraments, and the status of the Bible. Let us call true beliefs about such matters 'G-beliefs'. Using that definition, AC may be formulated as follows:

Formulation of the Argument

(A) If the God of evangelical Christianity were to exist, then:
   1. He would love all Christians and want a personal relationship with them.
   2. People would need to have G-beliefs (among other things) in order to have the sort of relationship with God that he would want them to have.

(B) Therefore, if the God of evangelical Christianity were to exist, then he would want all Christians to have G-beliefs.

(C) Thus, if the God of evangelical Christianity were to exist, then he would probably prevent Christians from becoming confused or conflicted about matters that are the subject of G-beliefs.

(D) But some Christians are confused about such matters.

(E) And many Christians disagree with one another about such matters.

(F) Therefore [from D & E], Christians have not been prevented from becoming confused or conflicted about matters that are the subject of G-beliefs.

(G) Hence [from C & F], probably the God of evangelical Christianity does not exist.

Discussion of AC

AC is in a way intermediate between the Argument from Evil (AE)[3] and the Argument from Nonbelief (ANB). It is like AE in that confusion is more clearly "evil" than is nonbelief, since it is disruptive among God's own people. The nonbelievers referred to in ANB might be shunted aside as "hopeless cases," but that outlook doesn't work with AC, as AC deals with the believers themselves. It is clearly a bad thing for *them* to have false beliefs about important matters. Although AC is like AE, it is not just a version of AE, for it is also like ANB in that it focuses on what is essentially an epistemic problem, namely, God's hiddenness, i.e., the failure of God to clearly reveal himself. That failure produces both confusion among believers and nonbelief among nonbelievers. All three arguments, AE, ANB, and AC, are powerful evidential arguments for the nonexistence of the God of evangelical Christianity, though only AE is widely known. It is a difficult question which of them is the most forceful, though my own view is that ANB and AC should be placed ahead of AE in that regard.

The word 'confusion' has at least two different senses. In one sense, a person is confused if he does not know his own mind and is undecided. In the other sense, we say that a group of people is confused about a given issue if its members hold conflicting positions on it. For example, if half the people in the world were to believe that the earth is flat and the other half believe it is round, then we could say that humanity would be confused about the shape of the earth. The first sense of 'confusion' applies to individuals, whereas the second sense applies only to groups. In the second sense, the group could be confused even if no individual in the group is confused. Where half the population believes that the earth is flat, each individual who believes that the earth is flat might be perfectly clear about his/her belief and thus not be confused. The person might be mistaken (i.e., have a false belief), but that is something else, not confusion. Yet, we could say of the entire population that *it* (the whole group) is confused on the matter.[4]

When the word 'confusion' is used in AC, it overlaps both of the above meanings (or types of confusion). With regard to the first sense, individual (mostly liberal) Christians are confused about such doctrinal issues as morality and salvation because they realize that the Bible is inconsistent or unclear on such matters, and so they are unsure what the truth is and are more or less bewildered by it all. With regard to the second sense, Christians, as a group, are confused about such issues because of the sharp splits that occur within their ranks on the issues. Necessarily, large numbers of Christians must be holding false beliefs. As individuals, they need not be confused, but, because of the disagreements, Christians as a group can be said to be confused. It is certainly a problem for Christians to explain why their God permits confusion of both types. One way to construe AC is in terms of *facts* which are *unexpected* given the hypothesis that the God of evangelical Christianity exists. The facts are that some individual Christians are confused about important doctrinal issues and that Christians as a group are confused (in the sense of conflicted) about such issues, with the result that many large subgroups of them must be holding false beliefs. We need an explanation for these facts and the best one seems to include the hypothesis that the God of evangelical Christianity does not exist.

Why believe AC's premise (E)? Why believe that many Christians actually disagree with each other about aspects of God's nature or system of governance that have importance to their lives? My reply is to provide examples of such disagreements. One example has to do with whether or not God hates or despises certain people (homosexuals, for example, or abortion providers, or atheists, etc.). Such disagreements could (and do!) have grave consequences. It is possible to list many important moral questions about which there is no unanimity or consensus within Christianity.[5] Such a list could be used in support of AC's premises (D) & (E), for whatever the correct answer may be to any of the questions, it is a G-belief, and all other answers that conflict with it would point to both sorts of confusion referred to within those premises. For each of the questions on the list, there would be both sorts of confusion among Christians as to the correct answer.

It is also possible to list additional areas of confusion within Christianity that go beyond those of morality.[6] For each of such areas, I make these claims:

(1) The Bible does not supply any answer that is clear and authoritative on the matter.
(2) Christians, as a group, are confused with regard to the issue.
(3) The issue is an important one.

Possibly for some of the questions, one might say that the matter is not so important and that God might be willing to permit lack of clarity and lack of unanimity with regard to it. But even if that were so for some of them, there would be *other* questions that really are fundamental issues about which it really is important to get clear. I would put *those* examples forward in support of AC's premises (D) & (E), along with the examples mentioned previously. I would say, then, that the premises in question can be supported quite strongly. AC is a most forceful argument.

There are at least three defenses of God's existence that might be raised against AC. They are called the Free-Will Defense, the Afterlife Defense, and the Unknown-Purpose Defense. According to the Free-Will Defense, God permits Christians to be confused about important doctrinal issues because if he were to clarify matters for them and thereby cause them all to have G-beliefs, it would interfere with their free will, which he does not want to do. It is more important to him that they retain their free will than that they have G-beliefs.

There are several objections to this defense. I shall just mention one of them here, and that is that it is simply false that educating people interferes with their free will. On the contrary, I would say that it does just the opposite: it enhances their free will. Knowledge is power. "The truth shall set you free" (John 8:32). For example, for Christians to be better aware of the nature of morality and salvation and God's connection with those matters would open up more options for them and allow them to better realize their goals in life. It would be a win-win situation, with both God and the Christians getting what they want from the other. It is clear, then, that the Free-Will Defense is a failure when applied against AC.[7]

The Afterlife Defense (AD) tries to belittle the problem. It grants that Christians are confused about doctrinal issues, but claims that all that will be rectified in the afterlife. What's a little bit of confusion on earth when everything will be clarified in heaven as we embark upon eternal bliss? Such confusion is a relatively minor matter and can be considered negligible from the perspective of eternity, which is how God views matters. This would be a way of attacking AC's premise (A2) and would, in effect, be an argument that there are no such things as G-beliefs.

There are many objections to AD. First, there is good reason to say that the very concept of an afterlife is, in the end, incoherent, but let us set that issue aside for now. Second, AD seems to presuppose universalism, the idea that everyone will eventually go on to eternal bliss in heaven, but that is definitely a minority outlook. AD does not work well once it is granted that some people, perhaps even including some Christians, will *not* achieve salvation. One big problem, in *that* case, is that people who would have gotten saved if they had had G-beliefs, end up not getting saved because they are confused about important matters and lack G-beliefs. How could God permit *that* to happen? And finally, for AD to belittle Christians' earthly confusion about doctrinal issues is, in effect, to belittle their earthly life itself. Why should God even put them here on this planet if their intellectual confusion and failure to acquire G-beliefs is such a minor matter as to be negligible? It makes their earthly life itself insignificant and meaningless. Since this is an unacceptable consequence of AD, we can infer that AD is another failure when applied against AC.[8]

Possibly the best of the defenses is the Unknown-Purpose Defense (UPD). According to UPD, although God wants Christians to be clear about morality and salvation and have G-beliefs, he has some *other* desire (which is at present unknown to us) which conflicts with that one and which overrides it. This is a very attractive defense because people are inclined to view God as a being that is so far beyond humans in mentality that it would be utterly hopeless, and perhaps presumptuous, to speculate about God's intentions or desires.

Nevertheless, I have various objections to UPD. One of them is that it merely appeals to the idea of mystery and so provides no explanation of anything. It is totally unenlightening. Another objection is that UPD is actually antithetical to the process of explanation. It makes huge portions of the Bible totally inexplicable. For example, all of the parts which play up the importance of morality and salvation would be rendered incomprehensible on the assumption that God has only limited concern that Christians are confused about those matters. Furthermore, all the verses that emphasize the importance of acquiring the truth would also be rendered incomprehensible. For example, why would God send his son "to testify to the truth" (as Jesus proclaimed at John 18:37) if the acquisition of the truth by God's own people here on earth were to be overridden by some other divine purpose? It would make no sense. (As pointed out above, Jesus himself said, "The truth shall set you free.") A similar point can be made regarding God's command that people "believe on the name of his son Jesus Christ" (I John 3:23) and Jesus' own command to his disciples that they spread the gospel message to all nations (Matt. 28:19–20) and to all creation (Mark 16:15–16). Such commands would be undercut and rendered unintelligible if God had some purpose which overrides his desire that people come to know the truth. Finally, consider all the claims of divine inspiration that are made in the Bible (such phrases as "And the Lord spake unto Moses, saying . . ." and "The word of the Lord came unto me, saying . . ."). In the Old Testament alone, there are 2,600 such claims of inspiration. Almost half the Book of Exodus and 90 percent of Leviticus consist of direct quotations from the words of God. Although the New Testament books only occasionally quote God directly, they were both claimed by the Apostles and recognized by the early church as authoritative revelations from God. According to II Tim. 3:16, "All scripture is given by inspiration of God, and is useful for teaching." It just does not make sense that God would do all that inspiring of Scripture for the purpose of instructing humanity if, indeed, he were to have some purpose which overrides his desire that humanity come to know the truth. We may infer that the "unknown purpose" God, an idea which would make much of the Bible incomprehensible, is not the God of the vast majority of Christians. On the contrary, they would say that God has revealed to us that the morality and salvation of his followers and their acquisition of the truth is a top priority with him. It is mainly to *their* God, the God of most Christians, that AC is directed.[9]

A further question is whether UPD might be used to defend against AC in the case of a more general Christian deity, one worshiped by so-called "liberal Christians." Certainly it would be more forceful, as a defense, in such a context. Christians who are not Bible-oriented could say that although God has some concern about the confusion and conflictedness of his followers, he also has some unknown purpose which overrides that concern. However, to say that God lacks great concern about his followers' unfortunate epistemic situation seems to imply that he also lacks great concern for humanity, lacks a strong desire for a close personal relationship with humans, and is not both omnipotent and perfectly loving. One would need to give up the sort of Christianity so prevalent in Western countries and, instead, go with some diminished view, perhaps something close to deism. That would be a kind of success for AC. Any Christian who is not willing to give up the idea of God as omnipotent, all-loving, and greatly concerned about humanity and desiring some close personal relationship with it, would have great difficulty in overcoming the Argument from Confusion.[10]

II. THE ARGUMENT FROM BIBLICAL DEFECTS (ABD)

Formulation of the Argument

(A) If the God of evangelical Christianity were to exist, then the Bible would be God's only written revelation.

(B) Thus, if that deity were to exist, then he would probably see to it that the Bible is perfectly clear and authoritative, and lacks the appearance of merely human authorship.

(C) Some facts about the Bible are the following:

1. It contradicts itself or is very unclear in many places.
2. It contains factual errors, including unfulfilled prophecies.
3. It contains ethical defects (such as God committing or ordering atrocities).
4. It contains interpolations (later insertions to the text).
5. Different copies of the same biblical manuscripts say conflicting things.
6. The biblical canon involves disputes and is apparently arbitrary.
7. There is no objective procedure for settling any of the various disputes, especially since the original manuscripts of the Bible have been lost and there has been no declaration from God that would help resolve any of the disputes.

(D) Therefore [from C], the Bible is not perfectly clear and authoritative, and has the appearance of merely human authorship.

(E) Hence [from B & D], probably the God of evangelical Christianity does not exist.

Discussion of ABD

Much of what was said above about AC also has application to ABD, for the two arguments are closely related. In the case of ABD, the critical facts, which have to do with the Bible, are the ones listed in its premise (C). Since those facts would be unexpected on the assumption that the God of evangelical Christianity exists, they constitute evidence for the nonexistence of that deity. Much support for the facts is provided in the literature. It is certainly true that the original manuscripts of the Bible have been lost and that copies (of copies . . .) of those originals, which do exist, conflict with one another.[11] It is also true that interpolations have been made in the biblical manuscripts[12] and that the biblical canon is arbitrary. Different Christian denominations have different canons. Also, it seems likely that the canon is incomplete (e.g., the so-called Q document is missing and probably some of Paul's letters have been lost). It is also well known that different translations of the Bible conflict with one another and there is no clear guide as to how to resolve such conflicts. Space limitations prevent me from supporting all that here.[13]

If the God of evangelical Christianity were to exist, then none of the facts in question would be expected. Instead, it would be expected that God's revelation to humanity would be free of defects and perfectly preserved. God would not permit the original manuscripts to get lost. He would not permit mistakes to be made in the writing, copying, or translating of the Bible. He would guide the selection of the canon in a way that would not give rise to disputes. He would see to it that the Bible is perfectly clear, especially with regard to important ethical and doctrinal issues. God's own people would not then be confused or conflicted about such issues. It is only by way of such guidance that God's aims, as formulated in the Bible and proclaimed by most Christians, might have a reasonable chance of being realized. Since the facts in question can't be easily explained on the hypothesis that the given deity exists, and are best explained on the basis of the alternate hypothesis that the deity does not exist, they thereby constitute good objective evidence for that alternate hypothesis.

ABD is the converse of the Argument from the Bible, which argues for God's existence from the alleged harmony and consistency of the Bible and alleged fulfilled prophecies.[14] This shows the pivotal role played by the issue of biblical errancy. If the Bible is errant, it is evidence that the Christian God does not exist, whereas if the Bible were inerrant and were to contain amazing fulfilled prophecies, then that would be evidence that the Christian God does exist. I was led to this result in part through the pioneering work of Niclas Berggren.[15]

One of the most important issues is the requirement for salvation (in other words, "What must I do to be saved?" a question once put to Jesus). The Bible contradicts itself on that matter. Consider, for example, repentance. According to Luke 13:3, one must repent in order to be saved. And yet there are passages which state or imply that everyone who is in a certain group will be saved, where no mention is made of repentance. For example, in John 3:16 it says, "whoever believes in him will not perish but have everlasting life."[16] There is no mention of repentance here. Furthermore, according to Matt. 25:46, the righteous (i.e., charitable people) will go away to eternal life. There is nothing in the description of them (verses 34–40) tht implies repentance. All those who have done good are said to be saved (John 5:29).[17] Thus, some biblical verses say that repentance is necessary for salvation but other verses imply that it is not necessary.[18]

Even aside from contradictions, there is simply the matter of biblical clarity. If there are wide disagreements on how to interpret a passage, then we can be sure that the subject being interpreted was not given in a clear enough manner to get everyone to understand it. People would have better understood God's message if it had been presented in a more straightforward manner. For example, if it were to say somewhere in the Bible: "Here is the list of things you *must do* in order to be saved . . . ," followed by a clear list of actions, then there would be considerably less confusion over what a person must do to be saved. And if Jesus had said, for example, "Abortion is *always* wrong in all circumstances," then that would greatly reduce the number of Christians who think abortion is acceptable under certain circumstances.

Consider an analogy. Suppose I am trying to tell a six-year-old that he must not play with matches, but I use advanced technical terms or poetic language and he fails to understand what I am saying. He goes on to burn the house down. The fault would lie with *me*. People would say I did not explain myself well enough to be understood. Obviously, if I am trying to get children to understand me, I should make my language as simple as possible to avoid confusion over what I meant. There may be nothing about my explanation that is generally unintelligible. The six-year-old may simply be too immature to understand my message, which would be perfectly clear to an adult. So, objective standards of clarity are not relevant here. What is relevant is that I need to explain myself in a way that the particular people I am addressing would understand. Both AC and ABD are claiming that God has not explained matters clearly enough for Christians to understand him, and the best evidence of that is the fact that there are sharp divisions among them regarding important points of doctrine. Although the fault may lie partly with the readers, it lies mainly with the author. He could have made the message perfectly clear to the readers, but failed to do so.

It might be objected that ABD is blunted by the fact that most Christians are not worried that the requirements for salvation are confusing or even contradictory and feel assured about their own salvation. Nevertheless, they should be bothered that there are other Christians out there who *are* distressed regarding salvation (both for themselves and for others, especially loved ones). They should wonder why God would permit there to be such distress among his own followers. Furthermore, even if the given objection were to deflect the force of ABD with regard to the harm caused by confusion to Christians themselves, it fails to address the harm to God. The Christian God is supposed to really care about the salvation of his people and to have gone to a great deal of trouble, with the crucifixion and all, to let them know just what they need to do. Even if some Christians think they know the correct requirements for salvation, they should still be bothered by other Christians' inability to see things their way and by God's apparent unwillingness to set matters straight. According to the Bible, there can be nothing more important regarding a person than his/her salvation.[19] So it is hard to see how God could be content to just leave it up to each person to figure out the requirements for salvation on an individual basis. Mistakes there would be too tragic for a loving God to allow. That whole idea runs counter to the great theme of God revealing his system of governance by way of Scripture. There is an inconsistency between God's apparent concern regarding salvation and his present hiddenness with regard to it. And the given objection fails to address that inconsistency.

In conclusion, like AC, ABD presents good objective evidence for the nonexistence of the God of evangelical Christianity. Believers in that deity need to explain why he would permit the Bible to have come to be the way it is, with all its defects and apparently human authorship, and thus far they have been unable to do so. The best hypothesis available to us, then, given the facts, is that that deity does not exist.

NOTES

1. See Theodore M. Drange, "The Argument from Nonbelief," *Religious Studies* 29 (1993): 417–32 (reprinted in this anthology), and *Nonbelief & Evil: Two Arguments for the Nonexistence of God* (Amherst, NY: Prometheus Books, 1998).

2. This is the first treatment of AC and ABD in print. For an earlier version of them, combined into a single argument in my debate with Doug Wilson, see "The Argument from Confusion" [online], www.infidels.org/library/modern/theodore_drange/drange-wilson/index.shtml [1999].

3. For my formulation of the AE, see chap. 2 in Drange, *Nonbelief & Evil.*

4. It might be objected that instead of saying of a group that it is confused, it would be more apt to say that it is *conflicted* and that I should be calling the argument "the Argument from Conflictedness." The matter of which label to use is not particularly important, but there are reasons for sticking with the term "confusion." First, "conflictedness" is a slightly more awkward term. Second, there is still confusion in the sense in which individuals are bewildered, and there the word is quite apt. And, third, "confusion" is even appropriate for conflicted groups, for people do sometimes call them "confused."

5. For example, questions about exceptions to the biblical commandments (e.g., "Is killing in self-defense or in defense of loved ones permissible?"), about which laws of the Torah are still applicable today, about the rights of women, children, and animals, about divorce and various sexual practices, etc. There are hundreds of them.

6. For example, which biblical verses are divinely inspired and which of them are to be taken literally? In what way and to what extent is human history divinely predestined? What is Satan? What are heaven and hell? What is the relation of Jesus to God? What are the requirements for salvation? What will the Second Coming be like? Again, there are hundreds of such issues.

7. For further material related to the Free-Will Defense, see the discussion of it as applied to ANB which occurs in sect. III of Drange, "The Argument from Nonbelief." There is a more extensive treatment of the topic in chap. 5 of Drange, *Nonbelief & Evil.*

8. In Drange, "The Argument from Nonbelief," AD, as applied to ANB, is represented by the Future-Kingdom Defense, which is discussed in sect. II. A more extensive treatment of the topic is given in chap. 9 of Drange, *Nonbelief & Evil.*

9. See the discussion of UPD, as applied to ANB, in sect. IV of Drange, "The Argument from Nonbelief." For a fuller treatment of the topic, see chap. 11 of Drange, *Nonbelief & Evil.*

10. Similar considerations can be raised in connection with the application of ANB to the God of liberal Christianity and to God in general. On those topics, see chaps. 13 and 14 of Drange, *Nonbelief & Evil.*

11. A. J. Mattill Jr., *Polluted Texts and Traditional Beliefs* (Gordo, AL: Flatwoods Free Press, 1998), supplies hundreds of examples of such conflicts.

12. This is amply supported by Patricia G. Eddy, *Who Tampered with the Bible* (Nashville: Winston-Derek Publishers, 1993).

13. Biblical criticism is an enormous topic. There are thousands of sources in print. Let me just mention two here: A. J. Mattill Jr., *The Seven Mighty Blows to Traditional Beliefs*, 2d ed. (Gordo, AL: Flatwoods Free Press, 1995), and C. Dennis McKinsey, *The Encyclopedia of Biblical Errancy* (Amherst, NY: Prometheus Books, 1995). There are also thousands more on the Internet.

14. On the Argument from the Bible (and biblical errancy in general), see appendix D of Drange, *Nonbelief & Evil*. For an expanded version of it, see "The Argument from the Bible" [online], www.infidels.org/library/modern/theodore_drange/bible.html [1996].

15. Niclas Berggren, "The Errancy of Fundamentalism Disproves the God of the Bible" [online], www.infidels.org/library/modern/niclas_berggren/funda.html [1996].

16. See also John 6:40, 11:25, Acts 16:31, Rom. 10:9. Furthermore, "whoever calls upon the name of the Lord will be saved" (Joel 2:32, Acts 2:21, Rom. 10:13).

17. For additional verses implying that people who are very moral and charitable are guaranteed salvation, see Matt. 19:16–17; Mark 10:17–21; Luke 10:25–37, 18:18–22; John 8:51; Rom. 2:5–7,10; and Jas. 2:24. These also imply that believing in God's son is not necessary.

18. For additional examples, see Theodore M. Drange, "Biblical Contradictions Regarding Salvation," *Free Inquiry* 14 (Summer 1994): 56–57. For an expanded version of it, see "Biblical Contradictions Regarding Salvation" [online], home.earthlink.net/~writetdrange/contradictions.html [2004].

19. Matt. 10:28, 16:26; Mark 8:36–37; Luke 12:15–21.

5

THE ARGUMENT FROM IGNORANCE

WALTER SINNOTT-ARMSTRONG

One principle that is accepted throughout science and everyday life is that we should not believe in entities for which we have no evidence. No good scientist would believe in a new element or particle or force without evidence. Any scientist who did claim to have discovered a new particle but who could not produce any evidence for it would be laughed out of town.

This rule applies with special force when an entity is unusual in important respects. If someone believes that there are clothes in my closet, then he might not seem to need any evidence for this belief other than his past experiences of closets, most of which contained clothes. However, no evidence like this is available, and the need for evidence seems especially strong, when someone believes in a kind of entity that is unprecedented. Nobody should believe that there is a perfect shirt or an invisibility cloak in the closet without any evidence for the existence of such an oddity. I hope everyone agrees in that case.

Religion might seem different. Religion is often said to be immune from the standards of science, because it lies outside the realm where evidence is possible. But this view leads to absurdity. If the fact that a religious belief cannot be subject to evidence did license one to accept that belief without evidence, then the same principle would also license many ridiculous beliefs.

An amusing example occurs in Charles Schultz's cartoon, *Peanuts*. Linus

---

From William Lane Craig and Walter Sinnott-Armstrong, *God? A Debate Between a Christian and an Atheist* (Oxford: Oxford University Press, 2004), pp. 101–105. Copyright © 2004 by Oxford University Press. Reprinted by permission of Oxford University Press.

believes in the Great Pumpkin, who visits pumpkin patches all over the world every Halloween. Linus has no evidence *for* his belief, since he has never seen the Great Pumpkin, and Linus can explain all of his beliefs and experiences without postulating any Great Pumpkin. On the other hand, Linus also ensures that nobody can have any evidence *against* the Great Pumpkin, since it is visible only to those with a pure heart. Linus stays in a pumpkin patch all Halloween night (at a great cost in candy). He looks constantly and carefully for the Great Pumpkin (at a great cost in sleep). But he sees nothing. Still, this does not show that the Great Pumpkin does not exist. All it shows is that Linus's heart was not pure, or not pure enough, at least according to Linus. This doctrine thus makes it impossible to prove that Linus is wrong. Moreover, Linus might be right. It is possible (just barely!) that there is a Great Pumpkin. However, most people agree that Linus is not justified in believing in the Great Pumpkin. More strongly, Linus *should not* believe in the Great Pumpkin. That is what makes the cartoon so funny. Linus is the butt of jokes in a cartoon for kids, because Linus believes something that he should not believe, given his evidence, on standards that are obvious even to children.

Linus illustrates why we should not believe in unusual entities without evidence for their existence and why this common restriction cannot be avoided by formulating one's beliefs to make them incapable of refutation. If we weaken our epistemic standards to accommodate irrefutable beliefs, then we might end up believing in the Great Pumpkin or, at least, holding that many absurd beliefs like this are justified.

The same standards apply to beliefs about God.[1] If there is no evidence for God's existence, then we ought not to believe that God exists. This follows even if God were defined so as to remove any possibility of evidence against His existence.

But is there evidence for God? [William Lane] Craig claims that there is. That is why he gave several arguments for the existence of God in ["Five Reasons God Exists"].[2] However, I refuted every one of his arguments [in "There Is No Good Reason to Believe in God"].[3] Craig might have overlooked an even better argument. Or maybe there is some way to get around my criticisms. But I don't see any.

Religious experiences are sometimes seen as evidence for God. Many people have feelings that seem to them to come from a higher power outside of them. But many people also think that they see and hear ghosts. Their experiences are not evidence for ghosts because we and they have no independent reason to think that their experiences are accurate rather than illusions. By the same standards, when people seem to experience God, that is no evidence for God because they and we have no independent reason to believe that their religious experiences are accurate rather than illusions. Moreover, we and they have plenty of reason to suspect that there is some better explanation of why they seem to see God. Just as people see ghosts only when they are afraid and predisposed to believe in ghosts, so people experience God only when they are predisposed to believe in God and are gripped by emotions that often distort experiences. God might appear only to those who seek or believe in Him, but then those experiences cannot count as evidence for God. Finally, even if religious experiences were evidence for something, they could not be evidence that their source is all-good and all-powerful. The most vivid religious experience could result from a God who is very powerful and pretty good, so they cannot be evidence for a traditional God.

Miracles are also often claimed to be evidence for God. However, secondhand reports of miracles are dubious at best, for obvious reasons.[4] On the other hand, if you think that you have witnessed a miracle first-hand, then the circumstances need to be considered carefully. Even if you and I cannot come up with any natural explanation for what you observed, that is no more miraculous than most magic tricks are. Besides, no miracle can be evidence that God is all-powerful or all-good, which is the kind of God at issue here.

I conclude that neither arguments nor experiences nor miracles provide any good evidence for the existence of God. This conclusion, together with common standards for justified belief, implies that we ought not to believe that God exists and, hence, that we ought to believe that God does not exist.

Theists often respond that it is fallacious to argue from "We have no evidence for it" to "It does not exist." This is called an argument from ignorance. Many logic textbooks label it a fallacy.

I admit that many arguments of this form are fallacious. One cannot say that there is no gold on Uranus just because we do not have any evidence for gold on Uranus. The problem is clear: Even if there were gold on Uranus, we still would not (or, at least, might not) have evidence for it. That is why we cannot conclude that there is no gold on Uranus.

However, this point cannot be used to defend the claim that there is gold on Uranus. If there is no evidence for gold on Uranus, maybe we should not conclude that there is none, but we also should not believe that there is some. We should suspend belief until we have adequate evidence one way or the other. Consequently, this analogy cannot provide solace to religious believers. If belief in God is like belief in gold on Uranus, then the lack of evidence for God does not show that God does not exist. However, the lack of evidence also cannot be used to defend a belief in God, since it supports agnostics who hold that we should suspend belief until we have evidence (even if this is a very long time).

More importantly, arguments from ignorance are not *always* fallacious. Arguments of this form work fine when the phenomenon is something that we would know if it were true. If I had a pot-bellied pig on my head, I would know it, at least after I felt around up there. Thus, my lack of evidence for a pot-bellied pig on my head is adequate reason for me to believe that there is none. Not everything is as obvious as a pot-bellied pig. But doctors can also have adequate reason to believe that a patient does not have a virus, if they look closely, they find no evidence for that virus, and the patient would have easily detectable symptoms if the patient did have that virus.

That is the situation with God. If there were an all-good and all-powerful God who could act in time, then we would have better evidence than we have. He could easily reveal himself by appearing before us. Giving us better evidence would not harm us. Why would such a God hide?

Some theists answer that, if the evidence for God were stronger, believers would not need faith. However, better evidence could leave room for faith. I have faith in my wife's love, even though I also have strong evidence of her love, namely, that she puts up with me! I would not be better off if I had to rely more on faith because I had less evidence for her love. So why is it better to have less evidence for God?

One answer might be that better evidence would take away our freedom not to believe. However, evidence does not take away any valuable kind of freedom. If it did, teachers would restrict the freedom of their students every time the teachers told the students a fact about history or performed a science experiment. If any freedom is lost in such revelations, it is a kind of freedom that is not very valuable, since it is just the freedom to believe irrationally.

Finally, even if stronger evidence did have some costs, it would also have many benefits. The new evidence would remove or reduce nagging doubts, as well as any fears that your children or friends might disavow God and end up in Hell. It would bring assurance and solace, if God is as merciful as Christians claim. Most evil people would be scared away from their horrible deeds, since few, if any, people would rape and torture if they received strong evidence that such deeds would be punished with eternal torment.

With so little to lose and so much to gain, an all-good God would reveal Himself clearly to everyone. An all-powerful God could easily reveal Himself clearly to everyone. But God has not revealed Himself clearly to everyone. Even if you have been convinced by your religious experiences, there are billions of other people on this earth now and in the past who have little or no evidence of God. Just ask yourself honestly, "Could God reveal Himself more clearly?" The answer is bound to be "Yes," since God is supposed to be all-powerful. Now ask yourself honestly, "What reason does God have not to reveal Himself more clearly?" I doubt that you can come up with any reason that withstands honest and thorough reflection. Consequently, if there were a God, we would have more and better evidence than we do. That is why our lack of evidence for God supports my thesis that there is no God.

NOTES

1. Editors' note: On p. 83 in Walter Sinnott-Armstrong and William Lane Craig, *God? A Debate between a Christian and an Atheist* (Oxford: Oxford University Press, 2004), Sinnott-Armstrong writes, "God is defined to be:

- All-good (= God always does the best that He can)
- All-powerful (= God can do anything that is logically possible)
- All-knowing (= God knows everything that is true)
- Eternal (= God exists outside of time)
- Effective (= God causes changes in time)
- Personal (= God has a will and makes choices)."

2. William Lane Craig, "Five Reasons God Exists," in *God?* pp. 3–30. See also "Reason Enough," pp. 53–78.

3. Walter Sinnott–Armstrong, "There Is No Good Reason to Believe in God," in *God?* pp. 31–52.

4. Ibid., pp. 36–38.

6

THE REAL ARGUMENT FROM IGNORANCE

WALTER SINNOTT-ARMSTRONG

William Lane Craig charges my argument from ignorance with a "subtle but crucial shift." However, this criticism misrepresents my argument. Craig's point is that a certain principle—"we should not believe in entities for which we have no evidence"—"at best supports agnosticism, not atheism."[1] Of course, this principle *by itself* can't yield atheism! That's why my argument did not stop with this principle. Perhaps I was not clear enough, but the earlier passages in my . . . "The Argument from Ignorance"[2] were merely supposed to set the stage for my argument. After all, atheists need to agree with agnostics on one thing, namely, that we should not believe in God.

My argument for atheism comes later. When Craig does discuss my later argument, he accuses me of "a bizarre role reversal" in my discussion of gold on Uranus.[3] This discussion would have been bizarre if I had claimed that God was like gold on Uranus. But I never claimed anything like that. My point was to draw a crucial contrast between the issue of gold on Uranus and the issue of God's existence. The difference, as I tried to make clear, is that a lack of evidence for gold on Uranus would *not* show that we should believe that there is no gold on Uranus, whereas the lack of evidence for God *does* show that we should believe that there is no God. That is why I said that some arguments from ignorance are fallacious, but others are not.

This crucial difference is captured by a premise in my argument that Craig

---

From William Lane Craig and Walter Sinnott-Armstrong, *God? A Debate Between a Christian and an Atheist* (Oxford: Oxford University Press, 2004), pp. 129–34.

ignored until later in his discussion. With this premise added, my argument takes this form:

1. If there were an all-good and all-powerful God who could act in time, then we would have strong evidence for the existence of God.
2. We do not have strong evidence for the existence of God.
3. Hence, there is no all-good and all-powerful God who can act in time.

Background premise (1), which can be called *the strong evidence principle*, is what enables my argument to reach the conclusion of atheism and not just agnosticism. Its basic idea is simply that, if God existed, He would make it easier for us to know Him. God would not hide His light under a bushel, for the same reasons that Jesus tells his followers not to hide their lights under bushels (Matthew 5:15–16). The point of the argument from ignorance is that God Himself does not follow Jesus' advice!

The strong evidence principle is, admittedly, controversial. Some theists might deny it. That is why I argued for it. I listed many benefits of God revealing Himself more clearly to us. For example, believers would suffer less from doubt, and some potential criminals would be deterred by fear of divine punishment. I also argued against many commonly claimed costs of strong evidence for God, including supposed losses of faith and freedom. My point there was that the evidence for God could be *much* stronger than it is without undermining freedom or faith. These arguments showed that strong evidence for God would make our lives better overall, so an all-good, all-powerful God would give us strong evidence for God, just as the strong evidence principle claims.

Once premise (1) is established, all I need is premise (2). That premise was supported by my arguments in ["There Is No Good Reason to Believe in God"], which refuted the best evidence for God that Craig could produce in ["Five Reasons God Exists"].[4] . . .

One major flaw, as I have said, is that Craig's conclusions are badly bloated. Even if his arguments seem relevant to several (not all!) traditional features of God, all of his arguments together still cannot show that one single God has all of these features together. The creator of the universe (even if there were one) need not be the ground of moral value or the source of anyone's religious experiences today, much less the force that raised Jesus from the dead (even if this did happen). Craig cannot legitimately assume that all of his conclusions about various features apply to a single unified being. But he does assume this. This assumption is hidden when Craig formulates his arguments in terms of 'God', since to refer to God in all of his arguments is to assume that there is a single being with all of these features. If Craig's conclusions instead referred to a creator, a ground of moral value, an external source of religious experience, and a

Jesus-raiser, then it would be clear that these might be separate beings and that Craig has no reason to assume that these are all the same person (much less that the Christian Bible gives an accurate picture of that person). That conclusion goes far beyond anything that his arguments could establish even if they did work (which they do not). Moreover, this gap in his argument leads directly to the problem of ignorance: If there were an all-good and all-powerful God, He could, should, and would give us strong reason to believe that He exists as a single unified being. The fact that we have no strong evidence for a unified being with all of these features, thus shows that there is no such being.

Some readers still might be impressed by Craig's arguments that depend on recent scientific advances or historical scholarship. These references might seem sophisticated, but they feed right into my argument from ignorance. To see why, think back 200 years to times before those scientific theories were formulated, when nobody yet had heard of a Big Bang. People at those times could not use Craig's scientific arguments; so, even if those arguments do work today, those earlier people did not have any strong evidence for the existence of God. Thus, premise (2) was true *for them.* Premise (1) is also true for them, since any all-good God would care as much about them as about us, so He would reveal Himself to them. He would have no reason to let so many people in the past remain ignorant of Him for so long. Thus, premises that are only about those earlier people would be enough to reach my conclusion that there is no all-good and all-powerful God. Craig's appeals to recent science cannot solve this problem of ignorance.

It is still possible that other arguments, different from the ones that Craig gave, provide strong evidence that God exists. However, this is merely a possibility. Until we actually see much better arguments for the existence of God, there is reason to accept premise (2). With premises (1) and (2) in place, atheism follows.

Of course, Craig rejects both premises, but that does not show that those premises are flawed. In ["Theism Undefeated"], at least, Craig has not given us any good reason to doubt either premise. He does call premise (1) "enormously presumptuous," and he asks, "why should [God] want to do such a thing?"[5] I already answered that question when I discussed the many benefits for humans of God revealing Himself more clearly. So Craig's rhetorical question has no force at this point in our discussion.

Craig rejects my answer because, "in the Christian view, it is a matter of relative indifference to God whether people (merely) believe that He exists or not." The point of his qualification "merely" seems to be that belief in God without love of God will not satisfy God: "what God is interested in is building a love relationship with you, not just getting you to believe that He exists."[6] Fine, but God still should have *some* interest in mere belief, even if He *prefers* more than mere belief. One reason is that belief in God, even without love of God, has important benefits for humans. Imagine a contract killer who does not believe in God. Suppose that, if this contract killer did believe in God, then he would not love God, but he still would refrain from murder because he would fear punishment by God. This contract killer might be better off believing in God. Even if this killer did not benefit, this killer's potential victims would be better off if this killer believed in God. Thus, if God cares about the victims, then God has reason to make Himself more manifest to this killer and to other wrongdoers, regardless of whether they love Him.

Furthermore, even if mere belief is not sufficient to satisfy God, it is still necessary. You cannot have a love relationship with anything unless you believe that it exists. I can't love my sister if I don't know that I have a sister. Consequently, even if God does not want us "just" or "merely" to believe in Him, God still would want us to believe in Him, as a necessary condition for loving Him. This makes it hard to see any way around the conclusion that God cares about whether humans believe that God exists.

Here is where Craig's second response kicks in: "there is no reason at all to think that if God were to make His existence more manifest, more people would come into a saving relationship with Him."[7] No reason at all? Here's one: Those who now love and believe in God would not lose their faith or love for God if His existence were made more manifest in the proper way. Some others who do not now believe in God would come to believe in Him if His existence were more manifest. Not all of these new believers will love God, but some will, especially if God reveals His goodness. So there would be more people who believe in God and love God if His existence were more manifest.

The only way in which this argument could fail is if the new evidence made enough people lose their love for God. Craig talks about "a neon cross in the sky" and "brazen advertisements" that make people "chafe" and "resent such effrontery."[8] This parody misses my point. Such bungling is beneath God. Surely an all-knowing and all-powerful God could find and use some way to make Himself more manifest, at least to non-believers, without undermining believers' love for Him. God could appear to each person with just enough evidence of the right kind to convince that individual. Or, at least, God could provide rapists and murderers with enough evidence to dissuade them from their rampages. This evidence need not be seen by non-criminal believers, in which case the evidence for non-believers could not turn those believers against God. Moreover, even if God did give extra evidence to believers, possibly in order to relieve their doubts, this evidence could be limited to whatever is appropriate. An all-powerful God wouldn't need to be "brazen" in order to give people better evidence than they now have for His existence. If God gave additional evidence in some proper way, then "more people would come into a saving relationship with Him,"[9] and humans would benefit in many ways at little or no cost to anyone. I might not be able to specify exactly how God would do this, but an all-knowing God could figure out *how* to do it, an all-powerful God *could* do it, and an all-good God *would* do it.

Thus, if there were an all-powerful and all-good God who could act in time, then we would have strong evidence for the existence of God. This is premise (1), which I called the strong evidence principle, so that premise is secure. As I said, premise (2) is supported by my series of arguments in ["There Is No Good Reason to Believe in God"].[10] Together these premises imply atheism. Nothing that Craig has said undermines that argument from ignorance.

NOTES

1. William Lane Craig, "Theism Undefeated," *God?* in William Lane Craig and Walter Sinnott-Armstrong, *God? A Debate between a Christian and an Atheist* (Oxford: Oxford University Press, 2004), p. 107.
2. Walter Sinnott-Armstrong, "The Argument from Ignorance," *God?* pp. 101–105.
3. Craig, "Theism Undefeated," p. 108.
4. Editors' note: See William Lane Craig, "Five Reasons God Exists," in *God?* pp. 3–30; Walter Sinnott-Armstrong, "There Is No Good Reason to Believe in God," in *God?* pp. 31–52; and William Lane Craig, "Reason Enough," in *God?* pp. 53–78.
5. Craig, "Theism Undefeated," p. 109.
6. Ibid. Craig's guarding term "just" is misleading, because neither I nor anyone else believes that *all* God cares about is "getting you to believe that He exists." Any all-good God would care about many things other than belief in Him. But that does not mean that belief in God is not one of the things that God would care about, at least instrumentally as a means to other goods.
7. Ibid.
8. Ibid.
9. Ibid.
10. Sinnott-Armstrong, "There Is No Good Reason to Believe in God."

7

AN ARGUMENT FOR ATHEISM FROM THE REASONABLENESS OF NONBELIEF

J. L. SCHELLENBERG

Many religious writers, sensitive to the difficulties in which our evidence for God is involved, have held that God would wish (or at any rate, permit) the fact of his existence to be obscure. God, so it is said, is a *hidden* God. But upon reflection, it may well appear otherwise. Why, we may ask, would God be hidden from us? Surely a morally perfect being—good, just, loving—would show himself more clearly. Hence the weakness of our evidence for God is not a sign that God is hidden; it is a revelation that God does not exist.[1]

Here I seek to develop this line of thought. The argument that will emerge is, in broad outline, as follows. A perfectly loving God would desire a reciprocal personal relationship always to obtain between himself and every human being capable of it. But a logically necessary condition of such Divine-human reciprocity is human belief in Divine existence. Hence a perfectly loving God would have reason to ensure that everyone capable of such belief (or at any rate, everyone capable who was not disposed to resist it) was in possession of evidence sufficient to bring it about that such belief was formed. But the evidence actually available is not of this sort (the claim that it is 'weak' is to be read simply as the claim that it is not 'strong' in this sense). The most obvious indication that it is not is that inculpable—or as I prefer to term it, reasonable—nonbelief actually occurs.[2] Hence we can argue from the weakness of theistic evidence (where

From *Divine Hiddenness and Human Reason* (Ithaca: Cornell University Press, 1993), pp. 1-83 (edited excerpts). Portions of this chapter reprinted from J. L. Schellenberg, *Divine Hiddenness and Human Reason*.

this is understood as indicated), or more specifically, from the reasonableness of nonbelief, to the nonexistence of a perfectly loving God. But God, if he exists, is perfectly loving. Hence we can argue from the reasonableness of nonbelief to the nonexistence of God.

DIVINE LOVE

The concept of God is the concept of a being who is, among other things, perfectly loving. But what is it for God to be loving? More specifically, what is it for God to love *us*—to love human beings? One term that may seem important here is 'benevolence': if God is loving, he desires our well-being. And indeed, it can hardly be denied that a reference to benevolence must find its way into any adequate explication of Divine love, for the sort of love that can be viewed as a perfection of personal being is clearly other-regarding. But there is more to love than a general reference to benevolence can capture. What more there is cannot be fully detailed here, but most important for our purposes is the (often neglected) connection between Divine love and the seeking of *personal relationship*. I will seek to clarify this connection and to develop certain of its implications.[3] In particular, I will argue that if a perfectly loving God exists, all human beings capable of personal relationship with himself are, at all times at which they are so capable, in a position to believe that he exists.

"God seeks to be personally related to us." In claiming that this proposition is essential to any adequate explication of "God loves human beings," I am claiming that God, if loving, seeks *explicit, reciprocal* relationship with us, involving not only such things as Divine guidance, support, and forgiveness, but also human trust, obedience, and worship. So understood, this proposition seems obviously required. For only the best human love could serve as an analogy of Divine love, and human love at its best clearly involves reciprocity and mutuality.

Love *transcends* obligation. It is spontaneous and supererogatory, and naturally seeks the well-being of its object in relation to itself. This is true even of human love at its best. Parents who love their children fully do their best to ensure that it is always possible for their children to draw on the resources of personal relationship with them. If we add to this that love seeks personal relationship for its own sake, it seems that we have good reason to make the all-inclusive claim in question [that there is no time at which some human being is to some extent capable of personal relationship with God but at which God does not wish the potential represented by that capacity to be realized].

A qualification must, however, be entered here. For a personal relationship of the sort in question is not something God can bring about on his own: God may wish to be personally related to me, but if I choose not to respond to his overtures, personal relations will not exist between us. Indeed, there is reason to suppose that an emphasis on freedom is *itself* essential to the explication of Divine love. Love, as John Macquarrie puts it, involves "letting-be, a respect for the otherness, freedom and individuality of the beloved."[4] And as John Hick points out, freedom is essential to personal relationship: "In a [personal] relationship we apprehend and treat the other person as an autonomous mind and will, a responsible and self-directing consciousness with views and rights of his own which must be consulted and respected—in short, as another *person*."[5] Hence it may seem that our claim should be that God will bring it about that it is at all times possible for us to relate personally to him *if we so choose.*

The point about freedom, however, requires us to go farther still. For a loving God, out of respect for our freedom, might well allow us to shut him out altogether—not only to fail to respond to his overtures, but also to put ourselves in a position where these were *no longer noticed.* Such resistance of God would, of course, be culpable, for it would involve shutting out one whom we had seen to be our creator, and perfectly good, as well as the culpable activity of self-deception: in exercising our freedom in this way, we would be bringing it about through our own actions and/or omissions that what was once seen was seen no longer. But if God is perfectly loving, and treats us as persons, he will, we may suppose, permit even this extent of freedom over against himself. Hence the clarified claim should read as follows: God will bring it about that, unless we culpably put ourselves in a contrary position, it is at all times possible for us to relate personally to him if we so choose. Or to put it more formally,

> P1 If God exists and is perfectly loving, then for any human subject S and time t, if S is at t capable of relating personally to God, S at t is in a position to do so (i.e., can at t do so just by choosing to), except insofar as S is culpably in a contrary position at t.[6]

Our discussion so far, then, suggests that we have good reason to affirm P1. In the absence of our own attempts to bring it about that a contrary state of affairs obtains, a perfectly loving God must surely bring it about that we are in a position to relate personally to himself. But some will no doubt feel that this claim requires more in the way of defense than I have given. It may be thought, for example, that I am asking for the beatific vision in this life. But the "personal relationship with God" referred to here is not to be viewed as identical with the beatific vision, although it might *culminate* in such an experience. As my use of the word 'culminate' already suggests, the relationship I am thinking of is to be understood in developmental terms. Were it to obtain, it would admit of change, growth, progression, regression. It might be shallow or deep, depending on the response of the human term of the relation. This is, of course, what we would expect if the relationship is conceived as a relationship between God and beings caught up in the toil and vicissitudes of earthly life. Such a relationship *belongs* in this life: now, in the midst of earthly pain and conflict, is when we require Divine guidance, support, consolation, and forgiveness. In light of this, as well as of the other points we have adduced, I would suggest that there is indeed reason to suppose that a being who did not seek to relate himself to us explicitly in this life—who elected to remain elusive, distant, hidden, even in the absence of any culpable activity on our part—would not properly be viewed as perfectly loving.

SOME EPISTEMIC IMPLICATIONS OF DIVINE LOVE

A personal relationship with God entails belief in Divine existence, that is, entails a disposition to "feel it true" that God exists.[7] This claim seems obviously true. For I cannot love God, be grateful to God, or contemplate God's goodness unless I believe that there *is* a God. An adequate description of such attitudes and actions entails reference to belief in propositions such as the following: "God is the source of my being," "God loves me," "God is to be praised." And clearly, one can only believe propositions such as these if one believes that God exists.[8]

It is important to note that my point here is a logical one. There is something logically amiss in the suggestion that I could display attitudes and perform actions of the sort in question without being disposed to feel it true that God exists. It is not as though someone who cannot be grateful to God or praise God because she does not believe there is a God could do so if only she *tried* a little harder. Such attitudes and actions are not just contingently difficult but *logically impossible* for one who does not believe that God exists.

Since one cannot add to one's beliefs just by choosing to (since belief is involuntary), it follows that while in a state of nonbelief I am not in a position to relate personally to God. But then, given P1, we can infer that God will seek to bring it about that I am never in a state of nonbelief. More exactly, we can infer that

> P2 If God exists and is perfectly loving, then for any human subject S and time t, if S is at t capable of relating personally to God, S at t believes that God exists, except insofar as S is culpably in a contrary position at t.

For if God will bring it about that (insofar as I am capable and unless I resist) I am always in a position to relate personally to him, and if the latter state of affairs obtains only if I always believe that God exists, it follows that God will bring it about that (insofar as I am capable and unless I resist) I at all times believe that God exists.[9]

What will God do to facilitate belief in his existence? I would suggest, as a first approximation, that God would provide *evidence* that is sufficient to produce belief.[10] For if belief is involuntary, then, if I am to believe that G [i.e., God exists], there must be something or other apart from my own choice—some evidence—on account of which I feel it to be true that G. Now it may be objected that God could simply bring it about that it seems to me strongly that he exists—where the "strong seeming" is something analogous to what produces (for most of us) such beliefs as the belief that 2 + 2 = 4—instead of providing evidence. But on the broad understanding I am here assuming, 'evidence' refers to anything that can serve as a ground of belief, and so not only to propositions that provide the basis for deductive and inductive inference but also to non-propositional, experiential evidence in which belief may be directly (non-inferentially) grounded. Hence the objector's point can be accommodated. For presumably, if it seems strongly to S that p is true, S may point to *that experiential circumstance*—the circumstance of it seeming strongly to S that p is true—as the ground of his belief.[11] More generally, there is nothing to prevent God, on our understanding of 'evidence', from bringing it about that I have certain experiences instead of providing an *argument* that has G as its conclusion.

This is not yet the whole story, however. For it is compatible with what we have said so far that I be led to believe on inadequate grounds, and this is surely not to be expected: God, we might expect, would provide evidence that *adequately supports* belief. Let us now look at this a little more closely. Why should we have this expectation? The answer, it seems to me, must be given in terms of the requirements of resistance and the nature of God. We have said that God would bring it about that it is only if S has put herself in a contrary position culpably that S is not in a position to relate personally to himself. If this is true, then, clearly, God would not take actions to facilitate belief that left open the possibility of inculpable resistance. And so he would provide adequate evidence, for if the evidence was not adequate, S might very well come to see it as such and inculpably reject it.

Perhaps it will be replied here that God as omnipotent could easily prevent me from ever viewing the evidence he provided *as* poor (even when it was). But were God to take this route, he would systematically deceive us by bringing it about that whenever the (actually inadequate) evidence was examined, it was viewed as adequate; and this seems incompatible with his perfect goodness.[12] This point, indeed, provides us with an independent reason for supposing that the evidence provided would be adequate. For a perfectly good God would not permit his intentions to be fulfilled by deceitful means. And so, it seems, he would not permit me to believe that G on grounds I viewed as adequate, but that did not adequately support that belief. We might go farther and point out that even if I did *not* explicitly consider my grounds or the support they provided,

God would still deceive me by bringing it about that they were inadequate. For in that case, my degree of firmness in believing (whatever it was) would not correspond to the degree of support provided by the evidence; and so—although I would not believe a false proposition about the evidence—God would have brought it about that I was, so to speak, living out a lie. We may therefore conclude that if God provides me with evidence, intending thereby to produce belief in his existence, it will be evidence that not only is sufficient to produce belief but also adequately supports it.

If now we consider what sort of evidence would provide the degree of objective support required here, I think we must say *probabilifying* evidence—evidence that renders G probable.[13] As William Alston has argued, it is only if a ground renders a claim probably true that the formation of belief on that basis would be "desirable from the epistemic point of view."[14] But there is another reason too: it is just not possible for anyone who considers the evidence on the basis of which she believes to continue believing unless it seems to her to render the proposition in question probably true. For suppose S offers the following description of her mental state: "I feel that G is true—that G conforms to the way the world is. But the arguments for G known to me (i.e., the public evidence) do not seem to me to favor G: neither individually nor cumulatively do they seem to me to show G to be more probable than its denial. Nor do I have any *private* evidence—any hunch or feeling or experience—that favors a contrary view." This description seems clearly contradictory, and the contradiction is one that S could hardly fail to see:

(1) I feel G to be true and I do not feel G to be true.

Hence the claim that one could consider one's evidence and continue to believe while not holding it to render the proposition one believed probable entails that S could believe a contradiction. But this does not seem to me to be something anyone could do. Hence that claim is false. But if it is false, we do indeed have additional reason to suppose that the evidence God would provide would be probabilifying evidence. For only that way could God ensure (without deception) that anyone who examined her evidence continued to believe.[15]

Perhaps it will now be objected that while probabilifying evidence is necessary, it would not be sufficient. Someone might argue for this as follows: "For those who consider the evidence, only the belief that the evidence renders G *very* probable would be sufficient to produce the belief that G. And so there could be a situation in which God provided probabilifying evidence and S saw it as such, but in which S *did not come to believe*, or in which S came to see the evidence on which she believed as probabilifying and forthwith *ceased* to believe. To avoid this, God would have either to deceive S into supposing the evidence to be stronger than it was or to provide stronger evidence. But obviously, if perfectly good, God would not choose the former route. Hence he would choose the latter. But then we cannot rest content with the claim that God would provide evidence that rendered his existence probable. We must, instead, say that he would provide evidence that rendered his existence *very* probable."

In response to this objection, I would suggest that we have good reason to reject the claim about belief on which it depends. We might first point out, with Richard Swinburne, that it is "tidier" to suppose that belief will exist as soon as the probability of the proposition believed is perceived as greater than 0.5 than to identify the point at which belief arises with some (inevitably arbitrary) value of probability between 0.5 and 1.[16] But other reasons might also be adduced. Suppose I believe that G has a probability of 0.6. Then I believe that the world is to some extent in favor of G, and (it seems) I will have at any rate a *weak* disposition to feel it true that G. It is clear that I may have such a disposition when the perceived probability is less than 1—as the objector himself admits, if I view G as *very* probable, I believe that G—so why should I not believe weakly when the probability is taken to be 0.6? Of course, if I consider the evidence to be evenly balanced, I will be uncertain whether G is true. But if I see G's probability as greater than 0.5, it seems natural to suppose that I believe it to some extent.

Now all of this (as suggested above) is of course subject to the qualification at the end of P1 and P2, namely, that God will at all times leave it open to us to resist his facilitative endeavors—to resist the actions he takes to put us in a position to relate personally with himself. Transposing this into the key of the present discussion, we must say that S will remain free to bring it about that he is in a position incompatible with belief (and so no longer in a position to relate personally to God) by opposing the evidence that God provides. Since such resistance would be culpable, it follows that S would remain free to culpably bring about the loss of belief.

Taking this point (and the clarificatory points above) into account, we may now express P2 more fully as follows:

> P2′ If God exists and is perfectly loving, then for any human subject S and time t, if S is at t capable of relating personally to God, S at t believes that G on the basis of evidence that renders G probable, except insofar as S is culpably in a contrary position at t.[17]

P2′ represents my clarified estimate as to the sort of epistemic situation a perfectly loving God would seek to facilitate. If there is a perfectly loving God, S, unless prevented by her own culpable activity, will at all the times in question find herself in possession of evidence that renders G probable and will in some degree believe that G. If such a situation were to obtain, S could only fail to believe that G on good evidence culpably, and so (given my definition of "reasonable") G would be beyond reasonable nonbelief for S. What P2′ states, therefore, is that if a perfectly loving God exists, our situation will be one in which God's existence is beyond reasonable nonbelief for all who are capable of a personal relationship with God at all times at which they are so capable.[18]

THE REASONABLENESS OF NONBELIEF

In our world reasonable nonbelief occurs. This, at any rate, is my claim. I will now spell out what is meant by this claim and give several arguments in its defense.

Let us take a nonbeliever to be one who fails (for whatever reason and in whatever way) to believe that there is a God. Even allowing for some flexibility in the interpretation of 'God', it is clear that many human beings in the actual world fit this description. There are, first of all, individuals—primarily from non-Western cultures—who have never so much as entertained the proposition "God exists" (G), let alone considered the question of its truth or falsity. Second, there are those, from both Western and non-Western backgrounds, who are to some extent familiar with the idea of God, but who have never considered with any degree of seriousness whether it is instantiated. Individuals in these two categories exhibit what we may call *unreflective* nonbelief. They are to be contrasted with *reflective* nonbelievers—individuals who disbelieve or are in doubt about G as a result of reflection on its content and some attempt to discover whether it is true or false.[19] Those who disbelieve consider this proposition to be improbable or certainly false and so believe that not-G.[20] Individuals who are in doubt, on the other hand (to whose state I will be returning presently), are uncertain about the truth of this proposition, believing neither G nor not-G, typically as a consequence of believing that epistemic parity obtains between G and its denial.[21]

So much for the varieties of nonbelief.[22] What about *reasonable* nonbelief? In the introduction, I suggested that reasonable nonbelief is in this context to be understood as exemplified by any instance of failure to believe in the existence of God that is not the result of culpable actions or omissions on the part of the subject. The claim that reasonable nonbelief occurs is therefore the claim that the nonbelief of at any rate some nonbelievers is not the consequence of their culpable actions or omissions—that it arises through no fault of their own and so they are not in any sense to blame for it. In defending this claim, I will be looking at one particular form of nonbelief—doubt—and attempting to show that it is sometimes inculpable. This is not to suggest that other forms of nonbelief are *not* inculpable. It seems clear enough that each type is inculpably exemplified, especially the first. But it will be convenient, for our purposes, to narrow the discussion to some particular form of nonbelief; and it will be interesting in its own right to learn that even where there *has* been reflection on G, and on the evidence in its favor, inculpable nonbelief may remain.

So let us look more closely at the notion of doubt. As I have already indicated, it is here explicated in terms of uncertainty about the truth of some proposition (typically) generated by the belief that epistemic parity obtains between that proposition and its denial.[23] *Inculpable* doubt, therefore, obtains if such a belief is inculpably held. That is to say, for all S, if S inculpably believes that epistemic parity obtains between G and not-G, then S is inculpably in doubt about G.[24]

It is not difficult to see how we might have reason to say of some individual that she believes that G and not-G are at epistemic parity, for she may tell us that she does and we may have no reason to doubt her word.[25] But it may be useful to look a little more closely at what is involved in holding this belief. As I understand it, one who believes that G and not-G are at epistemic parity believes that, given her evidence, she is not justified in holding either proposition to be more probable than its denial—that neither is, for her, *epistemically preferable* to its denial. Given this understanding, it may seem that what the parity believer believes is that G and not-G are equally probable, but this is not necessarily so: I may hold beliefs about G and not-G that entail the belief that neither is epistemically preferable to the other without believing that they are equally probable. I may, for example, believe that given my evidence, the correct values for the relevant probabilities (whether precise numerical or comparative) *cannot be determined*.[26] This belief entails the belief that neither G nor not-G is epistemically preferable to its denial, but it clearly does not entail the belief that they are equally probable. Therefore, in deciding whether some individual holds the parity belief, we must not only look for evidence that she believes G and not-G to be equally probable.

The second part of our task may appear to pose more difficult problems. How could we ever have reason to say, upon evaluating S's parity belief, that it is inculpably held? How could this information be available to us?

It seems to me that in some cases there may *not* be enough relevant information available. But it seems equally clear that in certain circumstances a judgment in favor of the subject would be appropriate. Again, what S tells us of her investigation is not to be taken lightly. But we may also be witness to her investigation and see it to be an exemplary one. S may have given as much or even more time and energy to investigation than our beliefs about the issue's importance, probabilities in the field, the probability that investigation will achieve something, and S's other responsibilities suggest is adequate. If so (and provided that S's own beliefs on these matters of which we have knowledge do not suggest that more investigation is required), we will rightly judge that S has not knowingly failed to pursue adequate investigation.

It may seem to some that the question whether self-deception has occurred will be especially difficult to answer in individual cases. But here, too, under certain conditions (which may well be present), we would have to rule in the subject's favor. S's conduct in other contexts, especially other epistemic contexts, is particularly important. Has he shown himself to be honest, a lover of the truth? Does he resist his wants when his head tells him he ought not to give in to them? We may also have reason to believe that S *desires* to have a well-justified belief that G or that not-G. If this is clearly so in some particular case, then (unless there is very strong evidence to the contrary) we may surely conclude that S is not self-deceived in arriving at a parity belief. For, given such a wish, S is much more likely to find ways of avoiding a parity belief than to find ways of acquiring one.

This suggests a more general point as well. If S desires a well-justified belief that G, or that not-G, he will arrive at a parity belief only *reluctantly* and, therefore, only if careful attention to the matter seems to him to leave him with no other option. Thus, if we have reason to believe that S wishes to have a well-justified belief that G, or that not-G, we have reason to believe not only that S is not self-deceived, but, more generally, that his investigation was a thorough one.

A final point about assessing parity beliefs as culpable or inculpable is that, where beliefs of this sort are concerned, we may also ask whether the propositions in question are *controversial*—whether expert opinion is divided over which is true. If this is the case, it is likely that there is something to be said for each side's position and so likely that more cautious investigators will see this. In such circumstances, instances of honest doubt are to be expected. Now this is not to say that if G and not-G *are* controversial, every parity belief is automatically inculpable. However, such controversy, where it exists, provides us with useful additional information, allowing our judgment, when we are inclined to conclude on other grounds that S's parity belief is inculpable, to be more confident.

It is time now to apply these considerations to the question whether inculpable doubt about the truth of G actually occurs. It is clearly true that many philosophers do believe that G and not-G are at epistemic parity—that neither of these propositions is epistemically preferable to its denial. (Of course, many non-philosophers hold this belief as well.) The term commonly associated with this view is 'agnosticism'. The agnostic claims that it is impossible to judge on rational grounds that there is or is not a God. (She may have in mind the present state of the evidence, allowing that the epistemic status of G and not-G may change, or she may hold that a judgment is impossible in principle.[27]) Now clearly, if an individual believes that the evidence does not allow a judgment as to whether there is a God, she believes that neither G nor not-G is epistemically preferable to its denial—that is, she holds a parity belief. That there are persons who believe the former (i.e., agnostics) is a truism.[28] We may therefore infer with the highest degree of confidence that there are individuals who hold a parity belief.

The other conditions seem also to be satisfied in many cases. Many who doubt have investigated the question of God's existence with great care and concern for the truth over a period of years. To say of them that they have not knowingly failed to pursue adequate investigation is to say too little: if their doubt is inculpable at all, it is *strongly* inculpable, that is, their investigations are exemplary, even supererogatory, and match in quality those of the most scrupulous of their opponents.

Now it may be thought that I have neglected the possibility of self-deception. But although there are no doubt some cases in which we have reason to suppose that it has occurred, in many others we either do not have such reason or have good reason to suppose that it has not occurred. There are, in particular, individuals of whom we would have to say that if they have any desire at all with respect to this issue, it is to have a well-justified belief one way or the other. Their longing corresponds to that of Pascal:

> I look around in every direction and all I see is darkness. Nature has nothing to offer me that does not give rise to doubt and anxiety. If I saw no sign there of a Divinity I should decide on a negative solution: if I saw signs of a creator everywhere I should peacefully settle down in the faith. But seeing too much to deny and not enough to affirm, I am in a pitiful state, where I have wished a hundred times over that, if there is a God supporting nature, she should unequivocally proclaim him, and that, if the signs in nature are deceptive, they should say all or nothing so that I could see what course I ought to follow. Instead of that, in the state in which I am, not knowing what I am or what I ought to do, I know neither my condition nor my duty. My whole heart strains to know what the true good is in order to pursue it: no price would be too high to pay for eternity.[29]

In individuals such as the one represented here—who certainly exist—self-deception, if it occurred, would, it seems, be much more likely to produce *belief* than doubt.

As I suggested earlier, the fact that some individuals who doubt desire to believe also gives us an independent reason for saying that doubt is sometimes inculpable. For such persons, the parity view is only to be arrived at after all alternatives have been exhausted. We can infer from the fact that they strongly wish to settle the question for themselves one way or the other but nonetheless hold a parity belief that their investigation was thorough, and that their parity belief—although it may be mistaken—is not the result of negligence.

My final point in support of the view that inculpable doubt occurs is perhaps more obvious than any other I have made, namely, that the question of God's existence is *controversial*—a question over which expert opinion is divided. The individual who begins an inquiry into God's existence is faced with a plethora of arguments both for and against. There is no easy way to sort through these arguments, and it is not obvious a priori that one side's arguments are deficient. From this it would seem to follow that we should expect what we in fact seem to find, namely, that scrupulous doubt occurs. Of course, as I suggested above, this information should not on its own lead us to conclude that such doubt occurs. But it seems to me that when taken in conjunction with other points I have adduced (which suggest that there are individuals holding parity beliefs who pass various tests of inculpability), it ought indeed to have this effect.

It is my conclusion, then, in view of all the arguments considered, that in the actual world reasonable nonbelief occurs.

A SUMMATION OF THE CASE

Let us now summarize the argument developed above. At the outset we saw that

(1) If there is a God, he is perfectly loving.

Exploring this idea of Divine love further we found considerable support for the following claim:

(2) If a perfectly loving God exists, reasonable nonbelief does not occur.

Then it was shown that (2)'s consequent is false, that

(3) Reasonable nonbelief occurs.

But (3), in combination with (2), yields

(4) No perfectly loving God exists;

and from (4), together with (1), it follows that

(5) There is no God.

We have arrived, then, at an argument of considerable force from the reasonableness of nonbelief to the nonexistence of God.[30]

NOTES

1. Several contemporary writers have touched on this problem. See Terence Penelhum, *God and Skepticism* (Dordrecht: Reidel, 1983), pp. 156–58, esp. p. 158; John

Hick, *Faith and Knowledge*, 2d ed. (London: Macmillan, 1988), p. 121; Ronald Hepburn, "From World to God," in *Philosophy of Religion*, edited by Basil Mitchell (Oxford: Oxford University Press, 1971), p. 178; Frank B. Dilley, "Fool-Proof Proofs of God?" *International Journal for Philosophy of Religion* 8 (1977): 19–27, 35; Anthony O'Hear, *Experience, Explanation, and Faith* (London: Routledge and Kegan Paul, 1984), pp. 238–39; George Schlesinger, "The Availability of Evidence in Support of Religious Belief," *Faith and Philosophy* 1 (1984): 422–27; William Alston, "Religious Diversity and Perceptual Knowledge of God," *Faith and Philosophy* 5 (1988): 445; C. Robert Mesle, "Does God Hide from Us? John Hick and Process Theology on Faith, Freedom, and Theodicy," *International Journal for Philosophy of Religion* 24 (1988): 97; Thomas V. Morris, "The Hidden God," *Philosophical Topics* 16 (1988): 5–7, 11; Mark R. Talbot, "Is It Natural to Believe in God?" *Faith and Philosophy* 6 (1989): 160–61; and Robert McKim, "The Hiddenness of God," *Religious Studies* 26 (1990): 141–43. But few of these writers have offered suggestions as to how the weakness of theistic evidence might yield an argument for atheism; and the remarks of those who have are sketchy.

2. Nonbelief is reasonable, I will stipulate, if and only if it is not the result of culpable actions or omissions on the part of the subject.

3. Claims with respect to this connection are defended as true, not as necessarily true. Needless to say, if they are necessarily true as well, the argument will be none the worse for it.

4. John Macquarrie, *In Search of Humanity* (London: SCM Press, 1982), p. 180.

5. Hick, *Faith and Knowledge*, pp. 128–29.

6. It is important to note that 'capable of' and 'in a position to' are here understood in such a way that someone might be *capable* of a personal relationship with God at a time—have the requisite cognitive and affective machinery—without being in a position to *exercise* her capacity at that time and so enter into the relationship.

7. I am here following L. J. Cohen, who defines 'belief that p' as "a disposition to feel it true that p" ("Belief and Acceptance," *Mind* 98 [1989]: 368). Cohen's definition conforms quite closely, I think, to actual usage. It is at any rate very helpful in pinpointing what I am claiming to be logically presupposed by personal relationship with God.

8. As Robert Adams puts it, "it is our highest good to be related in love to God, and . . . we have to believe that he exists and loves us in order to be related to him in that way" (*The Virtue of Faith* [New York: Oxford University Press, 1987], p. 20). Adams's claim (as well as mine) echoes a much older claim: "anyone who comes to God must believe that he exists" (Hebrews 11:6, New International Version).

9. It might be held that belief is not just necessary but also *sufficient* to put one in a position to enter into personal relationship with God, since anyone who has the relevant emotional and intellectual capacities *and believes* can, just by choosing to, contemplate God's goodness, cultivate a loving and trusting attitude toward God, and so on. But then, it might be concluded, P2 is in fact *equivalent* to P1. I have considerable sympathy for this claim, but it is not necessary, for our purposes, to endorse it. And the weaker claim, which is required, is quite obviously true.

10. What I say here is meant to apply both to the initial acquisition of belief and (should it be retained) to its persistence.

11. This view is defended by Alvin Plantinga. See his "Reason and Belief in God," *Faith and Rationality*, edited by Alvin Plantinga and Nicholas Wolterstorff (Notre Dame: University of Notre Dame Press, 1983), pp. 78–79.

12. The qualification "whenever the evidence was examined" is to be carefully noted. S may believe *without* reflecting on her evidence and without articulating to herself exactly how it provides support for G or how *much* support it provides (how probable G is rendered by it). If we did not suppose this, we would have to say that individuals who do not have the capacity for such reflection and evaluation (e.g., small children) could not believe that G; and this is an implication to be avoided. I am indebted to William Alston for drawing the need for some such qualification to my attention.

13. I do not wish to be taken as suggesting that God would ensure that his existence was probable on the *totality* of the evidence that exists—whatever that might be—or on the *public* evidence available—that is, on the set of propositions that provide the premises for arguments in natural theology. All we have seen reason to suppose (and all that the arguments immediately below suggest) is that God would bring it about that his existence was probable on S's evidence; and this evidence, as we have seen, might well include not only propositions of the sort mentioned above but certain of S's experiences too.

14. William Alston, *Perceiving God: The Epistemology of Religious Experience* (Ithaca: Cornell University Press, 1991), p. 74.

15. I would add here that on my view, any claim to the effect that S holds that G is not more probable than not-G and yet (irrationally) believes that G is most charitably interpreted as ignoring *private* evidence held by S to favor G, or as confusing belief with acceptance (a commitment to *act-as-if* some proposition is true which does not necessarily involve belief that the proposition is true). It is of course also possible for S, through self-deception, to lose the belief she once held that G and not-G are at epistemic parity and *come* to believe that G is true. But I can make no sense of the suggestion that S could *at one and the same time* hold both that G is not more probable than not-G *and* that G is true.

16. Richard Swinburne, *Faith and Reason* (Oxford: Clarendon Press, 1981), p. 5.

17. It may be said that given the way P2′ is phrased, we may argue not only from reasonable nonbelief to the nonexistence of God, but also from reasonable (but inadequately grounded) *belief*. For P2′ states that all will believe on *good evidence*, and is it not obvious that many actual believers do not? This point may be conceded, but it does not cast into question the approach I am taking. For the claim of the one who argues from inculpable (but poorly grounded) belief to the nonexistence of God—who emphasizes that a loving God would provide good evidence—*depends on* the claim (and arguments for the claim) that God would provide evidence *at all*. The success of my argument, in other words, is a necessary condition for the success of any argument from inculpable (but poorly grounded) belief. To put it yet another way, the claim under consideration is really a conjunctive claim—"God will provide evidence, and the evidence God provides will be good evidence"—the first conjunct of which must be supported by an argument of the sort provided in this paper. If this argument does not succeed, there is no reason to suppose that the other will. And if it *does* succeed, the other will be superfluous.

18. It may be objected that this conditional is not in fact equivalent to P2′. For as we have seen, S could be fooled into believing that poor evidence was good and so might very well find that G was beyond reasonable nonbelief for her—might find that she could not

reject it without resisting what she took to be good evidence—without it being the case that G was in fact rendered probable by her evidence. I will simply assume, however, that what is meant by "G is beyond reasonable nonbelief for S" is "S can only fail to believe that G on good evidence culpably," in which case the equivalence holds.

19. Given present concerns, the expression "is in doubt about G" is to be preferred to "doubts whether (or that) G." The latter is most naturally construed as "is inclined to disbelieve G," and this is not a meaning I wish to convey. Doubt is also sometimes understood in such a way as to be compatible with *belief*, and this too is a view from which mine must be distinguished. On the understanding assumed here, one who doubts neither believes nor disbelieves that G. To put it another way: doubt is identified with the point *midway* between belief and disbelief.

20. For the sake of simplicity, I include in the "certainly false" subcategory those who consider G to be incoherent or meaningless.

21. There will be more on "epistemic parity" later.

22. No doubt more varieties of nonbelief could be distinguished, but these are the main ones and will suffice for our purposes.

23. "Typically" is inserted here to allow for the possibility of doubt occurring without being caused by a parity belief (see note 22), *not* to suggest that a parity belief need not generate doubt. In my view, it must do so.

24. As this formulation indicates, I am not assuming that S's inculpably holding a parity belief is a *necessary* condition of S's being inculpably in doubt. To suppose that it is would be, as William Alston has pointed out to me, unduly restrictive, forcing us to say that individuals incapable of a parity belief (e.g., small children) cannot be in doubt. That such a belief constitutes a *sufficient* condition for inculpable doubt is, in any case, all that is required for our purposes.

25. I am of course appealing here to the principle of testimony, which, as Swinburne puts it, states "that (in the absence of special considerations) the experiences of others are (probably) as they report them" (*The Existence of God* [Oxford: Clarendon Press, 1979], p. 272).

26. As we will see, this is in fact the more common assessment.

27. See Anthony Kenny, *Faith and Reason* (New York: Columbia University Press, 1983), pp. 87–88.

28. Prominent contemporary examples include Anthony Kenny and Ronald Hepburn. See ibid., p. 85, and Ronald Hepburn, *Christianity and Paradox* (London: Watts, 1966), p. 1.

29. Blaise Pascal, *Pensées*, translated by A. J. Krailsheimer (Harmondsworth: Penguin, 1966), fragment 429.

30. Editors' note: J. L. Schellenberg titled and edited this paper for this anthology from excerpts drawn from pp. 1–83 in *Divine Hiddenness and Human Reason*.

8
RESPONSE TO HOWARD-SNYDER

J. L. SCHELLENBERG

With characteristic insight and rigor, Daniel Howard-Snyder examines (what he calls) the Argument from Divine Hiddenness and finds it wanting.[1] I shall reach a similar conclusion about his criticisms, but I hope that before the discussion is at an end, something more interesting than the fact of our disagreement will have been revealed.

I

I cannot resist remarking at the outset upon Howard-Snyder's label for the argument. If the latter were *from* Divine hiddenness, it could hardly be *for* atheism. The claim that God is hidden entails that God exists! But let that pass. I am more interested in commenting on (i) the way Howard-Snyder sets up the discussion, his characterization of the argument, and of the conditions necessary for its success; and on (ii) his (relevant) proposed defeaters.

Let's begin with (i). While he relies on my work[2] in clarifying the argument and in showing how certain of its premises might be defended, Howard-Snyder (presumably acting on the Principle of Charity) adds a clause to one of the premises I employ, and also inserts into the argument a premise I do not employ. Now this sort of move is in itself perfectly legitimate, and if the result were a stronger argument, I would applaud Howard-Snyder's efforts here. But it seems to me that

From *Canadian Journal of Philosophy* 26, no. 3 (September 1996): 455–62. Published by the University of Calgary Press. Reprinted by permission.

these revisions in fact weaken the argument, leaving it open to objections I sought to avoid by constructing it as I did. Not surprisingly, these objections surface later in Howard-Snyder's paper, playing a crucial backup role at the end.

What are the changes? They are italicized in the following statement of the argument, taken from Howard-Snyder's paper:[3]

1'. If a perfectly loving God exists, then for any human S at any time t, if S is capable of a personal relationship with God at t, S believes at t that God exists on the basis of reasonable grounds, unless S culpably fails to have theistic belief at t *or unless God has overriding reasons to permit her to fail [inculpably] to have theistic belief at t.*[4]

2. Some people capable of relating to God personally inculpably fail to have theistic belief.

3. *There is no reason for God to permit them to fail inculpably to have theistic belief.*

4. So, there is no perfectly loving God.

This argument bears an interesting resemblance to William Rowe's much-discussed version of the evidential argument from evil. Rowe argues that we are justified in holding that *there is no reason* for God to permit certain evils, and that since God would not permit the evils in question *unless there were such a reason*, we are therefore justified in believing that God does not exist.[5] Perhaps Howard-Snyder's formulation of the hiddenness argument owes something to Rowe. Whatever the case, the defender of the argument would do well to distance herself from Rowe's form of reasoning. As recent discussion makes painfully obvious, the inductive inference—from "We can't think of a reason" to "There is no reason"—by which Rowe seeks to support his 3-type premise is somewhat less than secure.[6] Objections to this sort of inference are mentioned by Howard-Snyder at the end of his paper[7]—additional support for the Rowe connection?—and are there called upon to reinforce his case. Even if all the reasons we can think of for God to permit inculpable nonbelief are unsuccessful, Howard-Snyder argues, this cannot be made the basis for a successful inference to the conclusion that 3 is true. He seems to assume here that no other way of supporting 3 is likely to suggest itself, and so concludes that 3—and therefore the argument of which it is a part—is defeated whether the reasons for inculpable nonbelief he has put forward are deemed successful or not. It is important to note, however, that all of this is *quite beside the point* if it is possible to formulate the hiddenness argument without supporting it by means of some counterpart of Rowe's inference. I think it is. Indeed, I think the argument can dispense with 3 altogether. Since it is possible to in this way avoid the encumbrances of a Rowe-style argument, it would seem to be the better part of prudence to do so.

But *is* it possible to do so? Howard-Snyder will say that 1' is implausible or unsupportable without the second "unless" clause, and that this imposes on any defender of the argument an obligation to assert and defend 3. Now I agree that *if* that clause is in place, then 3 must be asserted and defended, but I think 1' can get along quite nicely *without* the clause. It seems to me that plenty of considerations support a trimmer 1': as I show in *Divine Hiddenness and Human Reason*, we can directly support the stronger and simpler claim that God would prevent inculpable nonbelief,[8] and none of various proposed undercutting defeaters seems capable of weakening that support. In that case, I there conclude (and would still conclude), should no *counter*-considerations—considerations showing that 1', so construed, is false or as likely as not false—be available, we have an undefeated reason (the conjunction of the original considerations) for affirming it, and so *justifiably* affirm it, and given 2, justifiably affirm the argument's conclusion.

But hold on, Howard-Snyder will say, there is an undercutting defeater I have not considered: The reason I have put forward does not support the claim that God would have an *all-things-considered* desire to prevent inculpable nonbelief, but only the weaker claim that God would have *a* desire to do so.[9] It seems to me, however, that *both* claims mentioned by Howard-Snyder are supported by the reason I present—though with differing degrees of force. In any event, we should think of 1' as referring to a Divine *intention*, not a Divine desire, and there is no way of distinguishing between intentions and all-things-considered intentions in the Divine case. Can we say, then, as Howard-Snyder might now wish to do, that my reason provides no support, on its own, for the claim that God *intends* to prevent inculpable nonbelief? Only, I would suggest, if we set up the argument as Howard-Snyder does, accepting his expansion of its first premise—in which case his only support is question-begging support. Certainly human analogues provide no support. We often take ourselves to have reasons for making judgments about people's intentions even when those reasons are inconclusive, and compatible with there being and their having overriding reasons for doing other than what our reasons suggest they will do. In the Divine and in the human case, there may *very often* be overriding reasons we are not aware of. If we had always to wait for arguments ruling these out, we would surely seldom be justified in judging what others will do. In any case, the very language of "overriding reasons" suggests that this requirement is misguided. There would be no point in looking for overriding reasons for God to permit inculpable nonbelief if we had no reason to override. Let me put this another way. Suppose we *knew* that there are no reasons *for* God to permit inculpable nonbelief—that Howard-Snyder's 3 is true. Were this (perhaps counterfactual) state of affairs to be realized, we would not wish to reserve judgment, but would unhesitatingly conclude that God would not permit inculpable nonbelief. Why? Because (taking Howard-Snyder's approach) the condition specified by the final "unless" clause of the expanded 1' has now been shown to be satisfied? Surely it is just as plausible to say that it is because we have a reason *against* his doing so (against the claim that God would permit inculpable nonbelief) which in that case emerges victorious.

Now, as is reflected in this discussion, the argument as I conceive it *is* sensitive to the relevance of the *denial* of Howard-Snyder's 3. If we have support for the denial of Howard-Snyder's 3, we have support for the denial of 1' as I construe it—for the claim that a perfectly loving God would *not* prevent inculpable nonbelief. It may also be allowed that something like the *basis* of a Rowe-style inference must be affirmed by anyone who holds that considerations of the sort I have put forward carry the day: such a one must be able to say "We can't think of a reason for God to permit inculpable nonbelief"—otherwise the reason represented by those considerations would be defeated. But this is not a concession to Howard-Snyder, since in the absence of 3, there is no need to use this statement *as* a basis for a Rowe-style inference. 3 itself simply is not explicitly affirmed and need not be affirmed, and so need not be defended. Hence the point that a Rowe-style inference from the absence of available counter-considerations to the truth of 3 is illegitimate—or more generally, that 3 cannot be independently supported—is simply irrelevant.[10]

It may still be tempting to suppose that this is implausible. Surely I *must* make 3's negative claim, for as we have seen, if that claim is false, so is mine. Applying contraposition: if my claim is true, so is 3. This is a conditional I accept and I am committed to its antecedent; hence I am committed to its consequent as well, that is, to the truth of 3.

So far so good. But it does not follow that I must argue *directly* for the consequent at any point. If my *positive* claim is correct and there are powerful considerations supporting the antecedent of the conditional, supporting the claim that a loving God would prevent inculpable nonbelief, then *this itself* gives me (some) reason to affirm the consequent, and justifies me in believing both antecedent and consequent if counter-considerations supporting the denial of the consequent cannot be found. So although the objection is right to point out my commitment to the negative existential claim in question, its emphasis on the need for some sort of independent argument here seems misguided. It fails to note that the proponent of my approach has her own way of defending it, based on her reason for believing a claim that entails it.[11]

II

I come now to Howard-Snyder's rich and insightful discussion of (what I have called) possible counter-considerations. These are possible defeaters of the hiddenness argument that are relevant on any view of the issues discussed above. Basically three suggestions are put forward as to reasons a God might have for permitting the occurrence of inculpable nonbelief. I shall respond to each in turn.

The first concerns inculpable nonbelievers who would certainly or very likely respond *inappropriately*—with rejection or indifference—upon coming to believe. Their inculpable nonbelief in the present prevents them from *confirming* themselves in their bad dispositions (by actually rejecting God or responding indifferently) and from thereby making it less likely that they will become better disposed in the future.[12]

As it seems to me, three points are overlooked here, the conjunction of which provides a defeater for this defeater. First, if those who would *certainly* respond inappropriately are (as Howard-Snyder assumes and as apparently must be assumed) powerless to do otherwise, then they are incapable of a personal relationship with God, and so fall outside the bounds of this discussion. A personal relationship with God implies *positive* interaction—or at the very least, it implies that this is possible. Second (and assuming now that we are dealing with persons *very likely* to respond inappropriately), *how* individuals come to belief is extremely important here. Howard-Snyder must claim that there are inculpable nonbelievers of whom it may reasonably be believed that they would very likely reject God or respond indifferently *no matter how they came to know of him*. But if we consider that this could occur through religious experience, through a direct encounter with an omnipotent love capable of softening even the most self-centered or embittered soul, then it seems that this class of individuals must be empty.[13] Third, even if there *are* individuals who would very likely respond inappropriately upon coming to believe, it does not follow that they would *remain* in their regrettable condition ever afterward. Howard-Snyder claims that their inappropriate response would make less likely a better disposition in the future. But are we to imagine that God would try once and then leave the scene? Especially if their resistance were inculpable (and we are assuming that it would be), a loving God would surely seek in various ways to facilitate a better disposition. Now perhaps continuing inculpable nonbelief is not incompatible with the realization of this goal, but it is hard to see how God's task here would not be more effectively prosecuted by means of the many influences presupposing belief.

Howard-Snyder's second suggestion concerns inculpable nonbelievers who would certainly or very likely respond *appropriately* upon coming to believe, i.e., with some measure of love and obedience, but who are not responsible for being in this state. Here confirmation of disposition is desirable instead of undesirable and is *facilitated* by inculpable nonbelief. Their inculpable nonbelief provides such individuals with the opportunity to confirm their stance, to own it, to make it genuinely their own; and prevents the undesirable state of affairs in which they reciprocate God's love but without ever having had a say in the matter.[14]

What strikes me here once again is that Howard-Snyder is curiously insensitive to the relevance of what may *follow* that initial response if God exists. Suppose an individual of the sort in question is brought to theistic belief and reciprocates God's love without having had a say in the matter. Surely this is unfortunate, making an initial period of inculpable nonbelief desirable, only if access to the sort of confirmation Howard-Snyder envisages has now been cut off. And surely it has *not* been cut off. Howard-Snyder refers to repeated confirmation of one's disposition "in the face of contrary desires and competing allegiances."[15] Well, why isn't this possible even after having been given access to belief and its benefits? God can make it tough for the inculpable believer as well as for the inculpable nonbeliever. (We might also note, developing this point a bit, that even if her initial loving response is not something about which she had a choice, an individual of the sort in question may be put in a position where she has to choose whether to *continue* it.) Since there is no way to go back and allow the individual to acquire her good disposition voluntarily in the first place on *either* scenario, I fail to see how confirmation *after* belief, given the many additional benefits with which only it is compatible, would not be viewed by a loving God as the better of the two possibilities.

Finally, we have the suggestion that a perfectly loving God might subject to inculpable nonbelief even those individuals who would certainly or very probably respond appropriately to belief and who *are* responsible for being in this state. Two ideas seem combined here: (1) that since the love to which such individuals are disposed may still be unfitting in some respect—not deeply centered or improperly motivated—God may keep his distance, rightly preferring, as any human lover would, a more admirable love; and (2) that the situation is not likely to improve *unless* God keeps his distance.[16]

The second of these ideas can, I think, be dealt with simply by adapting points already made: the nature of our love can be shaped and made more fitting after belief as well as before, and indeed, certain experiential resources which would facilitate this process apparently *presuppose* belief.[17] The first, however, introduces something new, and so we must ask: Does God, like any human lover in a comparable situation, remain perfectly good if he prevents the conditions of personal relationship from obtaining in response to a less than fitting (disposition to) love? It seems to me that the answer is no—and this because of certain relevant *dis*analogies which undermine the support Howard-Snyder's otherwise interesting analogy provides for his claim. First, God obviously has *more to offer* and (therefore) more to withhold than any human lover. Second, the beings from whom he would remain hidden have been *created* by him *for* such a relationship and cannot achieve true fulfillment in any other. Third, it is in the nature of the case that the Divine-human relationship cannot be an *equal* relationship, and so God, unlike human lovers, does not rightly expect to get as much as he gives. (If we say here that human lovers do not rightly expect this either, we only weaken the analogy in another way.) Fourth, we cannot suppose that God has *needs* which he rightly hopes to have fulfilled in the relationship. No doubt other disanalogies could be mentioned, but these four, I take it, are both relevant and sufficient to undermine Howard-Snyder's inference here.

III

Many interesting directions for thought are suggested by Howard-Snyder's piece—only some of which I have been able to pursue (and those only for a little way). But I think we have seen enough to conclude that the hiddenness argument—or alternatively, the argument from the reasonableness of nonbelief—escapes from the pages of his paper relatively unscathed. Good reasons for Divine hiddenness would seem to be exceedingly hard to come by. But given that the systematic search for such reasons is still in its early days, perhaps we may hope—as I do—that their discovery awaits us in the future.

NOTES

1. Daniel Howard-Snyder, "The Argument from Divine Hiddenness," *Canadian Journal of Philosophy* 26 (1996): 433–53.

2. See J. L. Schellenberg, *Divine Hiddenness and Human Reason* (Ithaca: Cornell University Press, 1993).

3. Howard-Snyder, "The Argument from Divine Hiddenness," pp. 435–37.

4. I have inserted the qualifier "inculpably" here since it is required by the context and, presumably, intended by Howard-Snyder.

5. See, for example, Rowe's contributions to *The Evidential Argument from Evil*, edited by Daniel Howard-Snyder (Bloomington: Indiana University Press, 1996).

6. A number of the papers appearing in *The Evidential Argument from Evil*, as well as quite a number not appearing in it, undertake to make this obvious; and I think the effort they represent has been attended with some success.

7. Howard-Snyder, "The Argument from Divine Hiddenness," p. 453.

8. For simplicity of exposition, I leave tacit here (and hereafter) the reference to capacity for personal relationship with God.

9. Howard-Snyder, "The Argument from Divine Hiddenness," p. 434.

10. The force of "independently" here will be apparent shortly.

11. It may seem that I have belabored these structural points, but they are important. For if my way of structuring the argument is correct (or at least a legitimate alternative), then in the absence of *available* counter-considerations of the sort Howard-Snyder seeks to provide in later sections of his paper, the argument is successful, whereas on Howard-Snyder's interpretation, this would not follow.

12. Howard-Snyder, "The Argument from Divine Hiddenness," pp. 441–42.

13. Note that it does not follow from this that their counterparts in the actual world would certainly or very likely *accept* God.

14. Howard-Snyder, "The Argument from Divine Hiddenness," p. 443.

15. Ibid.

16. Ibid., pp. 446–47.

17. There is even a sense of the absence of God *compatible* with belief, which may be more effective than any such sense prior to belief because of the accompanying poignant awareness of *loss*. The reader is referred to Part 2 of *Divine Hiddenness and Human Reason*—especially the discussion of Pascal—for a more thorough development of this and other arguments relevant to the assessment of Howard-Snyder's case.

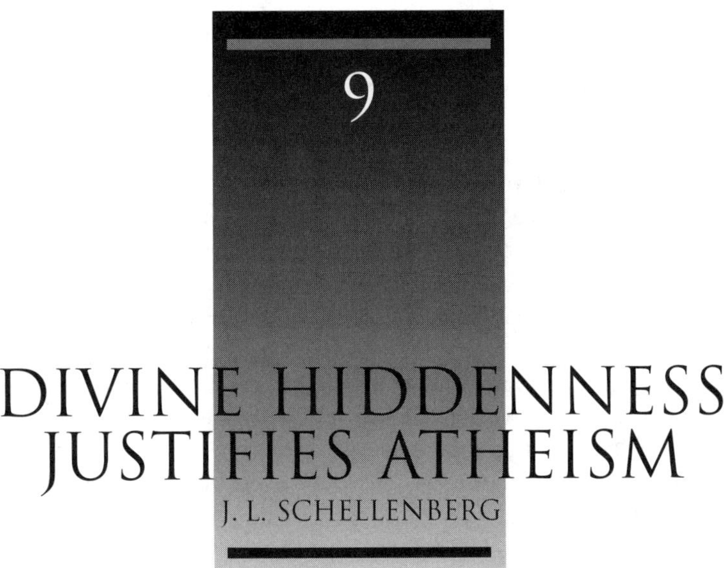

9

DIVINE HIDDENNESS JUSTIFIES ATHEISM

J. L. SCHELLENBERG

Arguments from divine hiddenness often go unnoticed in the consideration of arguments for and against the existence of God—where by 'God' is meant the *traditional* God: a separate but infinite consciousness, a personal and perfect creator of the universe. Perhaps the most interesting variety of this oversight occurs when people find themselves unable to settle the question of God's existence and therefore inclined toward agnosticism without noticing that these facts are *themselves* relevant to their quest and may support atheism. Of course, we need to be careful here. If by 'God is hidden' you mean "There is an actually existing God who hides from us," it will be short work proving that divine hiddenness provides no basis for atheism. For how could a premise asserting the *actual existence* of God lead to the conclusion that God *does not exist*? But perhaps the careful reader will be able to see that it is also possible to take the language of hiddenness less literally—as referring simply to the absence of convincing evidence for the existence of God, or, more specifically, to the absence of some kind of positive experiential result in the search for God. That is how it will be taken here. I begin with an argument from analogy focused on the latter, more specific form of hiddenness. The possibility of broadening and strengthening this argument through a closer look at the concept of divine love is then considered. The first argument will here be called "the Analogy Argument"; its sibling, naturally, is called "the Conceptual Argument."

From *Contemporary Debates in Philosophy of Religion*, edited by Michael L. Peterson and Raymond J. VanArragon (Oxford: Blackwell, 2004), pp. 30–41.

1. THE ANALOGY ARGUMENT

Imagine yourself in the following situation. You're a child playing hide-and-seek with your mother in the woods at the back of your house. You've been crouching for some time now behind a large oak tree, quite a fine hiding place but not undiscoverable—certainly not for someone as clever as your mother. However, she does not appear. The sun is setting, and it will soon be bedtime, but still no mother. Not only isn't she finding you, but, more disconcerting, you can't *hear* her anywhere: she's not beating the nearby bushes, making those exaggerated "looking for you" noises, and talking to you meanwhile as mothers playing this game usually do. Now imagine that you start *calling* for your mother. Coming out from behind the tree, you yell out her name, over and over again, "Mooooommmmm!" But no answer. You look everywhere: through the woods, in the house, down to the road. An hour passes, and you are growing hoarse from calling. Is she anywhere around? Would she fail to answer if she were around?

Now let's change the story a little. You're a child with amnesia—apparently because of a blow to the head (which of course you don't remember), your memory goes back only a few days—and you don't even know whether you *have* a mother. You see other children with their mothers and think it would sure be nice to have one. So you ask everyone you meet and look everywhere you can, but without forwarding your goal in the slightest. You take up the search anew each day, looking diligently, even though the strangers who took you in assure you that your mother must be dead. But to no avail. Is this what we should expect if you really have a mother and she is around, and aware of your search? When in the middle of the night you tentatively call out—"Mooooommmmm!"—would she not answer if she were really within earshot?

Let's change the story one more time. You're still a small child, and an amnesiac, but this time you're in the middle of a vast rain forest, dripping with dangers of various kinds. You've been stuck there for days, trying to figure out who you are and where you came from. You don't remember having a mother who accompanied you into this jungle, but in your moments of deepest pain and misery you call for her anyway: "MOOOOOMMMMM!" Over and over again. For days and days . . . the last time when a jaguar comes at you out of nowhere . . . but with no response. What should you think in this situation? In your dying moments, what should cross your mind? Would the thought that you have a mother who cares about you and hears your cry and *could* come to you but chooses *not* to even make it onto the list?

Now perhaps we could suppose, in each of these cases, that you *do* have a mother and that she *is* around, but that she simply *doesn't* care. We are inclined to think of mothers as almost by definition loving and caring, but just remember the mother of Hyde in *That '70s Show*, someone might say. Another possibility is that your mother has been prevented from doing what mothers tend naturally to do by factors external to her own desire and will: perhaps she fell into a deep well in the woods, or was kidnapped by that escaped convict who was spotted near town last week (from whose clutches you narrowly escaped, suffering only a memory-erasing blow to the head), or is fending off a crocodile even as you succumb to the jaguar. What we *can't* say is that a *loving* mother would in circumstances like these be hidden from her child *if she could help it*.

The first step in the Analogy Argument is the defense of this claim. As we might put it, our job is to find the proper filling for the blank at the end of the following sentence: "A loving mother would not be hidden from her child in circumstances like those mentioned if she could help it *because* —." What we need here are propositions specifying the properties of love *in virtue of which* the claim appearing in front of the "because" is true. These would, I suggest, include the following: (1) A loving mother would consider each of her child's serious requests important and seek to provide a quick response; (2) A loving mother would wish to spare her child needless trauma, or, more positively, would wish to foster her child's physical and emotional well-being; (3) A loving mother would seek to avoid encouraging in her child false or misleading thoughts about herself or about their relationship; (4) A loving mother would want personal interaction with her child whenever possible, for the joy it brings as well as for its own sake; (5) A loving mother would *miss* her child if separated from her. It is clear that each of these propositions is true. It is also clear that, *if* they are true, the claim we are defending is true—that no loving mother who could help it would be hidden from her child in circumstances like those mentioned. We may therefore conclude that the latter claim *is* true.

The next step in the Analogy Argument involves pointing out that there are, in the actual world, circumstances of *divine* hiddenness very similar to the circumstances we have highlighted in respect of our fictional mother and child. The relevant circumstances in our stories are those in which the mother is sought by the child but not found. Well, just so, God is (and has often been) hidden from many human beings: sought but not found. Some persons start out assured of the power and presence of God in their lives, and then *lose* all this—in the typical case because of reasoning that engenders doubt about the reliability of the support they have for theistic belief. And though they grieve what they have lost and seek to regain it, looking for God in all the old familiar places as well as in new, unfamiliar locales, they fail to do so: God seems simply absent, and their belief is gone. The situation of such individuals is relevantly similar to that of the child in the first story. Other persons don't start out in what they consider to be a relationship with God but, nonetheless, are, in their wanderings and in their attempts to determine where they belong, open to finding and being found by a divine parent; some of them seek long and hard for God, wishing to be related in love to God. But though they seek, they do not find. Their situation is relevantly similar to that of the second child. And many seekers, because of the inhospitable place this world can sometimes be, are at one time or another in a lot of *trouble*, and so have not only the usual and obvious reasons to seek to be united (or reunited) with a divine parent: they are also in serious need of divine help, calling out to God in conditions of great suffering and pain. But a divine answer to their calls is not forthcoming. What we see here is clearly relevantly similar to the situation of the third child.

Additional stories can be imagined, with features equally troubling from the perspective of motherly care, corresponding to other aspects of the form of divine hiddenness we are considering. We might have our first child, after many calls for her mother, hearing sounds in the woods that she is sure mark her mother's presence, but which turn out to come from nothing more than leaves rolling in the wind. This is like the experience of those who think they have detected traces of God in some happening or argument, only to have the former's theological significance undermined by convincing reinterpretation or the latter proved unsound. Our second child might come to be adopted by the strangers who take her in, and brought up in a manner that leaves her predisposed to be suspicious instead of trusting, calculatingly self-centered instead of generous and giving; or perhaps she comes to have experiences which cause her to deny the importance of personal relationship with a parent in the development of a child. This can be compared to what happens in the life of a seeker who, because of the influence of those who *do* answer her calls, is led to develop a character contrary to that which the God of traditional theism is said to desire for us, or whose search leads to religious experiences all right, but *nontheistic* ones. Clearly, the analogies between our fictional situations of parental hiddenness and the actual facts of divine hiddenness are very close.

So what can be done with these analogies? Well, the next step in the argument involves showing that what we have said about a mother's love applies to God as well. This is fairly easily done. For God, on the traditional theistic view we are challenging, is not only loving and caring, but *unsurpassably* loving and caring. Indeed, it seems that each of our propositions (1) to (5) above must specify a property that applies as much to God as to the mother. If God gives birth to the human race and is related to its members in a manner that is unimaginably close, caring, and loving, then surely: (1') God would consider each serious request submitted by God's human children important and seek to provide a quick response; (2') God would wish to spare human beings needless trauma or, more positively, would wish to foster their physical and emotional well-being; (3') God would seek not to encourage in human beings false or misleading thoughts about God or about the divine-human relationship; (4') God would want personal interaction with human beings whenever possible, for the joy it brings as well as for its own sake; and (5') God would *miss* such personal interaction if it were absent.

Now perhaps someone will say that God might be totally different from ourselves, and thus unlike a human mother. But there are certain conceptual constraints that need to be respected here. Of course we don't mean that God should be conceptualized as physical and as biologically female. But situations of human interaction and discussions of human interaction, including interaction between mothers and their children, do represent the primary contexts in which such concepts as those of 'closeness', 'care', and 'love' are used and acquire their meanings. What, then, could justify the supposition that God's closeness, caring, and loving would not be like those of the ideal mother, displayed in a manner appropriate to the divine nature (e.g., through religious experience instead of physical touching)? The question is rhetorical. Clearly what we have said about the best mother's love must in this way apply to God as well.

An important conclusion may now be reached quite easily. Let *P* be the conjunction of the various loving properties picked out by the original five propositions about a mother's love and the five propositions referring to God. We saw earlier that, in virtue of *P*, a loving mother who could help it would never be hidden from her child in the fictional circumstances we described. We also saw that the analogies between the latter circumstances and those of divine hiddenness are very close. But then we may infer that, very probably, *a God who could help it would never be hidden in those circumstances*: the operation of *P* would prevent this in the case of God, just as it would in the case of our fictional mother.

Thus far the Analogy Argument proper. Certain plausible additional moves may be made to bring us from this conclusion to atheism. In the case of the mother, we saw that there might be external actors that prevent her from responding to her child despite the presence of *P*—that she might be hidden and *not* able to help it. But if omnipotence means anything, it means that God couldn't *ever* be prevented from responding to the cries of God's human children. The disanalogy we see here, far from weakening the argument that starts out from the analogy, permits us to *complete* it. For it means that we may justifiably remove the little qualifier "who could help it" from our earlier conclusion and say simply that *God would never be hidden in the circumstances in question.* In other words, the Analogy Argument in conjunction with what we know about divine resourcefulness gives us a powerful reason to say that, if God exists, this form of divine hiddenness does not occur. But it *does* occur. Therefore, we have a powerful reason to believe that God does *not* exist.

2. IS THE ANALOGY ARGUMENT A SUCCESS?

Before getting too excited—or upset—about this argument, the reader should consider whether it can be defeated by counter-argument. It will, I think, be hard to question the claims we have made about how a loving mother would behave in our fictional scenarios. Most objections will quite naturally focus instead on questioning the closeness of the analogies we have drawn *between* those scenarios and the facts of divine hiddenness.

This can be done in various ways. One might argue, for example, that persons who seek God are not very much like *children*—the vulnerability and immaturity we attach to the latter and need to be able to transfer to the former if the argument is to succeed are in fact not transferable in this way. But this objection appears to assume that all who seek God in the relevant way are adult humans, and this is not at all obvious: actual children may (and do) seek God too, without in every case finding their search rewarded with positive results. More important, because of the evil we face and the evident frailty of our natures, even human grown-ups are not appropriately construed, theologically speaking, as mature adults. Theology has traditionally pictured us this way (while also referring to us as "God's children"), but a close look at the world suggests that a better picture would portray us as young and unformed, still needing a home—in particular, still in need of parental support and encouragement in the development of a character and self-esteem that can withstand the pressures toward fragmentation and despair that life presents and make the achievement of our full potential possible.

It might also be claimed that God is not appropriately thought of as mother—that in our application of human talk to the divine, non-motherly elements of human experience ought to predominate. Now it is clear that, traditionally, the notion of God as Father is much more common than that of God as Mother, but an appeal to "common practice" is always weak, especially when the practice in question has been (or can be) successfully challenged. Instead of getting into debates about feminism and patriarchy, though, let me simply point out that, whether presented under the label of "loving Father" or in some other way, such attributes as those of caring and closeness, compassion and empathy, are nonnegotiable in any theistic view that takes the moral perfection and worship-worthiness of God seriously. And these are the attributes at issue here. I have found it helpful to focus on the model of a mother because these attributes are still more closely linked in our experience and imagination with the notion of mother than with that of father. Indeed, the commonness in human experience of *distant* or *absent* fathers makes it possible for us to construe the connection between fatherhood and the attributes in question rather loosely. This fact, in conjunction with the tendency to think uncritically of God as Father, is, I think, a big part of the reason why so many are inclined to underestimate the force of arguments from divine hiddenness.

A third objection to our argument—a rather common sort—suggests that there is something presumptuous about *expecting* a response from God. God is not obligated to respond to our every whim; and if God responds, it will be in God's own way, not necessarily as we expect. Even if so-called seekers lack presumption, we ought still to consider that there may be some *other* human sin that prevents them from experiencing God. Perhaps God is hidden from us because of our *own* failings, instead of God's.

But the Analogy Argument, as you may have noticed, is not suggesting that God should satisfy our every *whim*, our every sudden, unreflective, unreasonable desire; only that God would respond to serious attempts to be united or reunited with God in a loving relationship. Observe how much more plausible the latter claim is than the former. The objection is here dealing with a caricature of our argument, not the real thing. As for presumption, the expectation of a seeker does not come in the form of a *demand*, but as anticipation or reasoned inference. Are we really to imagine seekers walking around demanding that God show himself? Some *philosophers* may do this, but these are usually individuals who have long since concluded that God does not exist and think the world is better off that way; it would be a mistake to confuse them with the earnest, hopeful seekers of our argument, or with those (perhaps the same individuals) who after careful reflection on all the available information conclude that it would be in the nature of God to be in some way revealed to anyone who calls upon God sincerely.

Turning now to the general reference to sin: this seems completely unsubstantiated—many who seek God seem in fact to be quite blameless in the relevant respects. It is important to notice here that beyond looking thoroughly and carefully for reason to believe in the existence of God and removing all observed impediments to success in the search, there is nothing the seeker *can do* to bring about belief. Belief as such is involuntary; it is something that happens to you when evidence adds up to a certain point, not something you can do directly (if you doubt this, just try to acquire right now, or to drop, as the case may be, the belief that God exists). Thus, if a search of the sort in question has been undertaken (as it often has), a nonbeliever cannot be "to blame" for not believing.

What about the possibility, also mentioned by the "sin" objection, that God *does* respond, and seekers simply miss the response, expecting something else—something other than what God has in mind? Well, what else might God have in mind? If the request is for the beginning or resumption of a loving relationship, and what is needed for this is, among other things, some measure of belief that there is someone there to relate *to*, what *could* count both as *loving* and as a *response* apart from some noticeable indication of God's presence? Certainly in the case of the unencumbered mother and her child, nothing apart from the mother actually coming to her child in a manner recognized by the child would qualify as a loving response. What makes us think that something else would do in the case of God's immeasurably greater love? Perhaps it will be said that God, unlike the mother, is able to be present to us all the time without us noticing it and is, moreover, responsible for every single good thing we experience. This is indeed true, if God exists. But it still doesn't qualify as a *response* to the cry of those who seek God. And we need to recognize that the absence of love in one respect is not compensated for by *other* forms of love when what we're dealing with is not the love of a finite being but the perfect love of an unlimited God. Indeed, it's starting to look as though the relevant differences between God and ourselves make it *harder* to mount an "other response" objection, not easier.

But maybe we can press this notion of differences between ourselves and God a little further, in a different direction. Perhaps there is some *great good* for the seeker that depends on the continuation of her search, and thus prevents God from responding. Perhaps no loving human mother would ever have reason to consider continued separation from her child, in circumstances like those we have described, to be "for his own good," but God, the critic will say, is aware of so many more forms of goodness than we are, and has a design plan that spans incomprehensible distances in time and space. We are therefore not justified in concluding that God would do what the mother does, even if they share the loving properties we have discussed.

Now various possible goods we know of might be enumerated and discussed in response to this objection, but the objector would only reply by saying that the relevant goods may be *unknown* to us. Fortunately, there is a way around all this. First, let's notice that if the ultimate spiritual reality is a personal God, then all serious spiritual development must begin in personal relationship with God. And if God is infinitely deep and rich, then any such relationship must be multileveled and developmental—indeed, the development of it would surely be potentially unending. Third, such relationship with a perfect and infinitely rich personal reality would have to be the greatest good that any human being could experience, if God exists—certainly this is the claim of all theistic traditions. But then why this talk of some *other* good, for which God would *sacrifice* such relationship?

Perhaps it will be replied that God sacrifices only *some time* in the relationship, not the whole relationship, and that what is gained thereby may contribute to the *flourishing* of a *future* relationship with God. But it is hard to see how someone seeking God, desiring a loving personal relationship, could possibly be in a state such that experience of God or evidence of some other sort would inhibit or prevent the success of the relationship in the long term, as this point requires. Indeed, such individuals would seem to be in just the *right* position in this respect—a position emphasized as eminently desirable by theistic traditions. Certainly their state is no less appropriate to relationship with God than that of many who would be declared by those traditions to be enjoying it already.

Consider also, in this connection, the infinite *resourcefulness* of God. If God indeed possesses this attribute and is, moreover, unsurpassably deep and rich, then there must at any juncture be literally an *infinite number* of ways of developing in relationship with God, which omnipotence and omniscience could facilitate, despite obstacles to continuing relationship that might seem to present themselves. To say less than this, a theist must surely contradict what she believes about the greatness of God! Hence, even if we were *not* dealing with seekers, individuals optimally placed to benefit from God's presence, we would *still* lack reason to maintain the present objection.

One particular form that the exercise of God's resourcefulness might take may be highlighted here. Strange as it may seem, there is an important form of "hiddenness" that is quite compatible with—and indeed *requires*—a situation in which God is revealed to every seeker. To see this, suppose that God exists, and that our seeker finds reason to believe in God and responds by entering into a personal relationship with God ("conversing" with God in prayer, feeling God's presence, living her whole life in the context of divine-human communion). Suppose also that she subsequently lapses into some inappropriate state—say, arrogance or presumption. What can God do? Well, there is still the possibility of a sort of divine withdrawal *within* the relationship. What I have in mind here is analogous to what has traditionally been called "the dark night of the soul"—a state in which there is evidence for God's existence on which the believer may rely, but in which God is not felt as directly present to her experience, and may indeed feel absent. While not removing the conditions of relationship, such a "withdrawal" would severely test the believer's faith, and, in particular, work against the sort of arrogance and presumption we have mentioned. Indeed, this form of hiddenness would seem capable of accomplishing much, perhaps all, of what theists sometimes say the *other* sort of hiddenness is designed to do! John Macquarrie, a Christian theologian, puts it nicely:

> As happens also in some of our deepest human relationships, the lover reveals himself enough to awaken the love of the beloved, yet veils himself enough to draw the beloved into an even deeper exploration of that love. In the love affair with God . . . there is an alternation of consolation and desolation and it is in this way that the finite being is constantly drawn beyond self into the depths of the divine.[1]

If this sort of hiddenness can produce the goods in question and is compatible with God having been revealed to the seeker, what possible reason could we have for insisting that God would leave the seeker in *doubt and nonbelief* in order to further those goods?

A final objection, significantly different from the rest, should briefly be mentioned. This is the claim that there are *other* reasons *for* belief in God which counterbalance or outweigh the reason *against* such belief that our argument represents. Our Analogy Argument, it should be emphasized, is broadly inductive, claiming only that its conclusion is very probable (i.e., much more probable than not). So it is always at least conceivable that the probability we assess for our conclusion on the basis of analogy may need to be adjusted when arguments *supporting* God's existence are taken into account. Someone, for example, who was deeply convinced of the soundness of a simple *de*ductive argument for God's existence (an argument with premises *entailing* the claim that God exists) and had only our Analogy Argument to consider on the side of atheism might well justifiably conclude, on the strength of her apparent proof of God's existence, that despite the closeness and persuasive force of the analogies, there must be *something* wrong with our argument and that God certainly exists, even if she cannot put her finger on what the mistake in our reasoning is.

For how many will this sort of move function as a successful defeater? It is hard to say: everything depends on how the independent evidence is assessed, and whether it is properly assessed. Even if we had the space for an exhaustive discussion of other evidence (and of course we do not), it would be possible for others to justifiably disagree with our assessment of it, given facts of personality, experience, time, intelligence, opportunity, and so on that nonculpably incline them in another direction. But some general points can be made, that are not without interest or effect. Most readers, it must be said, are likely to be *without* such proofs of God as were earlier mentioned—indeed, that such proofs are in short supply is one of the circumstances that helps to generate the problem of divine hiddenness in the first place! Certainly, anyone who finds that the other evidence for and against God's existence leaves her thinking that theism and atheism are about equally probable should find the balance tipping toward atheism when this *new* evidence is considered. And it is interesting to note that even those who came to this discussion convinced of the truth of theism may find their epistemic situation changing because of the apparent force of our argument. This is because its apparent force may *affect*—and *negatively* affect—the confidence with which other arguments or experiences are taken to support theism, especially in cases where this other evidence has not previously been carefully examined. We should therefore not suppose that just anyone who comes to these discussions justified in theistic belief will leave that way.

That concludes our discussion of objections to the Analogy Argument. Nothing we have seen takes away from its initial persuasiveness (even the last defeater we discussed must concede this much). Indeed, we have encountered points in this discussion that add to its force. Does the divine hiddenness referred to in its premises therefore justify atheism? Does it justify *you, the reader*, in believing atheism? Well, it seems plausible and would be accepted by most philosophers that the following proposition refers to conditions necessary and sufficient for justification of the relevant sort.

> An individual *S* is epistemically justified in believing that *p* in response to evidence *e* if and only if (i) *S* does to some degree believe that *p* on *e*, (ii) has considered all available epistemic reasons for not believing that *p* on *e*, (iii) finds none to be a good reason, and (iv) has fulfilled all relevant epistemic duties in the course of her investigation.

Thinking of yourself as *S*, of *p* as atheism, of *e* as the form of divine hiddenness we have discussed, of the defeaters we have considered (including the defeater relying on independent evidence) and any others known to you as the available reasons for *not* believing atheism because of divine hiddenness, and of the relevant epistemic duties as including such things as care, thoroughness, and openness to the truth, you may, by reference to this standard, work out for *yourself* whether our argument justifies you in believing that God does not exist.

3. THE CONCEPTUAL ARGUMENT

The Analogy Argument is not the only argument from divine hiddenness. Indeed, in my previous work on this topic it is only alluded to, and another form of argumentation is utilized instead.[2] I wanted to develop the Analogy Argument here, and had thought to leave the other aside. But after proceeding, I realized that in developing the former argument, a natural basis for an abbreviated but still forceful presentation of the latter would be laid. So let us briefly consider the additional moves which the latter argument requires.

The Conceptual Argument takes further a theme already touched upon: namely, the proper understanding of the concept of divine love. In examining this concept, developing our understanding of it as we must, by reference to what is best in human love, we are led to endorse claims from which it follows that, if God exists, evidence sufficient to form belief in God is available to everyone capable of a personal relationship with God and not inclined to resist such evidence. As can be seen, this argument not only focuses more closely on the concept of divine love (while drawing information from what we know of human love, including a mother's love) but embraces a wider range of nonbelievers in its premises. In this new argument, the notion of divine hiddenness is, as it were, *expanded* to include events (or the absence of certain events) in the lives of people who, without being closed toward the traditional God, are for one reason or another not aware of any need to seek God. If a label is desired, we may call all those belonging to this new and broader category of nonbelievers *nonresisters*. Nonresisters might include, in addition to seekers, individuals in the West whose upbringing has been completely secular. They certainly include the vast number of persons in both past and present living in parts of the world where the very *idea* of such a God is distant from human thought and imagination.

Now why should we suppose that the absence of evidence sufficient to form belief in God in the lives of nonresisters presents a problem for theism? Well, because reflection on the concept of divine love shows that a perfectly loving God would necessarily seek personal relationship with *all* individuals belonging to this type, and because such seeking entails the provision of evidence sufficient for belief in the existence of God. (As can be seen, here the emphasis is not on human seekers but on *God* as seeker.)

In defense of the first of these claims, we may point out that the seeking of a personal relationship is an essential part of the best human love. The best human lover encourages her beloved to draw from relationship with herself what he may need to flourish, but also quite naturally aspires to a kind of closeness between herself and her beloved: she reaches out to the one she loves immediately and spontaneously, and not only because of some prior calculation of advantages or disadvantages for either party. Something similar must apply to God's love for us: clearly an explicit divine-human relationship must do much to promote human flourishing, in which case God would seek it for that reason; and clearly God would also value personal relationship with human beings—creatures created in God's own image—for its own sake. No doubt God would not *force* such a loving relationship on anyone (the notion is logically contradictory and, in any case, contrary to love's respect for freedom), but surely a God who did not at least make such a relationship *available* to those who are *nonresisting* would not be perfectly loving.

This point sometimes has a hard time getting through. Due to a variety of social and religious factors, we seem to have got used to thinking of even God's love in a limited and limiting fashion, contrary to what all philosophical methods for working out an explication of the divine nature would indicate. But why suppose that if God exists there will be times when personal relationship with God will not be available to us? While a perfectly good and loving parent might occasionally stand to one side and let her child make the first move, and refuse to suffocate the child with her attentions, or even withdraw for a time to make a point, these are moments *within* the relationship, which *add* to its meaning. And while she might with deep sadness acknowledge that her child had completely cut himself off from the relationship, and not actively seek its resumption, it *would take* such resistance on the part of the child for the relationship to be put out of his immediate reach. What loving parent would ever willingly participate in bringing about such a state of affairs? And similar points apply to love as it occurs in the context of friendship and marriage relationships. So there seems no escaping this point: some form of personal relationship with God is always going to be available to nonresisters, if God is indeed loving.

A defense of our second claim—that for such relationship to be available, evidence sufficient for belief in God's existence would have to be similarly available—may now be added. The key point here is that it is logically impossible for you to hear God speaking to you or consciously to experience divine forgiveness and support or feel grateful to God or experience God's loving presence and respond thereto in love and obedience and worship or participate in any *other* element of a personal relationship with God while *not believing that there is a God*. Simply by looking at what it *means* to be in personal relationship with God, we can see that this is so. Since belief is involuntary, it follows that without evidence sufficient for belief in the existence of God, nonresisters are not in a position to relate personally to God. But where nonresisters are not in such a position, relationship with God has not been made available to them in the above sense. It follows that if relationship with God is to be made available to them, nonresisters must be provided with evidence sufficient for belief in God. This evidence, notice, would not need to be some thunderbolt from the sky or miracle or devastating theoretical proof. The quiet evidence of religious experience would do, and might also be most appropriate to the aims of any would-be divine relationship partner. But *some* such evidence must be available to nonresisters if they are to have the possibility of responding in love to God.

Taken in conjunction, the two points we have defended imply that if God exists, evidence sufficient for belief in God is *much more widely available than is in fact the case*. And from this it follows that God does *not* exist. Now this argument, like the other, has of course got to deal with objections. But as it turns out, the objections are pretty much the same ones, tailored to address the specifics of the new argument. And so are the replies. The reader is invited to go over the objections and replies again, this time with the Conceptual Argument in mind. She or he will see, I think, that the resources are there for a fully satisfying defense of the latter argument too. If so, we have not just the probable grounds of analogy but the more certain grounds of conceptual analysis for concluding that God does not exist.

NOTES

1. John Macquarrie, *In Search of Deity* (London: SCM Press, 1984), p. 198.

2. See my *Divine Hiddenness and Human Reason* (Ithaca: Cornell University Press, 1993). See also my "Response to Howard-Snyder" (and the paper to which it is a

response) in *Canadian Journal of Philosophy* 26 (1996): 455–62, and my "What the Hiddenness of God Reveals: A Collaborative Discussion," in *Divine Hiddenness*, edited by Daniel Howard-Snyder and Paul Moser (Cambridge: Cambridge University Press, 2001), pp. 33–61.

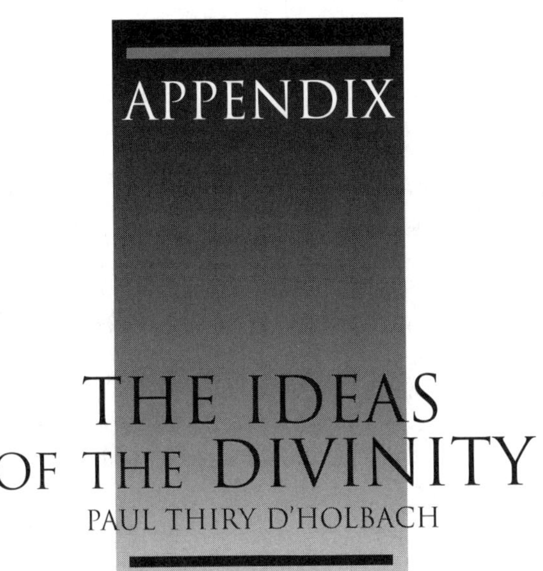

APPENDIX

THE IDEAS OF THE DIVINITY

PAUL THIRY D'HOLBACH

The existence of God, which is announced to us everywhere as an evident and demonstrated truth, is only so for those who have not examined the proofs upon which it is founded. These proofs frequently appear false or feeble to those themselves who, otherwise, do not by any means doubt of his existence; the inductions or the corollaries which are drawn from this pretended truth, said to be so clear, are not the same in two nations or even in two individuals; the thinkers of all ages and of all countries unceasingly quarrel amongst themselves upon religion, upon their theological hypothesis, upon the fundamental truths which serve for the basis of them, upon the attributes and the qualities of a God with whom they vainly occupy themselves, and the idea of whom varies continually in their own brain.

These disputes and these perpetual variations ought at least to convince us that the ideas of the Divinity have neither the evidence nor the certitude which are attributed to them, and that it may be permitted to doubt the reality of a being which men see so diversely, and upon which they are never in accord, and of which the image so often varies with themselves. In spite of all the efforts and the subtleties of its most ardent defenders, the existence of a God is not even probable. . . .

If God is desirous to be known, cherished, and thanked, wherefore does he not . . . manifest himself to all the earth in an unequivocal manner, much more likely to convince us than those particular revelations which appear to accuse the

---

From Baron D'Holbach, *The System of Nature* (1770), 2 vols. in 1, translated by H. D. Robinson (New York: Burt Franklin, 1970), vol. 2, chap. 8, pp. 247, 289–99.

Divinity of a fatal partiality for some of his creatures? Has the omnipotent no better means of showing himself to men than those ridiculous metamorphoses, those pretended incarnations, which are attested by writers so little in harmony with each other? Instead of such a number of miracles, invented to prove the divine mission of so many legislators held in reverence by the different people of the world, could not the sovereign of minds have convinced at once the human mind of those things with which he was desirous it should be acquainted? In [place] of suspending a sun in the vaulted firmament; in lieu of diffusing without order the stars and constellations, which fill up the regions of space, would it not have been more conformable to the views of a God so jealous of his glory, and so well-intentioned toward man, to have written, in a manner not liable to dispute, his name, his attributes, his everlasting will, in indelible characters, and equally legible to all the inhabitants of the earth? No one, then, could have doubted the existence of a God, of his manifest will, of his visible intentions; no mortal would have dared to place himself in a situation to attract his wrath; in short, no man would have had the audacity to have imposed on men in his name, or to have interpreted his will, according to his own whim and caprice.

Theology is truly the vessel of the Danaides. By dint of contradictory qualities and bold assertions, it has so shackled its God as to make it impossible for him to act. Indeed, when even we should suppose the existence of the theological God and the reality of those attributes, so discordant, which are given him, we can conclude nothing from them to authorize the conduct or sanction the worship which they prescribed. If God be infinitely good, what reason have we to fear him? If he be infinitely wise, wherefore disturb ourselves with our condition? If he be omniscient, wherefore inform him of our wants and fatigue him with our prayers? If he be omnipresent, wherefore erect temples to him? If he be Lord of all, wherefore make sacrifices and offerings to him? If he be just, wherefore believe that he punishes those creatures whom he has filled with imbecility? If his grace works everything in man, what reason has he to reward him? If he be omnipotent, how can he be offended and how can we resist him? If he be rational, how can he be enraged against those blind mortals to whom he has left the liberty of acting irrationally? If he be immutable, by what right shall we pretend to make him change his decrees? If he be inconceivable, wherefore should we occupy ourselves with him? If he has spoken, wherefore is the universe not convinced? If the knowledge of a God be the most necessary thing, wherefore is it not more evident and more manifest?

But, on the other hand, the theological God has two faces. Nevertheless, if he be wrathful, jealous, vindictive, and wicked, as theology supposes him to be, without being disposed to allow it, we shall no longer be justified in addressing our prayers to him nor in sorrowfully occupying ourselves with his idea. On the contrary, for our present happiness, and for our quiet, we ought to make a point of banishing him from our thought; we ought to place him in the rank of those necessary evils, which are only aggravated by a consideration of them. Indeed, if God be a tyrant, how is it possible to love him? Are not affection and tenderness sentiments incompatible with habitual fear? How could we experience love for a master who gives to his slaves the liberty of offending him, to the end that he may take them on their weak side, and punish them with the utmost barbarity? If to this odious character God has joined omnipotence, if he hold in his hands the unhappy playthings of this fantastic cruelty, what can we conclude from it? Nothing, save that whatever efforts we may make to escape our destiny, we shall always be incapacitated to withdraw ourselves from it. If a God, cruel or wicked by his nature, be armed with infinite power and take pleasure in rendering us eternally miserable, nothing will divert him from it. His wickedness will always pursue its course; his malice would, without doubt, prevent him from paying any attention to our cries; nothing would be able to soften his obdurate heart.

Thus, under whatever point of view we contemplate the theological God, we have no worship to render him, no prayers to offer up to him. If he be perfectly good, intelligent, equitable, and wise, what have we to ask of him? If he be supremely wicked, if he be gratuitously cruel, as all men believe, without daring to avow it, our evils are without remedy; such a God would deride our prayers, and, sooner or later, we should be obliged to submit to the rigor of the lot which he has destined for us.

This granted, he who can undeceive himself with regard to the afflicting notions of the Divinity has this advantage over the credulous and trembling superstitious mortal, that he establishes in his heart a momentary tranquility, which, at least, renders him happy in this life. If the study of nature has banished from him those chimeras with which the superstitious man is infested, he enjoys a security of which this one is himself deprived. In consulting nature, his fears are dissipated; his opinions, true or false, become steady; and a calm succeeds the storm which panic terrors and wavering notions excite in the hearts of all men who occupy themselves with the Divinity. If the human soul, cheered by philosophy, had the boldness to consider things coolly, it would no longer behold the universe governed by an implacable tyrant, always ready to strike. If he were rational, he would see that, in committing evil, he did not disturb nature; that he did not outrage his author; he injures himself alone, or he injures other beings, capable of feeling the effects of his conduct; from thence, he knows the line of his duties; he prefers virtue to vice, and for his own permanent repose, satisfaction, and felicity in this world, he feels himself interested in the practice of virtue, in rendering it habitual to his heart, in avoiding vice, in detesting crime, during the whole time of his abode amongst intelligent and sensible beings, from whom he expects his happiness. By attaching himself to these rules, he will live contented with himself, and be cherished by those who shall be capable of experiencing the influence of his actions. He will expect, without inquietude, the term when his existence shall have a period; he will have no reason to dread the existence which shall follow the one he at present enjoys. He will not fear to be deceived in his reasonings; guided by demonstration and honesty, he will perceive that, if contrary to his expectation, there did exist a good God, he would not punish him for his involuntary errors, depending upon the organization he should have received.

Indeed, if there did exist a God; if God were a being full of reason, equity, and goodness, and not a ferocious, irrational, and malicious genius, such as religion is pleased so frequently to depict him; what could a virtuous atheist have to apprehend, who, believing at the moment of his death he falls asleep forever, should find himself in the presence of a God whom he should have mistaken and neglected during his life?

"O, God!" would he say, "Father, who hast rendered thyself invisible to thy child! Inconceivable and hidden author, whom I could not discover! Pardon me, if my limited understanding has not been able to know thee in a nature where everything has appeared to me to be necessary! Excuse me, if my sensible heart has not discerned thine august traits under those of the austere tyrant whom superstitious mortals trembling adore. I could only see a phantom in that assemblage of irreconcilable qualities with which the imagination has clothed thee. How should my coarse eyes perceive thee in a nature in which all my senses have never been able to know but material beings and perishable forms? Could I, by the aid of these senses, discover thy spiritual essence of which they could not furnish any proof? How should I find the invariable demonstration of thy goodness in thy works, which I saw as frequently prejudicial as favorable to the beings of my species? My feeble brain, obliged to form its judgments after its own capacity, could it judge of thy plan, of thy wisdom, of thine intelligence, whilst the universe presented to me only a continued mixture of order and confusion, of good and of evil, of formation and destruction? Have I been able to render homage to thy justice, whilst I so frequently saw crime triumphant and virtue in tears? Could I acknowledge the voice of a being filled with wisdom in those ambiguous, contradictory, and puerile oracles which imposters published in thy name, in the different countries of the earth which I have quitted? If I have refused to believe thine existence, it is because I have not known either what thou couldst be, or where thou couldst be placed, or the qualities which could be assigned to thee. My ignorance is excusable, because it was invincible: my mind could not bend itself under the authority of some men, who acknowledged themselves as little enlightened upon thine essence as myself, and who, forever disputing amongst themselves, were in harmony only in imperiously crying out to me to sacrifice to them that reason which thou hast given men. But, O God! if thou cherishest thy creatures, I also have cherished them like thee; I have endeavored to render them happy in the sphere in which I have lived. If thou art the author of reason, I have always listened to it, and followed it. If virtue please thee, my heart has always honored it; I have never outraged it; and, when my powers have permitted me, I have myself practiced it. I was an affectionate husband, a tender father, a sincere friend, a faithful and zealous citizen. I have held out consolation to the afflicted: if the foibles of my nature have been injurious to myself or incommodious to others, I have not, at least, made the unfortunate groan under the weight of my injustice. I have not devoured the substance of the poor; I have not seen without pity the widow's tears; I have not heard without commiseration the cries of the orphan. If thou didst render man sociable, if thou wast disposed that society should subsist and be happy, I have been the enemy of all those who oppressed him, or deceived him, in order that they might take advantage of his misfortunes.

"If I have thought amiss of thee, it is because my understanding could not conceive thee. If I have spoken ill of thee, it is because my heart, partaking too much of human nature, revolted against the odious portrait which was painted of thee. My wanderings have been the effect of a temperament which thou hast given me; of the circumstances in which, without my consent, thou hast placed me; of those ideas which, in spite of me, have entered into my mind. If thou art good and just, as we are assured thou art, thou canst not punish me for the wanderings of my imagination, for faults caused by my passions, which are the necessary consequence of the organization which I have received from thee. Thus, I cannot fear thee, I cannot dread the condition which thou preparest for me. Thy goodness cannot have permitted that I should incur punishments for inevitable errors. Wherefore didst thou not rather prevent my being born, than have called me into the rank of intelligent beings, there to enjoy the fatal liberty of rendering myself unhappy? If thou punishest me with severity, and eternally, for having listened to the reason which thou gavest me; if thou correctest me for my illusions; if thou art wroth because my feebleness has made me fall into those snares which thou hast everywhere spread for me; thou wilt be the most cruel and the most unjust of tyrants; thou wilt not be a God, but a malicious demon to whom I shall be obliged to yield and satiate the barbarity; but of whom I shall at least congratulate myself to have for some time shook off the insupportable yoke."

It is thus that a disciple of nature would speak, who, transported all at once into the imaginary regions, should there find a God of whom all the ideas were in direct contradiction to those which wisdom, goodness, and justice furnish us here. Indeed, theology appears to have been invented only to overturn in our mind all natural ideas. This illusory science seems to be bent on making its God a being the most contradictory to human reason. It is, nevertheless, according to this reason that we are obliged to judge in this world. . . .

Let us balance the fictitious interests of heaven by the sensible interests of the earth. Let sovereigns and the people at length acknowledge that the advantages resulting from truth, from justice, from good laws, from a rational education, and from a human and peaceable morality are much more solid than those which they so vainly expect from their Divinities. Let them feel that benefits so real and so precious ought not to be sacrificed to uncertain hopes, so frequently contradicted by experience. In order to convince themselves, let every rational man consider the numberless crimes which the name of God has caused upon the earth; let them study his frightful history and that of his odious ministers, who have everywhere fanned the spirit of madness, discord, and fury. Let princes and subjects at least sometimes learn to resist the passions of these pretended interpreters of the Divinity, especially when they shall command them in his name to be inhuman, intolerant, and barbarous, to stifle the cries of nature, the voice of equity, the remonstrances of reason, and to shut their eyes to the interests of society.

Feeble mortals! How long will your imagination, so active and so prompt to seize on the marvelous, continue to seek, out of the universe, pretexts to make you injurious to yourselves and to the beings with whom ye live in society? Wherefore do ye not follow in peace the simple and easy route which your nature has marked out for ye? Wherefore strew with thorns the road of life? Wherefore multiply those sorrows to which your destiny exposes ye? What advantages can ye expect from a Divinity which the united efforts of the whole human species have not been able to make you acquainted with? Be ignorant, then, of that which the human mind is not formed to comprehend; abandon your chimeras; occupy yourselves with truth; learn the art of living happy. Perfect your morals, your governments, and your laws; look to education, to agriculture, and to the sciences that are truly useful; labor with ardor; oblige nature by your industry to become propitious to ye, and the Gods will not be able to oppose anything to your felicity. Leave to idle thinkers, and to useless enthusiasts, the unfruitful labor of fathoming depths from which ye ought to divert your attention; enjoy the benefits attached to your present existence; augment the number of them; never throw yourselves forward beyond your sphere. If you must have chimeras, permit your fellow creatures to have theirs also; and do not cut the throats of your brethren when they cannot rave in your own manner. If ye will have Gods, let your imagination give birth to them; but do not suffer these imaginary beings so far to intoxicate ye as to make ye mistake that which ye owe to those real beings with whom ye live. If ye will have unintelligible systems, if ye cannot be contented without marvelous doctrines, if the infirmities of your nature require an invisible crutch, adopt such as may suit with your humor; select those which you may think most calculated to support your tottering frame. Do not insist on your neighbors making the same choice with yourself; do not suffer these imaginary theories to infuriate your mind. Always remember that among the duties you owe to the *real* beings with whom ye are associated, the foremost, the most consequential, the most immediate, stands a reasonable indulgence for the foibles of others.